1991

ENVIRONMENTAL POLICY IN THE 1990s

ENVIRONMENTAL POLICY IN THE 1990s

TOWARD A NEW AGENDA

Edited by

Norman J. Vig
Carleton College

Michael E. Kraft
University of Wisconsin—Green Bay

A Division of Congressional Quarterly Inc.
1414 22nd Street, N.W., Washington, D.C. 20037

Printed in the United States of America

Third Printing

Library of Congress Cataloging-in-Publication Data

Environmental policy in the 1990s: toward a new agenda/edited by
Norman J. Vig, Michael E. Kraft.
p. cm.
ISBN 0-87187-544-6:
1. Environmental policy—United States. 2. Environmental policy.
I. Vig, Norman J. II. Kraft, Michael E.
HC110.E5E49876 1990
363.7' 056' 0973—dc20 89-70821
CIP

For
Teddy and Jesse
Steve and David

CONTENTS

III. Environmental Dispute Resolution and Policy Integration

IV. Toward Global Environmental Policy

V. Ethics, Values, and the Future of Environmental Politics

TABLES AND FIGURES

Tables

Figures

PREFACE

When the first "environmental decade" was launched twenty years ago, protecting our air, water, and other natural resources seemed a relatively simple proposition. The polluters and exploiters of nature would be brought to heel by tough laws requiring them to clean up or get out of business within five or ten years. The sense of urgency that swept Congress in 1970 as it passed the Clean Air Act with scarcely a dissenting voice reflected the rise of one of the most dramatic popular movements in American history. Since then, despite ebbs and flows, the tide of public opinion favoring greater environmental protection has continued to gather strength and conviction both from changing social values and from mounting scientific evidence of threats to our global life support systems. People perceive the environment as more endangered now than it was twenty years ago.

The making of public policy often resembles an awkward dance between idealistic ends and deficient means. The history of environmental protection is no exception. Implementing the major legislation of the 1970s on air and water pollution, hazardous waste, and preservation of public lands and other resources proved to be difficult and frustrating. Although genuine progress was made, few deadlines were met and results have fallen considerably short of expectations. At the same time, environmental protection has turned out to be a moving target. What appeared to be a relatively straightforward job of controlling a few key pollutants by mandating corrective technologies "at the end of the pipe" has become a far larger and more difficult task involving change in human behavior.

By the end of the 1970s it was evident that many of the most serious environmental problems had their origins in massive use and careless disposal of industrial chemicals whose cumulative health and environmental effects were largely unknown. These second-generation problems, requiring cleanup of thousands of leaking toxic waste dumps and other sources of chemical contamination, began to overwhelm the system in the

1980s, when the Superfund and other programs were put in place. By the end of the decade, a third generation of even larger ecological issues captured public attention: the greenhouse effect and global warming, thinning of the ozone layer, massive tropical deforestation, the extinction of species, and ocean and coastal pollution. The summer of 1988—with its record heat and drought, destructive fires, and sickening urban and beach pollution—along with the great Alaskan oil spill of March 1989 appeared to confirm that things were drastically wrong and had to be dealt with at a much more serious and fundamental level than in the past.

The presidential election of 1988 offered hope that the growing environmental crisis might be addressed. George Bush and Michael Dukakis vied to become the "environmental president," and both offered environmental programs that went well beyond their predecessors'. Bush distanced himself from the Reagan administration's record of environmental neglect, despite his contributions to it as vice president. But the formidable array of problems that have made their way onto the national and international environmental agenda will require an entirely different level of leadership if progress is to be renewed in the 1990s.

This book seeks to explain some of the most important developments in environmental policy and politics over the past two decades and to analyze the central issues that face us in the decade ahead. Unlike our previous volume, *Environmental Policy in the 1980s: Reagan's New Agenda*, it does not focus on policies of the current administration so much as on the underlying trends and policy dilemmas that all political actors will have to confront. As such, the book has broad relevance for the environmental community and everyone concerned with the difficulties of finding public solutions to our worsening environmental conditions.

Part I provides a retrospective view on policy development as well as a framework for analyzing policy change in the United States. Chapter 1 serves as an introduction to the book by outlining the basic issues in U.S. environmental policy over the past two decades, the development of institutional capacities for addressing them, and the successes and failures in implementing policies. The importance of presidential leadership is highlighted in Chapter 2, which examines the dismal environmental record of the Reagan administration, the 1988 election, and the potential for change under President Bush. Chapter 3 analyzes another phenomenon of the 1980s: the increasingly innovative and diverse roles of the states in environmental policy. Finally, Chapter 4 examines public opinion and the growth of environmental groups in the late 1980s and the support they will provide for renewed environmental activism in the 1990s.

Part II takes up some of the most intractable policy dilemmas that will need to be resolved if environmental progress is to resume. Chapter 5 examines the problem of policy "gridlock" in Congress and prospects for overcoming fragmentation and divisiveness on such issues as acid rain and pesticides. Chapter 6 looks at a similar problem played out in many local communities—the not-in-my-backyard (NIMBY) syndrome—and what new approaches may help to overcome it. Two other fundamental issues are considered in Chapters 7 and 8: to what extent should economic market incentives be incorporated into environmental regulation, and how useful is expert risk assessment in helping us to resolve difficult regulatory and environmental policy questions?

Part III shifts the discussion toward alternative institutional mechanisms for better reconciling conflicting interests and coordinating policies. Chapter 9 explains the traditional and more recent roles of the judicial system in deciding cases, reviewing administrative decision making, and sometimes reconciling parties. Chapter 10 then explores the rise of alternative methods for environmental dispute resolution, such as informal negotiation and mediation, and considers the pitfalls of these procedures as well as traditional adversary processes. Chapter 11 raises the much larger issue of whether truly comprehensive environmental policy is possible; that is, can we agree on a more general set of rational principles and institutional arrangements to guide decision making?

Part IV adds a comparative and international perspective on what is now seen as a global environmental agenda. Chapter 12 provides an intriguing comparison of cultural differences and environmental policy development in Europe and Japan, while Chapter 13 summarizes the grim pressures on environmental resources in much of the Third World and their implications for global ecological balances. Chapter 14 examines these and other "geophysical imperatives" and the need for the United States and other nations to cooperate on a much larger scale in developing global environmental policies for the future.

The last part raises the troubling issue of whether democratic political institutions are capable of resolving the crucial ethical and value conflicts that underlie environmental politics. In Chapter 15 it is argued that greater political activism, including expression of moral outrage, may be necessary as we are increasingly forced to choose among ecological, esthetic, efficiency, and equity values. This is followed by a discussion in Chapter 16 of how environmental protection as a "first-order value" is compatible with other basic democratic values, and how it can form the basis for new political coalitions that extend well beyond the present environmental community. Finally, Chapter 17 reviews and summarizes the arguments for major environmental policy changes in the 1990s and suggests courses of action that must be taken in the new "environmental decade."

We thank the contributing authors for their generosity, cooperation, and patience in response to our seemingly endless editorial requests. It was a pleasure to work with such a conscientious and punctual group of scholars. Special thanks are also due to Rebecca Spithill and Beth Hull, who provided valuable research assistance and commentary on chapter drafts. We also gratefully acknowledge financial support from the Technology and Policy Studies Program and Faculty Development Endowment at Carleton College and from the Herbert Fisk Johnson Professorship in Environmental Studies at the University of Wisconsin—Green Bay. Finally, we thank Joanne Daniels, Nancy Lammers, and Ann O'Malley of CQ Press for their encouragement and professional assistance in developing and completing this volume. As usual, any errors and omissions are our own responsibility.

Norman J. Vig
Michael E. Kraft

I. ENVIRONMENTAL POLICY AND POLITICS IN TRANSITION

1

Environmental Policy from the Seventies to the Nineties: Continuity and Change

Michael E. Kraft and Norman J. Vig

Environmental issues soared to a prominent place on the political agenda in the United States and other industrialized nations in the late 1980s. There was little mistaking the trend; the evidence for the rising saliency of the environment was everywhere. An intense drought and heat wave in the summer of 1988 dramatically raised public and governmental concern about global climate change, Europe and the United States gave new attention to elimination of chlorofluorocarbons (CFCs) and other chemicals responsible for depleting the earth's ozone layer, and in March 1989 the worst oil spill in U.S. history received extensive media coverage and vividly confirmed the environmental perils of energy development.[1] For the first time environmental issues played a highly visible role in a U.S. presidential election as George Bush and Michael Dukakis fought in the summer of 1988 over who was more committed to the environment. Just before Bush's inauguration, *Time* devoted an issue to the earth as "Planet of the Year," in which it analyzed the "looming ecological crisis" and provided an "agenda for urgent action." [2]

On cursory examination these recent developments resemble events of two decades ago when rapidly rising public concern about environmental issues and governments' eagerness to respond to this new political force initiated the "environmental decade." During the 1970s the United States and other industrialized nations adopted dozens of major environmental and resource policies, created new institutions such as the U.S. Environmental Protection Agency (EPA) to manage environmental programs, and greatly increased spending for them.[3] Under the Reagan administration in the 1980s, these programs were curtailed as the president adopted a

We wish to thank Beth Hull for her assistance in compiling data for the appendices and Rebecca Spithill for her assistance on the appendices and helpful comments on earlier drafts of the manuscript.

conservative policy agenda that included deep cuts in the budgets of EPA and other agencies. That strategy ultimately failed as Congress, the courts, and the American public resisted efforts to weaken or reverse environmental policy.[4]

On closer examination, however, it is clear that the 1990s will not be a replay of either the 1970s or the 1980s. While we can expect to see considerable continuity in environmental policies over the next decade, these policies will require careful evaluation and in many cases an imaginative search for more effective and efficient approaches. Important changes in the 1990s also can be expected in the kinds of environmental problems that will make their way onto governmental agendas and in the political responses to them. For example, governments are ill equipped to resolve many long-term and severe problems in the global environment; hence, institutional reforms and new methods of decision making will be critical to success in such cases.[5]

In this chapter we examine the continuities and changes in environmental politics and policy over the past twenty years and speculate on some of their implications for the 1990s. We discuss the nature of policy making, the development of environmental policies, and the performance of governmental institutions and political leadership, paying particular attention to the major environmental programs that were adopted in the 1970s. Many of the broad questions explored in this introduction are addressed more fully in the chapters that follow.

The Role of Government and Politics

The heightened political prominence of environmental problems in the late 1980s underscores the singularly important role of government and politics in devising solutions to the nation's and the world's mounting environmental ills. Effective response to problems such as global climate change, population growth, the spread of toxic and hazardous chemicals, threats to endangered species, and air and water pollution requires diverse actions by individuals and institutions at all levels of society. One major contribution will be scientific research and inquiry that draws from a wide range of disciplines, among them environmental and other natural sciences, economics, political science, sociology, history, and philosophy. There is also a wide range of response strategies. Some scholars and activists emphasize political initiatives and public policy responses more than others.[6] As political scientists, we believe government clearly has an indispensable role to play in environmental protection and improvement.

The major reason for the preeminent role of government is that most environmental ills are *public problems;* that is, they cannot be solved through purely private action. This does not mean that individuals and nongovernmental organizations cannot do much to prevent environmental deterioration, especially in local communities; it means only that individual efforts alone are insufficient. Moreover, self-interested individuals and a free economic marketplace guided mainly by a concern for short-term profits predictably create spillover effects or "externalities" such as pollution. Thus, the very character, scope, and urgency of environmental problems and the deficiencies in human institutions necessitate large-scale collective action, particularly by government.

Political Institutions and Public Policy

Public policy is a course of governmental action or inaction in response to social problems, and it is expressed in goals articulated by political leaders, formal statutes, rules and regulations, and the practices of administrative agencies charged with implementing programs. Policy states an intent to achieve certain goals and objectives through a conscious choice of means and usually within some specified period. In a constitutional democracy like the United States, policy making is distinctive in several respects: it must take place through constitutional processes, it requires the sanction of law, and it is binding on all members of society. Normally, the process is open to public scrutiny and debate, although secrecy may be justified in matters involving national security and diplomatic relations.

The constitutional requirements for policy making were established two hundred years ago, and they remain much the same today. The U.S. political system is based on a division of authority among three branches of government and between the federal government and the states. Originally intended to limit government power and protect individual liberty, this division of power can impede the ability of government to adopt timely and coherent environmental policy. Dedication to principles of federalism means that environmental policy responsibilities are distributed among the federal government, the fifty states, and thousands of local governments (see Chapter 3). Responsibility for the environment is divided within the branches of the federal government as well, most notably in the U.S. Congress, with power shared between the House and Senate and jurisdiction for environmental policy scattered among dozens of committees and subcommittees (see Table 1-1). The executive branch is also institutionally fragmented, with at least some responsibility for environmental and natural resource concerns located in eleven cabinet departments and in EPA, the Nuclear Regulatory Commission, and other agencies (see Figure 1-1). Although most environmental policies are concentrated in EPA and in the Interior and Agriculture departments, the Department of Energy (DOE) and the State Department are increasingly important actors as well. Finally, the more than one hundred federal trial and appellate courts play an important role in interpreting environmental

Table 1-1 Major Congressional Committees with Environmental Responsibilities

Committee	Environmental policy jurisdiction
House	
Agriculture	agriculture in general, soil conservation, forestry, pesticide policy
Appropriations	appropriations for all programs
Energy and Commerce	Clean Air Act, nuclear waste policy, safe drinking water, Superfund, hazardous waste and toxic substances
Interior and Insular Affairs	public lands, wilderness, surface mining, nuclear waste policy
Merchant Marine and Fisheries	National Environmental Policy Act, oceanography and marine affairs, coastal zone management, fisheries and wildlife
Public Works and Transportation	water pollution, rivers and harbors, oil pollution, water power
Science, Space, and Technology	nuclear waste policy, environmental research and development, energy research
Senate	
Agriculture, Nutrition, and Forestry	agriculture in general, soil conservation, forestry, pesticide policy
Appropriations	appropriations for all programs
Commerce, Science, and Transportation	coastal zone management; marine fisheries; oceans, weather, and atmospheric activities; technology research and development
Energy and Natural Resources	energy policy in general, nuclear waste policy, mining, national parks and recreation areas, wilderness, wild and scenic rivers
Environment and Public Works	air, water, and noise pollution; toxic and hazardous materials; Superfund; nuclear waste policy; fisheries and wildlife; ocean dumping, solid-waste disposal; environmental policy and research in general

Figure 1-1 Major Executive Branch Agencies with Environmental Responsibilities

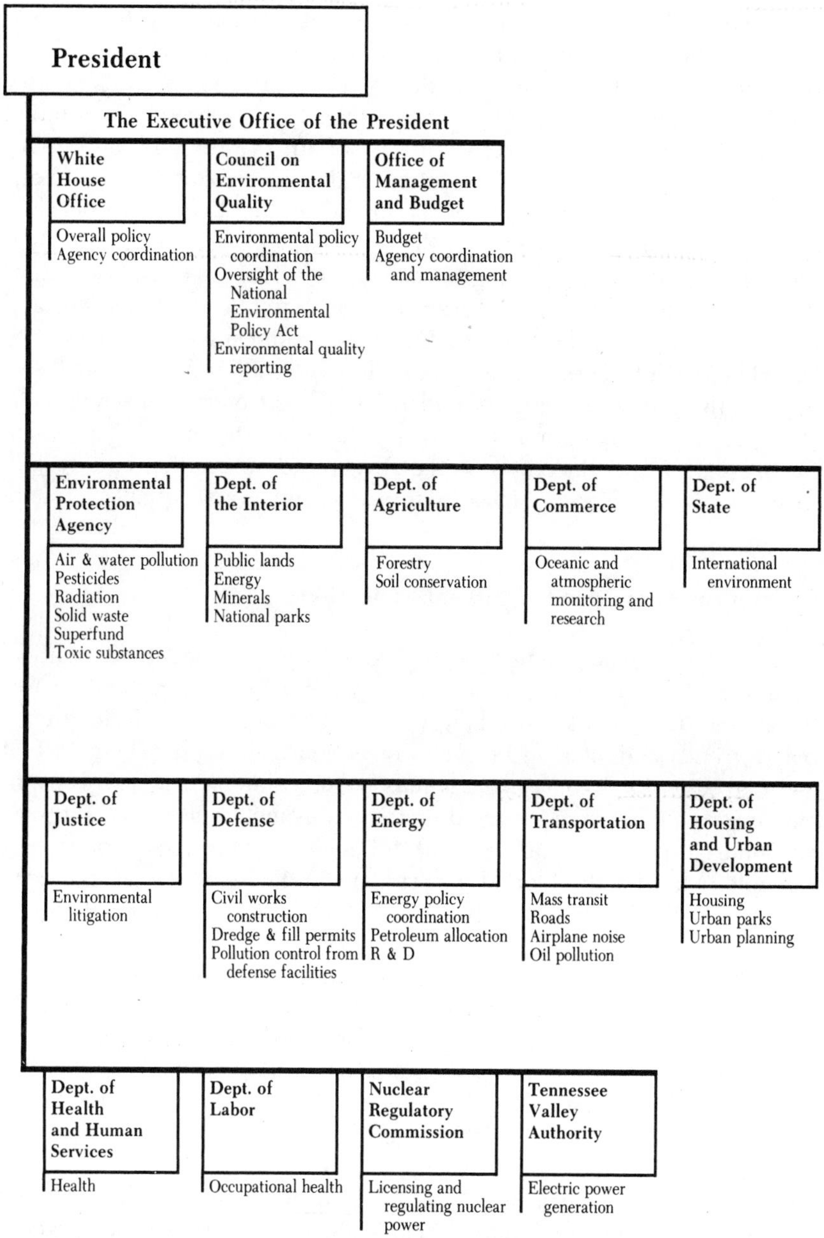

President

The Executive Office of the President

White House Office
- Overall policy
- Agency coordination

Council on Environmental Quality
- Environmental policy coordination
- Oversight of the National Environmental Policy Act
- Environmental quality reporting

Office of Management and Budget
- Budget
- Agency coordination and management

Environmental Protection Agency
- Air & water pollution
- Pesticides
- Radiation
- Solid waste
- Superfund
- Toxic substances

Dept. of the Interior
- Public lands
- Energy
- Minerals
- National parks

Dept. of Agriculture
- Forestry
- Soil conservation

Dept. of Commerce
- Oceanic and atmospheric monitoring and research

Dept. of State
- International environment

Dept. of Justice
- Environmental litigation

Dept. of Defense
- Civil works construction
- Dredge & fill permits
- Pollution control from defense facilities

Dept. of Energy
- Energy policy coordination
- Petroleum allocation
- R & D

Dept. of Transportation
- Mass transit
- Roads
- Airplane noise
- Oil pollution

Dept. of Housing and Urban Development
- Housing
- Urban parks
- Urban planning

Dept. of Health and Human Services
- Health

Dept. of Labor
- Occupational health

Nuclear Regulatory Commission
- Licensing and regulating nuclear power

Tennessee Valley Authority
- Electric power generation

Source: Council on Environmental Quality, *Environmental Quality, Sixteenth Annual Report of the Council on Environmental Quality* (Washington, D.C.: U.S. Government Printing Office, 1987).

legislation and adjudicating disputes over administrative and regulatory actions (see Chapter 9).

The implications of this constitutional arrangement were evident in the 1980s as Congress and the courts checked and balanced the Reagan administration's efforts to reverse the environmental policies of the previous decade. More generally, the effect of divided authority is slow and incremental alterations in policy, typically after broad consultation and agreement among diverse interests both within and outside of government. Such political interaction and accommodation of interests enhance the overall legitimacy of the public policies that result, but over time the cumulative effect for the environment has been disjointed policies that fall short of ecological or holistic principles of policy design.

Nonetheless, when issues are salient, the public is supportive, and political leaders act cohesively, the American political system proves to be flexible enough to permit substantial policy innovations.[7] As we shall see, this was the case in the early to mid-1970s, when Congress enacted major changes in U.S. environmental policy, and in the mid-1980s, when Congress overrode objections of the Reagan administration and greatly strengthened policies on hazardous waste and water quality, among others.

Policy Processes: Agendas, Streams, and Cycles

There are several models for analyzing how issues get on the political agenda and move through the policy processes of government. These theoretical frameworks are helpful in understanding both long-term policy trends and short-term cycles of action and response. One set of essential questions concerns *agenda setting:* how do new problems emerge as political issues demanding the government's attention, and why do some important problems fail to achieve such recognition? For example, why did the federal government initiate controls on industrial pollution in the 1960s and early 1970s but do little about national energy issues until well into the 1970s?

There are several hurdles to overcome in an issue's rise to prominence: it must first gain societal recognition as a problem, often in response to demographic, technological, or other social changes; then get on the docket of governmental institutions, usually through the exercise of organized group pressure; and finally it must get enough attention by governmental actors to reach the stage of decisional or policy action.[8] An issue is not likely to reach the decisional stage unless conditions are ripe (for example, unless specific "triggering events" focus public opinion sharply on the problems, and political leaders perceive the issue as salient to their constituents or supporters). One model analyzes agenda setting in terms of the convergence of three streams that flow through the political system—problems, policies, and politics. Although largely independent of one another, these streams can be brought together at critical times when "policy entrepreneurs" or issue activists are able to seize a "window of opportunity" for policy action.[9]

Once an issue is on the agenda, it must pass through several more stages in the policy process. These stages are often referred to as the *policy cycle.* Although terminology varies, most students of public policy delineate at least five stages of policy development beyond *agenda setting: policy formulation* (the actual design and drafting of policy goals and strategies for achieving them), *policy legitimation* (mobilization of political support and formal enactment by law or other means), *policy implementation* (provision of institutional resources and detailed administration of policy), *policy evaluation* (measurement of results in relation to goals and costs), and *policy termination or revision* (modification of goals or means).[10] The advantage of the policy-cycle model is that it emphasizes the importance of all phases of policy making; for example, how well a law is implemented is as important as the goals and motivations of those who drafted and enacted the legislation. The concept also suggests the continuous nature of the policy process: no policy decision or solution is "final," because changing conditions, new information, and shifting opinions will require policy reevaluation and revision. Other short-term cyclical forces and events, such as presidential elections or environmental accidents, can also profoundly affect the course of policy over its "life cycle." Thus, policy at any given time is shaped by the interaction of long-term social, economic, technological, and political forces and short-term fluctuations in the political climate. All of these factors are manifest in the development of environmental policy.

The Development of Environmental Policy: From the Seventies to the Nineties

As implied in the policy-cycle model, the history of environmental policy in the United States is not a record of continuous development and improvement in human relations with the natural environment. Rather it is one of fits and starts, with significant discontinuities, particularly since the late 1960s. It can be understood, to borrow from the concept of agenda setting described earlier, as the product of the convergence or divergence of two political currents, one that is deep and long-term and the other shallow and short-term.

Social Values and Environmental Policy Commitments

The deep current consists of fundamental changes in American values that began after World War II and accelerated as the nation shifted from an industrial to a postindustrial (or postmaterialist) society. Preoccupation with the economy (and national security) has gradually given way to a new set of concerns that includes quality of life issues like the environment.[11] These changes suggest that in the 1990s and the twenty-first century ecological issues will replace or be integrated with many traditional political, economic, and social issues, both domestically and internationally. This integration is implied, for example, in recent concern for sustainable development, and it is championed in *Our Common Future,* an influential report from the World Commission on Environment and Development.[12] The historian Samuel Hays describes these changes as a social evolutionary process that has affected all segments of American society. Political scientist Robert Paehlke characterizes environmentalism as a new ideology that has the potential to replace conventional political alignments.[13] In our terminology these long-term social forces are setting a new direction for the political agenda.

The shallow current consists of short-term political and economic forces, such as presidential elections, business cycles, and energy supply shocks, which may alter the saliency of environmental issues. These developments may either reinforce the long-term pro-environmental trends in society or temporarily weaken them. For example, in the early 1970s the deep and shallow currents converged, and there was an enormous outpouring of federal environmental legislation. Yet in the late 1970s energy shortages and a high level of inflation led the Carter administration to pull back from some of its environmental commitments, and the election of Ronald Reagan in 1980 shifted the environmental policy agenda sharply to the right for much of the 1980s.

Thus, the intersection of the deep and shallow currents helps to explain the fluctuations in environmental policy commitments from one year or decade to the next. Over time one can point to the continuity of environmental policy development: the trend is clearly one of strong public support for environmental protection, expanding government authority, and increasing effectiveness of policy implementation. From a near-term perspective, however, the discontinuity and inconsistency in policy direction capture our attention. We focus here on the changes from 1969 to 1989, and return to the long-term agenda for environmental politics and policy in the conclusion of the book.

Policies Prior to 1969

Until 1969 the federal government's role in environmental policy making was sharply limited. One major exception was in public land management, where for nearly a century Congress had set aside portions of the public domain for preservation as national parks, forests, grazing lands, recreation areas, and wildlife refuges. The "multiple-use" and "sustained-yield" doctrines that grew out of the conservation movement at the turn of the century ensured that this national trust would contribute to economic growth under the stewardship of the Interior and Agriculture departments. However, steady progress also was made in managing the lands in the public interest and protecting lands from development.[14] After several years of debate, Congress passed the Wilderness Act of 1964 to preserve some of the remaining forestlands in pristine condition, "untrammeled by man's presence." At the same time it approved the Land and Water Conservation Fund Act of 1964 to fund federal purchases of land for conservation purposes.

During the mid-1960s, the United States also began a major effort to reduce world population growth in developing nations through financial aid for foreign population programs, chiefly family planning and population research. President Lyndon B. Johnson and congressional sponsors of the programs tied them explicitly to a concern for "growing scarcity in world resources." [15]

Agenda Setting for the 1970s

Despite this long-time concern for resource conservation and land management, federal environmental policy was only slowly extended to control of industrial pollution and human waste. Air and water pollution long were considered strictly a local matter, and they were not prominent issues on the national agenda until the 1970s. In a very early federal action the Refuse Act of 1899 required individuals who wanted to dump refuse into navigable waters to obtain a permit from the Army Corps of Engineers; however, the corps largely ignored the pollution aspects of the act.[16] After World War II, policies to control the most obvious forms of pollution were developed gradually at the local, state, and federal levels. With passage of the Water Pollution Control Act of 1948, the federal government began assisting local authorities in building sewage treatment plants, and it initiated a limited program for air pollution research in 1955. Following the Clean Air Act of 1963 and amendments to the water pollution law, Washington began actively prodding the states to set pollution abatement standards and formulate implementation plans based on federal guidelines.[17]

By the end of the 1960s, it was widely recognized that this limited federal-state partnership was wholly inadequate to address what was then perceived as a national environmental crisis.[18] The environmental movement sweeping the country catapulted environmental policy onto the national political agenda. The movement drew its inspiration from the developing science of ecology and was spurred to action by books such as Rachel Carson's *Silent Spring*, which traced the impact of pesticides on birds and other wildlife, Paul Ehrlich's *The Population Bomb*, which warned of adverse effects on natural resources by a surging human population, and (after 1971) Barry Commoner's *The Closing Circle,* which introduced ecological principles to a lay audience.[19] In combination with a series of catalytic events—most notably an oil spill off the coast of Santa Barbara, California, in early 1969—and efforts by environmentalists to mobilize an American public newly alarmed by such reports and events, the stage was set for policy entrepreneurs in Congress and state legislatures to develop their own agendas for environmental action.[20]

The first Earth Day was April 22, 1970. Nationwide "teach-ins" about environmental problems symbolized the new place of ecology on the nation's social and political agendas.[21] Here we can see the clear effect of the long-term changes in social values, which became the bedrock upon which the rapidly growing environmental movement was built. An increasingly affluent and well-educated society placed new emphasis on the quality of life. Concern for environmental protection issues was an integral part of this change and was evident across all groups in the population, if not necessarily to the same degree.[22] The effect was a broadly based public demand for more vigorous and comprehensive federal action to prevent environmental degradation. In an almost unprecedented fashion a new environmental policy agenda rapidly emerged. Policy makers viewed the newly salient environmental issues as politically attractive, and they eagerly supported tough new measures, even when their full impacts and costs were unknown. As a result, laws were quickly enacted and implemented throughout the 1970s, but with growing concern over their effect on the economy and increasing realization that administrative agencies lacked the resources and the capacity to assume the new responsibilities given to them.[23]

Congress set the stage for the spurt in policy innovation at the end of 1969 when it passed the National Environmental Policy Act (NEPA). The act declared that,

> it is the continuing policy of the Federal Government, in cooperation with State and local governments, and other concerned public and private organizations, to use all practicable means and measures, including financial and technical assistance, in a manner calculated to foster and promote the general welfare, to create and maintain conditions under which man and nature can exist in productive harmony, and fulfill the social, economic, and other requirements of present and future generations of Americans.[24]

The law required detailed environmental impact statements on all major federal actions, and it established the Council on Environmental Quality (CEQ) to advise the president and Congress on environmental matters. President Richard Nixon then seized the initiative by signing NEPA as his first official act of 1970 and proclaiming the 1970s as the "environmental decade." In February 1970 he sent a special message to Congress calling for a new law to control air pollution. The race was on as the White House and congressional leaders vied for environmentalists' support.

Policy Escalation in the 1970s

By the spring of 1970 rising public concern about the environment galvanized the Ninety-first Congress to action. Sen. Edmund Muskie, then the leading Democratic hopeful for the presidential nomination in 1972, emerged as the dominant policy entrepreneur for environmental protection issues. As chair of the Senate Public Works Committee, he formulated proposals that went well beyond those favored by the president.[25] Following a process of policy escalation, both houses of Congress approved the stronger measures and set the tone for environmental policy making for much of the 1970s. Congress traditionally had played a more dominant role than the president in initiating environmental policies, and that pattern continued in the 1970s, particularly because the Democratic party controlled Congress during the Nixon and Ford presidencies. Although support for environmental protection was bipartisan, Democrats provided more leadership on the issue in Congress and were more likely to vote for strong environmental policy provisions than were Republicans.[26]

The increase in new federal legislation in the next decade was truly remarkable, especially since policy making in American politics is normally incremental. Appendix 1 lists the major environmental policies enacted between 1969 and 1989. They are arranged by presidential administration primarily to show a pattern of significant policy development throughout the period, not to attribute chief responsibility for the various bills to the particular presidents. These landmark measures covered air and water pollution control (the latter enacted over a presidential veto), pesticide regulation, endangered species protection, control of hazardous and toxic chemicals, ocean and coastline protection, better stewardship of public lands, requirements for restoration of strip-mined lands, the setting aside of more than 100 million acres of Alaskan wilderness for varying degrees of protection, and creation of a "Superfund" for cleaning up toxic-waste sites.

There were other signs of commitment to environmental policy goals as Congress and a succession of presidential administrations through Jimmy Carter's cooperated on conservation issues. For example, the area designated as national wilderness (excluding Alaska) more than doubled, from 10 million acres in 1970 to more than 23 million acres in 1980. Seventy-five units, totaling some 2.5 million acres, were added to the National Park Service in the same period. The National Wildlife Refuge System grew similarly. Throughout the 1970s the Land and Water

Conservation Fund, financed primarily through royalties from offshore oil and gas leasing, was used to purchase additional private land for park development, wildlife refuges, and national forests.

The government's enthusiasm for environmental and conservation policy did not extend to all issues on the environmentalists' agenda.[27] Two cases of note are population policy and energy policy. President Nixon recommended, and Congress in 1970 created, a Commission on Population Growth and the American Future. Its recommendations in 1972 that the nation should "welcome and plan for a stabilized population" were largely ignored, in part because birth rates in the United States were declining. After the early 1970s both domestic and international population issues virtually disappeared from the political agenda even though funding continued for the international aid programs begun during the 1960s.[28] The one major exception to the extremely low profile of population issues was the release in 1980 of the *Global 2000 Report to the President,* which concluded that "vigorous, determined new initiatives" were needed to deal with global problems of population, resources, and environment.[29]

For energy issues the dominant pattern was policy gridlock, not neglect. Here the connection to environmental policy was clearer to policy makers than it had been on population issues. Indeed, opposition to antipollution programs as well as land preservation came primarily from conflicting demands for energy production in the aftermath of the Arab oil embargo in 1973. The Nixon, Ford, and Carter administrations all attempted to formulate national policies for achieving "energy independence" by increasing energy supplies, with Carter's efforts by far the most sustained and comprehensive; Carter also emphasized conservation and environmental safeguards. For the most part, however, none of these presidents' efforts were successful. No consensus on national energy policy emerged among the public or in Congress, and presidential leadership was insufficient to overcome these basic constraints.[30]

Nevertheless, important changes in energy policy were enacted; these included removal of some price controls on oil and natural gas, creation of modest incentives for energy conservation, and requirements that state utility regulators consider ways to encourage conservation and use of renewable energy sources.[31] President Carter also formulated a national policy for permanent geologic disposal of high-level radioactive waste from nuclear power plants, which was submitted to Congress in 1980 and enacted during the Reagan presidency in late 1982. Congress and both presidents hoped that the waste disposal policy would brighten the otherwise dismal prospects for further development of nuclear energy. By late 1989 it had largely failed to do so, and the near-term outlook for resolving conflicts over nuclear waste is not promising.

Congress maintained its strong commitment to environmental policy throughout the 1970s, even as the saliency of these issues for the public seemed to wane. For example, it strengthened the Clean Air Act of 1970 and the Clean Water Act by amending them in 1977. Yet concern about the impact of environmental regulation on the economy and specific objections to implementation of the new laws, particularly the Clean Air Act, began creating a backlash of sorts by the end of the Carter administration.

The Reagan Interlude

The Reagan presidency brought to the federal government a very different environmental policy agenda (see also Chapter 2).[32] Virtually all environmental protection and resource policies enacted during the 1970s were reevaluated as part of the president's intent to reduce the scope of government regulation, shift responsibilities to the states, and rely more on the private sector. Confidence in the efficacy of "environmental deregulation" was predicated on the assumption that enforcement of environmental laws had a major adverse impact on the economy, a dubious proposition.[33] Whatever the merits of Reagan's new policy agenda, it was put into effect through a risky strategy that relied on ideologically committed presidential appointees to EPA and the Agriculture, Interior, and Energy departments, and on sharp cutbacks in budgets for environmental programs.

Congress initially cooperated with President Reagan, particularly in approving budget cuts, but it soon shifted to a posture of strong defense of existing environmental policy, and sharp and frequent criticism of the president's management of EPA and the Interior Department under Anne Burford and James Watt, respectively; both Burford and Watt were forced to resign by the end of 1983. Among the most notable achievements of the 1980s, Congress strengthened the Resource Conservation and Recovery Act (1984), Superfund (1986), the Safe Drinking Water Act (1986), and the Clean Water Act (1987) (see Appendix 1). It was less successful in overcoming policy gridlock on acid rain legislation, the Clean Air Act, and the nation's pesticides law (see Chapter 5). Only in the late 1980s did energy policy issues reappear on the congressional agenda, as concern mounted over the threat of global climate change. The same pattern of policy neglect and rediscovery characterized many other international environmental issues.

As we will show, budget cuts and the weakening of environmental institutions took a serious toll in the 1980s. Yet even the determined efforts of a popular president could not halt the long-term progress of environmental policy. Public support for environmental improvement, the driving force for policy development in the 1970s, increased markedly during the Reagan presidency and represented a striking rejection of the president's agenda by the American public.[34]

Paradoxically, Reagan actually strengthened environmental forces in the nation. Through his lax enforcement of pollution laws and prodevelopment resource policies, he created political issues around which national and grass-roots environmental groups could organize. They appealed successfully to a public that was increasingly disturbed by the health and environmental risks of industrial society and by threats to ecological stability. As a result, membership in environmental organizations soared, and a new grass-roots activism developed, creating further political incentives for environmental policy activities at all levels of government (see Chapter 4). By the fall of 1989, there was little mistaking congressional enthusiasm for continuing the advance of environmental policy into the 1990s, and a positive (if still cautious) stance on environmental issues was evident in the Bush White House.[35]

Institutional Development and Policy Implementation

Aside from the enactment of landmark environmental policies in the 1970s and 1980s, important institutional developments occurred that were essential to effective policy implementation and thus to actual improvements in environmental quality. Because Norman Vig discusses the Reagan administration at length in Chapter 2, we concentrate here on the institutionalization of environmental administration during the 1970s.

Institutionalizing Environmental Protection in the 1970s

The most notable institutional development in the 1970s was the establishment of EPA by President Nixon in December 1970. It was created as an independent agency that would report directly to the president, and it brought together environmental responsibilities that had been scattered among dozens of offices and programs. Under its first administrator, William Ruckelshaus, the legislative mandate of EPA grew rapidly as a consequence of the policy process we summarized earlier, and the agency acquired many new programs, offices, and staffs. EPA's budget (excluding construction grants for sewage treatment plants) grew from about $500 million in 1973 to $1.3 billion in 1980; full-time employees increased from 8,200 to 10,600, with two-thirds of them in the agency's ten regional offices. Even with its expanded budget and staff the nation's leading environmental agency found it increasingly difficult by 1980 to meet new program obligations with available resources.

During the 1970s virtually every federal agency was forced to develop some capabilities for environmental analysis under NEPA, which required that environmental impact statements (EISs) be prepared for all "major federal actions significantly affecting the quality of the human environment." Detailed requirements for the statements were set out by the Council on Environmental Quality and enforced in the courts. Provisions for public hearings and citizen participation allowed environmental and community groups to challenge administrative decisions, often by filing legal suits questioning the adequacy of the impact statements. In response to these potential objections, agencies changed their project designs—sometimes dramatically. Even the Army Corps of Engineers, which often had been castigated by environmentalists, learned to make adaptations in its designs.[36] Although the EIS process was criticized from all sides and was revised in 1979 to focus more sharply on crucial issues, most studies show that it forced greater environmental awareness and more careful planning in many agencies.[37]

Established natural resource agencies, such as Agriculture's Forest Service and Interior's Bureau of Land Management, generally made the transition to better environmental planning more easily. Long-standing doctrines of multiple use and strong professional norms of land management were gradually adapted to serve new environmental goals and interests. Wilderness preservation, never a dominant purpose of these agencies, came to be accepted as part of their mission.

Both in their compliance with new environmental laws and in their adjustment to democratic norms of open decision making and citizen participation in the 1970s, some agencies and departments lagged seriously behind others. Perhaps the most striking case is the Department of Energy. In the fall of 1988, following a series of news reports on severe environmental contamination at DOE nuclear weapons production facilities, Secretary of Energy James Watkins acknowledged the department's "years of inattention to changing standards and demands regarding the environment, safety, and health." He went on to announce initiatives intended to strengthen environmental protection at DOE facilities and to restore public confidence in the department. The cost to clean up the DOE sites was estimated at an astonishing $90 to $150 billion, to be spent over thirty years.[38] The Energy Department's record stands as a particularly clear example of the long-term costs of environmental neglect.

Successive administrations also gave modest support to the development of international environmental institutions. The United States played an active role in convening the United Nations Conference on the Human Environment held in Stockholm, Sweden, in June 1972. This conference, attended by delegations from 113 countries and 400 other organizations, addressed for the first time the environmental problems of less developed countries as well as those of industrialized nations. The result was the creation of the United Nations Environment Programme (UNEP) headquartered in Nairobi, Kenya. Although the United States disagreed with some of UNEP's initiatives, it provided the largest share (36 percent) of its budget between 1972 and 1980.[39]

Environmental Reform and Relief in the 1980s

By the time President Reagan assumed office in 1981, the effort to improve environmental quality at federal and state levels had been institutionalized, but not without a good many problems that demanded attention, including both legislative and administrative reform. Implementation often lagged years behind schedule because much of the legislation of the 1970s overestimated the speed with which new technologies could be developed and applied. The laws also underestimated compliance costs and the difficulty of writing standards for hundreds of major industries.[40] As regulated industries sought to block implementation and environmental organizations tried to speed it up, frequent legal challenges compounded the backlog.[41] Other delays were caused by personnel and budgetary shortages, scientific and technical uncertainties, and the need for extensive consultation with other federal agencies, Congress, and state governments.[42]

As a result of these kinds of difficulties, an extensive agenda for reforming environmental policies emerged by 1980. However, it was largely unaddressed by the Reagan administration, which was more concerned with providing short-term regulatory relief to industry.[43] The president's neglect of policy reform was compounded by his reliance on an administrative strategy that J. Clarence Davies described as "designed largely to reverse the institutionalization process" that had characterized the 1970s. This was accomplished through sharp budgetary reductions, weakening of the authority of experienced professionals in environmental agencies, and elimination or restructuring of many offices, particularly at EPA.[44] Staff morale and EPA credibility suffered under the leadership of Anne Burford, although both improved to some extent under EPA administrators William Ruckelshaus and Lee Thomas in the Reagan administration and William Reilly in the Bush administration. Nevertheless, the damage done in the early 1980s was considerable and long lasting. At the end of the Reagan presidency in January 1989, environmentalists still complained that there was no policy leadership at EPA and that little had been done to "restore the momentum of environmental protection." [45]

They also criticized Reagan for failing to pursue regulatory reform, saying he "blew the chance to streamline regulations and use marketplace incentives in an honest way to speed up environmental progress, lower regulatory costs, and foster economic growth." Business groups remained dissatisfied with what they believed was still an unnecessarily expensive and rigid system of federal environmental regulation. And even conservative critics of the Reagan administration expressed disappointment about what the Heritage Foundation termed a "squandered" opportunity to reform environmental protection laws and reduce their cost.[46] These same reform issues are likely to be prominent in the 1990s. As early as the summer of 1989, President Bush and leading members of Congress expressed interest in reform of environmental protection regulations, including greater use of market incentives (see Chapters 7, 8, and 11).[47]

Institutional Capacity:
Environmental Agency Budgets and Policy Implementation

As we try to assess the degree to which environmental quality might improve as a result of present laws and to consider the ability of government to meet the ecological challenges of the 1990s, there is little that is more important than budgets. Although spending more public money does not guarantee policy success, drastic budget cuts can severely undermine established programs. Thus, the massive cuts in environmental funding during the early 1980s have had long-term negative effects on the government's ability to implement environmental policies.

Appendix 2 shows spending for all natural resource and environmental programs in the federal government for fiscal years 1980 to 1990. In constant 1982 dollars, the total authorized by the federal government for these programs fell from $15.2 billion in 1980 to between $11 and $13 billion per year for most of the decade, before dropping to $9.6 billion in the proposed fiscal 1990 budget. The declines were steeper in some areas, particularly pollution control, where spending fell by 33 percent between 1980 and 1990.

Based on the president's budget for 1990, total federal spending on the environment will have increased (in constant dollars) by less than 20 percent over 1972 levels. Yet the same period saw the enactment of virtually all the major environmental laws listed in Appendix 1. Throughout most of the past two decades, funding fell far short of what was needed to implement these policies and to achieve the environmental quality goals they embodied.

In addition, the budgets of environmental and natural resource agencies did not increase enough to meet new program responsibilities (see Appendix 3). In constant 1982 dollars, EPA's operating budget in fiscal 1990 ($1.5 billion) was scarcely any higher than it had been in fiscal 1975 ($1.4 billion), despite the important new responsibilities given to the agency by Congress. Excluding Superfund employment, EPA's staff was also considerably smaller at the end of the 1980s than at the beginning of the decade (see Appendix 5).

A particularly vivid case of declining institutional capacity to make environmental policy can be seen in the Council on Environmental Quality. Adjusted for inflation, CEQ's budget dropped from $4.1 million in 1975 to $700,000 by 1990, or 83 percent (see Appendix 3). For all practical purposes, CEQ had ceased to exist for most of the 1980s. It was barely able to produce its mandated annual report on the nation's environmental quality, running several years behind schedule with a much more modest report than in earlier years. As shown in Appendix 5, CEQ's staff dropped from fifty-seven employees in 1977 to eleven by the late 1980s. The outlook for the council is more promising for the 1990s.[48]

An equally important indicator of the decline in institutional capacity is EPA's research and development budget (see Appendix 4). In the first three years of the Reagan administration, the budget declined by more than 50 percent. Although it has risen in recent years, it still remains well below its level in 1980 under the Carter administration. By 1988 the budget had suffered a 25 percent decline from 1980 in constant dollars. Research and development is presumably crucial to EPA's mission of improved environmental protection, and a budget comparison with other agencies is enlightening. At $421 million for fiscal 1990, EPA's research budget is far below that of the Department of Defense ($42 billion), the Department of Energy ($6.5 billion, most of which is for defense-related purposes), the National Aeronautics and Space Administration ($7.5 billion), and the Department of Agriculture ($1.1 billion), among other federal agencies. Although the research budget of the Energy Department is quite large, its spending on energy technology and development declined sharply (by some 60 percent) between 1980 and 1990, with spending on solar and renewable energy research especially hard hit (a 94 percent decline); the department's energy conservation budget was cut by 91 percent between 1981 and 1987.[49]

Somewhat the same picture of budget decreases characterizes natural resource agencies such as the Bureau of Land Management, the Fish and Wildlife Service, and the Forest Service (see Appendix 3). There were moderate and in some cases severe cuts during the 1980s and generally little increase in the number of employees.

Improvements in Environmental Quality and Their Costs

The most important test of any public policy is whether it achieves its objectives. Are air and water quality improving, hazardous-waste sites being cleaned up, wilderness areas being adequately protected? Unfortunately, there is no simple way to judge success.

Measuring Environmental Conditions and Trends

Environmental policies entail long-term commitments to broad social values and goals that are not easily quantified or measured. Short-term and highly visible costs are easier to measure than long-term, diffuse, and intangible benefits, and these differences often lead to intense debates over the value of environmental programs.

Variable monitoring of environmental conditions and inconsistent collection of data over time also make it difficult to assess environmental trends. To improve monitoring, data collection, and analysis, some have proposed a new and independent Bureau of Environmental Statistics to handle these important activities, now assigned to the Council on Environmental Quality under the National Environmental Protection Act of 1969.[50] Despite these limitations on measuring environmental conditions and trends, we will provide selective measures of changes in environmental quality.[51]

Air Quality. The ambient concentrations of six major air pollutants (sulfur dioxide, carbon monoxide, hydrocarbons, nitrogen dioxide, particulates, and lead) declined an average of 34.2 percent between 1970 and 1986. The declines in lead and particulates were most impressive, 95.8 percent and 70.5 percent, respectively. Sulfur dioxide and carbon monoxide concentrations each decreased by 25 percent, while nitrogen dioxide and hydrocarbon levels were up slightly, contributing to increased levels of ozone and smog. The number of unhealthful days due to air pollution has declined significantly in most parts of the country. Nevertheless, more than half of the nation's population still lives in areas where air pollution standards are exceeded at least once a year. More than one hundred urban areas still fail to meet federal standards for ozone or carbon monoxide or both.

Moreover, EPA has made little progress in dealing with toxic air pollutants; it set federal standards for only seven by mid-1989. That year information was finally reported on release of toxic air pollutants by industries; those manufacturers required to report under the 1986 Superfund amendments act released or disposed of some 22 billion pounds of hazardous substances in 1987, which included release of 2.7 billion pounds of chemicals into the air.[52] Thus, while significant progress was made in many areas, air pollution (including acid rain) remained a serious problem at the end of the 1980s, despite some $35 billion spent per year (largely by the private sector) to improve air quality. The Bush administration estimated in 1989 that the cost of compliance with its new clean air proposals would be an additional $14 to $19 billion per year; some industry estimates were much higher.

Several air pollutants are of concern primarily because of their effect on global environmental conditions rather than directly on human health. Aside from air emissions that contribute to acid rain, these include anthropogenic (human) sources of carbon dioxide, which contribute significantly to global warming, and chlorofluorocarbons, which deplete the earth's ozone layer as well as contributing importantly to global warming. Carbon dioxide emissions in the United States increased 31 percent between 1970 and 1985, and CFC emissions increased 28 percent in the same period. Without a reduction in fossil fuel use, the outlook for lower carbon dioxide emissions is not encouraging. The nation relies on fossil fuels for fully 90 percent of its energy consumption. After a long period of increased energy efficiency, energy use by the late 1980s was growing at the highest rate since 1979. The United States and Europe account for 75 percent of the world's CFC production, which is one reason consensus was reached in the 1987 Montreal Protocol to reduce worldwide CFC emissions by 50 percent by the year 1998. By 1989 most industrial nations favored a total ban on CFC production and use by the end of the century.

Water Quality. Even less tangible progress was made in other areas of pollution control. With some notable exceptions, the nation's water quality does not appear to have improved measurably since 1970. Monitoring data are less adequate for water quality than for air quality, but the available evidence shows that most rivers, streams, lakes, and estuaries maintained their quality, and a smaller number improved (in many cases strikingly so). About 25 percent of lakes declined in quality between 1972 and 1982, even though large sums were spent for water pollution control following passage in 1972 of the Federal Water Pollution Control Act (also known as the Clean Water Act); by 1987 cumulative spending by government, businesses, and individuals totaled $300 billion in constant 1984 dollars.[53] Still, prevention of further degradation of water quality in the face of a growing population and strong economic growth could be considered an important achievement. Most effort since 1972 has been on conventional point sources of water pollutants (where a particular source is identifiable), and most industries and municipalities have greatly reduced their discharges consistent with the intent of the Clean Water Act. Increasing emphasis on toxic pollutants and nonpoint sources such as agricultural runoff (the regulation of which is required by the Clean Water Act Amendments of 1987) is likely in the 1990s. To date almost no progress has been made in halting groundwater contamination despite passage of the Safe Drinking Water Act of 1974 and the Resource Conservation and Recovery Act of 1976 and their later amendments.

Toxic and Hazardous Wastes. Progress in dealing with hazardous wastes and other toxic chemicals has been the least satisfactory of all pollution control programs. Implementation of the major laws has been extraordinarily slow because of the complexity and extent of the problems, scientific uncertainty, industry opposition, people's fear of siting treatment and storage facilities in their communities, severe budgetary limitations, and lax enforcement by EPA. As a result, gains have been quite modest to date. For example, of the 1,224 sites on the national priority list of the most serious hazardous-waste sites, EPA had started cleanups at some 300 sites and completed work at fewer than 50 by mid-1989. The congressional Office of Technology Assessment has estimated that cleanup tasks could cost hundreds of billions of dollars and take decades to complete. Similarly,

EPA has followed a sluggish pace in testing toxic and hazardous chemicals. For example, under a 1972 law mandating control of pesticides and herbicides, only a handful of chemicals used to manufacture the 50,000 pesticides in use in the United States have received full testing or retesting. The track record over the past fifteen years on these various programs clearly suggests the need for reevaluation of federal policy. Congress partially addressed that need in its revision of the Superfund program in 1986, and both government and industry have experimented with promising new approaches (see Chapter 6).[54]

Natural Resources. Significant achievements have been more evident in protection of natural resources. Between 1970 and 1987 the number of acres of national parks increased by 169 percent (most of it by 1980) and the number of miles of wild and scenic rivers increased by 788 percent. By 1988 there were 119 rivers in this category totaling 9,200 miles, and the Agriculture and Interior departments proposed adding another 10,000 miles over five years. Similarly, the National Wilderness Preservation System increased in total acres by 786 percent from 1970 to 1987, the largest part added in Alaska. By 1989, twenty-five years after passage of the Wilderness Act of 1964, more than 90 million acres of wilderness had been set aside; according to the National Wildlife Federation, another 90 million acres of wildlands were unprotected. By 1989 the National Forest System consisted of 191 million acres, of which more than 32 million acres were protected as wilderness; an additional 50 million acres remain roadless, of which about 5 million acres have been recommended for wilderness designation.[55] Much less encouraging is the trend showing rapid loss of the nation's marshes, swamps, and other wetlands; more than 300,000 acres of these vital lands are lost to development each year.

Assessment. The nation made impressive gains between 1970 and 1990 in controlling many conventional pollutants and in expanding parks, wilderness areas, and other protected public lands. Despite some setbacks in the 1980s, progress on environmental quality continues, even if it is highly uneven. In the future, however, further advances will be more difficult, more costly, and more controversial. This is largely because the easy problems have already been addressed, and at this point marginal gains in air and water quality will cost more per unit of improvement than in the past (see Chapter 7). Moreover, "second generation" environmental threats such as toxic chemicals, hazardous wastes, and nuclear wastes are proving even more challenging than regulating "bulk" air and water pollutants in the 1970s. In these cases substantial progress may not be evident for years to come and will be expensive.

The same is true for the "third generation" of ecological problems, such as global climate change and protection of biodiversity. Solutions require an unprecedented degree of cooperation among nations, and substantial improvement in institutional capacity for data collection, research, and analysis as well as policy development and implementation. Hence, success is likely to come slowly as national and international commitments to environmental protection grow and capabilities improve. Some long-standing problems, such as rapid population growth, will continue to be addressed primarily within nation states even though the staggering effects on natural resources and environmental quality are worldwide. The earth's population in mid-1989 was 5.2 billion, it was increasing at 1.8 percent (or 93 million people) per year, and it is likely to reach 8.5 billion by 2025 and more than 10 billion by the end of the twenty-first century (see Chapter 13).[56]

The Costs and Benefits of Environmental Protection

The costs and benefits of environmental protection have always been vigorously debated. Critics of environmental policies believe that the kinds of improvements we have cited are often not worth the considerable costs imposed, particularly when regulations adversely affect economic growth or restrict technological development. In contrast, defenders of environmental policies are convinced that improvements in public health and in protection of "priceless" natural amenities such as wilderness areas and clean lakes are well worth the investment of governmental and private funds. Skepticism about the worth of environmental policies led to several attempts in the late 1970s and 1980s to impose regulatory oversight by the White House in the hope that costs could be limited by subjecting proposed regulations to cost-benefit analysis (see Chapters 2 and 7).[57] The imposition of these new controls (in a way that was widely thought to violate norms of administrative accountability) sharpened debate over the costs and benefits of environmental policies.

The impetus for these kinds of centralized control efforts, and the intensity of the debate over them, can be seen in the amount of money now spent on environmental protection by the federal government—as well as by state and local governments and the private sector. The federal government spends $16.5 billion per year in current dollars for all environmental and natural resource programs, or about 1.4 percent of the total federal budget. However, this is only about one-fifth of the nation's annual investment in environmental protection. Overall environmental spending in the United States, including that of state and local governments and the private sector, is estimated at 1.6 percent of the nation's Gross National Product, or about $80 billion per year. The benefits of environmental programs are more difficult to calculate, and thus there is a wide range of estimates offered by economists. Yet most studies suggest that the benefits are commensurate with the costs even if the equation varies considerably from one program to another.[58]

Debates over the costs and benefits of environmental policies will continue in the 1990s, but with several new twists. Government spending on natural resources and the environment, which rose sharply in the 1970s, is unlikely to increase much in the 1990s because of the persistent deficit in the federal budget, widespread reluctance to raise tax rates, and competing budget priorities. The burden of raising additional funds for environmental programs may be shouldered by the states, but some of them are more able and willing to do so than others (see Chapter 3). This pattern means that more of the additional cost of environmental protection will be borne by the private sector: by industry and eventually by the consumer. Another implication is that the federal government as well as the states will have to seek innovative policies that promise improvements in environmental quality without adding substantially to their budgets.

An example of what may become far more common in the 1990s is an effort by the Bush administration's EPA to draft legislation aimed at preventing rather than controlling pollution.[59] Also likely is an increase in industry programs of waste reduction, especially with new requirements of public reporting of pollution emissions. A parallel development among environmental groups, particularly the Nature Conservancy, is a successful venture into private purchase of ecologically important land for preservation. Private efforts to save endangered lands have recently been extended to financially strapped developing nations in so-called debt-for-nature swaps.

At another level the question of whether environmental programs are "worth it" must be answered in terms of the risks or costs of failing to respond or not acting soon enough. In some cases the risks to the environment and to society's well-being are so great that it would be extremely foolish to delay development of public policy. This is particularly so when prudent measures taken at an early enough date might forestall enormous costs of adjustment or remedial efforts in the future, whether paid for by governments or the private sector. That was clearly the lesson of environmental contamination at DOE nuclear weapons facilities, where cleanup will likely cost more than $100 billion. It is also apparent that such a prudent policy response is called for in the cases of acid rain, global climate change, and the thinning ozone layer, where there is great potential impact on the environment, human health, and the economy.[60] Much the same argument could be made for preservation of biodiversity and other compelling global environmental problems likely to be high on the agenda in the 1990s.[61]

Conclusion

Over the past two decades, public support for environmental protection has increased. This interest has spurred a vast array of new public policies that substantially increased the government's responsibilities, both domestically and internationally, for the environment and natural resources.

Implementation of these policies, however, has been far more difficult and controversial than their supporters imagined they would be. Partly for these reasons, the policies have been only partially successful, particularly when measured by substantive improvements in environmental quality. Further progress in the face of what are likely to be persistent and severe budgetary constraints requires that the nation search for more efficient and effective ways to achieve these goals, including the use of alternatives to conventional "command-and-control" regulation. Nevertheless, the record of the past two decades demonstrates convincingly that the U.S. government is able to produce significant environmental gains through public policies. Unquestionably, the environment would be worse today if the policies of the 1970s and 1980s were not in place.

Emerging environmental threats on the national and international agenda are even more formidable than the first generation of problems addressed by government in the 1970s and the second generation that dominated political debate in the 1980s. Responding to them will require new and imaginative efforts to improve the performance of government and other social institutions, and effective leadership to design appropriate strategies both within government and in society itself. Government is an important player in the environmental arena, but it cannot pursue forceful initiatives unless the public supports them. Only significant changes in society's values can provide the impetus for an ambitious governmental response to a rapidly changing world environment that, in all probability, will involve severe economic and social dislocations.

Notes

1. See, for example, Philip Shabecoff, "Suddenly, the World Itself Is a World Issue," *New York Times*, December 25, 1988, E3; Clifford D. May,"Pollution Ills Stir Support for Environmental Groups," *New York Times*, August 21, 1988, 20; and E. J. Dionne, Jr., "Big Oil Spill Leaves Its Mark on Politics of Environment," *New York Times*, April 3, 1989, 1, 12.
2. *Time*, January 2, 1989.
3. See Walter A. Rosenbaum, *Environmental Politics and Policy* (Washington, D.C.: CQ Press, 1985); J. Clarence Davies III and Barbara S. Davies, *The Politics of Pollution*, 2d ed. (Indianapolis: Bobbs-Merrill, 1975); and Helen M. Ingram and Dean E. Mann, "Environmental Protection Policy," in *Encyclopedia of Policy Studies*, ed. Stuart S. Nagel (New York: Marcel Dekker, 1983).
4. Norman J. Vig and Michael E. Kraft, eds., *Environmental Policy in the 1980s: Reagan's New Agenda* (Washington, D.C.: CQ Press, 1984).

5. See, for example, the World Commission on Environment and Development, *Our Common Future* (New York: Oxford University Press, 1987).
6. See John S. Dryzek and James P. Lester, "Alternative Views of the Environmental Problematique," in *Environmental Politics and Policy: Theories and Evidence,* ed. James P. Lester (Durham, N.C.: Duke University Press, 1989).
7. John W. Kingdon, *Agendas, Alternatives, and Public Policies* (Boston: Little, Brown, 1984); and Nelson W. Polsby, *Political Innovation in America: The Politics of Policy Initiation* (New Haven, Conn.: Yale University Press, 1984).
8. Roger W. Cobb and Charles D. Elder, *Participation in American Politics: The Dynamics of Agenda-Building* (Boston: Allyn and Bacon, 1972).
9. Kingdon, *Agendas, Alternatives, and Public Policies.*
10. For a more elaborate policy-cycle model, see Charles O. Jones, *An Introduction to the Study of Public Policy,* 3d ed. (Monterey, Calif.: Brooks/Cole, 1984).
11. Ronald Inglehart, *The Silent Revolution: Changing Values and Political Styles Among Western Publics* (Princeton, N.J.: Princeton University Press, 1977).
12. World Commission on Environment and Development, *Our Common Future.*
13. Samuel P. Hays, *Beauty, Health, and Permanence: Environmental Politics in the United States, 1955-1985* (New York: Cambridge University Press, 1987); and Robert C. Paehlke, *Environmentalism and the Future of Progressive Politics* (New Haven, Conn.: Yale University Press, 1989). For a discussion of public support for the new environmental paradigm, see also Lester W. Milbrath, *Environmentalists: Vanguard for a New Society* (Albany: State University of New York Press, 1984).
14. Paul J. Culhane, *Public Lands Politics: Interest Group Influence on the Forest Service and the Bureau of Land Management* (Baltimore: Johns Hopkins University Press, 1981), especially chap. 1.
15. Michael E. Kraft, "Population Policy," in Nagel, *Encyclopedia of Policy Studies,* 625-626. See also Phyllis T. Piotrow, *World Population Crisis: The United States Response* (New York: Praeger, 1973).
16. Davies and Davies, *Politics of Pollution.*
17. Helen M. Ingram and Dean E. Mann, "Environmental Policy: From Innovation to Implementation," in *Nationalizing Government: Public Policies in America,* eds. Theodore J. Lowi and Alan Stone (Beverly Hills, Calif.: Sage Publications, 1978); and Davies and Davies, *Politics of Pollution,* chap. 2.
18. See Walter A. Rosenbaum, *The Politics of Environmental Concern,* 2d ed. (New York: Praeger, 1977), chap. 5; and Charles O. Jones, *Clean Air: The Policies and Politics of Pollution Control* (Pittsburgh, University of Pittsburgh Press, 1975).
19. Rachel Carson, *Silent Spring* (Greenwich, Conn.: Fawcett Publications, 1962); Paul R. Ehrlich, *The Population Bomb* (New York: Ballantine Books, 1968); and Barry Commoner, *The Closing Circle: Nature, Man, & Technology* (New York: Knopf, 1971).

20. See Anthony Downs, "Up and Down with Ecology: The 'Issue Attention Cycle,'" *The Public Interest*, no. 28 (Summer 1972): 38-50; and Hazel Erskine, "The Polls: Pollution and Its Costs," *Public Opinion Quarterly* 36 (Spring 1972): 120-135. Erskine refers to the "unprecedented speed and urgency with which ecological issues have burst into American consciousness," and called the public's reaction "a miracle of public opinion."
21. See Garrett De Bell, ed., *The Environmental Handbook* (New York: Ballantine Books, 1970).
22. Hays, *Beauty, Health, and Permanence*. See also Riley E. Dunlap, "Public Opinion and Environmental Policy," in *Environmental Politics and Policy*, ed. Lester; and Robert Cameron Mitchell, "Public Opinion and Environmental Politics in the 1970s and 1980s," in *Environmental Policy in the 1980s*, ed. Vig and Kraft.
23. See Jones, *Clean Air;* and Lennart J. Lundqvist, *The Hare and the Tortoise: Clean Air Policies in the United States and Sweden* (Ann Arbor: University of Michigan Press, 1980).
24. Public Law 91-90 (42 USC 4321-4347), Sec. 101. NEPA was primarily the work of Sen. Henry Jackson, chair of the Senate Interior and Insular Affairs Committee; Rep. John Dingell, chair of the Subcommittee on Fisheries and Wildlife Conservation of the House Merchant Marine and Fisheries Committee; and Professor Lynton K. Caldwell, then a congressional adviser. See Lynton K. Caldwell, *Man and His Environment: Policy and Administration* (New York: Harper & Row, 1975), chap. 4; Lynton K. Caldwell, *Science and the National Environmental Policy Act: Redirecting Policy Through Procedural Reform* (University, Ala.: University of Alabama Press, 1982); and Richard A. Liroff, *A National Policy for the Environment* (Bloomington: Indiana University Press, 1976).
25. John C. Esposito, *Vanishing Air* (New York: Grossman, 1970).
26. Henry C. Kenski and Margaret Corgan Kenski, "Congress Against the President: The Struggle over the Environment," in *Environmental Policy in the 1980s*, ed. Vig and Kraft, 113-114.
27. For a review of the environmentalists' agenda as of 1977, see Gerald O. Barney, ed., *The Unfinished Agenda: A Citizen's Policy Guide to Environmental Issues* (New York: Crowell, 1977).
28. Kraft, "Population Policy," 626-629; and Michael E. Kraft, "Political Response to Population Stabilization and Decline in the United States and Western Europe: Implications for Population Policy," in *Public Policy and Social Institutions*, ed. Harrell R. Rodgers, Jr. (Greenwich, Conn.: JAI Press, 1984).
29. Council on Environmental Quality and Department of State, *The Global 2000 Report to the President*, vol. 1 (Washington, D.C.: U.S. Government Printing Office, 1980). For a major critique of the report, see Julian L. Simon and Herman Kahn, eds., *The Resourceful Earth: A Response to Global 2000* (New York: Basil Blackwell Inc., 1984).
30. See Dorothy S. Zinberg, ed., *Uncertain Power: The Struggle for a National Energy Policy* (New York: Pergamon Press, 1983); and James Everett Katz *Congress and National Energy Policy* (New Brunswick, N.J.: Transaction Books, 1984).

31. Walter A. Rosenbaum, *Energy, Politics and Public Policy* (Washington, D.C.: CQ Press, 1987); and Michael E. Kraft, "Congress and National Energy Policy: Assessing the Policymaking Process," in *Energy, Environment, Public Policy,* ed. Regina S. Axelrod (Lexington, Mass.: Lexington Books, 1981).
32. Vig and Kraft, *Environmental Policy in the 1980s.*
33. See, for example, Edwin H. Clark II, "Reaganomics and the Environment: An Evaluation," in *Environmental Policy in the 1980s,* ed. Vig and Kraft.
34. See Riley E. Dunlap, "Public Opinion on the Environment in the Reagan Era," *Environment* 29 (July/August 1987): 6-11, 32-37; and Mitchell, "Public Opinion and Environmental Politics." A CBS News/*New York Times* poll in late June 1989 showed that 80 percent of the American public agreed that "protecting the environment is so important that requirements and standards cannot be too high, and continuing environmental improvements must be made regardless of cost." The figure was up sharply from a year earlier. See "The Environment: A Higher Priority," *New York Times,* July 2, 1989, 1, 12.
35. See Trip Gabriel, "Greening the White House," *New York Times Magazine,* August 13, 1989, 25-26, 63, 66-68.
36. Daniel A. Mazmanian and Jeanne Nienaber, *Can Organizations Change: Environmental Protection, Citizen Participation, and the Corps of Engineers* (Washington, D.C.: Brookings Institution, 1979).
37. Richard N. L. Andrews, *Environmental Policy and Administrative Change: Implementation of the National Environmental Policy Act* (Lexington, Mass.: Lexington Books, 1976); Liroff, *A National Policy for the Environment;* and Caldwell, *Science and the National Environmental Policy Act.*
38. *Remarks by James D. Watkins, Secretary of Energy,* June 27 (Washington, D.C.: U.S. Department of Energy, 1989). See also Mark Miller, "Trouble at Rocky Flats," *Newsweek,* August 14, 1989, 19-20.
39. John McCormick, *Reclaiming Paradise: The Global Environmental Movement* (Bloomington: Indiana University Press, 1989), 110. This book provides a useful overview of international developments during this period.
40. Ingram and Mann, "Environmental Policy: From Innovation to Implementation"; Dean E. Mann, ed., *Environmental Policy Implementation: Planning and Management Options and Their Consequences* (Lexington, Mass.: Lexington Books, 1982); and Alfred A. Marcus, *Promise and Performance: Choosing and Implementing Environmental Policy* (Westport, Conn.: Greenwood Press, 1980).
41. Lettie McSpadden Wenner, *The Environmental Decade in Court* (Bloomington: Indiana University Press, 1982); and R. Shep Melnick, *Regulation and the Courts: The Case of the Clean Air Act* (Washington, D.C.: Brookings Institution, 1983).
42. See Marc K. Landy, Marc J. Roberts, and Stephen R. Thomas, *The Environmental Protection Agency: Asking the Wrong Questions* (New York: Oxford University Press, 1990).
43. George C. Eads and Michael Fix, *Relief or Reform? Reagan's Regulatory Dilemma* (Washington, D.C.: Urban Institute Press, 1984).
44. J. Clarence Davies III, "Environmental Institutions and the Reagan Administration," in *Environmental Policy in the 1980s,* eds. Vig and Kraft. See also Richard N. L. Andrews, "Deregulation: The Failure at EPA," in *Environ-*

mental Policy in the 1980s, ed. Vig and Kraft.

45. See Philip Shabecoff, "Reagan and Environment: To Many A Stalemate," *New York Times,* January 2, 1989, 1, 8.
46. Ibid., 8.
47. See *Project 88: Harnessing Market Forces to Protect Our Environment: Initiatives for the New President,* a public policy study sponsored by Sen. Tim Wirth, D-Colo., and Sen. John Heinz, R-Pa. (Washington, D.C.: Project 88, December 1988).
48. See Michael Weisskopf, "Reviving a Presidential Advisory Panel," *Washington Post National Weekly Edition,* August 21-27, 1989.
49. See Michael E. Kraft and Regina S. Axelrod, "Political Constraints on Development of Alternative Energy Sources: Lessons from the Reagan Administration," *Policy Studies Journal* 13 (December 1984): 319-330. Michael Kraft calculated the budget reductions after 1984.
50. See Paul R. Portney, "Needed: A Bureau of Environmental Statistics," *Resources,* no. 90 (Winter 1988): 12-15.
51. Unless otherwise noted, figures on environmental quality come from the CEQ annual report for 1989: Council on Environmental Quality, *Environmental Quality, 1987-1988* (Washington, D.C.: Council on Environmental Quality, 1989). In late 1989 the council plans to publish the third edition of its *Environmental Trends* sourcebook, the tables from which were included as an appendix in the 1989 annual report. For trends in global environmental conditions, see *State of the Environment: A View Toward the Nineties,* (Washington, D.C.: Conservation Foundation, 1987); *World Resources, 1988-89* (Washington, D.C.: World Resources Institute, 1988); and *State of the World* (Washington, D.C.: Worldwatch Institute, annual).
52. Philip Shabecoff, "Air Poisons Called Threat to Public," *New York Times,* March 23, 1989, 1, 8; and Shabecoff, "Industrial Pollution Called Startling," *New York Times,* April 13, 1989, 12.
53. Conservation Foundation, *State of the Environment,* 87.
54. See Daniel Mazmanian and David Morell, "The Elusive Pursuit of Toxics Management," *The Public Interest,* no. 90 (Winter 1988): 81-98.
55. Philip Shabecoff, "The Battle for the National Forests," *New York Times,* August 13, 1989, "Week in Review," 1.
56. Population Reference Bureau, "World Population Data Sheet" (Washington, D.C.: Population Reference Bureau, April 1989).
57. See *Regulatory Program of the United States Government: April 1, 1988-March 31, 1989* (Washington, D.C.: Executive Office of the President, Office of Management and Budget, 1988), 4-37.
58. A. Myrick Freeman III, *The Benefits of Environmental Improvement: Theory and Practice* (Baltimore, Md.: Johns Hopkins University Press, 1979); Daniel Swartzman, Richard A. Liroff, and Kevin G. Croke, eds., *Cost-Benefit Analysis and Environmental Regulations* (Washington, D.C.: Conservation Foundation, 1982); and Robert E. Litan and William D. Nordhaus, *Reforming Federal Regulation* (New Haven, Conn.: Yale University Press, 1983), chap. 2.
59. Margaret E. Kriz, "An Ounce of Prevention," *National Journal,* August 19, 1989, 2093-2096.

60. U.S. Environmental Protection Agency, "The Potential Effects of Global Climate Change on the United States" (Washington, D.C.: U.S. Environmental Protection Agency, 1988); Irving Mintzer, "Living in a Warmer World: Challenges for Policy Analysis and Management," *Journal of Policy Analysis and Management* 7 (Spring 1988): 445-459; Lester B. Lave, "The Greenhouse Effect: What Government Actions Are Needed?" *Journal of Policy Analysis and Management* 7 (Spring 1988): 460-470; and Stephen H. Schneider, "The Greenhouse Effect: Science and Policy," *Science* 243 (February 10, 1989): 771-781.
61. Conservation Foundation, *State of the Environment*, chap. 9. See also the special issue on "Managing Planet Earth" of *Scientific American* 261 (September 1989).

2

Presidential Leadership: From the Reagan to the Bush Administration

Norman J. Vig

The Reagan administration has an eight-year history of ignoring environmental reality and, as it limps into history, it seems intent on retaining the dubious virtue of being consistently wrong on environmental matters.

James Bradley
Environment Minister, Canada, 1988

I would be a Republican president in the Teddy Roosevelt tradition. A conservationist. An *environmentalist*.

George Bush

"I am an environmentalist," proclaimed George Bush during his campaign for the presidency in 1988. In one of the more dramatic scenes of the campaign, the vice president set sail in Boston Harbor and conducted a well-televised press conference on the alleged failure of his opponent, Governor Michael Dukakis, to clean up the sewage-clogged bay. The same day, an editorial in the *New York Times* carried the title "Electoral Dynamite: The Environment."[1]

It was the first time in nearly two decades that environmental problems had received such prominent attention in a presidential campaign. Not since 1972, when the environmental movement was near its peak, had public concerns over air and water pollution threatened to become a major election issue. The reasons were not difficult to discern. The summer of 1988 was the hottest and driest in memory, convincing much of the public that the "greenhouse effect" had begun. While crops withered and much of Yellowstone Park went up in flames, air pollution reached record levels in many cities. New evidence of ozone depletion in the upper atmosphere brought fears of cancer-causing radiation from the sun, while beaches along the New Jersey and Long Island coasts had to be closed as medical waste and other garbage washed up from the ocean. Capturing the ecological symbolism of these events, Bush warned solemnly that "Nineteen eighty-eight is the year Earth spoke back."[2]

This statement also symbolized a second reason for Bush's new emphasis on the environment: the failure of the Reagan-Bush administration's environmental policies over the previous eight years. On this issue Bush clearly wished to distance himself from the "Reagan revolution" and from his own public record as vice president. Shortly after taking office in 1981, Reagan had put him in charge of the Task Force on Regulatory Relief, a top-level group that eliminated, relaxed, and delayed scores of environmental regulations that the Reagan conservatives and the business community opposed. Although Bush later claimed that he personally supported some of these regulations—such as those requiring the phaseout of lead in gasoline—he displayed no visible leadership on environmental issues while vice president and earned highly negative ratings from environmental organizations along with the rest of the Reagan team. As concern for the environment mounted, Bush obviously felt vulnerable.

By 1988, moreover, it was evident that much of the initial thrust of the Reagan revolution had dissipated and that the public was looking for a different brand of leadership. The early push for deregulation had ground to a halt, and many new concerns such as air traffic safety, the collapse of the savings and loan industry, and the massive contamination discovered at nuclear weapons plants suggested the need for renewed government controls. The indifference of Reagan to these and other accumulating problems, such as the budget and trade deficits, contributed to the Republican loss of the Senate and weakened presidential authority in the second term. A series of scandals ranging from the Iran-contra affair to revelations of gross conflicts of interest in the White House and Pentagon further tarnished Reagan's leadership image. His perceived callousness toward the homeless and other disadvantaged groups indicated little concern for those left behind by the new economic growth.

Bush's campaign strategy was shaped by these weaknesses and by the consequent opportunity to define a program that would both maintain the perceived successes of the Reagan administration in economic and foreign policy and correct its excesses and mistakes. His promises of "no new taxes," prudent continuation of arms control negotiations with the Soviets, and tough new controls on crime and drugs spoke to the more popular elements in the Reagan record. But his call for a "kinder and gentler America" signaled a shift toward a less strident and ideological stance on social issues. Bush promised to work with Congress in finding practical solutions to many of the problems neglected in the Reagan era, including those affecting the environment.

The questions posed in this chapter are whether President Bush's environmental agenda is a significant break from that of the Reagan administration and how the powers of the presidency are likely to be used to assert environmental leadership. In order to understand the significance of the transition and prospects for the 1990s, it is first necessary to review the Reagan record on environmental policy. We can then examine the catalyzing effect of the 1988 campaign and the early initiatives of the Bush administration to evaluate the potential for change. Although any conclusions at this stage must remain tentative, the president's agenda is largely set during the first year in office and usually offers strong evidence of the direction policy will take in the future.

The Legacy of the Reagan Administration

Ronald Reagan entered office with the most conservative agenda and ideological perspective in half a century. Not since the New Deal had any president tried to reorient American government in so fundamental a manner. In Reagan's view, developed during long years of speaking for General Electric before serving as governor of California, government was the problem rather than the solution. He perceived the growth of the federal government, particularly its regulatory functions, as a basic threat to political liberty as well as the source of many of the country's economic and social ills. Thus, he attacked the new laws of the 1970s covering occupational safety and health, consumer protection, energy conservation, and the environment. These and other instances of "social regulation," he argued, were an unnecessary burden on the economy that was undermining our competitive position and world leadership.

During the campaign of 1980, Reagan showed little appreciation of environmental issues, at one point stating that trees were a major source of air pollution and calling for relaxation of the Clean Air Act. He also endorsed the "sagebrush rebels," a group of politicians, ranchers, and miners from several western states who were demanding that federal public lands be turned over to their control. Echoing his views, the Republican platform "declare[d] war on government overregulation" and called for "cost-benefit analysis of major proposed regulations." It also called for maximum growth of domestic energy production by moving "forward on all fronts simultaneously, including oil and gas, coal, and nuclear," and warned that "environmental protection must not become a cover for a 'no-growth' policy and a shrinking economy." [3]

Although public opinion surveys indicated strong public support for environmental protection, the perilous state of the economy and national defense were evidently uppermost in people's minds when they elected Reagan by a landslide on November 4, 1980 (Reagan received 50.7 percent of the vote, Jimmy Carter 41.0 percent, and John Anderson 6.6 percent). Reagan, who had promised to reduce taxes, increase defense spending, and balance the budget by eliminating "waste, fraud, and abuse," interpreted his victory together with Republican recapture of the Senate as a mandate for radical change.

The First Term

The goal of the Reagan revolution was to sharply curtail the role of the federal government in regulating the economy and redistributing wealth through social programs. In terms of economic theory, it rejected traditional Keynesian techniques for managing aggregate demand through fiscal and monetary policies in favor of a new "supply-side" doctrine, which held that reductions in marginal income tax rates would so stimulate work, saving, and investment that the resulting economic growth would balance the budget.[4] Deregulation was also seen as a tool for economic revival, especially by the new chairman of the Council of Economic Advisers, Murray Weidenbaum, and the director of the Office of Management and Budget (OMB), David Stockman. Before taking office, Stockman and then-Rep. Jack Kemp, R-N.Y., had written a widely circulated memorandum warning of an "economic Dunkirk" unless regulatory burdens were eased within the first few months of the new administration.[5] OMB was soon to become the center for deregulatory efforts.

President Reagan's first term was largely dominated by his priorities calling for a massive supply-side tax cut and an enormous increase in defense spending. The former was accomplished by the seminal legislative achievement of the Reagan presidency, passage of the Economic Recovery Act of 1981, which provided for a 25 percent cut in personal income taxes over three years as well as huge tax breaks for business corporations. The expansion of military spending, already begun under President Carter, greatly accelerated in the budgets for fiscal years 1982-1985. Cuts in domestic programs proved much harder to achieve, however, particularly since the bulk of social spending goes to middle-class entitlement programs such as Social Security and Medicare that Congress holds sacred. Moreover, high inflation rates led the Federal Reserve Board to maintain steep interest rates in the early 1980s, contributing to a severe recession in 1981-1982 that slowed business activity, threw millions out of work, and reduced tax revenues. The resulting unprecedented federal budget deficits were to plague the administration for the remainder of its tenure.

President Reagan's approach to environmental policy must be seen in this context. More than in any previous administration, government policies across the board were subordinated to a few overriding economic and political objectives. Thus, programs such as those for the environment received relatively little independent attention and were largely viewed as targets for deregulation efforts.

Although he had appointed an environmental transition team that included such moderate Republicans as William Ruckelshaus and Russell Train, both former heads of the Environmental Protection Agency (EPA), Reagan ignored their recommendations in favor of more radical proposals submitted by Stockman, Weidenbaum, and such organizations as the conservative Heritage Foundation.[6] As if to symbolize the change, the new Council on Environmental Quality, whose staff was cut from about sixty to eleven shortly after Reagan took office, echoed the new philosophy in its first report. The principles to guide environmental policy making were:

- use of cost-benefit analysis to determine the value of environmental regulations
- reliance as much as possible on the free market to allocate resources
- decentralizing environmental responsibilities to the states
- continuation of cooperation with other nations to solve global environmental problems.[7]

Although the latter remained largely a dead letter until the second term, the administration energetically pursued the first three goals from the outset as part of its deregulatory effort.

One of Reagan's first acts was to create the Task Force on Regulatory Relief headed by Vice President Bush. During its initial two-and-one-half years of existence, the task force reviewed hundreds of new and existing environmental regulations, rescinding some and returning many others to EPA and other agencies for further study and modification.[8] In February 1981 the president issued Executive Order 12291, which required cost-benefit analysis of all proposed regulations. The order provided that,

> to the extent permitted by law, all agencies must adhere to the order's substantive criteria in their regulations. These include: (1) refraining from regulatory action unless potential benefits outweigh potential costs to society; (2) choosing regulatory objectives that maximize net benefits to society; (3) selecting the alternatives that will impose the least net cost to society while achieving regulatory objectives; and (4) setting regulatory priorities to maximize aggregate net benefits to society, taking into account factors such as the condition of the national economy and of particular industries.[9]

Economic criteria were thus to be considered in all agency decision making. "Regulatory impact analyses" focusing on the costs of proposed regulations were to be prepared by all agencies and submitted to the new Office of Information and Regulatory Affairs (OIRA) within OMB. This process became a primary tool for slowing the growth of new regulation.[10]

Previous presidents had attempted to establish centralized controls over the bureaucracy, but Reagan's efforts to create an "administrative presidency" went much further.[11] In addition to the OMB review process and task force, Reagan attempted to ensure loyalty to his ideology and program by carefully screening all political appointees to agency positions. He appointed ideological conservatives to head both the Environmental Protection Agency (Anne McGill Gorsuch; her name later became Anne Burford in 1983) and the Interior Department (James D. Watt), as well as to key positions in all of the offices of these and other agencies. Virtually all of these appointees came from the business corporations to be regulated or from legal foundations or firms that had fought environmental regulations for years. Very few had previous experience in Washington or in environmental science. The result in the early years was a highly politicized and ideological form of environmental administration that drove many senior executives and professionals out of the environmental agencies.[12]

Perhaps an even more significant way of taming the regulatory agencies was to cut their budgets and personnel. Adjusted for inflation, EPA's operating budget was cut by more than one-third between 1981 and 1983, reducing it to a level comparable to a decade earlier. Funding for conservation programs in the Interior Department was also cut as emphasis was shifted to resource development, and support for energy conservation and renewable energy sources was virtually eliminated. EPA lost approximately 20 percent of its personnel as a result of these initial cuts. Although Congress later restored some of the funding cuts of 1981-1982, EPA's real operating budget (excluding grants for sewer construction and Superfund cleanup) has remained at pre-1980 levels (see Appendix 3).

Finally, President Reagan attempted to maintain control and coordination of administrative policy making through a series of "cabinet councils" consisting of several cabinet secretaries and members of the White House Office of Policy Development, the president's domestic policy staff. The Cabinet Council on Natural Resources and Environment was chaired by James Watt, giving it a strongly developmental orientation.

All of these tools—the Task Force on Regulatory Relief, Executive Order 12291 and the OMB regulatory review process, political appointments, budget and personnel cutbacks, and coordination through cabinet councils—reflected a conscious strategy for expanding the powers of the presidency to control the administrative state. The purpose was to achieve deregulation through administrative control rather than legislative reform. This effort to deregulate without congressional authorization or statutory revision proved highly controversial, to say the least. Environmental groups, members of Congress, and much of the public viewed the Reagan strategy as illegitimate. The result was a pitched battle over environmental policy during the first three years of the Reagan administration that culminated in the forced resignations of both EPA Administrator Burford and Interior Secretary Watt in 1983.

These officials aroused a storm of protest over both their abrasive, confrontational style and the substance of their decisions. They made it abundantly clear that they intended to use their full administrative powers to reverse the thrust of past environmental policies—which they considered fanatically pro-environmental—to achieve a "balanced approach" that recognized the interests of business and economic development. In part the shift was manifested by the appointment of business and industry executives to key agency positions and deliberate exclusion of environmental groups from the policy-making process. At one point James Watt issued a memorandum forbidding Interior Department staff to talk to environmentalists, but in any case they were no longer consulted. Burford announced that EPA would seek "cooperation" rather than "confrontation" with regulated industries, leading to frequent informal meetings with their representatives. These closed meetings and attempts to reach voluntary agreements with regulated parties raised questions about proper administrative procedures and suspicions about "sweetheart deals" that violated statutory requirements.

But Watt, Burford, and their subordinates also felt free to reorganize their agencies and reinterpret environmental laws to modify regulations in line with the Reagan agenda. Burford caused turmoil at EPA by abolishing the Enforcement Division, then reestablishing it, and then reorganizing it. Watt "streamlined" the Office of Surface Mining by abolishing its field offices and reducing its staff. He announced his intention to rewrite his department's operating manuals and regulations to permanently alter the "institutional memory" at Interior. But his decision to support and promote oil, gas, and mineral development aroused the greatest controversy. His plan for offshore oil drilling would have opened up the entire outer continental shelf to oil and gas exploration, including fragile areas off the coasts of California and Alaska. Watt also accelerated the leasing of western public lands for coal mining and approved a massive sale at Powder River Basin in Montana and Wyoming at prices later determined to have been well below market value. Most controversial of all, however, were Watt's attempts to open up national wilderness areas to mineral exploration, a cause he had previously espoused as an attorney for the prodevelopment Mountain States Legal Foundation.[13]

These actions provoked the wrath of environmental groups, whose memberships began to grow by leaps and bounds in response to the perceived threat. In March 1982, ten leading environmental and conservation groups issued an "indictment" of the president, charging that he had "broken faith with the American people on environmental protection" by taking or proposing "scores of actions that veered radically away from the broad bipartisan consensus in support of environmental protection that has existed for many years." [14] The document listed 227 ways in which environmental policies allegedly were being subverted. In another effort, more than a million signatures were collected on a petition calling for Watt's resignation.

Congress also revolted against the Reagan policies. Members of both parties, including key leaders of the Republican-controlled Senate Environment and Public Works Committee, fought Watt's unilateral attempts to rewrite regulations to permit exploitation of wilderness areas and other public lands. In the House of Representatives, several riders were attached to appropriations bills to prohibit such actions. A bipartisan majority also opposed revision of the major environmental statutes, leading to stalemate with the Reagan administration over amendment of the Clean Air Act and other major laws that were up for renewal between 1981 and 1984 (see Chapter 5).

Congress conducted numerous oversight hearings and other investigations into EPA and Interior Department activities. In late 1982, five House subcommittees and a Senate committee were investigating rumors of scandal in EPA's Superfund program. Charges were made that political influence had been exercised in the distribution of waste cleanup funds in California and elsewhere, and that secret deals had been made with some polluting industries. When a House committee attempted to subpoena documents from EPA, Burford, acting on White House instructions, refused to release them on grounds of executive privilege. As a result, she was cited for contempt of Congress, the highest executive official ever so charged. In the ensuing battle, President Reagan was forced to back down on the issue of executive privilege. Burford resigned, and some twenty other top EPA officials were fired in the spring of 1983.[15]

James Watt's demise came in October, after some tactless remarks about the racial composition of a commission set up to investigate his coal-leasing policies. By this time, however, it was obvious that his policies had little public support and that he had become an electoral liability. Even more than Burford, he had come to symbolize the political and ideological excesses of the early Reagan administration.

Although President Reagan praised both Burford and Watt, he was evidently little concerned with the details of policy making and eager to create a more positive environmental image. His appointment of William Ruckelshaus to replace Burford won wide public approval, while the surprise selection of his national security adviser, Judge William P. Clark, to succeed Watt at least indicated that he wanted to avoid further controversy and embarrassment at Interior. Contacts were restored with environmental groups, and Ruckelshaus brought in a new team that gradually restored credibility to EPA. Ruckelshaus was able to increase EPA's budget somewhat and get its regulatory program back on track (for example, regulations were issued to phase lead out of gasoline, and hazardous-waste legislation was strengthened), but no new initiatives were allowed on acid rain and other pending issues during the remainder of the term.

Reagan's first administration thus was a failure if the goal was to achieve major deregulation or changes in the basic framework of environmental law. The "administrative strategy" of seeking changes through the executive agencies while bypassing Congress and ignoring environmental constituencies and public opinion largely backfired. Reagan's ideological appointees proved to be such an embarrassment that he was forced to drop them when the scandals they perpetrated threatened to engulf the White House. As conservatives have since pointed out, the opportunity for reforming environmental regulation was squandered amidst these political controversies and the pro-environmental backlash that resulted.[16] On the other hand, from an environmental perspective, much damage had been done. Although the major environmental laws of the 1970s remained intact, their implementation had been seriously weakened by budgetary and staff reductions and by the political turmoil at EPA. The president's lack of leadership was an even greater travesty from this perspective.

The Second Term

In November 1984 Ronald Reagan was reelected by a landslide over former vice president Walter Mondale, who carried only one state and the District of Columbia. The election was generally seen as a strong endorsement of the president's first-term performance, especially in reviving the economy in 1983 and 1984. Environmental issues were barely mentioned during the campaign, mainly because the removal of Burford and Watt had defused most of the controversy before the election year.

Reagan interpreted his decisive victory as a mandate to "stay the course" and "complete the Reagan revolution," but it was by no means clear what this meant since the president failed to articulate any agenda comparable to that of 1981. Except for simplification of the tax system, which led to the bipartisan Tax Reform Act of 1986, the administration proposed no major initiatives in domestic policy during the second term. Much of both executive and congressional attention was focused on one overriding problem inherited from the first term: the budget deficit, which averaged more than $200 billion from 1983 to 1986. The Gramm-Rudman-Hollings amendment enacted by Congress in 1985 provided for automatic spending cuts if budget reduction targets were not met, but the deficit still hovered at $155 billion in 1988. Reagan's budget proposals were increasingly ignored by Congress, which began imposing its own priorities. Still, the deficit remained the single most important constraint on government programs, including those for the environment.

President Reagan took no obvious leadership on environmental issues during the second term. He appeared even less involved in the details of domestic policy than in the first term, a tendency that may have been furthered by centralization of powers in his new chief of staff, Donald Regan. On one issue, however, he remained steadfast: Reagan continued to insist that more research was needed before any action could be taken to control acid rain, much to the chagrin of Prime Minister Brian Mulroney and the Canadian government. He also threatened to veto a new Superfund law and did veto the new Clean Water Act twice, only to have both pass, the latter over his veto.

The Office of Management and Budget continued to resist new regulatory actions and proposed further reductions in environmental and resource conservation programs. OMB actually extended its control over regulation. Executive Order 12498, which supplemented Executive Order 12291 in 1985, required agencies to submit information on their regulatory calendars that outlined "significant regulatory actions" they planned to take during the following year, thus allowing OMB to influence regulatory priorities at an earlier stage.[17]

Congress was no longer cowed by the Reagan presidency, however, and increasingly ignored the administration, even before the Democrats regained control of the Senate in 1986. Several of the major environmental statutes were reauthorized and strengthened, notably the Superfund and Clean Water Acts—though Congress remained deadlocked over others, including the Clean Air Act and pesticide reform (see Chapter 5). Congressional committees, especially the House Energy and Commerce Committee, led by Rep. John D. Dingell, D-Mich., also fought a running battle with OMB over its attempts to impose what were regarded as political controls on EPA and other agencies. These congressional investigations, along with legal challenges to the constitutionality of OMB authority, forced OIRA to modify its regulatory review procedures during the second term. The review process by 1989 was somewhat more accountable since an open public record of OMB-agency transmittals is kept and *ex parte* contacts between OIRA staffers and outside interests are forbidden once regulatory actions have begun.[18]

The restoration of EPA's mission begun under Ruckelshaus in 1983 and 1984 continued under his successor in the second term, Lee M. Thomas. Thomas, who had been brought in to clean up the Office of Toxic Waste Management under Ruckelshaus, was a competent, low-key professional administrator who attempted to obtain support from both industry and environmentalists. To his credit, the number of EPA enforcement actions against polluters reached record levels and significant progress was made in issuing required environmental regulations, although many still lagged far behind schedule. Passage of the Superfund and Clean Water Act amendments led to substantial increases in EPA responsibilities and budget in these areas, but its general operating budget and staff increased little and morale remained low in many sections of the agency.

Within these constraints and the multiplicity of statutes under which EPA operates, Thomas attempted to concentrate EPA resources in areas of highest priority. Like Ruckelshaus, he furthered the use of risk assessment and cost-benefit analysis as techniques for defining these priorities (see Chapters 7 and 8). He also extended the use of economically efficient regulatory methods such as the "bubble policy," under which firms may use any combination of controls on specific pollution sources as long as overall emissions do not exceed allowable limits.[19] Finally, Thomas joined forces with the State Department to launch a new effort in global environmental diplomacy, perhaps the administration's most significant environmental achievement of the second term. Thomas and his staff played a crucial supporting role in negotiations leading to the Montreal Protocol of 1987, by which some thirty nations agreed to reduce chlorofluorocarbon (CFC) production by 50 percent by 1998. Although this goal is no longer considered adequate (as EPA predicted in 1987), the Montreal accords established an important precedent for multinational agreements on environmental protection that is likely to be followed in the future (see Chapters 14 and 17).

The Interior Department, on the other hand, continued the general orientation of the early Reagan years toward making public lands and resources available for private development. Donald P. Hodel, who served as secretary of interior from 1985 to 1989, pursued the same basic policies as his predecessors in less controversial ways. (He had served as James Watt's under secretary before moving to the Energy Department and then back to Interior.) Although more accessible and willing to negotiate than Watt, Hodel continued to push for maximum energy and resource exploitation on public lands, including oil exploration on the continental shelf and in unspoiled areas such as the Arctic National Wildlife Refuge (ANWR). Hodel also opposed the Montreal treaty, at one point suggesting that people don hats and sunglasses to avoid excess exposure to ultraviolet radiation.[20]

Although Hodel had moderate success in leasing oil, coal, and timber lands, low oil prices and other market conditions limited demand for rapid exploitation of these resources. Still, the administration continued to press for more private access to national forests and grazing lands, often against strong opposition from environmental groups determined to protect such unique amenities as virgin timber stands in Oregon and Washington. Other administration efforts to "privatize" public assets included transferring water rights on Bureau of Land Management

(BLM) lands to ranchers and oil shale lands to companies at prices far below market levels.[21] On the other hand, despite its opposition to adding any lands to the public domain, the administration did agree to establish a new park, Great Basin National Park in Nevada, and acquiesced in congressional addition of several million acres to the National Wilderness System.

One area in which the Reagan administration lost great opportunity was energy policy. From the beginning, the president favored deregulation of oil prices and reliance on free-market incentives to increase supplies and encourage conservation. But as a world oil surplus developed and fuel prices fell, incentives for conserving energy evaporated, and by 1986 energy consumption per unit of gross national product had leveled off and begun to grow.[22] Oil imports also began rising rapidly in the late 1980s, amounting to nearly as large a share of national consumption as before the oil crisis of 1979. Despite these trends, the Reagan administration suspended requirements for raising the fuel economy standards of new automobiles and opposed legislation enacted in 1987 requiring energy efficiency standards for new appliances. The Department of Energy (DOE) provided almost no support for either energy conservation or the development of renewable energy supplies (adjusted for inflation, funding for energy conservation fell by 91 percent between 1981 and 1987).

As if to symbolize these failures, massive nuclear and chemical contamination was revealed in 1987 and 1988 at all nuclear weapons plants managed by DOE. Other safety problems forced the shutdown of military nuclear reactors producing plutonium and tritium for bombs. (It should be noted that DOE facilities are not subject to the same Nuclear Regulatory Commission safety standards that civilian nuclear power plants are.) DOE has estimated the cost of cleaning up and rehabilitating its nuclear facilities at between $90 billion and $150 billion over the next thirty years. Ironically, funds shifted from environmental and safety programs to weapons construction in the Reagan years have not only destroyed the plants, but will end up costing society many times over in health and environmental damages.[23] This kind of neglect of long-term costs in favor of short-term gains was typical of many aspects of an administration that left its successor with enormous debts to pay.

The Transition to the Bush Administration

George Bush inherited a host of environmental problems, many of which had been exacerbated by eight years of negative presidential leadership. To be fair, others such as ozone depletion and the greenhouse effect had barely been recognized eight years earlier and were beyond the control of any one government. But he also inherited a presidency that was no more powerful than when Reagan took over, and was in some ways weaker. Unlike Reagan, Bush had no coattails and made no gains in Congress; instead the Democratic party increased its already solid margins in both houses. Thus, what had appeared to be a conservative victory turned into a "split-level realignment," entrenching each party in control of a different branch of government.[24] President Bush would thus face continuing stalemate unless he sought bipartisan cooperation with Congress.

Bush was in many ways suited to this task by experience and temperament. He had begun his political career in the House of Representatives and had held many other important administrative and diplomatic posts. He was considered a moderate, pragmatic, consensus seeker who respected competence and expertise. His service as a loyal and even enthusiastic lieutenant to Reagan, however, had tarnished these credentials in the eyes of many. This was certainly true in the field of environmental policy, mainly because of his role as chairman of the Task Force on Regulatory Relief. The League of Conservation Voters, an environmental organization that rates candidates according to their positions on environmental issues, gave Bush no better than a "D+" at the outset of his campaign. His running mate, Dan Quayle, was also rated as having one of the worst environmental records in the Senate; as senator he voted on the pro-environmental side of key issues only 20 percent of the time.[25] Bush thus faced an uphill fight in convincing the public that he would become an "environmental president."

The Election Campaign

Bush had been searching for issues on which to differentiate himself from Reagan during the year before the 1988 election. One issue that surfaced repeatedly among his campaign advisers was the environment. During the spring of 1988 his policy advisory staff, headed by pollster Robert Teeter, identified this as one of several key issues (along with education, drugs, and crime) that could swing independent voters to Bush, and the campaign conducted extensive research on the environmental record of Bush's likely opponent, Gov. Michael Dukakis. During June and July polls indicated rapidly rising public concern over the drought and other environmental issues. Meanwhile, the Bush campaign staff had identified six key "swing" states that were likely to determine the outcome of the election: California, New Jersey, Ohio, Illinois, Michigan, and Missouri. These were all states with a large number of suburban voters interested in "quality of life" issues. In the absence of major economic and foreign policy crises, these issues took on increasing significance among Bush's campaign strategists. In mid-August, the campaign staff, headed by James Baker and Teeter, decided to schedule

Bush for a week of environmental speeches at the end of August and in early September. Robert Grady, a former aide to New Jersey governor Thomas Kean who had emerged as the staff's environmental adviser, drafted the speeches for Bush.[26]

On August 31, Bush broke symbolically with the Reagan record on environmental policy. After weeks of attacking Dukakis as a "card-carrying liberal," Bush, in a surprise speech at the Detroit Metropark, declared himself an environmentalist in the Teddy Roosevelt tradition. "The time for study alone has passed," he stated in reference to the Reagan position on acid rain, promising a detailed plan to "cut millions of tons of sulfur dioxide emissions by the year 2000." He also promised to end ocean dumping of garbage by 1991 and to prosecute illegal disposers of medical waste; supported a major national effort to reduce waste generation and promote recycling; committed himself to a program of "no net loss" of wetlands and protection of lakes and fisheries; promised to convene a conference of world leaders to discuss global environmental problems during his first year in office; and called for strict enforcement of toxic waste laws, saying EPA should use its authority to "sue for triple damages" to force operators to clean up waste sites.[27] The next day he launched his famous attack on Dukakis's environmental record in Boston Harbor.

The sudden importance accorded the environment by Bush was unexpected not only because it seemed out of character with his previous record and agenda, but also because neither party had devoted much attention to environmental issues during their national conventions earlier in the summer. The Democratic platform contained a brief and general statement of environmental concerns that differed little in content from that of the Republicans. Gov. Dukakis had devoted only one sentence of his acceptance speech to the topic, while Bush had spent two short paragraphs on water and air pollution.[28]

Dukakis and the Democratic campaign staff were caught off guard by Bush's environmental attack in late August and were slow in responding to it—perhaps because they thought the environment was "their" issue. Dukakis did set out an environmental agenda during September and October that compared favorably with Bush's, but it received less attention in the last hectic weeks of the campaign. Although many of the themes were similar, Dukakis's proposals were somewhat more specific and differed on several points. For example, to reduce acid rain he promised to cut sulfur emissions by 12 million tons and nitrogen oxide emissions by 4 million tons by 2000, while Bush failed to specify any numbers (his subsequent plan was less ambitious, as indicated below). While Bush agreed to postpone offshore oil drilling in certain fragile areas of the California and Florida coasts, he approved oil exploration in the Arctic National Wildlife Refuge in Alaska; Dukakis opposed opening

ANWR to oil development and offered a more specific plan to protect the California coast. Bush strongly supported all forms of energy development, including nuclear, while Dukakis opposed further licensing of nuclear power plants until safety and nuclear waste disposal problems were solved, and placed more emphasis on energy conservation and alternative fuel sources. Both promised to convene an international conference or "summit" on the environment, but Dukakis also pledged to restore U.S. funding for international population control programs. Finally, Dukakis proposed to make the Environmental Protection Agency a cabinet department, which Bush opposed (in part because he was already committed to establishing a new department for veterans' affairs).[29]

Bush won the election easily on November 8 with 53 percent of the popular vote and 79 percent of the electoral college tally, carrying all six of the critical states. Although no single issue appears to have been decisive, exit polls suggested that Bush benefited most from his positions on national defense, taxes, crime, and abortion—the same issues that contributed to Reagan's popularity.[30] However, other issues may have tipped the balance in states such as California and New Jersey, where environmental concerns were strongest.

What about environmental issues generally? Were they salient to voters, and if so, how did they affect the outcome? According to one exit poll, reported in Table 2-1, "protecting the environment" was considered one of the most important reasons for choosing one candidate over the other by 11 percent of the voters, ranking it considerably below the budget deficit, defense, abortion, and crime as a motivating issue. Of those who did consider environmental issues among the most salient factors in their vote, Dukakis was favored by 70 percent, a positive rating exceeded only by Bush's advantage on defense. The poll results suggest that Bush's campaign promises were not very convincing, at least among strongly committed environmentalists (or, alternatively, that most of the latter are Democrats). Bush's environmental stance may have been important, however, in keeping some wavering voters from defecting to Dukakis on this issue.[31] In any event, all survey evidence suggests that a majority of the American public would support a vigorous environmental program such as *either* candidate proposed (see Chapter 4).

The Transition

Bush interpreted his victory as a mandate for his environmental policies and after his election moved quickly to open a dialogue with a broad range of environmental and conservation groups. Even before appointing a transition staff, he and his White House counsel, C. Boyden Gray, met with representatives of some thirty environmental organiza-

Table 2-1 Issues in the 1988 Presidential Election

	Percentage voting for Bush	Dukakis
Which issues were most important to your vote?		
The federal budget deficit (25%)	39	60
National defense (23%)	84	15
Abortion (20%)	63	36
Crime (18%)	67	31
Ethics in government (17%)	31	67
Taxes (15%)	70	29
Drugs (14%)	41	58
Unemployment (10%)	35	64
Protecting the environment (11%)	28	70
Foreign Trade (5%)	57	42
No issue, really (12%)	52	45

Source: Michael Nelson, ed., *The Elections of 1988* (Washington, D.C.: CQ Press, 1989), 84. Cable News Network/*Los Angeles Times* exit poll.

Note: The percentages that follow each issue indicate the percentage of respondents who mentioned the issue. Respondents could name more than one issue.

tions who submitted a list of more than 700 proposals for consideration by the new administration.[32] A transition team consulted further with these and others, including a bipartisan study group sponsored by Sen. Tim Wirth, D-Colo., and Sen. John Heinz, R-Pa., which prepared "Project 88," an influential report suggesting ways of using market forces to protect the environment.[33] Other long-time environmental advisers, notably William Ruckelshaus and Russell Train, were key in the selection of top environmental appointees such as the new EPA administrator.

The transition process thus went smoothly, particularly in comparison to when Reagan first took office. By inauguration day Bush's environmental agenda, derived from his campaign speeches, was reasonably well set.[34] The president also began his administration with considerable optimism and support from environmental groups, in marked contrast to his predecessor. But their continuing support and his success in implementing the agenda would depend heavily on three factors: (1) his appointments to key environmental positions, (2) his budget support for environmental programs, and (3) his specific proposals for environmental action. The picture is decidedly mixed on all of these criteria.

Appointments

During the campaign Bush promised to appoint a leading environmentalist to head EPA. In December 1988 he nominated William K. Reilly, president of the World Wildlife Fund and Conservation Foundation. Reilly's selection was warmly received by most environmental groups and in Congress. He had established a reputation as an effective leader at the Conservation Foundation, a moderate environmental think tank in Washington that advocates pollution prevention, comprehensive "cross-media" approaches to pollution control, and voluntary collaboration and mediation between industry and environmentalists to solve environmental problems.[35] Although Reilly is widely respected in the environmental community, concern was expressed that he might be too willing to compromise in seeking environmental consensus. He quickly developed a close personal relationship with Bush, however, and emerged as a strong environmental advocate within the administration.[36]

Some of Bush's other environmental appointees, such as Michael Deland as chairman of the Council on Environmental Quality (CEQ), also received wide support. Deland, a strong environmentalist and former director of EPA's regional office in Boston, took the position on condition that he would have regular access to the president and that CEQ would be restored to its former status in the Executive Office of the President. Robert E. Grady, Bush's environmental speechwriter, has been appointed associate director of the Office of Management and Budget for Natural Resources, Energy, and Science and is also considered a spokesman for the environment. The same can be said for Dr. Frederick Bernthal, who was appointed to head the State Department's Bureau of Oceans and International Environmental and Scientific Affairs, which is conducting negotiations on global warming and other international environmental problems.

On the other side of the coin, President Bush's choices for agencies dealing with public lands and other natural resources were strongly criticized by environmental groups. His new secretary of interior, Manuel Lujan, Jr., compiled a dismal environmental record as a ten-term U.S. representative from New Mexico and is regarded as a strong supporter of western development interests.[37] Although more accessible and pragmatic than his predecessors James Watt and Donald Hodel, Lujan is not likely to depart from their basic policies; for example, he supports old-growth timbering in the Northwest and oil exploration in the Arctic National Wildlife Refuge and other sensitive areas.

Bush's nominees to head the Bureau of Land Management and the National Park Service in Interior and the U.S. Forest Service in the Department of Agriculture appear similar to their counterparts in the Reagan administration. The new BLM director, Delos Cy Jamison, worked for James Watt and Rep. Ron Marlenee, R-Mont., who has one of the worst environmental records in the House. The National Park Service director, James M. Ridenour, is a former Republican party fund-raiser and associate of Vice President Dan Quayle who angered environmentalists while serving as head of Indiana's Department of Natural Resources. But most controversial was Bush's nominee to head the Forest Service, James E. Cason. As acting assistant secretary for land and minerals management at Interior, Cason was involved in below-market sales of oil shale lands and attempts to open national parks and wilderness areas to strip mining and oil drilling. Nine environmental groups charged him with "extreme bias in favor of those who financially benefit from the exploitation of the nation's public lands and resources," and the Senate later failed to confirm him.[38] However, Bush has compromised his environmental stance by awarding the key land-use agencies to the traditional ranching, mining, and timbering constituencies in the West.

Other Bush appointees, such as Adm. James D. Watkins as secretary of energy, received mixed reviews. A nuclear engineer who strongly supports energy development, Watkins has promised to elevate safety to top priority in the department. However, the nominee for DOE assistant secretary of environment, safety, and health, Diane K. Morales, was described as "a former Neiman-Marcus buyer and political appointee under James Watt" who inspired little confidence, and the Senate refused to confirm her.[39] Indeed, the confirmation process at DOE and other agencies proceeded so slowly that fourteen of the eighteen top positions were not filled during the first eight months of the Bush administration. It is thus difficult to say what the overall character of the administration will be, but it appears to have what *New York Times* reporter Philip Shabecoff has called a "split personality on appointments."[40]

Budgets

President Bush has made it clear that he intends to hold the line on federal spending to combat the budget deficit. His first budget, for FY 1990, called for the same level of expenditures for environment and natural resource programs as President Reagan had proposed. For future years to 1993, modest increases are proposed for pollution control, research and development, and international environmental programs, but outlays for all environment and natural resource functions are projected to increase only nominally (from $16.5 billion in 1989 to $17.9 billion in 1993 without allowing for inflation). Under Bush's budget the Environmental Protection Agency would receive only minor increases despite additional responsibilities for toxic waste cleanup, air pollution control, international programs, and other problems. Within a relatively static budget, EPA will devote increasing resources to research and development, an area singled out for exceptionally large cuts in the Reagan years. Expenditures will grow considerably for Department of Energy programs to develop "clean coal" and alternative fuel technologies, as well as for environmental cleanup and waste management at the nation's nuclear weapons facilities, but total outlays for energy programs were projected to *decline* by 1993.[41]

The strategy of the Bush administration is to emphasize enforcement and the "polluter pays" principle. Major increases in pollution control costs are to be borne by industry—and ultimately consumers—rather than by the federal government. Thus "off-budget" costs for environmental protection are expected to rise substantially despite the freeze on government spending. This approach is considered economically rational because it provides incentives to reduce pollution generation at the source, but whether it will prove politically feasible to off-load costs in this manner remains to be seen. Meanwhile, the continuing erosion of EPA's budget in real terms is a major concern to environmentalists.

Policy Initiatives

A new president usually has to act quickly during the first year in office if he is to achieve major domestic policy reforms.[42] The momentum gained by election and inauguration provides only a brief "honeymoon" for agenda setting before Congress and interest groups reassert their control over particular policy domains. The window of opportunity may be even narrower when both houses of Congress are controlled by the other party, as in the case of the Bush administration. Thus, to reassert leadership over environmental policy Bush had to honor his campaign promises quickly by proposing specific policy initiatives.

In fact, President Bush was heavily criticized for the slow, deliberate pace at which his administration began. On a number of issues he appeared to be reacting tardily to events or criticism rather than exerting leadership. For example, he was slow to respond and took little responsibility when the *Exxon Valdez* tanker ran aground in Prince William Sound off Alaska in March 1989, causing the worst oil spill in U.S. history. His administration relied heavily on Exxon's promises to clean up the spill—in line with its "polluter pays" philosophy—and only grudgingly turned supervision over to the U.S. Coast Guard when Exxon's initial efforts proved grossly inadequate. Similarly, the Bush administration held up negotiations for an international conference on global warming until it was acutely embarrassed by revelations that OMB had ordered one of the government's top scientists, Dr. James Hansen of NASA's Goddard Institute for Space Studies, to weaken his testimony before Congress on the greenhouse effect. When informed of this, the president quickly reversed the administration's position and called for a workshop on global warming to be held in Washington.[43]

This episode and others revealed deep divisions within the Bush administration over both national and international environmental policy. The Energy, Agriculture, Transportation, and Commerce Departments, as well as the Office of Management and Budget, have vigorously opposed EPA's proposals in cabinet meetings. OMB director Richard G. Darman, perhaps the most powerful holdover from the Reagan White

House, reportedly has gone so far as to argue that Bush should write off his pledge of an environmental presidency since they "could never make nature lovers a Republican constituency." [44] It thus appears that Bush's commitment is stronger than that of his administration and that environmental initiatives will not succeed without direct presidential intervention.

This was illustrated by the most important environmental initiative taken during the first year: Bush's plan for revising the Clean Air Act, announced at a press conference on June 12, 1989, to which environmental representatives were prominently invited. The sweeping proposals were much tougher than expected, but did not represent any consensus within the administration or its Domestic Policy Council. Instead they reflected a long and bitter struggle of interests that was finally resolved in favor of Reilly and the EPA's position by the president and his chief of staff, John Sununu.[45]

These proposals reflected what Bush himself referred to as "a new environmental philosophy" consisting of five objectives:

- to harness the power of the marketplace
- to encourage local initiative
- to emphasize prevention, instead of just cleanup
- to foster international cooperation
- to ensure strict enforcement; polluters will pay.[46]

While the first, second, and fourth of these principles were similar to those of the Reagan administration, they took on new meaning under Bush. The third and fifth points were significant departures from the Reagan philosophy (see page 37).

The Bush clean air proposals had three main goals: to control acid rain by reducing sulfur dioxide (SO_2) emissions from coal-burning power plants by 10 million tons (nearly half) and nitrogen oxide (NO_x) emissions by 2 million tons by the year 2000; to reduce urban air pollution (especially ozone and smog) enough to meet clean air standards in all but twenty cities by 1995 and in all cities within twenty years (mainly by reducing auto pollution by switching to cleaner fuels such as ethanol and natural gas and tightening up tailpipe emissions standards); and to reduce emissions of airborne toxics (chemicals suspected of causing cancer) by 75-90 percent by 2000. These are ambitious goals, but the methods proposed for achieving them were even more significant. Essentially, Bush adopted the arguments made by economists for years that flexible market incentives would achieve more at less cost than the present system of detailed technology standards mandated for each industry and type of plant under the Clean Air Act. Thus, under the Bush proposals power plants would be allowed to choose whatever combination of options for reducing SO_2 emissions they found least costly. Moreover, they would be allowed to buy and sell emission rights under a new system of marketable pollution rights. This form of emissions trading could eventually be extended to many other types of pollution generation, including air toxics and the right to produce such climate-damaging chemicals as CFCs.[47]

Bush's Clean Air Act proposals were almost immediately subject to attacks from industry and further infighting within the administration. The bill sent to Congress on July 21 was weaker than the original proposal on several points, and the White House subsequently failed to defend its provisions on clean automobile fuels.[48] But chances for reaching agreement during the 101st Congress appear better than at any time since the last revision of the Clean Air Act in 1977. President Bush's willingness to work with rather than against Congress on this issue may well determine the fate of his "environmental presidency."

Conclusion

George Bush deserves much credit for returning environmental policy to center stage after a decade of neglect. Although public opinion and electoral motivations played their part, there is no reason to doubt his sincerity in wishing to attack the mounting environmental problems we face. As a young representative from Texas he had a good environmental record, and he has now separated his presidency from Ronald Reagan's on issues relating to pollution, global climate change, and some facets of resource conservation. His first major environmental proposal, for drastic revision of the Clean Air Act, was both innovative and visionary. His recognition that environmental problems are serious and require renewed commitment in the 1990s amounts to a sea change of attitude in the Oval Office.

Bush's underlying philosophy is not very different from his predecessor's, however. Like Reagan, he believes that economic development and environmental protection are fully compatible; that the "free market" can solve environmental problems better than government regulators; and that no major changes are necessary in the American lifestyle to save the environment. His "conservation ethic," like that of Teddy Roosevelt at the beginning of the century, is based on the concept of wise management and use of resources rather than preservation of nature for its own sake.

The president will also continue to rely on the Office of Management and Budget to review and eliminate regulations that are not considered "economically rational" (Executive Orders 12291 and 12498 remain in effect). Although Bush now appears to favor regulatory reform rather than deregulation of the type advocated early in the Reagan administration, it remains to be seen whether he is willing to impose heavy costs on industry and consumers to achieve environmental goals.

Finally, it is by no means certain that any of the president's environmental policies will survive opposition in Congress and within his own administration. Many Democrats remain wary of concepts like marketable pollution rights, and traditional Republican constituencies and Reagan holdovers continue to oppose most environmental initiatives. Bush's appointments to the Interior and Agriculture Departments are especially disappointing in this regard and suggest an unwillingness to confront hard choices on western land and conservation issues. His refusal to consider tax increases or to provide any real budget increase for EPA suggests continuing failure to comprehend the institutional implications of policies required for the new decade. Rhetoric will not produce policy results without further commitment of resources.

The environmental jury is thus still out on Bush. But given the many interests at stake in environmental policy and the painful adjustments that may be necessary in coming decades, the importance of presidential leadership can scarcely be exaggerated. In our system, the president alone can exert unifying moral leadership in time of crisis, and he alone can lead in foreign affairs. The magnitude and complexity of the environmental problems we face at the close of the twentieth century are likely to require stronger leadership than we have seen from any president thus far—including Teddy Roosevelt.

Notes

1. Robin Toner, "Bush, in Enemy Waters, Says Rival Hindered Cleanup of Boston Harbor," *New York Times,* September 2, 1988, 9, 24.
2. George Bush, "Promises to Keep," *Sierra,* November/December 1988, 62.
3. For these and other excerpts from the 1980 party platforms, see Michael E. Kraft, "A New Environmental Policy Agenda: the 1980 Presidential Campaign and Its Aftermath," in *Environmental Policy in the 1980s: Reagan's New Agenda,* ed. Norman J. Vig and Michael E. Kraft (Washington, D.C.: CQ Press, 1984), 36-37.
4. See, for example, Herbert Stein, *Presidential Economics* (New York: Simon and Schuster, 1984); Benjamin A. Friedman, *Day of Reckoning* (New York: Random House, 1988); and William A. Niskanen, *Reaganomics* (New York: Oxford University Press, 1988).
5. See Richard A. Harris and Sidney M. Milkis, *The Politics of Regulatory Change: A Tale of Two Agencies* (New York: Oxford University Press, 1989), 97-98.
6. See Norman J. Vig, "The President and the Environment: Revolution or Retreat?" in Vig and Kraft, *Environmental Policy in the 1980s,* 84. See also Richard W. Waterman, *Presidential Influence and the Administrative State* (Knoxville: University of Tennessee Press, 1989), chap. 5.
7. Council on Environmental Quality, *Environmental Quality 1981* (Washing-

ton, D.C.: U.S. Government Printing Office, 1981), iii-iv and chap. 1.

8. Presidential Task Force on Regulatory Relief, *Reagan Administration Regulatory Achievements,* August 11, 1983. See also Harris and Milkis, *Politics of Regulatory Change,* 6-8 and chaps. 4 and 6.
9. As summarized in Richard A. Liroff, "Cost-Benefit Analysis in Federal Environmental Programs," in *Cost-Benefit Analysis and Environmental Regulations: Politics, Ethics, and Methods,* ed. Daniel Swartzman et al. (Washington, D.C.: Conservation Foundation, 1982), 39.
10. See Joseph Cooper and William F. West, "Presidential Power and Republican Government: The Theory and Practice of OMB Review of Agency Rules," *Journal of Politics* 50 (November 1988): 864-892; Harris and Milkis, *Politics of Regulatory Change,* 100-113, 257-265; and V. Kerry Smith, *Environmental Policy under Reagan's Executive Order: The Role of Cost-Benefit Analysis* (Chapel Hill: University of North Carolina Press, 1984).
11. George C. Eads and Michael Fix, *Relief or Reform? Reagan's Regulatory Dilemma* (Washington, D.C.: Urban Institute Press, 1984), chap. 3; and Richard P. Nathan, *The Administrative Presidency* (New York: Wiley, 1983).
12. Chester A. Newland, "The Reagan Presidency: Limited Government and Political Administration," *Public Administration Review* 43 (January/February 1983): 1-21. For a critique of Reagan's "administrative presidency" in this area, see Michael E. Kraft and Norman J. Vig, "Environmental Policy in the Reagan Presidency," *Political Science Quarterly* 99 (Fall 1984): 414-439.
13. For a more detailed summary of Watt's policies, see Paul J. Culhane, "Sagebrush Rebels in Office: Jim Watt's Land and Water Policies," in Vig and Kraft, *Environmental Policies in the 1980s,* 293-318.
14. *Ronald Reagan and the American Environment* (San Francisco: Friends of the Earth, 1982).
15. J. Clarence Davies, "Environmental Institutions and the Reagan Administration," in Vig and Kraft, *Environmental Policy in the 1980s,* 154-157. Burford tells her side of the story in Anne M. Burford (with John Greenya), *Are You Tough Enough?* (New York: McGraw-Hill, 1986).
16. Niskanen, *Reaganomics,* 125-129; Nolan Clark, "The Environmental Protection Agency," in *Mandate for Leadership III: Policy Strategies for the 1990s,* ed. Charles L. Heatherly and Burton Yale Pines (Washington, D.C.: Heritage Foundation, 1989), 213; and Robert W. Crandall, "What Ever Happened to Deregulation? " and Fred. L. Smith, Jr., "What Environmental Policy? " both in *Assessing the Reagan Years,* ed. David Boaz (Washington, D.C.: Cato Institute, 1988).
17. See *Regulatory Program of the United States Government,* published annually since 1986 by the Office of Management and Budget.
18. Interview with S. Jay Plager, director of the Office of Information and Regulatory Affairs, OMB. However, Congress continues to threaten to impose stricter time limits on OMB reviews to prevent regulatory delays; see also Margaret E. Kriz, "Good Riddance? " *National Journal,* July 22, 1989, 1930.
19. Richard A. Liroff, *Reforming Air Pollution Regulation: The Toil and Trouble of EPA's Bubble* (Washington, D.C.: Conservation Foundation, 1986).

20. Rochelle L. Stanfield, "Tilting on Development," *National Journal*, February 17, 1987, 313-318; Philip Shabecoff, "Watt's Goals at Interior, But in a Different Style," *New York Times*, March 3, 1986; and Rochelle L. Stanfield, "Greenhouse Diplomacy," *National Journal*, March 4, 1989, 512.
21. Philip Shabecoff, "Interior Dept. Acts to Speed Sales of Public Lands for Development," *New York Times*, January 8, 1989.
22. Matthew L. Wald, "U.S. Progress in Energy Efficiency Is Halting," *New York Times*, February 27, 1989.
23. "They Lied to Us," *Time*, October 31, 1988, 60-65; David C. Morrison, "Pentagon Polluters," *National Journal*, July 1, 1989, 1689-1691.
24. See Michael Nelson, ed., *The Elections of 1988* (Washington, D.C.: CQ Press, 1989); and David Rapp, "Reagan Added Luster but Little Clout to Office," *Congressional Quarterly Weekly Report*, January 7, 1989, 3-12.
25. "Presidential Candidate Report Card" (Washington, D.C.: League of Conservation Voters, 1988); and Philip Shabecoff, "Quayle Is Rated on Environment," *New York Times*, October 7, 1988, 10.
26. Interview with Robert Grady.
27. John Holusha, "Bush Pledges Aid for Environment," *New York Times*, September 1, 1988; Bill Peterson, "Bush Vows to Fight Pollution, Install 'Conservation Ethic,'" *Washington Post*, September 1, 1988.
28. For platform statements, see *Congressional Quarterly Weekly Report*, July 16, 1988, 1969, and August 20, 1988, 2387-2388. For acceptance speech comments, see ibid., July 23, 1988, 2054, and August 20, 1988, 2355.
29. The candidates' positions are summarized in "Promises to Keep," *Sierra*, November/December, 1988, 62-65, 116-117; "From Afar, Both Candidates Are Environmentalists. . . ," *New York Times*, September 24, 1988, 15; see also "Bush Pledges Aid for Environment," ibid., September 1, 1988; "Bush, in Enemy Waters, Says Rival Hindered Cleanup of Boston Harbor," ibid., September 2, 1988; "Dukakis Asserts Foe Somersaults on Environment," ibid., September 18, 1988; "Dukakis Turns Attack on Bush to Environment," ibid., September 30, 1988; "Dukakis Vows a Vast Coastal Sanctuary," ibid., October 2, 1988.
30. Paul J. Quirk, "The Election," in Nelson, *Elections of 1988*, 83-85.
31. Interview with Robert Grady.
32. Philip Shabecoff, "Bush Lends an Ear to Environmentalists," *New York Times*, December 1, 1988, 13. The "blueprint" presented to Bush by the environmental coalition was later published as *Blueprint for the Environment: A Plan for Federal Action*, ed. T Allan Comp (Salt Lake City: Howe Brothers, 1989).
33. *Project 88, Harnessing Market Forces to Protect Our Environment: Initiatives for the New President*, a public policy study sponsored by Sen. Tim Wirth, D-Colo., and Sen. John Heinz, R-Pa., (Washington, D.C.: Project 88, December 1988).
34. Bush's policies are summarized in *Building a Better America*, White House, February 9, 1989; and George Bush, *Leadership on the Issues* (Washington, D.C.: Republican National Committee, 1988).
35. Margaret E. Kriz, "Reilly at EPA," *National Journal*, January 14, 1989, 101;

"An Interview with William K. Reilly," *EPA Journal* 15 (March/April 1989): 2-6. For a critical perspective, see Dick Russell, "We Are All Losing the War," *The Nation*, March 27, 1989, 403-408.

36. *Congressional Quarterly Weekly Report*, February 4, 1989, 231; and Trip Gabriel, "Greening the White House," *New York Times Magazine*, August 13, 1989, 25.
37. John B. Oakes, "Bush's Shell Game," *New York Times*, January 12, 1989, 19; Cass Peterson, "No Cheers for Lujan," *Washington Post Weekly Edition*, May 22, 1989, 9-10.
38. John Lancaster, "Environmentalists Hit 'Shocking' Appointment," *Washington Post*, July 11, 1989, 23; "Mixed Reviews on Environmental Appointees," ibid.; John B. Oakes, "Bush 'Environmentalists'—Who's Watt, and Why," *New York Times*, April 29, 1989, 15; and Allan R. Gold, "Bush Nominee Withdraws Under Senate Pressure," *New York Times*, November 21, 1989, 11.
39. Judith Havemann, "Choice for Top Environmental Post in Energy Department Criticized," *Washington Post*, June 29, 1989; and Joseph A. Davis, "Watkins: New Management, Tighter Controls at DOE," *Congressional Quarterly Weekly Report*, February 25, 1989, 384.
40. Shabecoff, "Environment," *New York Times*, April 11, 1989; and Thomas W. Lippman, "Plenty of Room at the Top," *Washington Post National Weekly Edition*, October 2, 1989, 33.
41. For budget proposals, see *Building a Better America*, 84, 147-148, 185. However, DOE Secretary Watkins has proposed a large increase in cleanup spending; see also Keith Schneider, "$21 Billion Cleanup Is Proposed at Nuclear Sites in Next 5 Years," *New York Times*, August 1, 1989, 11.
42. Paul C. Light, *The President's Agenda* (Baltimore: Johns Hopkins University Press, 1982); and James P. Pfiffner, *The Strategic Presidency: Hitting the Ground Running* (Chicago: Dorsey, 1988), especially chaps. 7 and 8.
43. Edward P. Morgan, "Waiting for George," *The Amicus Journal* (Spring 1988): 14-17; "Fishing for Leadership," *Time*, May 22, 1989, 91; "Feeling the Heat on the Greenhouse," *Newsweek*, May 22, 1989, 79; and George Hager, "OMB Tampering of Testimony Hurts Bush's Credibility," *Congressional Quarterly Weekly Report*, May 13, 1989, 1112.
44. Gabriel, "Greening the White House," 66.
45. Ibid.; Michael Duffy, "Mr. Consensus," *Time*, August 21, 1989, 18-19; Margaret E. Kriz, "Politics in the Air," *National Journal*, May 6, 1989, 1098-1102.
46. White House Press Secretary, "Text of Remarks by the President on the Clean Air Act Announcement" (mimeo), June 12, 1989, 2.
47. George Hager, "Bush Sets Clean-Air Debate in Motion with New Plan," *Congressional Quarterly Weekly Report*, June 17, 1989, 1460-1464; Philip Shabecoff, "President Urges Steps to Tighten Law on Clean Air," *New York Times*, June 13, 1989, 1; Richard W. Stevenson, "Concern over Bush Clean-Air Plan," *New York Times*, June 14 1989, IV1; and Robert D. Hershey, Jr., "New Market Is Seen for 'Pollution Rights,' " ibid. For reactions, see Barbara Rosewicz and Michel McQueen, "Bush, Resolving Clash in Campaign Promises, Tilts to Environment," *Wall Street Journal*, June 13, 1989, A1; and

Curtis A. Moore, "Why Wait 20 Years for Clean Air?" *Washington Post*, June 18, 1989, C3.

48. John Lancaster, "Clean Air Proposal Weakened," *Washington Post*, July 12, 1989, A1; Philip Shabecoff, "Draft of Anti-Pollution Bill Falls Short, Critics Say," *New York Times*, July 12, 1989, B5; and Bill Richardson, "Watering Down Clean Fuels," *New York Times*, November 19, 1989, 23.

3

A New Federalism? Environmental Policy in the States

James P. Lester

For several reasons the early 1990s are a particularly exciting time to examine state environmental politics and policy. First, the 1980s were a period of state implementation of important environmental laws enacted during the previous decade: the Clean Air Act Amendments of 1970, the Federal Water Pollution Control Act Amendments of 1972, the Resource Conservation and Recovery Act of 1976, the Safe Drinking Water Act of 1974, the Surface Mining Control and Reclamation Act of 1977, and the Comprehensive Environmental Response, Compensation, and Liability Act of 1980.[1] Like the 1980s, the decade of the 1990s will be an "implementation era" in environmental policy, as well as in other areas of public policy.

Second, intergovernmental relations (meaning the relationships among the federal, state, and local governments) have recently taken on greater significance than ever before. During the 1980s, the doctrine of New Federalism stressed devolution of authority from the federal level to state and local levels in many areas of public policy. As part of the legacy of Ronald Reagan's presidency, states and local communities are taking on many responsibilities for protecting the environment that were previously assumed by the federal government. Indeed, the head of Vermont's environmental agency, Jonathan Lash, has said that the most important innovations in environmental protection are now occurring at the state level.[2] Many others agree with this assessment. More specifically, the Reagan administration had a number of objectives—including regulatory reform, reliance on the free market to allocate resources, and decentralization—whereby responsibilities for environmental protection were to be shifted to state and local governments whenever possible.[3] Early assessments, however, suggest that the states vary substantially in the extent to which they are able to maintain the level of commitment to environmental protection that was originally fostered by the federal government.[4]

Finally, the states themselves have undergone important transformations in their institutional capacities for implementing federal programs during the past twenty-five years. Presumably, states are no longer the weak link in the intergovernmental system of the United States. These changes of the past two decades are so far-reaching as to constitute a clear break with the past.[5] For all of these reasons, then, it is important to review changes in intergovernmental relations over the previous two decades and to assess the implications of these changes for the future of environmental management in the states.

In this chapter several questions are addressed. First, what is the New Federalism, and what are the implications of this change in federal-state relations for environmental management? Second, how are the states responding to the New Federalism, as indicated by environmental policy innovations, environmental policy implementation, and environmental policy impacts at the state level? Third, what are some of the explanations for states' behavior as a reaction to the New Federalism? Finally, what are the prospects for state environmental management in the 1990s, given the transfer of responsibility for environmental management from the federal government to state and local governments?

Federal Devolution of Authority and Resurgence of the States

Two dramatic developments affected the states during the 1970s and the 1980s. First, the Nixon and Reagan administrations, under their programs of New Federalism, attempted to return power and authority to the states and cities. New Federalism, which began with the State and Local Fiscal Assistance Act of 1972, mandated an expanded role for state and local governments. Among other things, states would become less subject to fiscal control by the federal government. Initially, New Federalism involved a number of short-term inducements, such as programmatic flexibility, elimination of de facto dual planning requirements for categorical grant applications, and increased consultation with state and local decision makers prior to the initiation of "direct development" activities.[6] By 1981, however, the objectives of President Reagan's New Federalism were to *decentralize* and *defund* federal environmental protection activities.

Proponents of the Reagan administration's program argued that the states, with their enhanced institutional capacities, were in a position to assume greater responsibilities than ever before. States and cities would simply make difficult choices about which programs they wanted to retain (and thus replace federal cuts with their own funds) and which ones they wanted to terminate. In this sense, then, public pressure would force state decision makers to take actions that reflected localized policy preferences. Critics, on the other hand, argued that the administration shifted responsibilities to the states, at least in the environmental area, for another reason as well—as a way to eliminate some programs altogether.[7]

During Reagan's first term, the states were subject to substantial cuts in a number of environmental program areas, including air pollution control, water pollution control, hazardous-waste management, pesticide enforcement, wastewater treatment, and safe drinking water. Although there is evidence that the states have strengthened their institutional capacity to deal with contemporary public policy problems, it is questionable whether state administrators can assume greater program responsibilities on such short notice.[8] Some programs are less amenable to decentralization of jurisdictional authority than are others because environmental pollution crosses state boundaries or because local industry pressures policy makers to adopt less stringent environmental protection policies. Nor is there convincing evidence that all states are prepared politically, economically, or administratively to adopt a more autonomous role in the management of some federal environmental programs. In fact, early assessments of the extent to which the states were willing or able to replace the federal cutbacks with their own funds suggested that most of the states did not do so in the environmental area, at least during the period from 1981 to 1984.[9]

The second dramatic development that affected the states during the past two decades was the transformation of their institutional capabilities. The states revised their constitutions, professionalized their legislatures (for example, by increasing salaries and staff support), modernized and strengthened the governor's office, reorganized their executive branches, reformed their courts, increased their revenues through tax diversification, and provided greater opportunities for citizen participation in state government through "open meeting laws" and other reforms.[10] Not all states adopted such reforms, nor were all equally able to make these modifications.[11] Hence, not all of them are able effectively to assume their new environmental responsibilities under the New Federalism of the 1990s.

The States' Response to New Federalism: 1972-1989

So much attention has been focused on activities of the federal government that many important developments at the state level have been given less attention than they deserve. Some states exhibit striking examples of innovative activity, while others are more conventional and less active. In fact, studies suggest a great deal of diversity in responses by the states to the challenges posed by the New Federalism of the 1970s and 1980s. A number of researchers in "think tanks" and university settings have studied innovative state actions, state environmental policy implementation, and the impacts of state environmental policy. Some of the more impressive state activities are discussed here.

Environmental Policy Innovations

The Council of State Governments has collected information on innovative environmental and natural resource policies since 1976. This information indicates that the total number of innovations in the states increased dramatically during the 1980s and that the quality of the innovations improved as well.

Innovative state actions include a groundwater discharge permit system in Arizona; statewide recycling mandates in some states; Proposition 65 in California on toxic use reduction; and source reduction programs in half a dozen states. In addition, a number of states (for example, New York, Connecticut, New Jersey, Maine, Massachusetts, New Hampshire, Rhode Island, and Vermont) have announced restrictions on the amount of gasoline vapor that may be emitted by automobiles.[12] In another regional effort, Virginia, Maryland, Pennsylvania, and the District of Columbia are cooperating to clean up the badly polluted Chesapeake Bay.[13] Denver has worked hard to reduce its air pollution, and New Jersey has imposed new environmental taxes and fees, and set up revolving loan funds. Variations in state groundwater quality protection programs suggest some states like Arizona have been quite innovative while other states like Texas have been much less so.[14]

Recent innovative programs in three states deserve special mention. The first is Southern California's attempt to reduce air pollution by imposing drastic restrictions on everyday activities. If put into effect, the three-phase plan would require that all cars be converted to electric power or other "clean" fuels by the year 2007. Other provisions, beginning as early as 1989, tighten restrictions on the use of automobiles, encourage public transportation, and limit household and industrial activities that produce chemical emissions. These measures include a ban on lighter fluid for barbecue grills and a requirement that restaurants that use charcoal broilers install special vents to reduce emissions. In addition, gasoline engines on lawn mowers would be banned, bias-ply tires would be banned, additional pollution control equipment would be required on some cleaning plants, and, to reduce traffic and automobile exhaust pollution, free parking would be virtually eliminated.[15] Although the plan must still receive federal approval, it is the most stringent air pollution control scheme ever formulated in the United States.

California also enacted the Beverage Container Recycling and Litter Reduction Act in 1986, the purposes of which are to promote a strong recycling industry; to reduce the amount of litter and solid waste going to landfills, thereby conserving landfill space; and to provide accessible sites for recycling. Consumers receive cash back for labeled beverage containers at recycling centers located within one-half mile of every major supermarket. There are more than 2,300 recycling centers throughout the state.

Another innovative state program is Florida's "Amnesty Days," days once a year when a free, mobile hazardous-waste collection program visits each county. The program provides the opportunity for each citizen, school, business, or government agency to properly dispose of up to one fifty-five-gallon drum of hazardous waste. One of the first in the nation, this program has been a model for other cities and states to follow as they implement new requirements for small-quantity generators under the Hazardous and Solid Waste Amendments of 1986.

Finally, North Carolina's "Pollution Prevention Program" represents a fundamentally different approach to environmental pollution in the United States. In the past both the federal government and the various subnational governments used an "end-of-pipe" approach to regulation, whereby laws were enacted to clean up environmental pollution after the fact. In this new approach "front-end" regulations are written to prevent pollution before it occurs. The goal of the program is to identify and apply methods to reduce, minimize, or recycle hazardous wastes before they become pollutants. Technical assistance, on-site consultation, and research and education are the cornerstones of this program, which was a useful model for the congressional Office of Technology Assessment's study on hazardous-waste minimization in 1986.[16]

During the 1990s, more innovative actions by the states are likely as they attempt to deal with environmental problems. Some states, however, have been far less active in changing their environmental policies during the past decade. This latter category of states is a cause of concern regarding their willingness and ability to deal with the diversity of environmental threats in the 1990s.

State Commitments and Environmental Management

As noted earlier, the states vary substantially in their commitment to environmental protection policies and in their ability, economically and institutionally, to carry out strong environmental protection programs. The Conservation Foundation has studied this variation, as indicated by both fiscal and nonfiscal measures.[17] Its overall focus is on regulatory programs and expenditures for environmental quality. The data (collected mostly in 1983) suggest that Minnesota, California, New Jersey, Massachusetts, and Oregon are among the states most heavily committed to the environment, while Oklahoma, New Mexico, Idaho, Mississippi, Missouri, and Alabama are some of the least committed.

The Fund for Renewable Energy and the Environment (FREE) has provided another source of data on what the states have done to protect the environment.[18] Since 1987, FREE has conducted an annual study that is nonfiscal in nature and reports an assessment of where the states stand on key environmental issues such as air pollution reduction, soil conservation, solid waste and recycling, hazardous-waste management, groundwater protection, and renewable energy and conservation. According to these data, Massachusetts, Wisconsin, California, and New Jersey are the most active states, and Arkansas, Mississippi, West Virginia, and Wyoming are the least active. In FREE's most recent study, other states in the top ten are Oregon, Minnesota, Iowa, Florida, Maryland, and Connecticut.[19] FREE and the Conservation Foundation identified the same states as the most environmentally concerned over time.

States' capabilities to protect the environment vary as well as their commitment to environmental protection. The Council of State Governments recently studied the fifty states' institutions for environmental management, their expenditures for environmental and natural resource programs, and the numbers of state government employees with environmental or natural resource responsibilities.[20] Table 3-1 presents a state-by-state comparison of the numbers of state employees devoted to environmental protection.

The data in the table suggest some potential problems in the states' ability to effectively manage the environment, no matter how progressive or innovative they may be. Some environmental problems, such as toxic waste, cannot be effectively managed without enormous sums of money and highly trained staff. Yet these data, and interviews with environmental personnel at both federal and state levels, suggest that the states suffer from inadequate fiscal resources, inadequate numbers of staff, inexperienced staff, staff turnover, and other problems that will adversely affect these states' abilities to implement federal directives in the 1990s.[21]

Environmental Policy Implementation

Mere enactment of a policy does not guarantee that the policy will be put into effect. Effective implementation of environmental policies is essential, and it varies from state to state. For example, implementation may be achieved by delegation of authority from the federal government to the states to manage their environmental programs after they have met federal guidelines. A number of scholars have studied the extent to which various states have assumed responsibility to run environmental programs, and thereby increased the speed of implementation.[22] Between 1972 and 1980, some states accepted primary responsibility for enforcing national environmental standards within their boundaries. States that scored highest in this regard included California, Michigan, Minnesota, New York, Washington, and Wisconsin.[23]

In addition, environmental policy implementation may be indicated by the amount of money spent on state environmental programs. The U.S. Department of Commerce collected data on environmental quality control expenditures from 1969 to 1980.[24] These data show that Califor-

Table 3-1 Environmental Department Personnel by State

State	Authorized positions	Actual employees	Permit reviewers	Inspectors	Laboratory personnel	Enforcement personnel	Technicians/ field data	Policy analysts	Administrators
Alabama	260	245							
Alaska	250	215			22			32	
Arizona									
Arkansas	217	170							
California	583	586	14	23	88	56	185	110	110
Colorado[a]	1,247								
Connecticut	1,947	1,618	127	50	1	213	180	38	202
Delaware									
Florida	1,222	1,106							
Georgia									
Hawaii	302	278	28	32	0	27	134	45	36
Idaho									
Illinois	834	770							
Indiana									
Iowa									
Kansas	255	230	58	50	20	5	37	[c]	45
Kentucky	1,322	1,239	147	295	22	294	51	45	385
Louisiana	396	356	36	175	17	5		26	91
Maine									
Maryland	682	639	92	214	0	28	126	38	184
Massachusetts									
Michigan	671	619	84	170	42	23	80	110	110
Minnesota									
Mississippi	749	621							
Missouri	446	413	31	92	13	33	63	27	132
Montana	112	103	14	24	19	4	15	11	18
Nebraska	114	102	12	16	6	3	7	25	32
Nevada	46	44	14	10	0	4	4	5	9
New Hampshire									

(Table continues)

Table 3-1 continued

State	Authorized positions	Actual employees	Permit reviewers	Inspectors	Laboratory personnel	Enforcement personnel	Technicians/ field data	Policy analysts	Administrators
New Jersey	3,294	3,184							
New Mexico	301	264	44	65	0	37	49	16	90
New York	3,647								
North Carolina	1,931	1,931							
North Dakota	84	80	25	37	0	12	20	18	24
Ohio	700	660							
Oklahoma		1,063	301	558	43	29		26	164
Oregon	387	310	50	92	63	5	37	10	140
Pennsylvania	3,756	3,518							
Rhode Island		489							
South Carolina	477		55	60	50	25	120	58	109
South Dakota									
Tennessee	815	790	56	416	0	28	81	59	150
Texas	351	332	28	104	45	10	38	23	103
Utah[b]	1,014	1,014							
Vermont	517	552	43	67	22	7	153	73	131
Virginia									
Washington	796	750	73	64	30	36	123	94	255
West Virginia	60	60	4	22	0	0	0	9	19
Wisconsin	2,595	2,409							
Wyoming	151	139		83	5		6	6	49
TOTALS	32,531	26,899	1,336	2,719	508	884	1,509	904	2,588

Source: R. Steven Brown and E. Garner, *Resource Guide to State Environmental Management* (Lexington, Ky.: The Council of State Governments, 1988).
Notes: Departmental duties vary considerably from state to state. The data should not be interpreted as an indicator of a state's commitment to environmental programs. Blanks indicate not applicable or data not available. In some cases the actual employees column does not equal the breakdowns in the other seven columns. Totals may vary for a variety of reasons: one position may be listed in more than one category because of job responsibilities or some positions do not fit in one of the seven categories listed.
[a] Department of Natural Resources. [b] Department of Natural Resources and Energy. [c] Included with administrators.

nia, Delaware, Maryland, Massachusetts, New Hampshire, Ohio, Rhode Island, and Vermont spent the most in terms of per capita expenditures, while Mississippi, Oklahoma, South Carolina, Texas, Utah, and Virginia spent the least. Unfortunately, due to budgetary cutbacks in 1981, this data collection effort was halted. Without continuous data from 1981 to the present, it is difficult to assess fully the impact of President Reagan's New Federalism on state environmental spending.

Nevertheless, recent efforts by the Council of State Governments have provided new data on state environmental protection expenditures that will help to fill the vacuum created by the elimination of the Department of Commerce data (see Table 3-2). California, Pennsylvania, Wisconsin, New York, New Jersey, Illinois, Michigan, Florida, Washington, and Alaska lead the nation in terms of total environmental expenditures. Note, however, that the top ten rankings shift significantly when spending per capita is considered or when expenditures are measured as a percentage of the total state budget, which is perhaps the best indicator of the priority of environmental protection activities within a state.[25]

A very different indicator of environmental policy implementation by the states is whether they replace federal environmental grant-in-aid reductions with state funds. During the period 1981 to 1984, most states did not allocate their own funds to replace federal budget cuts in several environmental areas, including wastewater treatment grants, air pollution control grants, hazardous-waste management grants, safe drinking water grants, pesticide enforcement grants, and water pollution control grants. This raises the important question of how wastewater treatment and other environmental programs will be funded in the 1990s.[26]

In addition, there is growing evidence of the phenomenon of "environmental gridlock" at the state level, especially in the areas of Superfund cleanups, hazardous-waste facility siting, and land-based and at-sea incineration of hazardous wastes (see Chapters 5 and 6). There has been, however, some research on the use of economic incentives to ameliorate gridlock.[27]

Environmental Policy Impacts

One would hope that the environmental legislation that was enacted in the 1960s and the 1970s, and implemented in the 1980s, would eventually result in a cleaner environment. However, as one might expect, the states have exhibited substantial variation in the extent to which they have effectively cleaned up their environments. The Conservation Foundation reviewed America's progress in improving the condition of its environment and the management of its resources in 1982, in 1984, and again in 1987. The most recent evaluation in 1987

Table 3-2 Environmental Expenditures by State, Fiscal Year 1986

Total environmental expenditures		Environmental expenditures per capita		Environmental expenditures as a percentage of total state expenditures	
California	$1,199,938,000	Alaska	$326.00	Wyoming	15.00
Pennsylvania	332,549,763	Wyoming	135.33	Oregon	4.44
Wisconsin	260,289,169	South Dakota	75.90	South Dakota	4.31
New York	227,274,090	Montana	69.55	California	3.53
New Jersey	200,750,000	Wisconsin	55.31	Idaho	3.49
Illinois	181,897,000	Idaho	51.97	Montana	3.46
Michigan	173,007,900	California	50.70	Alaska	3.00
Florida	171,267,941	Oregon	49.01	New Hampshire	2.89
Washington	160,334,318	Delaware	47.74	Wisconsin	2.79
Alaska	130,973,900	Vermont	42.94	Pennsylvania	2.71
Oregon	129,052,806	Washington	38.80	Vermont	2.39
Missouri	123,279,074	New Hampshire	32.41	Missouri	1.96
Massachusetts	122,313,035	North Dakota	31.08	Washington	1.91
Texas	100,921,072	Pennsylvania	28.03	Mississippi	1.83
Ohio	92,169,500	New Jersey	27.25	North Dakota	1.82
Kentucky	88,448,194	Rhode Island	26.16	West Virginia	1.60
Virginia	87,316,466	Missouri	25.07	Delaware	1.57
Maryland	85,748,214	Utah	24.60	Kentucky	1.51
North Carolina	77,193,938	New Mexico	24.59	Nevada	1.41
Minnesota	73,482,950	Mississippi	24.38	New Jersey	1.39
Louisiana	73,079,329	Kentucky	24.16	Utah	1.36
Tennessee	70,911,499	West Virginia	23.68	Massachusetts	1.32
Georgia	68,986,592	Maine	22.31	Colorado	1.30
Colorado	64,319,886	Colorado	22.26	Michigan	1.25
Wyoming	63,604,967	Nevada	21.77	New Mexico	1.25

Mississippi	61,453,623	Massachusetts	21.32	Rhode Island	1.23
Alabama	60,252,564	Maryland	20.33	Maine	1.21
Montana	54,739,315	Hawaii	19.21	Tennessee	1.18
South Dakota	52,450,000	Michigan	18.68	Illinois	1.14
South Carolina	50,018,484	Minnesota	18.03	Louisiana	1.12
Idaho	49,063,734	Florida	17.57	Nebraska	1.09
Iowa	47,090,046	Louisiana	17.38	Iowa	1.07
Indiana	46,551,743	Virginia	16.33	Maryland	1.06
West Virginia	46,183,752	Iowa	16.16	Virginia	1.04
Oklahoma	43,892,933	South Carolina	16.02	North Carolina	1.04
Arizona	41,287,553	Illinois	15.92	Alabama	0.99
Connecticut	38,666,000	Alabama	15.47	Florida	0.98
Utah	35,947,156	Tennessee	15.45	South Carolina	0.97
New Mexico	32,046,123	Arizona	15.19	Arizona	0.95
Kansas	30,445,137	North Carolina	14.62	Connecticut	0.89
Arkansas	30,372,330	Oklahoma	14.51	Arkansas	0.88
New Hampshire	29,850,570	Nebraska	13.32	Minnesota	0.88
Delaware	28,359,508	Arkansas	13.29	Kansas	0.87
Maine	25,096,481	New York	12.94	Oklahoma	0.85
Rhode Island	24,767,942	Kansas	12.88	Georgia	0.83
Vermont	21,944,786	Georgia	12.63	Hawaii	0.72
Nebraska	20,918,705	Connecticut	12.44	Indiana	0.69
North Dakota	20,293,798	Ohio	8.54	Ohio	0.60
Hawaii	18,540,533	Indiana	8.48	Texas	0.55
Nevada	17,413,195	Texas	7.09	New York	0.54

Source: R. Steven Brown and E. Garner, *Resource Guide to State Environmental Management* (Lexington, Ky.: The Council of State Governments, 1988).

notes that the American public continues to strongly support environmental programs.

Air quality has significantly improved since 1975. While many of the nation's waters are becoming cleaner, others are degrading.[28] In the area of hazardous waste, the federal government continues to have problems collecting accurate information about the amount of hazardous waste generated in the United States, how it is managed, and how much risk it poses. Data on state cleanups of hazardous-waste sites during the period 1980 to 1987 suggest that very few of the Superfund sites have been cleaned up. As of September 1987, only 3 percent of the total number of National Priority List sites had been completely "remediated."[29]

In sum, the evidence indicates that some states exhibit innovative and responsible behavior in implementing environmental policy by setting up appropriate environmental institutions, staffing them with capable personnel, and spending the necessary resources. Other states, however, are noninnovative and largely unresponsive to environmental needs. They fail to provide the necessary resources, and thus it is doubtful that their environmental quality is improving. The next section reviews various explanations of effective state environmental management.

Explaining State Environmental Management

Political scientists have sought to explain the variation in state environmental protection policies and program implementation. Such information is useful in two respects. From a purely pragmatic point of view, an understanding of why states behave as they do can be used to formulate strategies for political action that could stimulate inactive states to be more responsive to environmental concerns. Second, this information may be used for scientific purposes as well; research findings can be used to suggest policy reforms that might encourage more effective implementation of environmental policies by the states.

There are at least four basic explanations for effective policy responses to the problems posed by environmental pollution: the severity argument, the wealth argument, the partisanship argument, and the organizational capacity argument.[30]

The "severity argument" is that rapid and concentrated population growth, extensive industrialization (especially a reliance on the petrochemical and metallurgical industries), and steady rates of public consumption of goods and services create severe pollution problems that, in turn, bring about strong pressures for environmental protection policies. Thus, an obvious source of environmental policy differences among the states is the severity of the pollution problem itself.[31] In other words, it is assumed that states with more severe environmental pollution problems will take the necessary steps to deal with this pollution. However, studies suggest that the relationship between problem severity and state environmental protection is mixed, at best, and that more refined indicators of pollution severity are needed before a final assessment of its effect on state environmental policy can be known.[32] Factors other than problem severity (such as politics or economics) appear to be affecting states' behavior in this area.

The "wealth argument" posits a direct relationship between the socioeconomic resource base of a state and the level of its commitment to environmental protection.[33] States with greater fiscal resources are assumed to spend more on environmental protection than those with fewer fiscal resources. Those who assume that the failure of government to act in the environmental area is caused by states' "backwardness" or nonresponsiveness to environmental problems often overlook the wealth factor. Wealth accounts for a significant amount of the variation in state efforts to protect the environment.[34]

The "partisanship argument" is based on possibly the most common generalization in environmental politics literature: environmental policy formation can be explained, to a large extent, by political party (or ideological) differences. Riley Dunlap and Richard Gale argue that there are important reasons for expecting significant partisan differences to emerge on environmental issues, with Democrats being more supportive of such efforts than Republicans. These reasons largely concern differences between the two major parties in their support for business interests, which are often opposed to environmental protection policies that regulate their behavior and impose compliance costs on them.[35] In a recent review of the literature, Jerry Calvert found that for these reasons Democratic partisanship is strongly related to environmental voting within state legislatures and Congress.[36]

Finally, the "organizational capacity argument" focuses on administrative and legislative reforms as predictors of environmental policy outputs. For example, proponents of this view contend that reorganization (especially centralization) of the environmental bureaucracy promotes environmental protection policy by helping to eliminate jurisdictional overlaps, jealousies, and conflicts among multiple agencies in this area.[37] Moreover, consolidation of the environmental bureaucracy increases the governor's span of control and, with regard to crucial appointments in environmental agencies, improves the governor's ability to mobilize the bureaucracy in support of his or her objectives.

In addition, it is often argued that "professional" legislatures facilitate environmental protection more effectively than do unprofessional legislatures.[38] Presumably, professional legislatures are more responsive to environmental needs, generous in spending and services, and "interventionist" in the sense of having powers and responsibilities of broad scope. The evidence suggests that, in some instances, consolidated environmental bureaucracies and professional legislatures do make a positive contribution to the states' efforts to protect the environment.[39]

While each of these four arguments provides some insight into the determinants of state environmental protection policies, none captures the complexity of the policy process or sufficiently explains the multiple forces that influence states' commitment to environmental quality. Each argument simply assumes that conditions within the states themselves are the sole (or even primary) influences on state environmental management. Given the intergovernmental influences on state environmental behavior described earlier in the chapter, it seems appropriate also to consider external influences on state efforts to protect the environment.[40] The four explanations of state environmental management should be considered in a wider context that includes federal-level and local-level, as well as state-level, influences.[41] What the states do in the environmental area will be shaped within an intergovernmental framework.

The Future of State Environmental Management

President George Bush has said nothing to indicate whether he will reverse the flow of responsibility to the states and cities that has occurred since the 1970s. Nor has he said whether the states will receive more money to fund environmental programs. His pledge not to raise taxes suggests that the states will be left to their own resources to carry out their environmental responsibilities. Decentralization of federal environmental programs and federal reductions in environmental grants-in-aid are likely to continue into the 1990s. Thus, state environmental management in the 1990s largely will be governed by two considerations that are internal to the states themselves. The first concerns state government capability and the second concerns state commitment to environmental protection. While federal and local influences should be considered in future studies of state environmental policy, it is these within-state influences that are most useful in projecting what the states will do in the area of environmental management in the 1990s.

Some argue that state governments lack the expertise available to national governments, that they tend toward parochialism, that they are unwilling or unable to raise revenues to meet service demands, and that they are dominated by a conservative, business-oriented elite. Proponents of decentralization contend, however, that the institutional reforms of the 1970s and 1980s changed all this. Compared with the federal government, state governments, they argue, are in closer touch with problems to which proposed rules will be applied, more flexible and innovative, and better able to fashion responses that are appropriate to their individual conditions and preferences.[42]

But not all the states have taken initiatives to revitalize their institutional structures. A state's response to New Federalism will depend upon two different, but nevertheless complementary, dimensions: its commitment to environmental protection activities and its institutional capabilities. Based on these two dimensions, the states can be divided into four groups—progressives, strugglers, delayers, and regressives—that describe the most probable path for state environmental policy development in the 1990s.

The Progressives

The first group of states are those with a high commitment to environmental protection coupled with strong institutional capabilities. These include California, Florida, Illinois, Maryland, Massachusetts, Michigan, New Jersey, New York, Ohio, Oregon, Pennsylvania, Washington, Wisconsin, and Virginia. In these states substantial improvements in the quality of the environment and in the implementation of federal environmental legislation are expected. As these states move ahead with regard to environmental quality, they may adopt policies that are independent of federal mandates. Environmental conditions will likely get better, not worse.

California, for example, considers the natural environment a very important issue. For almost three decades "air pollution bills have been winning approval in Sacramento, well ahead of the national government." [43] For states such as California, the major issue will be the extent to which the private and public sectors can reach a consensus on the rather drastic environmental policies that these states will likely pursue. Significant tensions may arise in the course of these deliberations.

The Strugglers

A second category of states includes those with a strong commitment to environmental protection but with limited institutional capacities. These include Connecticut, Delaware, Hawaii, Indiana, Iowa, Kentucky, Maine, Minnesota, Montana, South Dakota, and Vermont. These states are willing, but often structurally unable, to implement federal environmental programs effectively. In other words, they have the will but not the resources (fiscally and institutionally) to pursue aggressive environmental protection policies. Progress probably will be made in these states, but it will be slower and possibly less innovative than in the progressive states. The "strugglers" will do the best they can within the constraints imposed on them. The major issues in these states will revolve around finding the means to implement aggressive environmental protection policies. Much of the debate will focus on issues associated with tax increases as these states seek to increase their resource base for environmental protection.

Vermont, for example, is staunchly protective of its environmental assets, but historically has been described as a "low service, high unemployment, communal" state.[44] That is, it has kept the costs of government low and has preferred a decentralized, "town-meeting" approach to its problems as opposed to the development of strong state-level institutions that are necessary for effective environmental policy.

The Delayers

The third group of states are those with a strong institutional capacity but with a limited commitment to environmental protection. These include Alabama, Alaska, Arkansas, Georgia, Louisiana, Missouri, Oklahoma, South Carolina, Tennessee, Texas, and West Virginia. They will probably maintain the status quo with respect to the environment and move very slowly in implementing federal legislation. Whatever progress is made will be painstakingly slow.

States that are dominated by the energy industry, such as Louisiana, Oklahoma, Texas, and West Virginia, comprise this group. West Virginia, for example, has been characterized as "still struggling," which means that it has few if any areas of exceptional program management, save for welfare policy.[45] It is a state that depends heavily on the federal government for intergovernmental aid and one that has not been able to build up its political institutions in a way that would sustain innovative environmental policies. The major issue in these states will be apathetic state bureaucracies that seem unwilling to effectively respond to state environmental crises.

The Regressives

States with weak institutional capacities as well as a weak commitment to environmental protection include Arizona, Colorado, Idaho, Kansas, Mississippi, Nebraska, Nevada, New Hampshire, New Mexico, North Carolina, North Dakota, Rhode Island, Utah, and Wyoming. For these states decentralization of environmental programs will likely be a disaster. They may fail to adequately implement federal laws in this area, and they are unlikely to take independent actions. The quality of life may deteriorate so much that large numbers of the population may move to other states (especially the more progressive ones). Dirty industries may continue to move into these states, making them even more unattractive to the inhabitants. These states will continue to promote economic development at the expense of environmental quality. At some point a catastrophe may turn the states in this category around, but at present they seem to be captured by an obsessive optimism that prevents their taking necessary precautions against further damage to the environment.

Colorado, for example, has been described by Neal Peirce and Jerry Hagstrom as a "tragedy in the making." By this they mean that Coloradans have never become serious in deciding how they are going to accommodate their love of unfettered growth with their love of the outdoors. Colorado governor Richard Lamm once said that "it was a never ending irony to me that I can be elected governor of this state, then reelected by a substantial margin, but I can't get through the legislature the policies which almost everyone agrees are necessary to protect the state." [46] Colorado is characterized as a state that has been lulled into thinking that there will be no crisis, and that a solution can be found to all growth problems.[47]

Conclusions and Implications

In this assessment of state environmental policy under the doctrine of New Federalism, I have described changes in federal-state relations and reforms of state institutions. I also have examined environmental policy innovations in the states (including their commitment to and capacity for environmental policy making). Implementation and impacts in the states are discussed, and several explanations are offered for the way states manage their environments. Finally, I have suggested four possible classifications of the states in the 1990s: progressives, strugglers, delayers, and regressives. These scenarios range from extremely optimistic (the progressives) to extremely pessimistic (the regressives) with regard to the effectiveness with which states will address environmental problems. The scenarios assume no major changes in state commitments or institutional capabilities, but public opinion and the media could cause some legislators to adopt very different strategies if conditions become intolerable.

The policy implications of this discussion are significant. If future empirical research suggests that federal-level factors are crucial influences on state environmental management, then the argument for centralization of environmental management would once again acquire enhanced credibility. That is, if federal inducements (such as federal legislation and intergovernmental aid) are necessary conditions for successful state environmental management, then a policy of decentralization probably will not work effectively for all states. On the other hand, if state-level and local-level resources strongly influence state environmental management, then arguments about decentralization of environmental management would acquire even more credibility. Or decentralization may work well in some states (for example, the innovative states), but poorly in others (for example, the regressive states). Thus, "selective decentralization," a policy in which some programs are decentralized for some states while other programs for other states are not, may be the most appropriate strategy.[48]

In any case policy makers need to reconsider the nature of intergovernmental relations as it affects state and local environmental management. The federal government may or may not be the most appropriate governmental institution to tackle environmental pollution, but the fifty states are not equally able to muster the necessary resources to deal with environmental problems in the 1990s. Novel approaches will thus be required and are particularly appropriate in an era of "regulatory federalism," which will likely characterize the 1990s.

Notes

1. Advisory Commission on Intergovernmental Relations (ACIR), *Regulatory Federalism: Policy, Process, Impact, and Reform* (Washington, D.C.: ACIR, 1984), 19-21.
2. Philip Shabecoff, "The Environment as Local Jurisdiction," *New York Times*, January 22, 1989, E9.
3. Council on Environmental Quality, *Environmental Quality: 1981* (Washington, D.C.: U.S. Government Printing Office, 1982), 16-18.
4. See, for example, Richard Nathan et al., *The Consequences of Cuts: The Effects of the Reagan Domestic Program on State and Local Governments* (Princeton, N.J.: Princeton University Press, 1983); and Richard Nathan et al., *Reagan and the States* (Princeton, N.J.: Princeton University Press, 1987). See also James P. Lester, "New Federalism and Environmental Policy," *Publius* 16 (Winter 1986): 149-165; and Michael E. Kraft, Bruce B. Clary, and Richard J. Tobin, "The Impact of New Federalism on State Environmental Policy: The Great Lakes States," in *The Midwest Response to the New Federalism*, ed. Peter K. Eisinger and William Gormley (Madison: University of Wisconsin Press, 1988), 204-233.
5. Ann O'M. Bowman and Richard C. Kearney, *The Resurgence of the States* (Englewood Cliffs, N.J.: Prentice-Hall, 1986), 1-46.
6. These points are dealt with at length in the following texts on intergovernmental relations: Laurence J. O'Toole, Jr., ed., *American Intergovernmental Relations* (Washington, D.C.: CQ Press, 1985); David C. Nice, *Federalism: The Politics of Intergovernmental Relations* (New York: St. Martin's Press, 1987); and Thomas J. Anton, *American Federalism and Public Policy* (Philadelphia, Pa.: Temple University Press, 1989).
7. J. Clarence Davies, "Environmental Institutions and the Reagan Administration," in *Environmental Policy in the 1980s: Reagan's New Agenda*, ed. Norman J. Vig and Michael E. Kraft (Washington, D.C.: CQ Press, 1984), 150.
8. Bowman and Kearney, *The Resurgence of the States*, 47-134. See also Parris N. Glendening, "The States in the Fiscal Federal System" (Paper delivered at the annual meeting of the American Political Science Association, Washing-

ton, D.C., August 30-31, 1984); and the Advisory Commission on Intergovernmental Relations, *The Question of State Government Capability* (Washington, D.C.: U.S. Government Printing Office, 1985).

9. Charles E. Davis and James P. Lester, "Federalism and Environmental Policy," *Environmental Politics and Policy: Theories and Evidence*, ed. James P. Lester (Durham, N.C.: Duke University Press, 1989), 57-84.
10. See the Advisory Commission on Intergovernmental Relations, *The Question of State Government Capability;* Advisory Commission on Intergovernmental Relations, *The Transformation in American Politics* (Washington, D.C.: U.S. Government Printing Office, 1986); and Bowman and Kearney, *The Resurgence of the States*, 47-134.
11. Ann O'M. Bowman and Richard C. Kearney, "Dimensions of State Government Capability," *Western Political Quarterly* 41 (June 1988): 341-362.
12. The Council of State Governments, *Innovations in Environment and Natural Resources* (Lexington, Ky.: The Council of State Governments, 1986); The Council of State Governments, *Suggested State Legislation* (Lexington, Ky.: The Council of State Governments, various years); and U.S. Congress Office of Technology Assessment, *Serious Reduction of Hazardous Waste* (Washington, D.C.: U.S. Government Printing Office, 1986).
13. Shabecoff, "The Environment as Local Jurisdiction," E9.
14. James L. Regens and Margaret A. Reams, "State Strategies for Regulating Groundwater Quality," *Social Science Quarterly* 69 (September 1988): 53-59.
15. Robert Reinhold, "Southern California Takes Steps to Curb Its Urban Air Pollution," *New York Times*, March 18, 1989, 1.
16. U.S. Congress Office of Technology Assessment, *Serious Reduction of Hazardous Waste*.
17. Christopher J. Duerksen, *Environmental Regulation of Industrial Plant Siting* (Washington, D.C.: Conservation Foundation, 1983), 224-225.
18. Scott Ridley, *The State of the States: 1987* (Washington, D.C.: Fund for Renewable Energy and the Environment, 1987). Similar reports have also been produced for 1988 and 1989.
19. Mark Obmascik, "Survey Places Colorado 26th in Environmental Efforts," *Denver Post*, March 1, 1989, A1.
20. See R. Steven Brown and L. Edward Garner, *Resource Guide to State Environmental Management* (Lexington, Ky.: The Council of State Governments, 1988), 2-96.
21. Interviews with staff at the U.S. Environmental Protection Agency, Office of Solid Waste, State Programs Branch, July 1987.
22. See Pinky S. Wassenberg, "Implementation of Intergovernmental Regulatory Programs: A Cost-Benefit Perspective," in *Intergovernmental Relations and Public Policy*, ed. Edwin Benton and David R. Morgan (Westport, Conn.: Greenwood Press, 1986), 123-137; Patricia M. Crotty, "The New Federalism Game: Primacy Implementation of Environmental Policy," *Publius* 17 (Spring 1987): 57-63; James P. Lester, "Superfund Implementation: Exploring Environmental Gridlock," *Environmental Impact Assessment Review* 8 (June 1988): 159-174; and James P. Lester and Ann O'M. Bowman, "Implementing Intergovernmental Environmental Policy: A Test of the Sabatier-Mazmanian Model," *Polity* 21 (Summer 1989): 73-86.

23. Crotty, "The New Federalism Game," 53-55.
24. U.S. Department of Commerce, Bureau of the Census, *Environmental Quality Control* (Washington, D.C.: U.S. Government Printing Office, 1982).
25. Brown and Garner, *Resource Guide to State Environmental Management*, 83-94. The Council of State Governments hopes to continue its data collection effort and eventually to obtain data for 1981 to 1985 and 1987 to the present.
26. Laurence J. O'Toole, Jr., "Goal Multiplicity in the Implementation Setting: Subtle Impacts and the Case of Wastewater Treatment Privatization," *Policy Studies Journal* (forthcoming); and Laurence J. O'Toole, Jr., "Alternative Mechanisms for Multiorganizational Implementation: The Case of Wastewater Management," *Administration and Society* (forthcoming 1990).
27. Kent E. Portney, "The Potential of the Theory of Compensation for Mitigating Public Opposition to Hazardous Waste Treatment Facility Siting: Some Evidence from Five Massachusetts Communities," *Policy Studies Journal* 14 (September 1985): 81-89.
28. See *State of the Environment: 1982* (Washington, D.C.: Conservation Foundation, 1982); *State of the Environment: An Assessment at Mid-Decade* (Washington, D.C.: Conservation Foundation, 1984); and *State of the Environment: A View Toward the Nineties* (Washington, D.C.: Conservation Foundation, 1987).
29. See James P. Lester, "Superfund Implementation," 163-165.
30. James P. Lester et al., "Hazardous Wastes, Politics and Public Policy: A Comparative State Analysis," *Western Political Quarterly* 36 (June 1983): 257-285.
31. Lettie M. Wenner, *One Environment Under Law: A Public Policy Dilemma* (Pacific Palisades, Calif.: Goodyear, 1976).
32. Kingsley W. Game, "Controlling Air Pollution: Why Some States Try Harder," *Policy Studies Journal* 7 (Summer 1979): 728-738.
33. James P. Lester and Patrick M. Keptner, "State Budgetary Commitments to Environmental Quality Under Austerity," in *Western Public Lands*, ed. John G. Francis and Richard Ganzel (Totowa, N.J.: Rowman and Allenheld, 1984), 193-214.
34. Ibid.
35. Riley E. Dunlap and Richard P. Gale, "Party Membership and Environmental Politics: A Legislative Roll-Call Analysis," *Social Science Quarterly* 55 (December 1974): 670-690.
36. Jerry W. Calvert, "Party Politics and Environmental Policy," in *Environmental Politics and Policy*, 158-178.
37. James L. Garnett, *Reorganizing State Government: The Executive Branch* (Boulder, Colo.: Westview Press, 1980).
38. See *The Sometime Governments: A Critical Study of the Fifty American Legislatures* (Kansas City, Mo.: Citizens Conference on State Legislatures, 1971).
39. Lester and Keptner, "State Budgetary Commitments," 201-207.
40. Douglas Rose, "National and Local Forces in State Politics: The Implications of Multi-level Policy Analysis," *American Political Science Review* 67 (December 1973): 1162-1173.
41. Russell Hanson, "The Intergovernmental Setting of State Politics," in *Politics*

in the American States, ed. Virginia Gray, Herbert Jacob, and Kenneth N. Vines (Boston: Little, Brown, 1983), 27-56.

42. See Jeffrey Henig, *Public Policy and Federalism* (New York: St. Martin's Press, 1985); and John Scholz, "State Regulatory Reform and Federal Regulation," *Policy Studies Review* 1 (June 1981): 347-359.
43. Neal Peirce and Jerry Hagstrom, *The Book of America: Inside Fifty States Today* (New York: Warner Books, 1984), 776.
44. Ibid., 199.
45. Ibid., 345.
46. Ibid., 659.
47. Ibid., 659-668.
48. Paul E. Peterson, Barry G. Rabe, and Kenneth K. Wong, *When Federalism Works* (Washington, D.C.: Brookings Institution, 1987), 216-236.

4

Public Opinion and the Green Lobby: Poised for the 1990s?

Robert Cameron Mitchell

The celebration of Earth Day 1990 marks the twentieth anniversary of the original Earth Day, April 22, 1970, an event that heralded the arrival of the environment as a major social problem and the environmental movement as its advocate. Despite (or perhaps because of) competition from the antiwar protest movement and other radical causes of the time for media space, "ecology" captured the attention of television and newspaper reporters who portrayed it as a dynamic cause supported by people of all ages and political persuasions. However, few political observers at the time would have predicted that environmental issues would prove to be the enduring addition to the national policy agenda that they have become.

The environment has long enjoyed strong support in the public opinion polls, whose findings helped environmental groups keep the issue alive during the Reagan era. Now, as we enter the 1990s, survey data suggest that the public's commitment to a cleaner environment is stronger than ever. This chapter examines this important development and its implications for environmental politics in Washington.

The Rise of the Modern Environmental Movement

The modern environmental movement was born in the early 1960s. Its midwife was Rachel Carson, whose 1962 best seller, *Silent Spring,* was the first popular book to expose the destructive side effects of the pesticide DDT and to articulate the subtle cumulative perils of modern technology. Its parents were the old-line conservation groups that had been founded thirty to seventy years earlier: the Izaak Walton League, National Audubon Society, National Parks and Conservation Association,

The author wishes to thank Jean McKendry for her able research assistance.

National Wildlife Federation, and Sierra Club. Throughout the 1960s these groups made increasingly successful efforts to alert the public to various environmental threats and to mobilize support for such causes as wilderness protection and air pollution control. During this pre-Earth Day period, the rising tide of environmental concern not only swelled their membership ranks, but also facilitated the formation of new national organizations, such as Friends of the Earth and two leading environmental law groups: the Environmental Defense Fund (EDF) and the Natural Resources Defense Council (NRDC). These efforts created the climate that made the 1970 Earth Day a success, even though it was organized by student environmental activists who acted independently of the existing environmental movement.

Following Earth Day, the major environmental groups established or strengthened their Washington offices and hired full-time staff to lobby for their issues. In Washington the assumption gained currency that the environment was a "motherhood" issue and that the leaders of the environmental groups were the legitimate spokespeople for a large and powerful constituency. Congress, influenced by this assumption, passed a series of landmark laws to protect the environment and supported the efforts of government agencies to enforce these laws (see Chapter 1 and Appendix 1). In 1973 the Arab oil embargo briefly put this view to the test, but environmentalists successfully fought off attempts in Congress to weaken environmental laws on grounds of energy security. Presidents Nixon and Ford professed support for environmental quality; President Carter placed it high on his agenda and appointed committed environmentalists to important government posts.

In 1980 the Reagan administration, responding to what it believed to be a shift in public priorities prompted by the nation's economic problems and the high costs of pollution control, attempted to curtail the federal government's commitment to strong environmental regulation. Those chosen to execute this shift, most notably James Watt, the secretary of the interior, and Anne Gorsuch (later Burford), the administrator of the Environmental Protection Agency (EPA), publicly challenged the prevailing pro-environmental assumptions and sought to redirect their agencies toward policies they believed were more cost-effective and supportive of economic growth. Watt went so far as to question the legitimacy of the public's conception of environmental groups as guardians of the environmental mandate, calling their leaders "hired guns" concerned about "membership, dollars, and headlines."[1] They were, he asserted, out of touch with their rank and file. The Republican Study Committee, a conservative caucus made up of approximately three-quarters of the 192 Republican members of the House of Representatives at that time, publicly declared that "environmental groups represent only a minority fringe of the American public."[2]

The Reagan administration's attack on mainstream environmentalism can be regarded as a powerful test of the movement's claim to represent the views of a large segment of the public. Here was a popular president—blessed with a reassuring manner, an ability to make convincing speeches, a coherent and appealing view of the world, and working from a sincere belief that he had been granted a mandate by the electorate in his landslide 1980 election to get government off the people's backs—supporting what environmentalists regarded as a significant cutback in the nation's efforts to improve environmental quality. In a time of economic adversity he sought to legitimize this policy change by citing the nation's economic and foreign policy priorities and by branding his opponents as "environmental extremists." [3]

It took only three years for the Reagan administration to be proved wrong.[4] By 1983 public opinion surveys showed even stronger public support for environmental protection efforts than in the Carter years. In response to direct-mail appeals for support in their fight against Reagan's environmental policies, national environmental groups gained tens of thousands of new members and the level of donations increased sharply. Watt and Burford were forced to resign and the administration was obliged to adopt a more conciliatory approach to the demands of environmentalists and their allies in Congress during the rest of the Reagan years (see Chapter 2).

Current Public Support for Environmental Protection

In 1989, six years after Watt's resignation and one president later, public support for environmental protection stands higher than at any time since the early 1970s.[5] There is, moreover, evidence that the issue has gained in salience. These trends, if they continue, may help tip the balance in the decade-long standoff between environmental and industry groups toward the environmental side.

Two important dimensions of public opinion about policy issues are *strength* and *salience*. Strength refers to the degree to which people regard an issue as a matter of national or personal concern and want to improve the situation. Polls measure strength by asking people to say how serious or how important they think a problem is, or how concerned they are about the problem. Pollsters also may ask people to make choices between improving the problem or not, when the possible costs of improvement include such things as higher prices, closed factories, and reduced energy production.

Salience, in contrast, is the amount of immediate personal interest people have in the issue. The most common poll measure of an issue's salience is whether people spontaneously mention it when asked to name the one or two problems they believe to be the most important facing the nation. According to this measure, the environment has been a low salience issue for most of the past fifteen years, as only a few percent of the public named it as a most important problem. The handful of issues that receive significant mention are issues that dominate the evening news: the economy, inflation, unemployment, war, and, more recently, drugs.[6]

Because salience measures are headline-sensitive, they are an untrustworthy guide to how the public will respond to policy changes in apparently nonsalient issues. The Reagan administration discovered this when it fell into the "salience trap": because people did not spontaneously list the environment as a most important problem, the Reagan team believed that there was a weakening of the previous decade's environmental consensus. In making this assumption, the president's advisers ignored the fact that during Reagan's 1980 campaign the polls continued to show high levels of concern about environmental issues and backing for environmental protection, even when the questions invoked the costs entailed in providing this protection. As it turned out, the strength of environmental concern measured by those polls proved to be a more accurate predictor of public support for the environmental movement in its battle with the Reagan administration over the direction of environmental policy than the low salience ratings.

Salience

It now appears that environmental issues are gaining in salience as well as in strength. Evidence of a possible salience shift comes from a "most important problem" question asked four times a year of a large national sample by Cambridge Reports.[7] At the end of 1987 only 2 percent of respondents told the Cambridge interviewers that the environment was "one of the two most important problems facing the United States today." This level was typical of many earlier askings of this type of question in other national surveys. By the end of 1988, however, mention of the environment recorded a modest increase to 6 percent. Then in Cambridge Reports' second quarter (April-June) 1989 survey, the percent citing the environment as a most important problem jumped to 16 percent, an increase that may confidently be attributed to the *Exxon Valdez* oil spill, which occurred in late March. Significantly, the level of salience did not fall in the third quarter (July-September) 1989 survey, when 16 percent again named the environment.

Strength

Turning now to the strength dimension, poll after poll has shown that the environment has fared increasingly well during the 1980s. Questions that measure concern and support reveal that only a very small minority of the public in 1989 sympathizes with the Reagan administration's approach to environmental policy. Roper polls, for example, show that the percentage of a national sample favoring "a cutback in environmental regulations and pollution controls" declined from 30 percent in January 1981, just as Reagan was taking office, to 15 percent in January 1989, at the beginning of the Bush administration.[8] Almost three-quarters (74 percent) of the public now oppose such a cutback. Similarly, Cambridge Reports finds that the percentage of people who say the amount of government regulation and involvement in the area of environmental protection is "too little" increased from 35 percent in 1982 to 53 percent in 1988.[9]

A particularly striking example of the increase in support for environmental protection during the 1980s is found in a series of seven polls conducted by the *New York Times*/CBS News.[10] In each survey interviewers asked a national sample of Americans whether they agreed or disagreed with the following statement: "Protecting the environment is so important that requirements and standards cannot be too high, and continuing environmental improvements must be made regardless of cost." Given the strongly pro-environmental wording of the statement, the fact that in 1981 a plurality of 45 percent said they agreed with it was regarded as strong evidence of public support for environmental protection.[11] Thus, it is striking that subsequent askings during the 1980s traced an ever-upward level of support for this position, as shown in Figure 4-1. By the end of Reagan's first term, the percentage of respondents saying that environmental improvements must be made regardless of cost had increased to 58 percent. In 1988, shortly before he left office, the percentage had climbed to 65 percent. Two successive surveys in 1989 recorded an increase of an additional 15 percentage points for those who took this uncompromisingly pro-environmental position—another effect of the *Exxon Valdez* oil spill.

It is important to ask how support for environmental protection fares in comparison with other pressing social problems. According to Roper poll findings, the environment is one of a set of problems that commands the greatest level of public willingness to spend more to solve them, a position that has strengthened since the early 1970s. In December 1988 Roper asked a national sample of Americans whether they thought we were spending too much, too little, or about the right amount of money on solving seventeen problems. Seventy percent said we were spending too little money on "helping the homeless," the problem with the highest level of support for greater spending. "Improving and protecting the environment" was not far behind at 62 percent, immediately following such important problems as poverty, drug addiction, health, and crime, and just above "improving the nation's education system." The trends for

Figure 4-1 Views About Environmental Protection "Regardless of Cost," 1981-1989

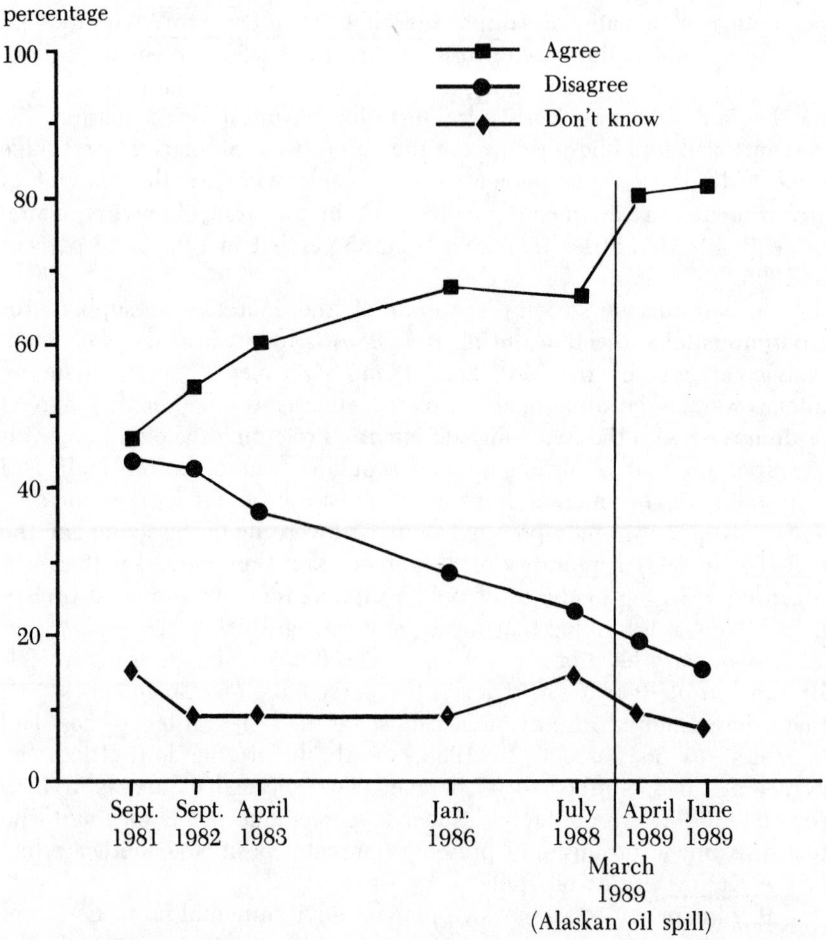

Source: National telephone surveys conducted by the *New York Times*/CBS News, *New York Times*, July 2, 1989, 1.

Note: The question asked was: "Do you agree or disagree with the following statement: Protecting the environment is *so* important that requirements and standards cannot be too high, and continuing environmental improvements must be made *regardless* of cost."

these survey responses (see Table 4-1) show how support for spending more on improving the environment increased from 1973 to 1989. This increase is both absolute, the percentage in favor increases from 45 in 1973 to 62 in 1988, tying with education for the largest increase, and relative, over this time period several issues, such as energy and transportation, declined relative to the environment.

Table 4-1 Percentage of the U.S. Public Saying We Are Spending Too Little to Solve National Problems, Various Years, 1973-1988

	1973	1980	1983	1984	1985	1986	1987	1988
Helping the homeless	*	*	*	*	*	*	*	70
Helping the poor	*	*	*	*	*	*	*	67
Dealing with drug addiction	57	63	58	62	60	63	59	66
Improving and protecting the nation's health	57	58	56	58	59	58	63	64
Halting the rising crime rate	62	73	64	62	64	62	58	64
Improving and protecting the environment	45	47	48	54	56	59	54	62
Improving the nation's education system	44	52	59	56	60	59	60	61
Dealing with the problem of AIDS	*	*	*	*	*	*	*	51
Solving the problems of the big cities	42	38	39	39	43	41	35	40
Increasing the nation's energy supply	66	63	40	40	36	34	34	36
Improving public transportation	54	45	35	33	36	32	29	30
Welfare	18	16	20	25	25	26	23	27
Space exploration program	3	19	10	9	9	13	18	14
The military, armaments, and defense	14	56	21	14	15	15	13	10

Source: Roper Reports 89-1 (January 1989), 63.

Note: The question asked was: "Turning now to the business of the country—we are faced with many problems in this country, none of which can be solved easily or inexpensively. I'm going to name some of these problems, and for each one I'd like you to tell me whether you think we're spending too much money on it, too little money, or about the right amount. First, the space exploration program—are we spending too much, too little, or about the right amount on the space exploration program?" Those items not included in this table and the percentage saying we are spending too little on them in 1988 are: rebuilding the nation's roads, bridges, and tunnels, 33 percent; unemployment insurance benefits, 31 percent; and foreign aid, 5 percent.

Causes of the High Level of Environmental Concern

Environmental problems have several characteristics that help explain why they continue to command such a high level of public attention and concern.[12] One is the shift that occurred around 1970 in the dominant value system from one that regarded economic development as the preeminent goal to one that emphasized that economic growth should be pursued in a way consistent with the need to maintain the quality of the natural environment and protect the public from unnecessary risks.[13] Another is the inherently broad appeal that environmental problems have because everyone is potentially affected by many of them and diverse constituencies have an interest in an array of environmental issues. Citizens with little interest in nature may be concerned about the public health threat posed to their localities by toxic wastes or drinking water contamination. Indeed, recent polls have shown that several of the environmental issues with the highest percentages of people saying they regard them as "very serious" involve this kind of local threat. The issues named in a 1988 Roper survey are: hazardous-waste sites, water pollution, worker exposure to toxic chemicals, and drinking water contamination.[14]

While they help explain the persistence of environmental concern, these factors alone cannot account for the recent upswing in support. Major factors behind this shift are environmental trends and events and how they are presented in the news media. Editors of weekly news magazines such as *Time* and *Newsweek* choose for cover placement stories they believe have wide appeal. Table 4-2 lists the topics of every cover story on an environmental topic run by the three major weekly news magazines during 1987, 1988, and the first ten months of 1989. In 1987 only *Time* ran environmental cover stories (for a total of three). In 1988 all three magazines ran environmental stories on their covers; the total number of cover stories doubled from three to six. Featured topics included the global issues of climate change, ocean pollution, as well as the general vulnerability of the earth to human change. From January to October 1989, the number of environmental cover stories doubled again to twelve. Journalists and pundits began to predict another round of environmental activism like the one that surrounded the first Earth Day in 1970.[15]

The top environmental story in 1989 was the March 24 oil spill in Alaska by the *Exxon Valdez* (four of the twelve environmental covers). This largest oil spill in U.S. history dumped crude oil on more than one thousand miles of shoreline in the biologically rich and heretofore pristine Prince William Sound. The cleanup cost the Exxon oil company more than $1 billion for the first year's efforts alone. Newspaper and television coverage of this event was extremely heavy. In the first month after the spill the main daily television newscasts carried an average total of 3.2

Table 4-2 News Magazine Cover Stories on Environmental Topics, 1987-1989

Year	*Newsweek*	*U.S. News and World Report*	*Time*
1987	none	none	African wild animals, vanishing U.S. coastline, global climate change
1988	greenhouse effect, ocean pollution	planet earth, general environment	ocean pollution, government nuclear facility pollution
1989[a]	the environment, Alaskan oil spill	air pollution, wilderness preservation, Alaskan oil spill, endangered species (Africa)	planet of the year, food contamination, Alaska and the environment, Alaskan oil spill, Amazon rainforest, African ivory trade

[a] First ten months only.

stories and the top four national newspapers ran an average total of 7.4 stories a day.[16]

A notable characteristic of the media's handling of the Alaskan oil spill was that it was treated as emblematic of an already recognized environmental dilemma. Since it fell into a pattern that the media had already identified, it helped confirm that pattern.

Once the media's growing appetite for environmental stories was stimulated, environmentalists did their best to feed it. In the early spring of 1989 a report issued by the Natural Resources Defense Council about the potential health risks posed to children by pesticides and other chemicals, especially Alar, created a big media splash and made the cover of *Time*.[17] In late 1989 the Wilderness Society and the Sierra Club, after years of effort and the help of the endangered northern spotted owl, succeeded in making the logging of old-growth or virgin timber in the national forests of Washington and Oregon a newsworthy topic that found its way to the cover of *U.S. News and World Report*.

Related to the intensified coverage of environmental issues in the media is a growing belief among the public that environmental problems have worsened and that this trend will continue in the future. This type of belief is particularly likely to mobilize people to support environmental and other movements.[18] One set of survey findings suggests that pessimism about past environmental progress increased in 1988 and that pessimists continued to outnumber optimists in 1989.[19] Table 4-3 presents the findings

Table 4-3 Public Expectations about Problem Severity in the Future (in percentages)

Problem area	Expectation for next fifteen years			
	Worse	About the same	Better	Don't know
Quality of environment	46	35	18	0
Personal safety from crime	46	27	26	1
Availability of good jobs	31	38	30	1
U.S. influence in world affairs	29	35	35	1
Health of Americans	28	24	48	1
Outlook for world peace	27	31	41	1
Quality of life in local community	21	41	38	0
Quality of public education	19	27	53	1

Source: ABC News/*Washington Post* telephone survey of 1,505 persons selected by random digit dialing nationwide. Interviews were conducted from January 17, 1988, to January 23, 1988.

Note: The question asked was: "Do you expect the outlook for (name of item) to be better, about the same, or worse in another fifteen years or so?" The items are rank ordered by the percentage saying the problem will get worse over a fifteen-year period.

of another survey, conducted in 1988, which found that more than twice as many Americans believe that the quality of the environment will get worse in the next fifteen years as believe it will get better. This is the highest level of pessimism recorded for any of the eight major social problems covered in the survey. Thus, more people think that crime, the economy, the role of the United States in the world, and the outlook for world peace will get better than think the quality of the environment will improve.

Environmental Groups in Washington

The pro-environmental findings of public opinion polls on environmental issues have been an important political resource for the environmental movement over the past twenty years. Environmental protection is costly and politicians are reluctant to impose these costs on taxpayers and consumers without evidence that there is a significant demand for environmental improvements. In recognition of this, early in the Bush administration the National Wildlife Federation and the Sierra Club, along with a group called Americans for the Environment, published a report entitled *The Rising Tide*. This document contained a summary of poll findings on the environment similar to those given above, as well as commissioned commentaries by three prominent political pollsters. According to the report, "The strength of public opinion [for environmental protection] will lead the way towards substantial shifts in the way we live, and in the way elected officials respond to a real and growing crisis. . . ."[20]

Although the current strength of environmental public opinion is undeniable, "substantial shifts" of the sort predicted in *The Rising Tide* are not likely to occur spontaneously, at least not in Washington where a small army of corporate and trade association lobbyists and publicists are paid to persuade elected officials not to jump on any environmental bandwagon that happens to roll down the street. A strong environmental lobby also will be necessary in Washington if environmentalists are to make effective use of the environmental events that nature (and Exxon) has dealt them and translate heightened public concern into future public policy.

Overall the "green lobby" appears to be in a favorable position to press its advantage. This lobby includes a core of twelve national groups that maintain a significant staff in Washington to lobby Congress on legislative matters and the executive branch agencies, such as EPA, on the often crucial details of how legislation will be implemented and enforced.[21] Although these core groups will be the focus of the discussion that follows, it must be emphasized that environmental lobbying is by no means restricted to these groups. Depending on the issue the core groups may be joined by one or more of a host of more specialized national or local environmental groups or by other public interest groups, such as Ralph Nader's Congress Watch or the Union of Concerned Scientists, whose interests sometimes overlap those of the environmentalists.[22]

The green lobby's current strength is the result of several factors, the most important of which is the groups' success during the 1980s in translating increased public concern for environmental issues into membership growth without succumbing to the managerial and morale problems that rapid growth can cause. Other factors include a healthy balance between intergroup cooperation and competition; the ability to expand their set of issues in a creative, often anticipatory way; and the likelihood that the increase in tensions between grass-roots environmentalists and the national groups will strengthen rather than weaken the national groups' lobbying effort.

There is no question that the Reagan administration's attack on the environmental movement in the early 1980s ultimately strengthened the groups even though, in the short run, many incurred budget deficits as they battled to defeat Watt.[23] During the Carter years the groups' direct-mail campaigns generally yielded just enough new members to replace those who failed to renew. Thanks to the furor created in response to moves by Reagan and Watt, the response rates to their mail appeals began to improve. The first to benefit were the Sierra Club and the Wilderness Society—two groups that follow public lands issues and fought Watt aggressively; they almost doubled their membership in the first three

Table 4-4 Membership in Selected Environmental Groups, 1980 and 1989

Group	1980	1989	Average yearly increase (%)
Defenders of Wildlife	44,000	80,000	9
Environmental Defense Fund	45,000	100,000	14
National Audubon Society	412,000	575,000	4
Natural Resources Defense Council	42,000	117,000	20
Sierra Club	180,000	496,000	20
Wilderness Society	45,000	317,000	67

Sources: James A. Tober, *Wildlife and the Public Interest* (New York: Praeger, 1989); and Charles Mohr, "Environmental Groups Gain in Wake of Spill," *New York Times*, June 11, 1989, 31.

Note: The 1989 membership figures are for May 1989 and do not reflect any increases as a result of the *Exxon Valdez* oil spill.

years after Reagan's election and their memberships continued to grow even after Watt resigned. Many other groups also benefited, with results such as those shown in Table 4-4.[24]

The fastest growth recorded during this period was by the newest group, Greenpeace. The first Greenpeace group was founded in 1971 in Vancouver, Canada, to protest U.S. nuclear weapons testing in the Aleutian Islands through what was to become its trademark activity: the headline-grabbing, ecoactivist tactic of sailing a vessel into the test area. In 1975 Greenpeace activists began to pursue direct-action tactics against whalers in international waters. Informal Greenpeace groups quickly sprang up in various countries, including the United States. In 1979 the international Greenpeace organization incorporated in the Netherlands, and in 1980 the American headquarters moved from San Francisco to Washington, D.C. There Greenpeace USA entered the mainstream, at least in part, by initiating legislative work focusing on air pollution, toxic waste, ocean wildlife, and nuclear issues.[25] The group's growth indicates the popular support available for an activist group that pursues environmental issues with a proven capacity to get results. By 1989, just ten years after it began its direct-mail membership campaign, Greenpeace USA could claim an astonishing 1.35 million members in the United States—an average growth rate exceeding 100 percent per year.

Rapid membership growth and financial stability were not universal, however. Two of the national groups failed to grow over this period and suffered financial problems that led them to merge with other financially marginal environmental groups in the hopes that their combined strength would allow them to survive. Friends of the Earth underwent a protracted period of internal conflict in the mid-1980s, during which it neglected its direct-mail program. Friends of the Earth subsequently decided to move its headquarters to Washington, D.C., and, somewhat later, to merge with the Oceanic Society and the Environmental Policy Institute. The new organization is expected to keep the Friends of the Earth name. In 1988 Environmental Action, another small and relatively radical group that lacked the financial resources to exploit the direct-mail opportunity created by conflicts with Reagan's policies merged with the Environmental Task Force, a grass-roots group in Washington, D.C.

The largest and most powerful environmental groups were spared these problems, but instead had to cope with the opportunities and problems presented by their membership expansion. The influx of new members and the increase in contributions from their old members made it possible to expand programs and staff. These increases also meant greater clout in Congress, whose members respect groups with large constituencies, especially those whose cause is acknowledged to have widespread public support.

Growth was not without its costs, however. The biggest problem was achieving managerial control without losing the group's sense of mission. The challenge to organize effectively is great. Large amounts of money are needed for the elaborate recruitment campaigns; once recruited, the members must be serviced. The expanded staff must be coordinated and their performance evaluated. The group's finances require professional management. Planning horizons lengthen, issue campaigns become more numerous and complex, reorganizations become commonplace, and meetings proliferate. In the case of the environmental lobbies, the organizational problem is exacerbated by the fact that the groups have been fighting environmental battles in Washington for twenty years, most of the time as the underdog.[26] Under such circumstances, and pursuing an activity—lobbying—where compromise is often an essential ingredient for success, it is difficult for groups to maintain their cutting edge and avoid staff burnout.

All things considered, most of the groups enter the 1990s in good organizational shape. With the exception of Friends of the Earth, whose future does not yet seem secure, they have survived the financial insecurity of the Watt era. More than half of the groups have also endured a change of leadership, some more than once, with generally positive results.[27] The new leaders typically did not come from within the organization—evidence that the groups' boards of directors placed a premium on perceived managerial competence. At the staff level, turnover has been at a tolerable level. Not infrequently, the older, more experienced staffers shift from one group to another. This practice helps prevent burnout and stagnation, but at the same time weakens the communal ties that bolstered staff members in earlier times. The continued presence of veteran environmental lobbyists among the groups' staffs is an important resource, as personal contacts on Capitol Hill built up over a long period of time can pay off in influence. As one congressional staffer said of the Environmental Defense Fund's longtime wildlife specialist, Michael Bean, "[He] doesn't have to file a lawsuit to have an impact." [28]

The multiplicity of groups that comprise the green lobby is, overall, a source of strength given the wide range of issues that fall under the environmental umbrella and the degree to which the Washington environmental groups are willing to cooperate even though they must all compete for members and contributions from the same pool of "liberal givers." Coalitions on behalf of issues such as clean air or the Alaska wilderness bill have long been commonplace, as is the practice of having groups "sign off" on agreed legislative positions. More recently, in the early 1980s, leaders of ten of the groups established an informal coalition, known as the Group of Ten, which meets on a regular basis to discuss common strategies and problems.[29] Other cooperative ventures include producing consensus reports outlining environmental priorities, such as *An Environmental Agenda for the Future*, issued in 1985 by ten of the national groups, and the more recent *Blueprint for the Environment*, prepared by a coalition of more than thirty organizations and aimed at influencing the Bush administration's environmental agenda.[30]

Another source of the green lobby's strength is its ability to respond to changing circumstances by recognizing new issues and developing new approaches. Six groups joined together to issue a report in 1984 that sought to place the industrial policy debate in the context of environmental considerations. Long before global issues made the news magazine covers, the groups were issuing statements about global ecological impacts and funding staff to work on the international dimensions of environmentalism.[31] An example of a new approach is the willingness of some groups, such as the Wilderness Society and the Environmental Defense Fund, to develop and promote market-based strategies for environmental management. The Wilderness Society created an economics research unit headed by an economist whose title is vice president of resource planning and economics. This group prepares economic and ecological critiques of Forest Service plans. EDF has for years promoted energy conservation programs as a more cost-effective strategy for public utilities than building new power plants. It was also a major force behind Project 88, a bipartisan effort sponsored by Sen. Tim Wirth, D-Colo., and Sen. John Heinz, R-Pa., to find innovative solutions to major environmental and natural resource problems. The project's final report received considerable recognition in Washington and President Bush incorporated part of its recommendations in his Clean Air Act proposals.

Tensions between the national organizations and local environmentalists, the so-called grassroots, have always been present.[32] In recent years, however, the level of rhetoric has escalated. Radical or "deep" environmentalists accuse the national groups of being reformist, caught up in Washington power games. They fault the national organizations for failing to recognize how serious things are and not addressing the fundamental issues. National leaders, for their part, have accused the radicals of being utopians.[33] Those small bands of activists that undertake property destruction to protect such threatened resources as old-growth forests (Earth First!) and whales (Sea Shepherds) scorn environmental lobbyists as careerists who are out of touch with what is really happening and find themselves disavowed by national leaders as terrorists.[34]

Finally, a host of community and neighborhood groups have sprung up in response to local threats, such as abandoned waste facilities, operating chemical factories, or proposed waste-treatment facilities.[35] These groups, several thousand of which are served at the national level by the Citizen's Clearinghouse for Hazardous Waste (founded by Lois Gibbs, the Love Canal activist), represent a populist strand in the environmental movement that is adamantly opposed to any compromise with industry and unsympathetic to market-oriented initiatives.

Thus far, these manifestations of grass-roots activism pose little threat to the national groups' lobbying effectiveness in Washington or to their fund raising. In fact, they appear to offer some positive benefits. The national groups are able to differentiate themselves from extremist acts and probably gain political clout by appearing to be reasonable as a result. The association of environmentalism with populist issues helps counter the elitist label that the movement's critics like to use, and the challenge from below gives the national groups reason to avoid spiritual decline and overprofessionalization. Indeed, it is inaccurate to make too much of the dichotomy between the grass-roots and the national groups, as the grass-roots groups have ideological links with several of the national lobbies (the Citizen's Clearinghouse does not lobby) who actively support their goals and help represent them at the national level. These include two of the smallest groups, Friends of the Earth and Environmental Action, as well as one of the largest, Greenpeace.

Conclusion

This chapter has examined the state of public opinion and the environmental movement in the first year of the Bush administration, some twenty years after the original Earth Day, and discussed some possible implications for environmental politics in the 1990s. Within the past two years the already high level of support for environmental protection has strengthened further, and the *Exxon Valdez* oil spill has helped to raise the salience of environmental issues for the first time in years. This level of public concern helps the environmental lobbies by reinforcing their legitimacy as genuine representatives of a large constituency.

For many years environmentalists have found themselves fighting a holding action in Congress. The public's heightened concern about environmental issues may help create a new political climate more favorable to environmental initiatives. There are already signs that this is happening both in the White House and in Congress. The degree of public concern about the environment recorded by Republican tracking polls led President Bush's advisers during the 1988 presidential election to stage the famous and successful preemptive strike on what had hitherto been a Democratic issue by having Bush make a television commercial featuring Boston Harbor in which he declared his support for environmental protection. Thus committed, the newly elected president appointed William Reilly to head EPA, and subsequently backed a revision of the Clean Air Act that some environmentalists praised. In Congress, veteran observers were startled by a unanimous October 1989 vote on a Clean Air Act provision by the House Subcommittee on Health and the Environment that ended twelve years of stalemate by tightening automobile emissions to an extent previously rejected by industry lobbyists and their congressional supporters. Congressman John Dingell, D-Mich., long resistant to compromise on this issue and powerful enough to block any legislation in this area that he did not agree with, was said to have realized that the political climate had shifted and that it was time to get the best deal possible.[36]

Notes

1. Joanne Omang, "Watt Finds Time to Hear Audubon Society," *Washington Post*, May 15, 1981, A23.
2. Tim Peckinpaugh, "The Specter of Environmentalism: The Threat of Environmental Groups," Republican Study Committee, Special Study, February 12, 1982.
3. "Transcript of Reagan News Parley on Nomination of Ruckelshaus to E.P.A.," *New York Times*, March 22, 1983, A24.
4. For a further discussion of why the environmental movement was successful in opposing the Reagan administration's policies, see Robert Cameron Mitchell, "Public Opinion and Environmental Politics in the 1970s and 1980s," in *Environmental Policy in the 1980s: Reagan's New Agenda*, ed. Norman J. Vig and Michael E. Kraft (Washington, D.C.: CQ Press, 1984).
5. For a major assessment of environmental public opinion trends see Riley E. Dunlap, "Public Opinion and Environmental Policy," in *Environmental Politics and Policy: Theories and Evidence*, ed. James P. Lester (Durham, N.C.: Duke University Press, 1989).
6. For a typical "most important problem" series, see the *New York Times*/CBS News poll, "January Survey," January 12-15, 1989, which gives the findings of this question for each poll taken during the Reagan years.

7. Cambridge Reports, *Cambridge Reports Trends and Forecasts,* September 1989, 6. The environment tied with poverty for fifth place, after drugs (39 percent), "other social problems" (22 percent), foreign affairs (21 percent), and government spending (17 percent).
8. *Roper Reports* 89-2 (February 1989), 4.
9. Cambridge Reports poll, cited in Americans for the Environment, Sierra Club, National Wildlife Federation, *The Rising Tide: Public Opinion, Policy & Politics* (Washington, D.C.: Americans for the Environment, Sierra Club, National Wildlife Federation, April 20, 1989), 5-15.
10. *New York Times,* July 2, 1989, A1, A18.
11. The wording of this question was intentional because the survey researchers wanted to identify those who held more than casual pro-environmental views.
12. See Mitchell, "Public Opinion and Environmental Politics"; and Robert Cameron Mitchell, "From Conservation to Environmental Movement: The Development of the Modern Environmental Lobbies," in *Government and Environmental Politics: Essays on Historical Developments Since World War II,* ed. Michael J. Lacey (Washington, D.C.: Woodrow Wilson Center Press, forthcoming).
13. See Riley E. Dunlap, "Paradigmatic Change in Social Science: From Human Exemptionalism to an Ecological Paradigm," *American Behavioral Scientist* 25 (1980): 5-14; and Lester W. Milbrath, *Environmentalists: Vanguard for a New Society* (Albany, N.Y.: State University of New York Press, 1984).
14. For example, *Roper Reports* 88-1 (January 1988), 19; *Roper Reports* 88-2 (February 1988), 39. Wildlife and wilderness issues were not included in these questions.
15. Ben J. Wattenberg, "Environmental Activism: Here We Go Again," *U.S. News and World Report,* April 17, 1989, 29.
16. This is the combined average of the main daily newscasts on CBS, ABC, NBC, CNN, and the "McNeil-Lehrer News Hour," and of the daily stories in the *New York Times, Wall Street Journal, Los Angeles Times,* and *Washington Post.* The data are from the *Anchorage Daily News,* September 3, 1989, A1.
17. Natural Resources Defense Council, *Intolerable Risk: Pesticides in Our Children's Food* (New York: Natural Resources Defense Council, 1989).
18. See Mitchell, "Public Opinion and Environmental Politics," 58-59; and Robert Cameron Mitchell, "National Environmental Lobbies and the Apparent Illogic of Collective Action," in *Collective Decision Making: Applications from Public Choice Theory,* ed. Clifford S. Russell (Washington, D.C.: Resources for the Future, 1979), 87-121.
19. In 1988 the pessimists outnumbered the optimists for the first time since 1983, when Cambridge Reports began asking respondents each year whether the quality of the environment "around here" is better or worse than it was five years ago. In 1983, 38 percent said it was better and 34 percent worse, of whom 5 percent said it was "very much worse." In 1988 the responses were: 32 percent better, 46 percent worse, of whom 9 percent stated it was "very much worse." In 1989 the optimists stood at 27 percent, the pessimists at 44 percent, of whom 18 percent said it was "very much worse." (Twenty-five percent in 1989 thought it was about the same.) Cambridge Reports,

Cambridge Reports Trends and Forecasts, 6.

20. Americans for the Environment, Sierra Club, National Wildlife Federation, *The Rising Tide*, 1-2.
21. The twelve national groups are the Environmental Defense Fund, Friends of the Earth, Izaak Walton League of America, National Audubon Society, National Parks and Conservation Association, National Wildlife Federation, Natural Resources Defense Council, Sierra Club, Wilderness Society, Environmental Action, Defenders of Wildlife, and Greenpeace USA. Another group, the Environmental Policy Institute, has merged with Friends of the Earth. The first nine groups (plus the Environmental Policy Institute) comprise the coordinating leadership group known as the Group of Ten.
22. Some groups do not claim lobbying as one of their functions, although they may attempt to influence policy on issues in their area of expertise or work with others who do the lobbying. Among the largest of the many groups in this category are: the Nature Conservancy, a group that preserves land nationwide; the Conservation Foundation/World Wildlife Fund, two groups that have administratively merged while preserving separate identities; the Citizen's Clearinghouse for Hazardous Waste, which serves local groups protesting hazardous-waste sites and facilities; the League of Conservation Voters, which offers campaign help and money at election time for politicians friendly to the environmental cause; and the World Resources Institute, a think tank on global issues. In what follows I will focus on the core lobbying groups.
23. Peter Borrelli, "Environmentalism at a Crossroads," in *Crossroads: Environmental Priorities for the Future*, ed. Peter Borrelli (Washington, D.C.: Island Press, 1988), 17.
24. See James A. Tober, *Wildlife and the Public Interest* (New York: Praeger, 1989), 38; and Charles Mohr, "Environmental Groups Gain in Wake of Spill," *New York Times*, June 11, 1989, 31.
25. Michael Harwood, "Daredevils for the Environment," *New York Times Magazine*, October 2, 1988, 72, 74-76. Grass-roots lobbying and direct action in the United States are the province of a companion organization, Greenpeace Action.
26. Environmental lobbying has a longer history, but prior to 1970 it was more episodic and was performed by the groups' leadership rather than by junior hired hands.
27. Rochelle L. Stanfield, "Environmental Lobby's Changing of the Guard Is Part of Movement's Evolution," *National Journal*, June 8, 1985, 1350-1353.
28. Tober, *Wildlife and the Public Interest*, 115.
29. A number of other national environmental organizations do not include lobbying among their activities. See note 22.
30. Robert Cahn, ed., *An Environmental Agenda for the Future* (Washington, D.C.: Island Press, 1985); Rochelle L. Stanfield, "The Green Blueprint," *National Journal*, July 2, 1988, 1735-1737; and T Allan Comp., ed., *Blueprint for the Environment: A Plan for Federal Action* (Salt Lake City: Howe Brothers, 1989).
31. See Cahn, *An Environmental Agenda*, chap. 12; and Tober, *Wildlife and the Public Interest*.

32. The Sierra Club and National Audubon Society have their own grass-roots chapters and experience the grass-roots/national tension within their organizations.
33. Kirkpatrick Sale, "The Forest for the Trees," *Mother Jones,* November 1986, 25-33, 58.
34. Joe Kane, "Mother Nature's Army," *Esquire,* February 1988, 98-106.
35. Robert Gottlieb and Helen Ingram, "The New Environmentalists," *The Progressive,* August 1988, 14-15.
36. Allan R. Gold, "Shift in Fight on Air Rules," *New York Times,* October 5, 1989, B15.

II. PUBLIC POLICY DILEMMAS

5

Environmental Gridlock: Searching for Consensus in Congress

Michael E. Kraft

Environmental policy is paralyzed in Congress and mired in the courts. Congress failed to agree on important revisions of the acts governing clean air, clean water, drinking water and abandoned toxic dump sites.

New York Times editorial
November 30, 1984

Gridlock is expensive, both in terms of the usual definition of expense, namely dollars, but also in terms of public and environmental health. If we do not do anything about a problem because we cannot decide what to do about it, whatever health threat or environmental threat exists is certainly not going to be mitigated or alleviated to any significant extent.

William Ruckelshaus, former administrator
Environmental Protection Agency (1988)

In vivid contrast to the environmental policy activism and innovation of the 1970s, the 1980s have been widely characterized as a period of policy paralysis. As the *New York Times* editorialized in late 1984, Congress seemed unable to advance on virtually any front in furthering America's environmental progress, including renewal of the Clean Air Act and other measures on acid rain, clean water, pesticide regulation, energy use, and toxic chemicals. In assessing the problem, former Environmental Protection Agency (EPA) administrator William Ruckelshaus and others found an apt metaphor in urban traffic gridlock.[1] Whether the reference was to community opposition to siting hazardous-waste facilities or to congressional immobility on important national policies, the United States seemed afflicted with intractable environmental problems that frustrated all policy actors, governmental and nongovernmental.[2]

By the late 1980s the tide had turned in Congress for some

environmental issues, and there were encouraging signs of easing gridlock related to the NIMBY syndrome in local siting disputes (see Chapter 6). Despite opposition or indifference by the Reagan administration, Congress revised and strengthened the Clean Water Act, the Safe Drinking Water Act, and the Superfund program, among other major policies. At the end of 1989, with George Bush in the White House and environmental issues high on the political agenda, renewal of the Clean Air Act for the first time since 1977 appeared certain. The new act was also likely to include provisions that would sharply reduce acid rain.

What accounts for such shifts in our willingness and capacity to devise solutions to the nation's environmental ills? Why did we have environmental gridlock in the early 1980s, and to what extent had the pattern changed by the late 1980s? Will the 1990s be a period of increased consensus and progress on environmental legislation or will it be a replay of the "deferral politics" of the early 1980s, when Congress was unable to act on environmental issues? [3]

In this chapter I look back briefly at the 1970s to assess environmental policy making in its most favorable decade. I then compare this to policy making in the 1980s in several important areas, including air quality, acid rain, and pesticides. I focus on the U.S. Congress, even though gridlock also occurs in the states and in federal bureaucracies. Finally, I ask what we might expect in the 1990s, as the United States faces a broader and more formidable agenda of global ecological threats.

Environmental Gridlock and Its Causes

Policy gridlock refers to an inability to resolve conflicts in a policy-making body such as Congress, which results in governmental inaction in the face of important public problems. There is no consensus on *what* to do and therefore no movement in any direction. Present policies, or slight revisions of them, continue until agreement on change is achieved.

The environmental policy stalemate in Congress and elsewhere reflects a fundamental reality of American politics. Policy making is often a difficult and tortuous process. For decades political commentators have bemoaned the "deadlock of American democracy" that derives from the U.S. political system's highly fragmented authority, weak political parties, and uncertain presidential leadership, especially when control of the White House and Congress is divided between the major parties. The brunt of the criticism is directed at the constitutionally mandated separation of powers among policy-making institutions (for example, the division of authority in a bicameral Congress, the presidential veto, and the congressional power of appropriations) and other structural features that make governing difficult. Some have complained that congressional reforms in the 1970s worsened the problem of fragmentation by dispersing power to more than two hundred subcommittees led by highly independent legislators owing little to either party leadership or the president.[4]

Institutional structure *is* important, but it is hardly the sole reason for environmental gridlock. A fuller list of explanations would include the complexity of environmental issues in the 1980s, the high cost of solutions, uncertain scientific knowledge, ineffectual presidential and congressional leadership, the variable political climate in the nation, and intense competition among powerful interest groups.

The standoff between environmental groups and industry is one of the most significant factors, as Christopher Bosso has shown in the case of pesticide policy.[5] The late 1970s and 1980s witnessed an explosive growth in the number of interest groups, nearly all of which found it essential to open offices in Washington to be near the center of policy action. The environmental lobby greatly improved its access to the corridors of power, and its political influence grew as opinion polls indicated a public highly supportive of environmental protection. In response, groups representing industry and resource development interests sharply increased their own presence in Washington. By the late 1970s they were a powerful force often aligned against environmentalists.[6] Business groups also began a multifaceted effort to shift the political climate of the nation to the right, particularly away from increased regulation. Because of this realignment of interest groups, consensus building became far more difficult and action on controversial environmental policy initiatives often became impossible.

The consequences of policy gridlock attract more attention than its causes. Concern has focused on what difference it makes to environmental quality and public health when collectively we are unable to make tough decisions in a timely manner. As demonstrated by a recent *Time* cover story entitled, "Is Government Dead?" and a Brookings Institution book, *Can the Government Govern?* there has been no shortage of either popular or scholarly criticism of the government's capacity for effective decision making on a range of important policy problems.[7]

For environmental as well as other issues, the policy dilemma associated with gridlock derives from the tension between two competing expectations for the policy process. One emphasizes prompt and rational problem solving; the other stresses representation of pertinent interests and policy legitimation. From the first perspective, gridlock is a needless, and possibly dangerous, blockage of sensible policy making. Dire consequences are foreseen unless immediate action is taken to institute preventive measures. From the second perspective, it is essential to improve understanding of the problems faced and to formulate policies that are broadly acceptable to the diverse interests affected by governmental action.

For many environmental issues (for example, expansion of wilderness areas or appropriations for municipal sewage treatment facilities), short-term legislative stalemate is not necessarily cause for alarm. A relatively slow movement toward enactment may help to legitimize the policy ultimately approved. It allows time for research, review, and deliberation, and thus the building of scientific knowledge and political support crucial to successful implementation. Poorly designed and hastily approved policies run a significant risk of failure, as Charles Jones argued was the case with the Clean Air Act of 1970. Scholars and activists have criticized the environmental and resource policies of the Reagan administration on the same basis.[8]

Apprehension over environmental gridlock is clearly warranted, however, in those instances where excessively long delays in addressing a problem may cause severe or irreversible damage to public health and environmental quality. This may be the case for such problems as the thinning ozone layer, global climate change, maintenance of biodiversity, and rapid population growth.[9]

It is essential that we make these distinctions. Not all environmental threats are equally great and not all require "crisis decision making." If we fail to recognize the difference, we confuse the question of what constitutes a proper governmental response to the environmental challenge. Where risks are moderate to low, slow or incremental decision making is more acceptable than where the risks of inaction are high. While we may aspire to improve our capacity for environmental policy making in all cases, the latter condition presents a more compelling case for doing so.

Where the risks of indecision or ineffective action are great, we have to question the normal expectation that policy making should not proceed without a high degree of scientific certainty, demonstrably favorable benefit-cost ratios, and agreement among all significant parties in a dispute. As many writers have argued, we need to think more seriously about other bases for decision making, such as what is ecologically rational and what best promotes our long-term, collective well-being.[10] If conventional decision making cannot adequately address the problems likely to be faced in the 1990s and in the twenty-first century, we need to develop the political and institutional capacity for governing the planet's future more successfully.

An examination of environmental gridlock in Congress cannot address all these questions, but it can illuminate some of the key issues. There are conflicting interpretations of policy stalemate, its impact on both public policy and environmental quality, and necessary solutions. Review of the ways in which policy making in the 1970s and 1980s differed, and closer study of several cases of environmental gridlock in recent years, helps clarify the reasons for its greater frequency in the 1980s and the implications for environmental policy in the 1990s.

Environmental Policy Making in the 1970s

The 1970s offer abundant examples of both successful and unsuccessful efforts at environmental policy making. The record for this "environmental decade" is remarkable, particularly in comparison to the 1980s (see Appendix 1). When the issues are highly salient, public concern is high, media coverage is favorable, environmental groups are well regarded and effective, and bipartisan leaders in Congress and the White House support legislative initiatives, the usual impediments to nonincremental policy change can be overcome.[11] The enactment of the National Environmental Policy Act, Clean Air Act, Clean Water Act, Endangered Species Act, and Resource Conservation and Recovery Act, among others, demonstrated that major environmental policies could be approved in fairly short order in the United States.

The legislative accomplishments owed much to some basic changes in American society and politics in the 1960s and 1970s. Public concern over environmental threats increased sharply, as did the membership and political clout of environmental groups. As these new players entered the political arena, the "scope of conflict" was widened, new issues received attention, and the older political coalitions were irrevocably altered. The "subgovernments" that once dominated policy areas such as pesticide use, public lands, nuclear power, and water projects were forced to accommodate new and broader issue networks.[12] Congress itself was transformed by a series of internal changes that made it more open to public scrutiny and more responsive to new political forces such as those represented by environmental and other public interest groups.[13]

To these factors we can add the presence in Congress of an extraordinary group of environmental policy entrepreneurs who provided the leadership essential to enactment of the landmark policies of the 1960s and 1970s. They included Senators Edmund Muskie, D-Maine, chair of the influential Subcommittee on Air and Water Pollution, Henry Jackson, D-Wash., chair of the Committee on Interior and Insular Affairs, and their counterparts in the House, such as Representatives Morris Udall, D-Ariz., and Paul Rodgers, D-Fla. Along with other key legislators, they identified and publicized emerging environmental problems and assembled the necessary legislative coalitions for policy enactment.

These early environmental victories were deceptive in some respects. Congressional support was broadly based but thin. Relatively few members of Congress were activists on the issues or well informed about ecology and environmental protection.[14] Most members favored environmental policies because they were popular and relatively free of conflict. Even the active members had little idea of the implications of the policies they enacted, the complaints the policies would eventually provoke from the business community, and the many technical, administrative, and economic concerns that would arise during implementation.

It is hardly surprising that enthusiasm in Congress for the advance of environmental policy gradually dissipated as growing experience and familiarity bred increasing concern about its impact on the economy and as the saliency of the issues among the American public declined. In comparison to the 1980s, the achievements in the 1970s were victories made easy by a fortuitous convergence of political forces that was not to last.

Even during the 1970s, some environmental and natural resource policy initiatives were unsuccessful. The most striking case is energy policy. Despite a succession of presidential proposals to Congress in the wake of the Arab oil embargo of 1973, including a major push by President Jimmy Carter in 1977 and 1978, Congress failed to adopt a comprehensive national energy policy. That outcome, which had a negative impact on the economy and environmental quality in the 1980s, was understandable. No consensus on energy policy goals existed either among the public or on Capitol Hill, presidential leadership was feeble, and there was intense opposition to the energy initiatives by a diversity of organized interests. The resulting policy stalemate portended what would occur under similar conditions in the 1980s.[15]

Environmental Policy Making in the 1980s

For a variety of reasons, environmental gridlock became the norm in the early 1980s. Although a ranking of the various causes is not easy, among the most important were the election of Ronald Reagan in 1980, the capture of the Senate by the Republican party in the same year (for the first time since 1955), and a shift in the political climate of the nation that made proposal of new regulatory programs exceedingly difficult. The economic recession of 1980 to 1982 and the high cost of energy were important factors shaping Reagan's decision to make environmental policy goals subordinate to economic recovery.

As a result of these alterations in the political environment in 1981, Congress was thrown into a defensive posture. It was forced to *react* to the Reagan administration's radical policy shifts, and it did so by defending existing policy. Rather than proposing new programs or expanding old ones, it focused its resources on oversight and criticism of the Reagan administration. Between the Ninety-sixth Congress (1979-1980) and the Ninety-seventh Congress (1981-1982), the frequency of oversight hearings increased appreciably on all the major environmental committees.[16] Partly because of the intensity of the Reagan administration's efforts to reverse environmental commitments of the 1960s and 1970s, bipartisan leadership on these issues also became more difficult in the 1980s. Thus, for most of Reagan's first term political conditions were ripe for protracted conflict between the president and Congress.

Environmental Gridlock: 1981-1984

In assessing environmental policy making from 1981 to 1984, Mary Etta Cook and Roger Davidson argue that Congress was practicing "deferral politics." As environmental issues became more complex, less salient to the public, and more contentious, there were fewer incentives for policy leadership on Capitol Hill. Members were increasingly cross-pressured by environmental and industry groups, partisanship on these issues increased, and Congress and President Reagan battled over budget and program priorities.[17] Some Democrats also feared that if the existing statutes were opened to amendment, they might be weakened, given the antiregulatory climate of the early 1980s.

The fragmentation of environmental policy responsibilities added to Congress's inability to respond expeditiously and coherently to the president. Dozens of committees and subcommittees have jurisdiction over these issues (see Table 1-1 in Chapter 1), and they often compete with one another. This dispersion of authority affects congressional oversight of the administration as well. Hearings by different committees are typically uncoordinated, as each seeks political attention and credit for its activities.[18]

The cumulative effect of these conditions in the early 1980s was that Congress increasingly adopted a posture of deferring action. It had become impossible to form majority coalitions to act definitively on most of the major environmental statutes coming up for renewal. Thus members opted to keep programs alive through continuing appropriations and short-term extensions of the existing acts. During the Ninety-seventh Congress, eight comprehensive environmental programs were due for reauthorization; only two were enacted. Although it renewed the Toxic Substances Control Act and the Endangered Species Act in 1982, Congress deferred action on programs for clean air, clean water, pesticide regulation, noise control, safe drinking water, and hazardous-waste control.

Moreover, there were virtually no *new* environmental policies proposed in this Congress. Divided party control of the House and Senate and a conservative president in the White House made congressional policy initiation improbable. It was more expedient for Congress to enter a holding pattern and wait for an improved political climate.

Gridlock Eases: 1984-1989

The legislative logjam began breaking up in late 1983, as President Reagan's environmental agenda was repudiated by the American public and as Anne Burford and James Watt were forced from office. Those developments altered what John Kingdon has called the "politics stream," [19] and environmental groups took advantage of the favorable political mood to push ahead on their deferred policy agenda. The new pattern was evident in 1984 when, after several years of deliberation, Congress approved major amendments to the 1976 Resource Conservation and Recovery Act that strengthened the program and set tight new deadlines for EPA rule making on control of hazardous chemical wastes. Reauthorization of other major acts followed in the next two years.

Although the Republicans still controlled the Senate, the Ninety-ninth Congress (1985-1986) compiled a record dramatically at odds with the deferral politics of the Ninety-seventh and Ninety-eighth Congresses. Congressional action was helped by the occurrence of two environmental catastrophes: At Bhopal, India, in December 1984, the world's worst industrial accident killed more than three thousand people and injured several hundred thousand, and at Chernobyl in the Soviet Union in April 1986, the worst nuclear power plant accident in history exposed hundreds of people to high levels of radiation and spread radioactive fallout across northern Europe. The accidents increased the credibility of arguments for additional environmental protection. They also created windows of opportunity for environmental groups to press their case for renewal of the Superfund program and related policies on toxic chemicals and pollution control.

In May 1986, the Safe Drinking Water Act was strengthened and expanded in scope, incorporating a three-year timetable for regulation of eighty-three chemical contaminants. In the fall of 1986, after years of bitter controversy, Congress enacted the Superfund Amendments and Reauthorization Act (SARA), which renewed the program for hazardous-waste cleanup for five years at a total budget of $8.5 billion, far greater than the spending level favored by the Reagan administration. As a reflection of public concern following the Bhopal accident, Congress added to SARA a separate Title III, the Emergency Planning and Community Right-to-Know Act. This was an entirely new program mandating nationwide reporting requirements for toxic and hazardous chemicals produced, used, or stored in communities, as well as state and local emergency planning for accidental releases.[20]

Another notable accomplishment of the Ninety-ninth Congress that received strong backing from both environmentalists and industry was the adoption of energy efficiency standards for appliances. The Appliance Energy Conservation Act was signed by President Reagan in March 1987 after an earlier veto. In addition, in late 1986 Congress reauthorized the Clean Water Act, with a price tag of $18 billion over nine years. The water bill was vetoed by President Reagan as too expensive, but in February 1987, the One-hundredth Congress (1987-1988) easily passed the same bill (with the authorization raised to $20 billion), and overrode the president's second veto by large margins.

Environmentalists were pleased with these results. At the end of 1986 the Natural Resources Defense Council described actions of the Ninety-ninth Congress as "a complete turnaround from recent years," and noted that "the original statutes were substantially strengthened. . . ." In early 1987 the Sierra Club congratulated Congress for its "solid record on environmental quality and public lands issues." It added that "bipartisan majorities supported the improvement of key laws despite resistance from President Reagan." [21]

The Democrats regained control of the Senate following the 1986 election and the newly elected members of both the House and Senate were more environmentally oriented than those leaving Congress. Yet despite what is by any measure a highly productive record, several major environmental policy measures were unsuccessful not only in the Ninety-ninth Congress, but in the One-hundredth Congress as well. These included renewal of the Clean Air Act and the major pesticide control act, the Federal Insecticide, Fungicide, and Rodenticide Act (FIFRA), and new legislation on acid rain.

Cases in Policy Paralysis: Clean Air, Acid Rain, and Pesticides

"Congress stayed largely stalemated on a range of old environmental and energy problems in 1988, even while a generation of new ones clamored for attention." So wrote Joseph Davis for Congressional Quarterly's assessment of environmental issues at the end of the One-hundredth Congress.[22] The reasons for environmental gridlock discussed above help explain why Congress made so little progress in resolving persistent conflicts over air quality, acid rain, and pesticide policies.

Air Quality

Environmental gridlock has been typified by Congress's inability to reauthorize the costly and controversial Clean Air Act after its 1977 amendment. By 1981, when funding authorization for the act was to expire, critics had compiled a long list of grievances about air pollution regulation. There was also wide agreement that the 1977 act, itself a product of a fragile coalition, needed at least modest revision.[23] But consensus on the *particulars* of reform proved to be nearly impossible between late 1981 and 1989. During this period the act was funded on a year-to-year basis through the appropriations process, thus maintaining the 1977 statute but not correcting its many defects.

Having pledged in the 1980 campaign to ease the burden of federal regulation, President Reagan was expected to lead a fight to weaken the act. Just before his inauguration his nominee to head the Office of Management and Budget, David Stockman, had criticized the Clean Air Act for its "staggering excess built upon dubious scientific and economic premises." [24] However, the combination of a sharply critical response to leaks of early drafts of possible White House changes and poll results showing broad public support for strong air pollution laws led the administration to issue only a vague set of "basic principles" on clean air policy.

With no presidential leadership on the clean air issue, attention in Congress focused on a bill sponsored primarily by Rep. John Dingell, D-Mich., chair of the House Energy and Commerce Committee. Introduced in late 1981 and referred to as a "moderate compromise," the bill drew its major support from business interests, and won endorsement by the Reagan White House. Environmentalists quickly labeled it the "dirty air" bill, and faulted it for omission of acid rain provisions. These first skirmishes in the clean air battles hinted at what lay ahead for the rest of the decade as each side dug in its heels on this important symbol of commitment to environmental protection.

Conflicts over clean air policy throughout the 1980s were personified by the incessant wrangling between the powerful Dingell, who was protective of Michigan's automobile industry, and Rep. Henry Waxman, D-Calif., chair of the Energy and Commerce Committee's Subcommittee on Health and the Environment after 1979, whose district in Los Angeles was one of the smoggiest in the nation. Debate in the Energy Committee was bitter, and the committee was described in the press as "polarized and paralyzed." No bill emerged from the committee in 1981 or 1982; after that the initiative fell to Waxman and his subcommittee. They spent the next eight years, in his words, "painting the picture and setting the agenda" for clean air legislation.[25] Policy incubation of this kind was the best Waxman could hope for given the political environment in Congress and White House disinterest in legislative action.

After 1982 President Reagan played no active role on clean air, but he promised to veto any strong revision of the act out of concern for the economic burden it would place on industry. At the same time, the EPA under Anne Burford pursued an aggressive administrative strategy of undercutting the Clean Air Act's implementation.[26] In August 1982, the Republican-controlled Environment and Public Works Committee rejected Reagan's call for sweeping changes in the act and agreed on a modest revision. However, the bill never reached the Senate floor.

From 1982 to 1988, the politics of clean air remained similarly stalemated. The Senate's Environment and Public Works Committee reported out clean air bills in 1984 and 1987 that went nowhere (although the full Senate would likely have approved the measures). In the House, the Energy and Commerce Committee, less pro-environment than the full House, remained mired in controversy over the stringency of air pollution control measures.

In 1988 there was a new atmosphere of moderation in both houses and Congress came close to breaking the gridlock. For the third time, the Senate Environment and Public Works Committee had reported out a comprehensive bill, endorsed by environmentalists, that included sections on ozone, toxic air pollutants, and acid rain control, as well as tougher emission limits on motor vehicles and industry.[27] But Senate Majority Leader Robert Byrd, D-W.Va., worried about the impact of the acid rain provisions on his state's coal miners, would not bring it to the floor. Sen. George Mitchell, D-Maine, chair of the Environment and Public Works Committee's Subcommittee on Environmental Protection, hoped the election-year popularity of clean air policy would allow him to piece together a compromise bill, but the coalition fell apart at the end of the session, largely over acid rain measures.

In the House, an informal caucus of moderate and conservative industrial state Democrats on the Energy and Commerce Committee, known as the Group of Nine, made a parallel effort. Saying they were "tired of deadlock," they developed a compromise bill on urban smog that failed to satisfy either side completely.[28] John Dingell continued to oppose proposals to strengthen the Clean Air Act, and, like Waxman in 1982, he made full use of parliamentary rules to delay action in Waxman's subcommittee, for example, by not appearing for quorum calls. The two coalitions of opposing interest groups—the Clean Air Working Group (representing industry) and the National Clean Air Coalition (representing environmental, public health, and consumer groups)—were strong enough to block each other's initiatives.

George Bush's election in 1988, an improved political climate for environmental issues, and several changes in party leadership on Capitol Hill finally offered the promise of a breakthrough on clean air legislation. In one of the key shifts, Senator Mitchell, the chief proponent of clean air laws in the Senate, replaced Robert Byrd as the majority leader, making floor action more likely. Sen. Max Baucus, D-Mont., the new chair of the Subcommittee on Environmental Protection, reflected this optimistic consensus for passage by citing public support for environmental protection, the rising saliency of environmental issues, and legislative backing: "Everyone wants a bill this year—the Speaker, the majority leader, and the president."[29] Reports of worsening ozone levels in urban areas and the release in mid-1989 of new data on air toxics improved prospects as well. Shortly after the data on air toxics were released, the Chemical Manufacturers Association said it would support some changes in the Clean Air Act, a significant reversal of its long-standing opposition.[30]

"It's time to break the gridlock on this issue," George Bush said in

July 1989 as he sent his clean air bill to Congress. Directed at the three problems of urban smog, toxic air pollutants, and acid rain, the bill was criticized by environmentalists as too weak and by industry as too demanding.[31] Nevertheless, both the House and the Senate committees moved quickly to complete work on the various clean air proposals, with compromises made by both sides. These efforts had mixed consequences. The Senate Environment and Public Works Committee voted unanimously for stronger provisions on urban smog and toxic air pollutants than Bush had endorsed. In addition, in what the press celebrated as a historic occasion in the House, Waxman and Dingell agreed on tough auto emissions standards, which would be phased in beginning in 1994.[32] However, the subcommittee weakened the president's proposal for use of alternative, cleaner fuels in cars amid contradictory signals from the White House, and controversies erupted once again over acid rain control. Despite these conflicts, the outlook in both houses remained favorable for enactment of Clean Air Act amendments in 1990.

Acid Rain

The shift in the political environment in 1989 also seemed likely to break the long-term deadlock over national acid rain policy. Although intimately tied to debate over renewal of the Clean Air Act, several unique features that explain gridlock on acid rain measures merit brief discussion. These include the often intense regional conflicts over distribution of the costs of control and strong presidential opposition during much of the 1980s.

Acid rain is a generic term used to describe both the wet and dry deposition of acids formed by sulfur dioxide (primarily from coal combustion) and nitrogen oxides (primarily from motor vehicle exhaust and electric utilities) emitted into the atmosphere. Although scientific evidence is not conclusive on the severity of all the impacts, acid rain adversely affects aquatic life in lakes and streams, forests, crops, and buildings, and may threaten human health.[33] The effects are particularly serious in the Northeast; the contributing sources are chiefly in the industrial Midwest, especially areas using older, coal-fired generating facilities. This accounts for the regional conflict over policies that concentrate costs on one region to provide benefits for another.

As concern over the effects of acid rain mounted during the 1980s, repeated attempts were made to formulate policies that would sharply reduce sulfur dioxide and nitrogen oxide emissions, but they were consistently opposed by the affected industries and blocked by congressional leaders sympathetic with their plight. Central to these disagreements was who should bear the costs of emissions reduction. Midwestern utilities insisted that the costs be shared nationally. Utilities in the East and West rejected such "burden-sharing" approaches as unfair, saying they already had reduced their sulfur dioxide emissions at great expense. They, as well as the Bush EPA, maintained that the Midwest was only being asked to pay in proportion to what it contributed to the acid rain problem.

Another major reason for the extended gridlock on acid rain policy was opposition to control measures by the Reagan White House. The Carter administration had declared that immediate action on acid rain was necessary, and signed an agreement with the Canadian government in 1980 pledging to develop "policies, practices and technologies to combat acid precipitation's impact." Despite pressure from states in the Northeast and mounting scientific evidence of the damage, the Reagan administration held consistently to the view that further research was needed before any costly regulatory program could be adopted.[34] Even a modest and experimental emissions reduction effort proposed by Reagan's newly appointed EPA administrator, William Ruckelshaus, was rejected by the White House in 1983 as too expensive.

Congressional efforts to adopt an acid rain policy were no more successful during the 1980s than was Ruckelshaus's overture to the White House. By 1986 Representative Waxman finally was able to get his Subcommittee on Health and the Environment to approve a widely supported measure he called a "breakthrough." But the bill did not survive in the full House Energy and Commerce Committee, whose chair, John Dingell, had opposed control plans throughout the decade out of concern for the auto industry.[35] Dingell won the backing of midwestern members who had comparable fears about economic impacts in their districts. Beginning in 1982 the Senate Environment and Public Works Committee was able to agree on bills mandating sizable reductions in emissions. However, the committee's enthusiasm for acid rain control was not shared by Majority Leader Byrd, who refused to bring the measures to the floor.

While critics have singled out Dingell and Byrd for blocking acid rain policy making, there are other reasons why Congress was deadlocked on acid rain. The major one was the difficulty of fashioning an acceptable bill given the regional divisiveness the subject evoked and the uncompromising positions taken by both environmentalists and industry. The challenge became even more apparent at the end of 1988.

For months, Senator Mitchell, chair of the Subcommittee on Environmental Protection, had negotiated quietly with Byrd and others, and he drafted acid rain provisions in the clean air bill that he thought all sides could support. When the bill was derailed at the end of the session in October 1988, Mitchell delivered a blistering twenty-three-page speech on the Senate floor. He blamed both environmentalists and the utilities and coal companies for remaining "rigid and unyielding . . . even when faced with the certainty that their rigidity would result in no action this year." In an interview just after his speech, Mitchell described the difficulty of acid rain politics:

> The problem remains as it has for over a decade. . . . It is a complex problem requiring a complex solution affecting virtually every part of the country. The costs can be specifically identified, while the benefits are general in nature. It's very difficult to arouse public support for it, and it is hard to translate public support into legislative support.[36]

As environmentalists had hoped in rejecting Mitchell's compromise bill, the prospects for stronger legislation improved markedly in 1989. The key factor was President Bush's decision to break with his predecessor's implacable opposition to acid rain control measures. By doing so he lent crucial White House backing to congressional efforts to devise a solution to the stalemate.[37] Bush's proposal of a 50 percent reduction in sulfur dioxide and nitrogen oxide emissions from utilities was one of the strongest components of his clean air bill, and it quickly changed the prospects for acid rain policy. Mitchell's election as majority leader would also help coalition building in the Senate. In addition, a decade of policy incubation, which allowed further scientific research and assessment of innovative and successful acid rain control programs in several states like Wisconsin and Minnesota, made agreement on some technical and economic issues more likely by 1989. Regional divisions over the distribution of costs continued, and some predicted "full-scale floor battles" on the bills. However, the prospects for passage were still better than at any time in the previous decade.[38]

Pesticides

Federal pesticide policy differs greatly from clean air and acid rain policy, but the reasons for policy gridlock are similar. Since 1981, sharp conflicts between chemical companies and environmentalists blocked reauthorization of the Federal Insecticide, Fungicide, and Rodenticide Act. Both sides were well represented in Congress and neither was willing to compromise. Like clean air and acid rain, pesticide legislation is highly complex, but unlike those relatively "glamorous" policies, pesticide control is a low-salience issue. Few members of Congress are motivated to spend the time necessary to understand the problem, thereby leaving the playing field to more experienced hands with well-entrenched positions.

For eight years, the House Agriculture Committee and the Senate Agriculture, Nutrition, and Forestry Committee tried to balance the competing demands of pesticide manufacturers (chemical companies) and environmentalists. The latter argued that pesticide regulation was governed by an "anachronistic statute that falls far short of other modern health and environmental laws," and was "riddled with loopholes and industry-oriented provisions."[39]

In 1986, the Ninety-ninth Congress came close to passing a comprehensive pesticide bill when a coalition of environmentalists and chemical companies supported a compromise plan. The House and Senate agreed, as did a conference committee, but at the last minute the measure failed to clear the Senate. When the One-hundredth Congress convened, the coalition had fallen apart. Environmentalists thought that with the Democrats now in charge of the Senate, they could work out a more favorable deal, and the process of coalition building began anew in 1987.[40]

The Campaign for Pesticide Reform, which includes some forty-one environmental, health, consumer, and labor groups, has sought an array of changes in recent years. These included speeding up the testing of pesticides (which has been an extremely slow process in EPA), strengthening the law to help control contamination of groundwater, limiting pesticide residues in food, protecting farm workers from exposure to harmful pesticides, improving public access to health and safety information, and providing for the so-called reregistration of older pesticides that were "grandfathered in" by the 1972 act but never adequately tested for health effects. Industry groups, organized as the National Agricultural Chemicals Association (which included some ninety-two companies), have protested that such changes would cost millions of dollars, yield no appreciable benefits, and jeopardize trade secrets.

The politics of pesticides turns on the challenge by environmentalists to the subgovernment (the alliance of congressional agriculture committee members, bureaucrats in the Agriculture Department, and agricultural interests—both farmers and the chemical industry) that dominated this policy arena for years. As some environmentalists put it, pesticides are "legalized poisons" that are deliberately released into the environment to promote economic gain. Historically, pesticide policy was concerned chiefly with the safety of use by farmers and the benefits of improved and more abundant crops. Both farmers and the sizable pesticides industry (with $4 billion per year in sales) have fought to continue that policy.[41] In recent years the issue has been framed differently—to include the effects of pesticides on groundwater, food supplies, and wildlife. As a result, the old players in this arena have been forced to deal with additional issues and the new groups concerned with them. Within Congress, the challenge has taken the form of jurisdictional battles between the old-line agriculture committees (dominated by representatives from farming districts and states) and the environment committees, particularly on issues like groundwater contamination. The present alignment of groups, with such divergent perspectives on the issues, makes agreement on pesticide policy exceptionally difficult.[42]

As one indication of the strength of these political forces, by late 1988 amendments to FIFRA were approved in both houses and signed by the president. However, the bill represented only a modest change in the law, and was promptly dubbed "FIFRA Lite" by its critics. It was aimed largely at speeding EPA's review and reregistration of older pesticides (with a nine-year timetable to complete health tests on some 600 active ingredients in pesticides) and easing the removal of dangerous products from the market. With the potential for consensus limited, particularly on control of groundwater contamination, other issues were put off once more. Some proponents of change talked about a new strategy of avoiding a comprehensive rewrite of FIFRA and instead trying a "brick-by-brick" rebuilding of the law in the future. By 1989 the environmentalist position on revision of the act was reenforced by a report by the National Academy of Sciences that concluded the nation should sharply decrease its reliance on pesticides.[43]

Conclusion

These cases in congressional gridlock illustrate the general difficulty government has in setting environmental policy, particularly when public consensus is lacking or the issues are low in salience. In particular, the cases of clean air, acid rain, and pesticide policy suggest that there are many reasons for stalemate in a legislative body like Congress, and thus no single solution to the problem. The technical complexity of environmental problems, lack of scientific agreement on crucial issues, weak presidential and congressional leadership (or outright opposition), and especially the proficiency with which well-organized groups are able to frustrate coalition building and compromise are all important impediments to action.

Scientific knowledge, leadership, and the political climate change over time, making gridlock more common in some periods, such as the early 1980s, than in others. However, the institutional characteristics of Congress, such as the dispersion of authority, continue unchanged, and the capacity of interest groups to thwart one another's proposals seems to have increased of late. All these forces have implications for the environmental gridlock we can expect in the 1990s, and for what might be done to improve the nation's capacity for environmental policy making.

The Future of Environmental Gridlock

Environmental policy making in the 1990s will be both similar to and different from the patterns of the past twenty years. The similarities will be seen when the major acts are up for renewal and battles are fought over the adequacy of implementation efforts and the level of resources to be made available. For example, the Resource Conservation and Recovery Act will need revision to be used effectively to curb the nation's rising volume of solid waste. As the cases reviewed above make clear, the periodic renewal of environmental policies presents the potential for conflict and deadlock. On the one hand affected interests (especially industry) seek to reduce their financial and other burdens, while on the other hand environmental groups press for strengthening the policies. Ironically, in the 1980s stalemate in Washington contributed to important policy innovation at the state level. The pre-1970 pattern of weak state response to environmental issues was reversed in the 1980s as many states grew tired of waiting for Congress to act. They moved ahead on their own in areas as diverse as energy conservation, recycling, clean air, and acid rain control.[44] We may see a continuation of such state action in the next decade.

For other issues in the 1990s, the policy-making process may well depart from previous patterns. For example, the government's ability to address "third-generation" environmental problems (such as global climate change, deforestation, and population growth) is especially likely to suffer from factors which contribute to gridlock in policy making, with more serious consequences than were evident in the 1970s and 1980s. The most important effects of these environmental problems will be felt in the future, which offers few political incentives for policy leadership. Scientists disagree over the causes and appropriate remedies, and responding to these problems effectively will impose significant economic and social costs. Dealing with global environmental threats will require unprecedented international cooperation, and achieving political consensus on solutions will thus be problematic. Many of these issues will affect people's lifestyles and personal values and not simply the fortunes of regulated industries; hence, environmental policies may well become less popular in the 1990s.

The potential for policy stalemate is evident in regard to global climate change and proposals to cut fossil fuel use sharply. As the United States prepared for international meetings on global warming in late 1989, the Bush administration was deeply divided over what position to take. The president's chief of staff, John Sununu, and his science adviser, D. Allan Bromley, argued for further scientific study before development of any policy. They also wanted a careful assessment of the potential economic impact of European proposals to stabilize carbon emissions by the year 2000 at 1988 levels and to reduce them by 20 percent by 2005. In contrast, EPA administrator William Reilly, key legislators such as Senators Albert Gore, D-Tenn., and Tim Wirth, D-Colo., and leaders of environmental groups pressed for aggressive policies to lower carbon emissions that were comparable to the European proposals.[45] Such disagreements over the U.S. response to the threat of global warming suggest the difficulty of setting ambitious policy goals on other international environmental policies. Addressing that broader issue in late 1989, Richard Benedick, chief U.S. negotiator of the historic 1987 Montreal agreement on protection of the ozone layer, warned that the "most formidable obstacles to action [are] the entrenched economic and political interests" of the world's industrial nations.[46]

For these reasons, there are several possible scenarios for the 1990s. One is that we might expect protracted political conflict and gridlock in policy making, especially if the issues become more complex, scientific evidence remains inconclusive, economic costs and social impacts are perceived to be great, there are unresolved regional inequities, and public opinion is divided. In a second scenario, we might see a much reduced level of political conflict as consensus among the public on environmental policy goals increases, as a durable political constituency for environmental protection provides political incentives for action, and as Congress and the White House agree on needed measures. The propensity to act might be increased by periodic crises, such as the *Exxon Valdez* oil spill, and new scientific findings about impending environmental problems. A third possibility is a blend of the first two scenarios. The political response would depend on the particular issue, as well as the other variables discussed in this chapter: the issue's saliency, the perceived costs and impacts, the relative influence of environmental and industry groups, the effectiveness of political leadership, and institutional capacity for policy making.

If the first scenario seems likely, what might be done to lessen the impending gridlock and improve the chances of enacting sound policy that is responsive to public concerns about the world's deteriorating environment? A variety of strategies come to mind. We should try to reduce scientific uncertainties through increased funding for environmental research and development. We also need to improve the government's capacity to anticipate and respond to emerging environmental problems, particularly long-term and global threats. Both of these needs are discussed in Chapter 17. Political leadership on environmental issues is important as well, and depends critically on the public's willingness to educate itself on environmental problems and to take an active role in the political process.

In earlier years, broad public concern moved policy makers to adopt far-reaching and costly efforts to reverse environmental degradation. Given budgetary constraints and other political obstacles to action in the 1990s, diffuse public support is no longer sufficient to overcome the intense economic, regional, and other interests often aligned against environmental progress. Public opinion remains a powerful force in environmental policy making. But as policy choices become increasingly difficult and contentious, concerned citizens will have to improve their ability to translate their beliefs into effective political influence. They will also have to struggle to define their own interests and preferences in a world filled with policy dilemmas and tough choices.

Notes

1. See "Remarks of William D. Ruckelshaus," in *Breaking the Environmental Gridlock,* ed. Carl E. Van Horn (New Brunswick, N.J.: Eagleton Institute of Politics, 1988), 23-33.
2. See, for example, Daniel A. Mazmanian, Michael Stanley-Jones, and Miriam J. Green, *Breaking Political Gridlock: California's Experiment in Public-Private Cooperation for Hazardous Waste Policy* (Claremont, Calif.: California Institute of Public Affairs, 1988); and Mary Etta Cook and Roger H. Davidson, "Deferral Politics: Congressional Decision Making on Environmental Issues in the 1980s," in *Public Policy and the Natural Environment,* ed. Helen M. Ingram and R. Kenneth Godwin (Greenwich, Conn.: JAI Press, 1985).
3. Cook and Davidson, "Deferral Politics."
4. See, for example, the classic treatment of James McGregor Burns, *The Deadlock of Democracy* (Englewood Cliffs, N.J.: Prentice-Hall, 1963). On the congressional reforms of the 1970s, see Roger H. Davidson, "Subcommittee Government: New Channels for Policy Making," in *The New Congress,* ed. Thomas E. Mann and Norman J. Ornstein (Washington, D.C.: American Enterprise Institute for Public Policy Research, 1981).
5. Christopher J. Bosso, *Pesticides and Politics: The Life Cycle of a Public Issue* (Pittsburgh: University of Pittsburgh Press, 1987).
6. See Jeffrey M. Berry, *The Interest Group Society,* 2d ed. (Glenview, Ill.: Scott, Foresman/Little, Brown, 1989), 16-43; and Kay Lehman Schlozman and John T. Tierney, *Organized Interests and American Democracy* (New York: Harper and Row, 1986), 58-87.
7. See *Time,* October 23, 1989; and John E. Chubb and Paul E. Peterson, eds., *Can the Government Govern?* (Washington, D.C.: Brookings Institution, 1989).
8. Charles O. Jones, *Clean Air: The Policies and Politics of Pollution Control* (Pittsburgh: University of Pittsburgh Press, 1975). On Reagan's policies see Norman J. Vig and Michael E. Kraft, eds., *Environmental Policy in the 1980s: Reagan's New Agenda* (Washington, D.C.: CQ Press, 1984), and chap. 2, "Presidential Leadership: From the Reagan to the Bush Administration," in this volume.
9. See, for example, The World Commission on Environment and Development, *Our Common Future* (New York: Oxford, 1987); and "Managing Planet Earth," special issue of *Scientific American* 261 (September 1989).
10. John Dryzek, *Rational Ecology: Environment and Political Economy* (New York: Basil Blackwell, 1987), esp. chap. 3; Robert V. Bartlett, "Ecological Rationality: Reason and Environmental Policy," *Environmental Ethics* 8 (Fall 1986): 221-239; and William Ophuls, *Ecology and the Politics of*

Scarcity (San Francisco: W. H. Freeman, 1977).

11. A useful summary of key legislative actions can be found in the reference work *Congress and the Nation* (Washington, D.C.: Congressional Quarterly Inc., various dates), vol. III, 1969-1972, 745-849; vol. IV, 1973-1976, 201-320; and vol. V, 1977-1980, 451-597.
12. See, for example, Bosso, *Pesticides and Politics,* chaps. 6 and 7; and James R. Temples, "The Politics of Nuclear Power: A Subgovernment in Transition," *Political Science Quarterly* 95 (Summer 1980): 239-260.
13. Norman J. Ornstein, "The House and Senate in a New Congress," in *The New Congress;* Lawrence C. Dodd and Bruce I. Oppenheimer, "The House in Transition: Change and Consolidation," in *Congress Reconsidered,* 2d ed., ed. Lawrence C. Dodd and Bruce I. Oppenheimer (Washington, D.C.: CQ Press, 1981); and Davidson, "Subcommittee Government."
14. See Michael E. Kraft, "Congress and Environmental Policy," in *Environmental Politics and Policy: Theories and Evidence,* ed. James P. Lester (Durham, N.C.: Duke University Press, 1989), esp. 182-187.
15. Bruce I. Oppenheimer, "Congress and the New Obstructionism: Developing an Energy Program," in *Congress Reconsidered;* and Michael E. Kraft, "Congress and National Energy Policy: Assessing the Policymaking Process," in *Environment, Energy, Public Policy: Toward a Rational Future,* ed. Regina S. Axelrod (Lexington, Mass.: Lexington Books, 1981).
16. Cook and Davidson, "Deferral Politics"; Gary C. Bryner, "Science, Law, and Politics in Environmental Policy" (Paper presented at the annual meeting of the American Political Science Association, Chicago, September 2-6, 1987); and Henry Kenski and Margaret Corgan Kenski, "Congress Against the President: The Struggle Over the Environment," in *Environmental Policy in the 1980s.*
17. Cook and Davidson, "Deferral Politics"; and Kenski and Kenski, "Congress Against the President."
18. Gary Bryner reported in 1987 that fourteen committees and twenty subcommittees in the Senate and eighteen committees and thirty-eight subcommittees in the House had at least some jurisdiction over EPA. See Bryner, "Science, Law, and Politics in Environmental Policy."
19. John W. Kingdon, *Agendas, Alternatives, and Public Policies* (Boston: Little, Brown, 1984).
20. Susan G. Hadden, *A Citizen's Right to Know: Risk Communication and Public Policy* (Boulder, Colo.: Westview, 1989), esp. chap. 2.
21. Sierra Club, "Scorecard," *Sierra* 72 (January/February 1987): 16-17; and Natural Resources Defense Council, "The 99th Congress—A Strong Voice for the Environment," *NRDC Newsline* 4 (November/December 1986): 1-3.
22. Joseph A. Davis, "Environment/Energy," *1988 Congressional Quarterly Almanac* (Washington, D.C.: Congressional Quarterly Inc., 1989), 137.
23. Richard J. Tobin, "Revising the Clean Air Act: Legislative Failure and Administrative Success," in *Environmental Policy in the 1980s.* See also Michael Weisskopf, "A Qualified Failure: The Clean Air Act Hasn't Done the Job," *Washington Post National Weekly Edition,* June 19-25, 1989, 10-11. On the compromises made in enactment of the 1977 act, see Bruce B. Ackerman and William T. Hassler, *Clean Coal/Dirty Air* (New Haven: Yale

University Press, 1981).

24. Tobin, "Revising the Clean Air Act," 230.
25. Josh Getlin, "Mr. Clean's Air Act," *Sierra* 74 (November/December 1989): 77-81.
26. For details, see Tobin, "Revising the Clean Air Act."
27. Rochelle L. Stanfield, "Punching at the Smog," *National Journal,* March 5, 1988, 600-602.
28. Joseph A. Davis, " 'Group of Nine' Determined to Break Clean-Air Deadlock," *Congressional Quarterly Weekly Report,* April 16, 1988, 984-990.
29. Personal interview, Washington, D.C., July 14, 1989.
30. Margaret E. Kriz, "Politics in the Air," *National Journal,* May 6, 1989, 1098-1102.
31. Philip Shabecoff, "President Urges Steps to Tighten Law on Clean Air," *New York Times,* June 13, 1989, 1, 10; Philip Shabecoff, "President's Plan for Cleaning Air Goes to Congress," *New York Times,* July 22, 1989, 1, 7; George Hager, "Critics Disappointed by Details of Bush Clean-Air Measure," *Congressional Quarterly Weekly Report,* July 22, 1989, 1852-1853; and Richard W. Stevenson, "Concern Over Bush Clean-Air Plan," *New York Times,* June 14, 1989, D1, D6, city edition.
32. George Hager, "Senate Panel One-Ups Bush on Clean Air Controls," *Congressional Quarterly Weekly Report,* October 28, 1989, 2864-2865; and George Hager, "Energy Panel Seals Pact on Vehicle Pollution," *Congressional Quarterly Weekly Report,* October 7, 1989, 2621-2624.
33. See James L. Regens and Robert W. Rycroft, *The Acid Rain Controversy* (Pittsburgh: University of Pittsburgh Press, 1988), chap. 2.
34. See Tobin, "Revising the Clean Air Act," 242-246; and Regens and Rycroft, *The Acid Rain Controversy,* chap. 5.
35. See Joseph A. Davis and Amy Stern, "Marathon Markup Succeeds, Acid Rain Bill Moves Forward," *Congressional Quarterly Weekly Report,* May 24, 1986, 1174; and Amy Stern, "House Acid Rain Legislation Criticized from Several Sides," *Congressional Quarterly Weekly Report,* May 3, 1986, 970.
36. Rochelle L. Stanfield, "For Acid Rain, 'Wait Till Next Year,' " *National Journal,* October 15, 1988, 2606.
37. See Philip Shabecoff, "An Emergence of Political Will on Acid Rain," *New York Times,* February 19, 1989, E5; and George Hager, "Acid-Rain Controls Advance on Both Sides of Aisle," *Congressional Quarterly Weekly Report,* April 1, 1989, 688-691.
38. Hager, "Acid-Rain Controls Advance on Both Sides of Aisle"; and George Hager, "Bush's Tough Acid Rain Bill Puts Midwest on the Spot," *Congressional Quarterly Weekly Report,* November 4, 1989, 2934-2937.
39. Joseph A. Davis, "House Members Push Pesticide Law Changes," *Congressional Quarterly Weekly Report,* June 8, 1985, 1107-1109.
40. Mark Willen, "Senate Panel Takes a Swing at Pesticides Bill," *Congressional Quarterly Weekly Report,* February 20, 1988, 368-369.
41. Rochelle L. Stanfield, "Legalized Poisons," *National Journal,* May 2, 1987, 1062-1066.
42. Bosso, *Pesticides and Politics.*
43. Margaret E. Kriz, "Pesticidal Pressures," *National Journal,* December 10,

1988, 3125-3127; and Keith Schneider, "Science Academy Recommends Resumption of Natural Farming," *New York Times*, September 8, 1989, A1, B5, city edition.

44. Sharon Begley, "E pluribus, plures," *Newsweek*, November 13, 1989, 70-72; and Matthew L. Wald, "Recharting War on Smog," *New York Times*, October 13, 1989, 1, 13. See also chap. 3, "A New Federalism? Environmental Policy in the States" in this volume.
45. Allan R. Gold, "Administration Is Divided on Stance to Take in Fighting Global Warming," *New York Times*, October 27, 1989, 7; and Sharon Begley, "Is It All Just Hot Air?" *Newsweek*, November 20, 1989, 64-66. For an overview of economic analyses of proposals to reduce carbon emissions, see Peter Passell, "Cure for Greenhouse Effect: The Costs Will Be Staggering," *New York Times*, November, 19, 1989, 1, 10.
46. Glenn Garelik, "A New Item on the Agenda," *Time*, October 23, 1989, 62; see also William D. Ruckelshaus, "Toward a Sustainable World," *Scientific American* 261 (September 1989): 166-174.

6

The "NIMBY" Syndrome: Facility Siting and the Failure of Democratic Discourse

Daniel Mazmanian and David Morell

> Nimbys are noisy. Nimbys are powerful. Nimbys are everywhere. Nimbys are people who live near enough to corporate or government projects—and are upset enough about them—to work to stop, stall, or shrink them. Nimbys organize, march, sue, and petition to block the developers they think are threatening them.
>
> William Glaberson
> *New York Times*, June 19, 1988

> The democratic process as we know it today—the institutions of liberal, representative democracy—seem incapable of achieving democratic control of the 'crucially important and inordinately complex' issues of modern technological society.
>
> H. D. Forbes (1988)

America has set lofty goals for cleaning up the nation's polluted air, water, and land. Reaching these goals will require industry to introduce safer and more efficient facilities and to alter dramatically its hazardous-materials management practices. The ability of business to carry out these tasks is stymied in part by the equally compelling effort of local citizens and communities to protect themselves and their immediate surroundings from the degradation that might result from having even a state-of-the-art facility in their midst. When faced with a siting proposal, local residents often "just say no." [1] To kill a project they need only demonstrate an ability to use the legal and political systems to cause intermina-

---

The authors would like to thank Michael Stanley-Jones, Michael Kraft, and Norman Vig for their review and helpful comments on this chapter.

ble delays and oftentimes kill a project. The specter of endless cost overruns associated with such delays prompts many project developers to retreat and inhibits many other proposals entirely. Major energy, industrial, or waste-management projects once accepted as vital to the nation's growth and well-being are now routinely opposed because of their perceived adverse impacts. The clamor of "Not In My Back Yard" (NIMBY) is heard across the land.

What are the causes of this NIMBY syndrome? Does it help or hinder in carrying out the nation's environmental agenda? How does it fit in the broader context of modern American politics? These are the questions that will be addressed in this chapter.

The good news in the eyes of many, especially those living near a proposed site, is that most projects can currently be stopped through concerted action by local citizens working with environmental and health advocates from outside the community. The bad news is that society pays a high price for such local vetos, in terms of the economic viability of the communities and the regions where the new facilities are not being admitted, with the end result being a weakening of the nation's economy.[2] Furthermore, rarely are opponents (and, indeed, proponents) able to distinguish between those facilities that are truly necessary for society and can be expected to be operated safely, and those that are not. When "needed" facilities are rejected, there are serious consequences. The successful opposition to a modern hazardous-waste treatment facility, for example, leaves society dependent on the leaky landfills of the past, despite federal and state laws mandating radical new practices.

One of the most important questions of the 1990s is how to move beyond the current gridlock created by NIMBYism in siting power plants, major industrial facilities, and hazardous-waste facilities in ways that make sense ecologically, technologically, politically, and economically. A workable answer is central to realizing the nation's environmental goals.

Causes of the NIMBY Syndrome

In one sense the NIMBY syndrome is a response to an inherent imbalance in the distribution of a project's benefits and costs. Costs in terms of human health and environmental and aesthetic decay are concentrated in one community, while benefits accrue across a much broader area and to distant corporations.

NIMBYism goes beyond narrow self-interest, however. It springs from an awareness in our atomic age that science and technology have the capacity not only to improve the human condition, but also to change it for the worse. The widely shared sympathy with project opponents ("it could have been my town") reveals an underlying sense of guilt about shifting too many health and environmental costs explicitly onto others.

The modern paradox is that the industrial system that spawns America's material affluence is simultaneously the source of enormous pollution loads for the air, water, and land.

In recent years, the most strident environmental opposition has been aimed at projects designed to handle hazardous wastes and hazardous materials—toxins, petroleum, chemicals, and industrial by-products—and this experience will form the backdrop of the discussion. NIMBYism is exacerbated by a widespread fear of hazardous substances—from asbestos to food preservatives, pesticides, and PCBs (polychlorinated biphenyls)—and a growing "chemophobia." [3] This fear often takes the form of outrage when citizens suspect that someone, knowingly or otherwise, has placed (or proposes to place) the lives of their family, friends, and community in jeopardy by exposing them to toxic and hazardous materials.[4] Outrage then clouds the ability of a community to consider a proposed project on its merits: how can one expect otherwise? A disposal facility for hazardous-waste chemicals, for example, is generally seen as akin to a nuclear power plant in the eyes of the public, and few people want either one located within one hundred miles of where they live.[5]

As fear and outrage about toxics have risen, the public's confidence in business and government leaders to make well-informed, impartial, safe, and prudent decisions has severely diminished.[6] This has created a profound crisis of legitimacy in American politics. The conventional public policy process, from the smallest community up through the states and federal government, has been rendered incapable of effectively balancing needs for growth, development, and facility siting with those of health and environmental protection for current and future generations.

In this context 1970 is a key date. That year ushered in the environmental movement as a major social and political force in the United States. Earth Day, the signing of the National Environmental Policy Act, and the creation of the president's Council on Environmental Quality and the Environmental Protection Agency were followed quickly by the initiation of dramatic revisions in the nation's air and water pollution laws. Decisions about major infrastructure projects, industrial facilities, and waste management have not been the same since.

Solutions to NIMBYism

To respond appropriately to the NIMBY syndrome, these causal factors will have to be effectively addressed. Successful action of necessity will challenge conventional thinking and the past practices of business, government, and individual citizens.

Several promising approaches have emerged. They balance the need for siting economically and socially critical facilities with the needs of the host communities to preserve their fundamental political rights and have their health and safety concerns addressed. The basic goal is to achieve a process whereby "good" facilities will be sited in a timely manner in "good" locations; at the same time, the process would not site "good" facilities in "bad" locations, and would not approve "bad" facilities for siting anywhere. While disagreements will persist over criteria for "good" and "bad" in this context, attention must be paid to both facility characteristics and locational quality if NIMBY concerns are to be addressed. Facility proponents may need to reassess their designs and site preferences, while opponents review their reasons for opposition. Both groups may need to approach the whole siting dilemma in new ways. As such, the methods most successful in responding to the NIMBY syndrome hold profound implications not only for dramatically accelerating the cause of environmental protection, but also for ensuring a more democratic American society.[7]

The Crucial Questions of Siting

Questions on five topics are central to every siting decision. To understand how projects are stymied today, and how this might be different in the future, it is important to recognize how the answers to these questions have changed in response to the environmental movement, first as the movement was conceived in the 1970s and then as it took on new dimensions in the 1980s.

1. Who takes the initiative in defining the need for a facility? Whose expertise is relied upon? Under what perception of need?

In the past, proposals to site major facilities were almost exclusively demand driven and market controlled. As America industrialized and grew, manufacturing plants, energy facilities, and petrochemical factories were built whenever business deemed it profitable. The decisions about which technology to employ, where to locate, what costs were involved, and how to manage the facility were left to the private sector. The marketplace was the driving force of society and the judgments of business leadership went essentially unchallenged.

With relatively inexpensive and abundant natural resources for industry to draw upon, the market system placed little value on capturing and reusing the waste by-products of manufacturing and business operations. These wastes went into the air and water, or onto the land. Scant attention was paid to the irreplaceability of the energy and material feedstocks that fueled the industrial order. Faith was placed instead in technological innovation and substitution. When oil ran low it would be replaced by nuclear energy (wood by plastics, rubber by synthetics, and so on.) Until the dawn of the environmental age, technological optimism was paramount.

The pollution caused by any one business was seldom significant enough or scientifically (or legally) documentable enough to cause alarm or engender action. If surroundings became too unpleasant, it was possible for people to pick up and move. The cumulative consequence was that America's major streams and rivers became open sewers; the air over major cities was polluted; and liquid and solid industrial wastes were routinely poured on the land to evaporate and percolate away, pumped into sewers or deep into the earth, or dumped into landfills.

The pollution regulations initiated in the contemporary era empowered those who opposed continuation of these practices to challenge them effectively. The opportunity to do so emerged with particular clarity when specific new projects were proposed for their communities. While project initiative remained with business and government proponents, federal and state laws required project proponents to notify communities more fully of their intentions and to produce extensive environmental impact reports on their proposals. These reports were supposed to disclose the implications regarding pollution and present information on feasible, less-polluting alternatives. Although an environmental impact report alone could not kill a project, it could be used to tie up the project for years, and provide the grounds for subsequent court challenges. The time so gained was often used to rally further political opposition. When the moment came for the local land-use decision, often city hall was no longer ready to just say "yes."

Another major change today is that opponents are usually able to recruit their own environmentally oriented scientists and technical experts to counter claims by business and the government that a proposed project is vitally important to the nation's well-being, or that a project's health and environmental impact will be insignificant. As a consequence, the present period has seen the successful derailing of a wide array of projects, from hundreds of proposed nuclear power plants in the 1970s[8] to radioactive-waste disposal facilities, new hazardous-waste landfills and treatment facilities, and solid-waste landfills in the 1980s.[9]

Meanwhile, the Clean Air Act, Clean Water Act, Resource Conservation and Recovery Act, and Superfund laws have begun forcing industry to include in their business calculations the cost of reducing or recapturing their wastes, and more safely disposing of that which remains. Costs that had traditionally been considered "economic externalities"—borne not by the generator but by the individuals or environments affected by polluted air, water, and land—are being progressively internalized.[10] Some hazardous substances used in business and commerce, such as DDT, asbestos, and lead in gasoline and paints, have been banned outright because of their extreme threat to human health and the environment.[11]

Especially hard hit have been proposals for newer, more effective waste-management facilities designed to treat hazardous wastes that traditionally have been sent to landfills or injected underground. The resulting paralysis impedes the needed upgrading of American industry and presents a broad threat to society.

2. *What are the economic/technical characteristics of the proposed project, and of its location?*

Traditionally, just as the demand for facilities was market-driven, so too were decisions about the technical configuration of a facility and its location. Governments directed facilities to industrial zones and away from residential communities, and required the facilities to meet health and safety codes.

The government's involvement did not extend to judging a facility based on the amount of pollution it generated or on its waste disposal practices. Waste disposal facilities themselves selected out-of-sight and self-contained (looking) locations to avoid nuisance complaints from neighbors. Little attention was given by anyone to the potential for despoiling the ground or contaminating underground aquifers. The legacy of poor on-site and off-site disposal practices has been exposed at the more than ten thousand Superfund sites identified since 1980 that the nation will be cleaning up over the next fifty or more years.[12]

At the onset of the environmental era in the 1970s, the predisposition was to set up broad guidelines for pollution reduction, along with limited government-sponsored research and development and some pilot projects. Beyond that, the needed transformations were left up to business. In some instances, this approach produced desired changes: (1) less polluting natural gas became favored over coal for powering major utilities, (2) the catalytic converter was added to automobiles to reduce air emissions, (3) the combination of energy conservation with cogeneration and small-scale hydroelectric power helped to meet the nation's electric energy needs, and (4) a massive campaign was undertaken to clean up the nation's waterways. At the same time, most new industrial facilities received land-use approvals and permits, even with NIMBY opposition.

By the 1980s the nature of concerns about pollution had changed. People feared that they were being exposed to toxic material in ways never before suspected, and not readily detected. It was no longer sufficient for a siting proposal simply to meet governmental requirements. Any proposal associated with nuclear power, nuclear waste, toxic and hazardous materials, and hazardous waste became taboo.[13] While most existing facilities continued to operate unfettered, new ones needed approval. NIMBY-led siting defeats became pervasive.

Throughout much of this period, industry continued to identify and press for facility sites based on conventional technical and economic considerations. Proponents were slow to learn that the dynamics of siting had changed. They continued to think of the pollution potential of a facility in terms of their own technical understanding, apart from the public attitudes at the host site. This created a serious disjuncture between the proposed facility's technical specifications and those best suited to the site. Too often, large facilities continued to be proposed for remote areas, which themselves generated few wastes, thereby exacerbating tensions over inequity and the inherent imbalance of costs and benefits.

Moreover, the marketplace has contributed to resistance to the introduction of new waste-management technologies. As long as the cost of disposal remains lower at conventional (though today, triple-lined) landfills and through deep-well injection, few companies will choose to send their wastes to new recycling and treatment facilities. In response, few are being built. This marketplace uncertainty has increased investors' reluctance to proceed with new technologies, particularly in the face of likely NIMBY-led opposition to any hazardous-waste facility siting proposals. Ironically, source reduction can exacerbate this situation since it threatens to reduce the waste volume needed to justify a treatment facility's economics.

Only recently have some businesses realized the necessity of designing facilities that are more responsive to the environmental ethic, thus reaching beyond their conventional technical and economic considerations. "Pollution prevention pays," the motto of the 3M Company for more than a decade now, went unheard until the mid-1980s, and only now has become the rallying cry around which all parties can agree. Dow, Union Carbide, and General Dynamics, for example, have all set significant targets for dramatically reducing their waste flow, and for achieving total management of those wastes that remain. Moreover, the potential now arises for a source reduction/siting compromise to emerge, with facility-siting advocates committing to more source reduction measures than they would have chosen on their own, in exchange for acceptance by NIMBY-style opponents of some siting proposals. Each party would profit from such a solution.

Even the best source-reduction technologies cannot eliminate hazardous wastes, however. A significant number of incinerators, hazardous-waste collection stations and treatment facilities, and long-term storage and repositories will be required. Still, no one wants these facilities in their back yards.

3. What standards of fairness are applied—substantively and procedurally—when dealing with competing interests in a siting controversy?

Public confidence in the fairness of public decision making—in the way decisions are made, and in their outcome—is vital to the success of the democratic political process. While people in a local community may never be pleased that a facility is being sited in their town, they may come to accept the process by which the decision is made. The public's definition of what is fair and proper can change over time, of course, and this is precisely what is occurring with the siting of major facilities.

Conventionally, a project was justified politically if it could satisfy the utilitarian test of the greatest good for the greatest number, as understood within the context of the host community. In practice, this meant that siting approval would be granted by duly elected public officials if the project would bring new jobs, pay local property taxes, and contribute to overall economic development. The second political criterion was that "might (i.e., money) makes right." Americans extend a great deal of deference to wealth, and it was expected—and thereby considered legitimate—that money would be used to influence the public policy process. Dependency on developers was (and, in many places, still is) the lifeblood of local politics, where siting decisions are usually made.

Concepts of what is just and acceptable in this regard are changing. The ethic of individual property rights and utilitarian economics now must compete with new definitions of individual and community political rights and considerations of equal treatment for minorities and women. Consequently, projects that will serve the economic interest of the greatest number are often challenged in light of individual or community interests—one's home, one's local environment, one's personal health, one's minority group—never before possible. The economic well-being of the majority has come into direct conflict with the growing political and social rights of various other interests, and the latter often prevail in a siting controversy.

This change has come in part from the growing realization of the potential health risks produced by the chemical and biotechnological revolutions of the post-World War II period. The public feels that it is an injustice to expose anyone to toxins, pollutants, and other hazardous materials, knowingly or otherwise. Legally and politically this means that the burden of moral (and legal) proof that harm has or has not occurred is being shifted to those who generate potentially harmful substances. We now err on the side of health and environmental caution. Indicative of this are the new stringent liability provisions of pollution laws, such as the "strict, joint and several liability" provisions of the federal Superfund law that hold the producers and handlers of hazardous waste fully responsible for its safe disposal, and California's Proposition 65, which makes the users of a lengthy list of substances known to cause cancer or birth defects liable if these chemicals are not managed and disposed of safely.

In a dramatic departure, as part of the new environmental ethos, legal protection is now accorded to a growing range of nonhuman species and even inanimate objects.[14] Potential harm to nonhuman entities and future generations is today an ethically and legally accepted reason to challenge a proposed development project.

Determining what is "just" is confounded today because project proponents typically appeal to conventional utilitarian and economic criteria, while opponents usually base their case on the newer ecological, community, or minority rights standards. Proponents of state-of-the-art toxics incinerators, for example, claim that the net pollution resulting from incineration is far less potentially harmful than continuing to dispose of hazardous wastes in landfills and through other conventional methods, and that incinerators are the most cost-effective waste-management alternative. They probably are right in the conventional way of thinking. At the same time, opponents argue that incinerators may pose unacceptable health risks to the nearby residents. They probably are right, too. No wonder proponents and opponents so often talk past one another in a classic failure of effective democratic discourse.

The result is public confusion and a sense that there is no consistent rationale for judging either the process or the outcome of a siting decision. Rather than make the tough choices between the old and new standards, policy makers in the 1980s have addressed siting proposals on a case-by-case basis, and this has placed them in an especially difficult position. Whenever a balance is struck at a specific site, those who remain dissatisfied are quick to shout, with some justification, that their rights have been violated. This is almost inevitable in periods of value transition, such as the present. Yet in trying to balance different criteria of fairness and justice, government officials appear indecisive and compromised, and suffer accordingly in the eyes of the public.

4. Who makes the siting decision, and through what process?

An unavoidable trade-off exists between the number of people involved in a decision and the costs—in time, money, and organization—associated with making that decision. Traditionally, siting decisions were weighted in favor of the lowest possible near-term decision costs. This was accomplished through limiting participation to the developer, community officials, and (when necessary) state officials. Formalities were minimal; environmental and health laws were not nearly as stringent as current regulations; and, once approved, the developer pretty much proceeded as desired. This satisfied the procedural requirements of representative democracy well enough, but did not incorporate all the potentially interested parties.

This pattern has now changed. In the late 1960s it became obvious to many Americans that siting decisions, once made locally with local interests in mind, had substantial impacts on neighboring communities, regions, and ultimately the states themselves. Air and water pollution did not recognize municipal boundaries; dense buildup in one community affected traffic and congestion in the next. As each community sought to increase its tax base by developing every available piece of land, the once readily accessible open spaces, such as ocean and lakefront shoreline, and outdoor recreational areas, quickly disappeared. Few in power seemed willing to protect these valuable assets within their own borders so that all could enjoy them. The effects of urban congestion and increasing population were taking their toll.

This triggered the "quiet revolution" in land-use planning in the 1970s, which was marked by a notable shift away from the localities in matters concerning land use. State governments asserted themselves in the decision-making process at several junctures. They required state review, and established new powers to override local decisions. They initiated state permitting of major facilities, and required comprehensive local plans that incorporated the concerns of the broader community.[15]

With the emphasis on community and state planning came a heightened awareness of the importance of land-use decisions by community groups and environmentalists. If these decisions were no longer matters of the marketplace and local discretion, then they wanted to be involved.[16] NIMBYism grows directly out of these developments. While not everyone is equally active or important, experience in the contemporary era has shown that just about anyone can participate in the decision-making process and almost any well-organized group can derail a proposal.

There have been several responses to this new reality. The case of hazardous-waste facilities is instructive. In the beginning, businesses tried to muscle their way through local siting procedures. When this met with failure, waste generators and waste managers united behind efforts to convince state legislatures that NIMBYism would prevent them from ever siting their needed facilities, and that the states must preempt local siting decisions. Several did, but to little avail. NIMBY resistance only increased—hazardous-waste facilities still could not be sited. Many politicians and public agencies responded by calling for greater dialogue and public involvement in the decision-making process. They assumed that once people were involved and informed, responsible local leaders would find some accommodation with industry, if only to secure their own economic future. This too did not prove to be the case. Public involvement seemed to facilitate NIMBY resistance.

Having an extremely active citizenry at the local level seems like the epitome of democracy to most Americans. But when, in effect, they only have the power to stop proposed facilities, the process is far from complete. Few mechanisms have yet been devised that bring competing interests together in ways that allow them to identify their common goals, narrow their differences, and move forward to identify and site in acceptable locations those genuinely necessary industrial facilities and public facilities that today are being vetoed. No viable democratic process exists to mesh the collective needs with those of individuals and localities. Clearly, a site-by-site approach has not succeeded. Recent experiences in

California and elsewhere suggest that it may be necessary for communities, regions, and states to first reach a "mega-consensus" on the overall need for facilities, and on a democratic decision-making process that ensures that burdens will be shared fairly, as a prelude to making decisions on specific proposals at specific sites.[17]

5. Who will protect the public's health and safety throughout the life of the proposed project?

Traditionally, this question was seldom asked. First, it was presumed that facilities were reasonably safe. If not, health hazards would be evident through the normal senses of sight and smell. Problems such as acid rain, contamination of underground aquifers, lead poisoning from paint and gasoline, and many other issues now known to be associated with hazardous materials simply were not part of the pubic consciousness. Some states were more stringent than others in their oversight of industrial facilities, but generally health and environmental concerns were not attended to by anyone.

This situation is changing rapidly. States like New Jersey, Minnesota, and California took the lead in the mid-1980s by requiring companies to develop inventories of their hazardous materials and to prepare emergency response plans for their facilities. Federal law now requires this nationwide, as well as the tracking from "cradle to grave" of almost all hazardous wastes. Across the nation, municipal fire departments and health departments have been drawn into the monitoring and compliance process as never before. The most common complaint now is not that monitoring and enforcement powers do not exist, but that there are not enough staff and resources available to local, state, and federal officials to do a thorough job.

Siting in the 1990s and Beyond

One suggestion for resolving the typical siting gridlock is to return siting decisions more fully to the marketplace. This idea first emerged on America's political right, where the environmental problem is seen as one of government mismanagement. The "tragedy of the commons" suggests that it is in everyone's self-interest to overconsume what is held in common, and shepherd what is theirs.[18] The solution? Privatize public lands, auction off water and other resource rights, and establish private ownership where it has never previously existed, as in the oceans.[19] When disputes arise or injury results from the management of private property, one can then rely on private claims and tort law, not on government regulators, to win relief. Advocates of this approach argue that better facility siting decisions could be achieved through an auction, with the highest bidder getting to decide the use of the property in question. In this way, proponents and opponents would be forced to reveal their "true" preferences and place a monetary value on them.[20]

Privatization has also been proposed by the more populist left, but for vastly different reasons. The argument here is made on behalf of an environmental and health protection "citizens' bill of rights," to which all polluters could be held accountable. If a clean and healthy environment were an individual's legal right, then anyone polluting could be brought to account through private litigation.

Privatization clearly has potential for helping to resolve NIMBY controversies and achieve successful facility siting. However, it does not provide a complete solution. The policing done under tort law and the citizen monitoring potentials are all after-the-fact remedies; they are activated after the harm has occurred to human health and environment. And as many questions are raised as are answered. Would a clean environment bill of rights mean that no person or business could generate pollution, at any time? If so, would all productive activities come to a halt? Also, while auctioning development sites may sound attractive, especially in this period of siting gridlock, the process would inevitably be weighted in favor of those with the most money, not in favor of health, ordinary citizens, or the environment. Furthermore, auctions would resolve siting controversies one at a time. The approach is not well suited to coordinated regional programs for hazardous waste and materials management, nor does it fit in any obvious way with the drive for source reduction and waste minimization.

Siting in the new environmental epoch needs to be guided by a broader set of principles than self-interested market behavior. A set of five guidelines has been suggested by Roger Kasperson:

1. The general well-being of society requires that some individuals will have to bear risks on behalf of others.
2. Wherever reasonable, such risks should be avoided rather than mitigated or ameliorated through compensation.
3. Reasonably unavoidable risks should be shared, not concentrated, in the population of beneficiaries.
4. The imposition of risk should be made as voluntary as reasonably achievable within the constraints of deploying sites in a timely manner, and the burden of proof for site suitability should be on the developer.
5. Reasonably unavoidable risks should be accompanied by compensating benefits.[21]

It is unlikely that all these principles can be satisfied by working strictly within a market framework. Equally true, they probably cannot be satisfied fully by a top-down, command-and-control type of government. And surely they are not met by the ineffective, fragmented regulatory regimes that have evolved to date. The challenge of the 1990s is to devise approaches to siting that incorporate these five principles within a democratic framework, while remaining ever sensitive to the complex political, economic, technical, and social contexts of modern American society.

The *process* of site selection and approval for hazardous-waste and hazardous-materials facilities must gain enhanced legitimacy by improving early public access to decisions, planning more effectively, avoiding state preemption, and providing for community oversight of facility operations. Likewise, the *substance* of facility proposals must be improved by shifting to smaller facilities to lessen local inequities, using transportable units, and insisting on stricter safety standards.

Industry and government both need to change their approach to the siting dilemma if the genuine concerns of citizens are to be met successfully. This is a challenge, but not an impossibility. Three available strategies aimed at moving beyond NIMBY gridlock while satisfying the Kasperson principles can be seen as models for the coming decade.

Siting a Single Facility: The Siting Contract

The potential to successfully site a facility that handles hazardous materials is illuminated in the quasi-experimental work of Michael Elliott. Elliott has been able to reach much deeper into people's concerns and fears than is possible through observation of actual siting controversies.[22] He finds that most project proponents and designers spend time attempting to scientifically predict possible problems with a plant's equipment and its operation and attempting to engineer technical solutions. In contrast, those in the surrounding community are more worried about detecting hazardous conditions that may develop at the plant and implementing mitigation measures to lessen or reverse the danger. They worry more about whether those measures will be applied speedily should a problem arise than about the capabilities of exotic, technically advanced equipment. These concerns fuel NIMBY tendencies. Community members might even accept a technically less sophisticated facility if its operator placed greater emphasis on rapid, effective detection and mitigation. In addition, Elliott has concluded that the only realistic way of convincing an ever-wary community that a facility's operator is committed to detection and mitigation is to open the plant's operations to community scrutiny and subject its safety practices to close community review.

To increase the likelihood of successfully siting good facilities in good locations, long-term oversight arrangements that provide for greater community involvement, power sharing, and risk sharing may need to be formalized between the facility operator and the host community. This could be accomplished through an enforceable contract between the owner/operator and the local community. With such a facility-siting and operations contract in place, the facility's neighbors would no longer have to rely on notoriously weak government permitting processes and regulatory enforcement activities. The contract's specific terms would be negotiated during the siting process. It would typically contain the operational provisions normally placed in the facility's regulatory permits. The contract could also embody the source reduction/siting compromise noted earlier. Violation of the contract's terms could be enforced by the community directly, through traditional breach-of-contract judicial proceedings. A court could even be asked to issue a temporary restraining order requiring the facility to cease operations until it was again able to fully observe its formal contractual obligations.

With an oversight committee of community members and a dialogue process in place at the facility, resort to legal action should not be necessary. But having this option may well be the price a community in the 1990s would expect to exact for local siting approval: no contract, no siting approval. This mechanism could guarantee stability over the term of future facility operations. Inviting the community to participate in the oversight of a facility is obviously a radical departure from past practices, yet it is clearly an inclusive, community-based, and democratic process. It provides a mechanism for ensuring that many of Kasperson's principles will be satisfied. If Elliott is correct in his assessment that the public does not so much fear technology and chemical substances per se, but fears how they are managed, then the contract approach may be useful in overcoming today's chemophobia. Most important, the approach may hold the key to successful community-based siting of particular facilities in the future.

A Public Utility Model for Hazardous-Waste Management

Throughout the 1980s, local communities have not only vetoed conventional hazardous-waste landfills, but proposed modern facilities that would recycle, neutralize, detoxify, incinerate, or provide short- or long-term storage of hazardous wastes. In Europe, the introduction of modern facilities for hazardous-waste management has developed far more rapidly, in part because hazardous-waste management has been undertaken as a public function, like highway building and sewage treatment.

Bruce Piasecki and Gary Davis have proposed a variation on the European approach for the United States. They believe that the regulated public utility model of close public-private cooperation can be used to move from conventional U.S. land disposal practices to a closed system that recycles, treats, stores, and protects society from hazardous wastes. These new institutions would be independently operated and managed profit-making corporations. Closely watched and regulated, they would receive liability waivers, charge regulated prices, and operate within set geographic or functional boundaries. Piasecki and Davis note:

> In exchange for treating all of the waste generated in an area, including hard-to-treat waste and household toxics, at set prices and using specified technologies, the private firm would have no competition in its service areas and would receive a guaranteed return on its investment in treatment facilities.[23]

Offering a comprehensive system of modern treatment facilities, the public utilities approach has much to recommend it and may prove to be a vital piece of the hazardous-waste and materials-management strategy of the 1990s. Local governments and citizens would presumably be more receptive to siting such facilities knowing that they would be operated like a utility, with close public scrutiny and with the goal of safe waste-management practices. At the same time, the new facilities would be operated with the effectiveness of a private business. The closest example today is the Gulf Coast Waste Disposal Authority in Houston, Texas. It operates as an independent, quasi-governmental, nonprofit corporation that plans and operates needed waste facilities. It has the power to issue tax-exempt bonds for financing and to condemn land to site its facilities.

The current siting dilemma is marked by continuing NIMBYism, ongoing gridlock, and little or no progress toward successful siting. The public utility model for hazardous-waste management may be the only viable option for the coming decade. The inherent problem of winning public assent for siting would not disappear under this model, of course. Moreover, dealing with hazardous wastes is only one, albeit important, component of hazardous materials use and of the overall siting dilemma facing society.

Comprehensive Regional Design for Hazardous Wastes

An unusual effort that in many ways incorporates some of the best features of both the siting contract and public utility models is currently unfolding in California. This hazardous-waste planning and siting process was initiated in 1986 in response to the state's facility-siting gridlock. Its objective is to enable every county to map its own plans for managing hazardous waste and hazardous materials. While the process is not mandatory, all of California's fifty-eight counties are participating. Each county must develop a profile of the hazardous waste generated within its borders and project what it will be through the year 2000. The counties also plan to inventory existing sites and evaluate the need for additional treatment capacity. They stipulate criteria for siting new facilities and, in general, where they might be located. Where hazardous wastes cross county lines for treatment, counties may enter into intercounty compacts to ensure safe waste management on a regional basis. The county plan must be prepared with extensive involvement of cities, industry, environmental and health groups, and the general public, all of which have a right to participate in the process and have a strong vested interest in the outcome. Local participants recognize that if they cannot agree on their own future, the state's Department of Health Services will eventually make the decision for them.

This statewide process builds directly on earlier experiences in Southern California, where eight counties and their associated cities carried out a regional planning process whose hallmark was the equitable distribution of needed new facilities based on each county's share of the region's total waste generation. The Southern California Hazardous Waste Management Authority first initiated this "YIMBY" (Yes In Many Back Yards) solution as an equity-based alternative to the NIMBYesque controversy over siting.[24] The YIMBY concept lies at the heart of the planning now underway in all the counties.

In this way, communities throughout California have been challenged to chart their own future and take responsibility for their hazardous wastes. Once approved by the state, a county's plan will serve as a strict guide to all subsequent local siting and toxics policy decisions. Ten million dollars have been provided for this planning effort by the state. In concept, though not yet in practice, the local profiles that emerge are also to be aggregated by the California Department of Health Services into an overall state plan.

If successful, California will be unique in the nation in having locally determined, community-based plans for hazardous-waste management. Developers will be able to request, and stand a reasonable chance of receiving, approval of new hazardous-waste management facilities if they are consistent with a county's plan. If the siting proposal meets all the technical and procedural requirements in the plan but is still turned down by local authorities (under NIMBY-style pressure, for example), the developer can then appeal to a state review board for an override of the local decision. Local vetoes of good facilities in good locations may thus no longer hold up in California. Given the realities facing local communities and that diverse business, environmental, and other interests are negotiating, bargaining, and cooperating through this new planning process, there is hope that the gridlock over facility siting will be broken in California, and that this will serve as a model for other states.

However, the counties and the state are still faced with an intense controversy over the precise definition of the "fair-share" and "equity-based siting" principles central to the county planning process, that may threaten final state approval of county plans and scuttle the whole effort.

Yet, no other criteria to allocate facilities appear able to survive the scrutiny of all the vested interests in and between communities when confronting one another over who will bear the burden of accepting new facilities. It is always difficult for an elected politician to advocate approval of a new hazardous-waste management facility before his or her constituents; if that facility is freestanding and designed primarily to manage wastes generated elsewhere, such a stance is politically suicidal. Equity-based, fair-share formulas thus become imperative in the dynamics of successful facility siting in a democratic setting. Also, before agreeing to new facilities, local communities and environmental groups can be expected to press business for the maximum in waste reduction, since this will decrease a county's need to host new facilities.

Conclusion

Opposition to proposed new facilities—the NIMBY syndrome—symbolizes the broader failure of democratic discourse in the 1970s and 1980s. When the issue of environmental protection thrust itself onto the political agenda, major confrontations occurred between conventional business and government interests and those championing the new environmentalism. The efforts by business to deflect the environmentalists or simply overpower them were played out in the political arena. The participatory nature of the American political system, with its many checks and balances, assured that the contending interests all had an entry into the political process and a major say in the outcome. Forces were sufficiently balanced so that none could impose their view on others. Both sides dug in their heels and the result was policy gridlock and widespread NIMBYism. To the extent that democratic political empowerment is the right to say "no," the system worked. The problem is that this is only a negative power and, ultimately, everyone is worse off.

While this situation will not change overnight, some potent harbingers of change are evident. Public-private partnerships are beginning to emerge, as all parties recognize the futility of continuing along the traditional path.[25] Facility-siting contracts can allow long-term community oversight of facility operations and provide a focus for effective mitigation and compensation measures and siting/source reduction compromises. Most significantly, regional and statewide siting efforts based explicitly on the politics of equity offer the potential to meld successfully the interests of both proponents and opponents in conventional facility-siting disputes. Equity principles can combine with new, smaller, and often transportable technologies to allow siting of good facilities in good locations and thus encourage communities to say "yes." Guided by Kasperson's five ethical principles of siting, YIMBY may then replace NIMBY as the hallmark of siting in the 1990s.

Notes

1. Susan G. Hadden, Joan Veillette, and Thomas Brandt, "State Roles in Siting Hazardous Waste Disposal Facilities: From State Preemption to Local Veto," in *The Politics of Hazardous Waste Management*, ed. James P. Lester and Ann O'M. Bowman (Durham, N.C.: Duke University Press, 1983), 197-211.
2. William Glaberson, "Coping in the Age of 'Nimby,'" *New York Times*, June 19, 1988.
3. It is alleged that the public suffers from an absence of the requisite technical information and a misperception of the genuine risk involved. See Paul Slovic and Baruch Fischhoff, "How Safe Is Safe Enough? Determinants of Perceived and Acceptable Risk," in *Too Hot to Handle? Social and Policy Issues in the Management of Radioactive Wastes*, ed. Charles Walker, Leroy Gould, and Edward Woodhouse (New Haven, Conn.: Yale University Press, 1983). However, at least for those opposing the siting of radioactive-waste facilities, the opposition has been well apprised of the risks involved. See Michael E. Kraft and Bruce B. Clary, "Citizen Participation and the NIMBY Syndrome: The Case of Radioactive Waste Disposal" (Paper delivered at the annual meeting of the American Political Science Association, Washington, D.C., September 1-4, 1988, revised April 1989).
4. Peter M. Sandman, "Risk Communication: Facing Public Outrage," *EPA Journal* (November 1987): 21-22.
5. U.S. Council on Environmental Quality, "Public Opinion on Environmental Issues: Results of a National Public Opinion Survey" (Washington, D.C.: U.S. Government Printing Office, 1980), 31.
6. Seymour Martin Lipset and William Schneider, *The Confidence Gap: Business, Labor, and Government in the Public Mind*, rev. ed. (Baltimore: Johns Hopkins University Press, 1987).
7. Daniel Mazmanian and David Morell, "The Elusive Pursuit of Toxics Management," *The Public Interest* 90 (Winter 1988): 81-98.
8. In the energy arena, public utilities were ultimately forced by public and political pressure, and the soundness of the energy conservation argument, to adopt the environmentalists' projections of future energy needs and the alternatives to nuclear energy for supplying it. Capital cost increases were equally important. See David Roe, *Dynamos and Virgins* (New York: Random House, 1984).
9. Rather than conform to new federal safety guidelines, risk financial exposure under new federal liability provisions, and combat intense local pressure, thousands of conventional landfills stopped accepting hazardous wastes. For example, in Illinois, a major industrial state, the number of commercial sites that accept hazardous wastes dropped from sixty to only three between 1974 and 1985. See Lettie McSpadden Wenner, "Commercial Landfilling Hazardous Wastes in Illinois" (University of Illinois: Institute of Governmental Affairs, 1987), 17.
10. See A. Myrick Freeman's full discussion in Chapter 7 of the market-type incentives that have been introduced in the environmental policy area.
11. The case for banning hazardous substances from use as the most effective

environmental policy is presented in Barry Commoner, "The Environment," *New Yorker*, June 15, 1987, 46-70.

12. U.S. Congress, Office of Technology Assessment, *Superfund Strategy*, OTA-ITE-253 (Washington, D.C.: U.S. Government Printing Office, March 1985).
13. Paul Slovic, "Perception of Risk," *Science* 236 (April 17, 1987): 280-285.
14. Christopher D. Stone, *Earth and Other Ethics: The Case for Moral Pluralism* (New York: Harper & Row, 1988).
15. See Robert Healy and John Rosenberg, *Land Use and the States*, 2d ed. (Baltimore: Johns Hopkins University Press, 1979).
16. David Morell and Christopher Magorian, *Siting Hazardous Waste Facilities: Local Opposition and the Myth of Preemption* (Cambridge, Mass.: Ballinger, 1982), 87-88.
17. Daniel Mazmanian and Michael Stanley-Jones, "Reconceiving LULUs: Changing the Nature and Scope of Locally Unwanted Land Uses," in *Confronting Regional Challenges: Approaches to LULUs, Growth, and Other Vexing Governance Problems*, ed. Joseph DiMento (Cambridge, Mass.: Lincoln Land Institute, forthcoming).
18. Garrett Hardin, "The Tragedy of the Commons," *Science* 162 (December 13, 1968): 1243-1248.
19. Robert J. Smith, "Privatizing the Environment," *Policy Review* (Spring 1982): 43.
20. For an overview of market-like approaches to siting see David E. Ervin and James B. Fitch, "Evaluating Alternative Compensation and Recapture Techniques for Expanded Public Control of Land Use," *Natural Resources Journal* 19 (January 1979): 21-44.
21. Roger E. Kasperson, "Hazardous Waste Facility Siting: Community, Firm, and Governmental Perspectives," in *Hazards: Technology and Fairness* (Washington, D.C.: National Academy Press, 1986), 139.
22. Michael L. Poirier Elliott, "Improving Community Acceptance of Hazardous Waste Facilities Through Alternative Systems of Mitigating and Managing Risk," *Hazardous Waste* 1 (1984): 397-410.
23. Bruce W. Piasecki and Gary A. Davis, *America's Future in Toxic Waste Management: Lessons from Europe* (New York: Quorum Books, 1987), 229.
24. David Morell, "Siting and the Politics of Equity," *Hazardous Waste* 1 (1984): 555-571.
25. Daniel A. Mazmanian, Michael Stanley-Jones, and Miriam Green, "Breaking Political Gridlock: California's Experiment in Public-Private Cooperation in Hazardous Waste Policy" (Claremont, Calif.: California Institute of Public Affairs, 1988); and Carl E. Van Horn, "Breaking the Environmental Gridlock: The Report on a National Conference" (New Brunswick, N.J.: Eagleton Institute of Politics, 1988).

7

Economics, Incentives, and Environmental Regulation

A. Myrick Freeman III

The environment is a scarce resource that contributes to human welfare in a variety of ways. It is the source of the basic means of life support—clean air and clean water. It provides the means for growing food. It is the source of minerals and other raw materials that go into the production of the goods and services that support modern society's standard of living. The environment can be used for a variety of recreational activities such as hiking, fishing, and observing wildlife. And it is the source of amenities and aesthetic experiences including scenic beauty and awe at the wonder of nature. Finally, and unfortunately in some respects, the environment can be used as a place to deposit the wastes from the production and consumption activities of the modern-day economy. It is this latter use, along with conversion of natural environments to more intensely managed agricultural ecosystems or to residential and commercial development, that give rise to today's environmental problems.

To say that the environment is a scarce resource means that it cannot provide all of the desired quantities of all of its services at the same time. Greater use of one type of environmental service usually means that less of some other type of service is available. Thus, the use of the environment involves trade-offs. Increasing the life-sustaining or amenity-yielding services it provides may require reducing the use of the waste-receiving capacities of the environment or cutting back on development, and vice versa.

Economics is about how to manage the activities of men and women, including the way they use the environment, to meet their material needs and wants in the face of scarcity. Environmental protection and the control of pollution are costly activities. Society wishes to protect the environment and reduce pollution presumably because the value it places on the additions to the life-sustaining and enhancing services that the environment provides is greater than the value placed on what it has to give up. Devoting more of society's scarce resources of labor, capital, and administrative and technical skills to controlling pollution necessarily means that less is available to do other things that are also valued by society. The protection of a particular environmental resource to preserve amenities or wildlife habitat typically means that other uses of that resource, such as mining of minerals and production of forest products, are precluded. The costs of environmental protection are the value of these alternative uses that are forgone and the labor, capital, materials, and energy that are used up in controlling the flow of wastes to the environment. Because pollution control and environmental protection are costly in this sense, it is in society's best interest to be "economical" in its decisions in these areas.

There are two senses in which this is true. First, society needs to be economical about its choices of environmental objectives. If Americans are to make the most of their endowment of scarce resources, they should compare what they receive from devoting resources to pollution control and environmental protection with what they give up by taking resources from other uses. They should undertake more pollution activities only if the results are worth more in some sense than the values they forgo by diverting resources from other uses such as producing food, shelter, and comfort. This is basically what benefit-cost analysis is about.

Second, whatever pollution control targets are chosen, the means of achieving them should be selected to minimize the costs of meeting these targets. Using more resources than are absolutely necessary to achieve pollution control objectives is wasteful. Yet many environmental protection and pollution control policies are wasteful in just this sense. One of the major contributions of economic analysis to environmental policy is that it reveals when and how these policies can be made more cost-effective.

In the next section of this chapter, I will describe the use of benefit-cost analysis in deciding how far to go in the direction of environmental protection. Also discussed are recent applications of benefit-cost analysis to environmental policy decisions and contributions that this economic approach to environmental policy making might make in the future.

In the third section I will briefly describe the basic approach to achieving pollution control objectives that is embodied in the major federal statutes—the Clean Air Act of 1970 and the Federal Water Pollution Control Act of 1972. The fourth section is devoted to the concept of cost-effectiveness.

Then in the last three sections I describe and evaluate a variety of economics-based incentive devices (such as pollution taxes, deposit-refund systems, and tradable pollution discharge permits), which encourage pollution-control activities by firms and individuals and which reduce the overall costs of achieving environmental protection targets. I also discuss the possibility of increasing the use of economic incentives in environmental policy in the 1990s.

Benefit-Cost Analysis and Environmental Policy

Two basic premises underlie benefit-cost analysis. First, the purpose of economic activity is to increase the well-being of the individuals who make up the society. Second, each individual is the best judge of how well off he or she is in a given situation. If society is to make the most of its scarce resources, it should compare what it receives from pollution control and environmental protection activities with what it gives up by taking resources from other uses. It should measure the values of what it gains (the benefits) and what it loses (the costs) in terms of the preferences of the people who experience these gains and losses. Society should undertake environmental protection and pollution control only if the results are worth more in terms of individuals' values than what is given up by diverting resources from other uses. This is the underlying principle of the economic approach to environmental policy. Benefit-cost analysis is a set of analytical tools designed to measure the net contribution that any public policy makes to the economic well-being of the members of society.

Although in some respects benefit-cost analysis can be considered as organized common sense, the term is usually used to describe a more narrowly defined, technical economic calculation that attempts to reduce all benefits and costs to a common monetary measure (that is, dollars). It seeks to determine whether the aggregate of the gains to those made better off is greater than the aggregate of losses to those made worse off by the policy choice, where gains and losses are both measured in dollars. If the gains exceed the losses, the policy should be accepted according to the logic of benefit-cost analysis. The gains and losses are to be measured in terms of each individual's willingness to pay to receive the gain or to prevent the policy-imposed losses.

Policies where the aggregate gains outweigh the aggregate costs can be justified on ethical grounds because the gainers could fully compensate the losers with monetary payments and still themselves be better off with the policy. Thus, if the compensation were actually made, there would be no losers, only gainers.[1]

Setting Environmental Standards

Selection of environmental quality standards illustrates some of the issues involved in using benefit-cost analysis for environmental policy making. An *environmental quality standard* is a legally established minimum level of cleanliness or maximum level of pollution in some part of the environment. For example, the U.S. Environmental Protection Agency (EPA) is required by law to establish maximum allowable levels (ambient air quality standards) for major air pollutants such as sulfur dioxide and ozone. A standard, once established, can be the basis for enforcement actions against a polluter whose discharges cause the standard to be violated. Benefit-cost analysis provides a basis for determining at what level an environmental quality standard should be set. In general, economic principles require that each good be provided at the level for which the marginal willingness to pay for the good (the maximum amount that an individual would be willing to give up to get one more unit of the good) is just equal to the cost of providing one more unit of the good (its marginal cost).

Consider, for example, an environment that is badly polluted because of industrial activity. Suppose that successive one-unit improvements are made in some measure of environmental quality. For the first unit, individuals' marginal willingness to pay for a small improvement is likely to be high. The cost of the first unit of cleanup is likely to be low. The difference between them is a net benefit. Further increases in cleanliness bring further net benefits as long as the aggregate marginal willingness to pay is greater than the marginal cost. But as the environment gets cleaner, the willingness to pay for additional units of cleanliness typically decreases, at least beyond some point, while the additional cost of further cleanliness rises. At that point where the marginal willingness to pay equals the marginal cost, the net benefit of further cleanliness is zero, and the total benefits of environmental improvement are at a maximum. This is the point at which the environmental quality standard should be set, if economic reasoning is followed.[2]

An environmental quality standard set by this rule will almost never call for complete elimination of pollution. As the worst of the pollution is cleaned up, the willingness to pay for additional cleanliness will decrease, while the extra cost of further cleanup will increase. The extra cost of going from 95 percent cleanup to 100 percent cleanup may be several times larger than the total cost of obtaining the first 95 percent cleanup. Seldom will it be worth it in terms of willingness to pay.

The logic of benefit-cost analysis does not require that those who benefit pay for those benefits or that those who ultimately bear the cost of meeting a standard be compensated for those costs. Whether compensation should be paid is considered to be a question of equity. Benefit-cost analysis is concerned exclusively with economic efficiency as represented by the aggregate of benefits and costs. If standards are set to maximize the net benefits, then the gainers could fully compensate the losers and still come out ahead. But when beneficiaries do not compensate losers, there is political asymmetry. Those who benefit call for ever stricter standards and more cleanup because they obtain the benefits and bear none of the costs, while those who must control pollution call for less strict standards.

Uses of Benefit-Cost Analysis

One possible use of benefit-cost analysis is retrospective (that is, to evaluate existing policies by estimating the benefits actually realized and comparing them with the costs of the policies). In an early effort to evaluate federal legislation on air and water pollution, I found that policies to control air pollution from stationary sources probably had yielded benefits (primarily in the form of improved human health) substantially greater than the economic costs of the control, while the opposite was true of the control of automotive air pollution and industrial and municipal sources of water pollution.[3] Where retrospective analysis shows that costs have exceeded benefits, it may be possible to find ways to reduce the costs through adopting more cost-effective policies. But excessive costs also may indicate that the targets or environmental standards need to be reconsidered.

Benefit-cost analysis is increasingly being used in the federal government to evaluate proposed regulations and new environmental policies. A major stimulus to this use of benefit-cost analysis is Executive Order 12291 issued by President Ronald Reagan in February 1981. This order mandates that major federal regulations be subject to an economic analysis of benefits and costs.[4] EPA has prepared benefit-cost analyses for several new regulatory initiatives and for revisions of existing air-quality standards. In some cases the results of these "regulatory impact analyses" have supported new regulations or tightening of existing air-quality standards.

Is Benefit-Cost Analysis Biased?

The typical textbook discussions of the use of benefit-cost analysis implicitly assume a disinterested decision maker who has access to all of the relevant information on the positive and negative effects of a policy and who makes choices based on this information so as to maximize social welfare. The real world, however, seldom corresponds to the textbook model. First, decision makers seldom have perfect information on benefits and costs. The physical and biological mechanisms by which environmental changes affect people may not be well understood. And the economic values people place on environmental changes can seldom be measured with precision. But even more important, environmental policy decisions are usually made in a highly political setting in which the potential gainers and losers attempt to influence the decision.

Some contend that in such a setting the benefits of environmental regulation tend to be underestimated and the costs of regulation overestimated. Consequently, benefit-cost analysis will appear to justify less environmental protection and pollution control than is really desirable. There are three responses to this argument.

First, this is not so much an argument for rejecting the benefit-cost criterion for decision making as it is an argument for electing and appointing decision makers who are more capable and for trying to achieve greater objectivity and balance of conflicting views. To be sure, pro-industry groups will present information that tends to minimize estimates of benefits and to maximize estimates of costs. But there is room in the process for the presentation of alternative estimates and points of view.

Second, the argument is based on a view of process that is, at best, oversimplified. Policy analysts within government seldom accept industry estimates at face value. For major regulations government agencies often prepare their own estimates of benefits and costs or have them prepared by consultants. Some agencies have adopted procedures that systematically overestimate the risks of chemicals to human health and therefore the benefits of controlling chemical exposures.[5] In addition, there have been important cases where an agency's careful analysis of the benefits and costs of a regulation has led to the adoption of stricter environmental protection. An example of this is the 1985 decision by EPA to reduce the maximum allowable lead in gasoline from 1.1 grams per gallon to 0.1 grams per gallon. The benefits of controlling lead in the environment include reduced incidence of adverse health and cognitive effects in children, reduced incidence of blood-pressure-related effects in adult males, and reduced automotive maintenance expenditures. Not all of the benefits can be easily measured in monetary terms, but counting only measurable benefits resulted in a benefit-cost ratio in excess of 10 to 1.[6] Consequently, the regulation was adopted.

The third response is to point to an area of environmental policy in which greater reliance on benefit-cost analysis would clearly lead to decisions that are economically sounder as well as more protective of environmental values. This is the area of federally financed water resources development. For many years decisions on funding for specific water resource development projects were based nominally on benefit-cost analyses. But it is well known that these analyses used techniques that systematically overstated the benefits of water resource development, understated the economic costs, and ignored environmental costs. The result was construction of a number of projects that were economically wasteful and environmentally damaging and serious consideration of such misguided proposals as the one to build a dam in the Grand Canyon.[7] Competently and objectively done benefit-cost analyses clearly demonstrate that many projects are uneconomical even without taking into account their environmental costs. People fighting against environmentally destructive water resource developments have found benefit-cost analysis to be a useful weapon. For example, a study showing that economic costs exceeded benefits helped to weaken congressional support for the Dickey-Lincoln School hydroelectric power project on the St. John River in Maine. The Army Corps of Engineers estimated the benefit-cost ratio to be about 2.1 to 1 in 1976, but a more reasonable accounting showed the ratio to be much less favorable—between 0.8 and 0.9 to 1. And this estimate was made without being able to put a dollar price tag on the cost of destroying a free-flowing wild river.[8] Not surprisingly, Congress eventually deauthorized this project.

The Future of Benefit-Cost Analysis

The United States has made substantial progress over the past twenty years in some areas such as reducing emissions of soot and dust from coal-burning power plants and municipal trash incineration and the disposal of sewage and other organic wastes into rivers. In part this is because these problems were highly visible and the costs of cleaning them up were relatively low. But the pollution problems of the future are likely to be much more costly to deal with. Thus, it is more important to know, or to estimate, what the benefits of cleanup will be. On some kinds of problems the decisions may have to be made before there is adequate information on benefits and costs. Examples include protecting the stratospheric ozone layer and preventing greenhouse-induced global climate change. Analysis of these problems is complicated by the long-term, irreversible consequences of environmental change. Nevertheless, recognition of the economic limits imposed by scarcity and some effort to describe and quantify benefits and costs may help decision makers avoid the errors of doing too much or doing too little, too late.

In a number of environmental policy areas, irreversibility is not a major consideration, and some knowledge already has been gained about benefits and costs. For example, consider the question of how much farther America should go in the direction of cleaning up its air and water. This is just the kind of question that benefit-cost analysis is best suited to answer. One of the most controversial issues of this type is how to control substances that form atmospheric ozone or smog. The authorities of the South Coast Air Basin, of which smog-ridden Los Angeles is a part, recently approved a new air quality management plan to further control the sources of ozone pollution. This plan specifies three tiers of control measures of increasing stringency. The total cost may exceed $13 billion per year.[9] To put this whopping sum in perspective, consider the cost in 1988 of all federal policies on air pollution control in the United States:

about $30 billion. Does it make sense to do all three tiers of the plan? Can each of the tiers be justified by comparing its benefits with its costs? Questions of this sort will become increasingly important in the 1990s, and economists will become increasingly busy seeking the information needed to answer them.

Direct Regulation in Federal Environmental Policy

The major provisions of the federal laws controlling air and water pollution embody what is often termed a *direct regulation* approach (or *command and control* approach) to achieve the established pollution control targets. This direct regulation approach is based on specific limitations on the allowable discharges of polluting substances from each source, coupled with an administrative and legal system to monitor compliance with these limitations and to impose sanctions or penalties for violations.

In this approach the pollution control authority must carry out a series of four steps:

1. Determine the rules and regulations governing the behavior of each source that are necessary to achieve the given pollution control targets. These regulations might include the installation of certain types of pollution control equipment, restrictions on activities, or control of inputs, such as limiting the sulfur content in fuels. Most typically, the regulations take the form of maximum allowable discharges of polluting substances.
2. Establish a set of penalties or sanctions to be imposed for noncompliance with the regulations and requirements.
3. Monitor the actions of sources so that incidents of noncompliance can be detected. Alternatively, the authorities might establish a system of self-reporting with periodic checks and audits of performance.
4. Punish violations. If violations of the regulations are detected, the authorities must use the administrative and legal mechanisms spelled out in the relevant laws to impose penalties or to require changes in the behavior of the sources.[10]

Economists have criticized the direct regulation approach to environmental protection on two grounds. First, the pattern of pollution control activities required by the regulations is likely to be excessively costly. In other words, the activities are not likely to be cost-effective. Second, the incentive structure created for firms and individuals is inappropriate. Since compliance with the regulations is costly, there is no positive incentive to control pollution, only the negative incentive to avoid penalties. Not only is there no incentive to do better than the regulations require, but the incentives to comply with the regulations themselves may be too weak to overcome the disincentive of bearing the costs. Reform of the incentive structure will be addressed in the last two sections of this chapter.

Efficiency and Cost-Effectiveness

Even if one objects, for either philosophical or pragmatic reasons, to basing environmental policy on benefit-cost analysis, it still makes good sense to be in favor of cost-effective environmental policies. Cost-effectiveness means controlling pollution to achieve the stated environmental quality standards at the lowest possible total cost. The importance of achieving cost-effective pollution control policies should be self-evident. Cost savings free resources that can be used to produce other goods and services of value to people.

Where there are several sources of pollution (for example in factories or electric power plants), a pollution control policy must include some mechanism for dividing the responsibility for cleanup among the several sources. The direct regulation form of policy typically does this by requiring all sources to clean up by the same percentage. But such a policy will rarely be cost-effective. A pollution control policy is cost-effective only if it allocates the responsibility for cleanup among sources so that the incremental or marginal cost of achieving a one-unit improvement in environmental quality at any location is the same for all sources of pollution. Differences in the marginal costs of improving environmental quality can arise from differences in the marginal cost of treatment or waste reduction across sources, and because discharges from sources at different locations can have different effects on environmental quality.

Suppose that targets for air pollution control have been established by setting an ambient air-quality standard for sulfur dioxide. To illustrate the importance of differences in marginal costs of control, suppose that two adjacent factories are both emitting sulfur dioxide. A one-ton decrease in emissions gives the same incremental benefit to air quality whether it is achieved by factory A or factory B. Now suppose that to achieve the ambient air-quality standard, emissions must be reduced by fifty tons per day. One way to achieve the target is to require each factory to clean up twenty-five tons per day. But suppose that with this allocation of cleanup responsibility, factory A's marginal cost of cleanup is $10 per ton per day, while at factory B, the marginal cost is only $5 per ton per day. Allowing factory A to reduce its cleanup by one ton per day saves it $10. If factory B is required to clean up an extra ton, total cleanup is the same, and the air quality standard is met. And the total cost of pollution control is reduced by $5 per day. Additional savings are possible by continuing to shift cleanup responsibility to B (raising B's marginal cost) and away from A (reducing A's marginal cost). This should continue until B's rising marginal cost of control is made equal to A's now lower marginal cost. Emissions of a pollutant may have different impacts on air quality depending upon the location of the source. This must also be taken into account in finding the least-cost or cost-minimizing pattern of emissions reductions.[11]

Nothing in the logic or the procedures for setting pollution control requirements for sources ensures that the conditions for cost minimization will be satisfied. In setting discharge limits, agencies do not systematically take into account the marginal cost of control, at least in part because of the difficulties they would have in getting the data. Thus, such limits are not likely to result in equal marginal costs of reducing discharges across different sources of the same pollutant. One analysis of the marginal cost of removing oxygen-demanding organic material under existing federal water pollution standards found a thirtyfold range of marginal costs within the six industries examined.[12]

Another way of looking at the question of cost-effectiveness is to ask how to get the biggest benefit in the form of environmental improvement for a given total budget or total expenditure on pollution control. The answer is to spend that money on those pollution control activities with the highest level of pollution control benefit per dollar spent (the biggest "bang for the buck"). For example, if society decides for whatever reason to spend $1 million to control organic forms of water pollution, it should require that the money be spent on those industries with the highest pollutant removal per dollar or, what is the same thing, the lowest dollar cost per pound of removal. The study cited in the preceding paragraph shows that spending an extra dollar for controlling organic pollution in a low-cost industry will buy thirty times more pollution removal than spending the same dollar in a high marginal cost industry.[13]

A number of environmental protection and public health policies are cost-ineffective because of large differences across activities in the marginal cost of control or the benefit of dollars spent. Curtis Travis, S. Richter Pack, and Ann Fisher examined the costs of regulating different chemicals in the environment and then compared them with estimates of the reduced incidence of cancer. The costs per cancer death avoided varied widely.[14] The clearest example of cost-ineffective regulation is the pesticide Chlorobenzilate. Its use in noncitrus fruits has been regulated at a cost of $4 to $14 million per cancer death avoided, but its use in citrus fruit has gone unregulated, even though substantially more cancer deaths could be avoided at costs perhaps as low as $38,000 each. Similarly, some sources of benzene emissions have been regulated at a high cost per death avoided while other sources have gone unregulated even though their control costs are lower by a factor of ten.

Probably the greatest opportunities for more cost-effective pollution control are in the realm of the conventional pollutants of air and water. The problem of cost-effectiveness has stimulated many empirical studies comparing the costs of direct regulation policies under provisions of the Clean Air Act and Federal Water Pollution Control Act with cost-effective alternatives to this legislation based on equalizing the marginal costs of meeting environmental quality standards across all pollution control sources. In his review of these studies, T. H. Tietenberg found that least-cost pollution control planning could generate cost savings of 30 to 40 percent, and in some cases savings could exceed 90 percent.[15] This means that in some instances pollution control costs are *ten times* higher than they need to be.

How can potential cost savings of this magnitude be realized? In other words, how can pollution control policies be reformed to bring about greater cost-effectiveness without causing further environmental degradation? The answer lies in changing the incentives faced by polluters.

Incentives Versus Direct Regulation

Economic analysis of environmental problems has pointed out that pollution arises because of the way individuals and firms respond to the incentives created for them by an unregulated market economy. For firms, using safe and nonpolluting methods of disposing of wastes is usually more costly than dumping these wastes into the environment, even though environmental disposal causes harm to others. Polluters are not usually required to compensate those who experience these damages, so they have no incentive to take the damages into account and alter their waste disposal practices.

Incentives Under Direct Regulation

In deciding how to respond to a system of regulations and enforcement, polluters are likely to compare the costs of compliance with the likely costs and penalties associated with noncompliance. The costs of compliance may be substantial, but the costs of noncompliance are likely to be uncertain. Incidents of noncompliance might not be detected. Minor violations, even if detected, might be ignored by the authorities. Rather than commit itself to the uncertain legal processes involved in imposing significant fees and penalties, the overburdened enforcement arm of the pollution control agency might negotiate an agreement with the polluter regarding compliance at some future date. And finally, if cases are brought to court, the court might be more lenient than the pollution control agency would wish. All of these factors add up to a weak incentive for polluters to comply with the regulations.

The consequences of these weak incentives for compliance have been studied little, but the evidence that exists is not encouraging. For an eighteen-month period in 1981 and 1982, the U.S. General Accounting Office compared the actual discharges of a sample of water polluters with the permissible discharges under the terms of their discharge permits. Because of limited resources for the study, the GAO had to rely on discharge data supplied by the sources themselves rather than on independently verified discharge data. Nevertheless, the GAO study found a major noncompliance problem. Eighty-two percent of the sources studied had at least one month of noncompliance during the study period. Twenty-four percent of this sample was in "significant noncompliance," with at least four consecutive months during which discharges exceeded permitted levels by at least 50 percent.[16] Since the sources have incentives to understate actual discharges in their reports to the state agencies, the extent of noncompliance for this group could be even greater.

Improving the Incentives

Economists have proposed an alternative approach to pollution control policy; it is based on the creation of strong positive incentives for firms to control pollution. Suppose that the government imposed a charge or tax on each unit of pollution discharged and set the tax equal to the monetary value of the damage that pollution caused to others.[17] Each discharger wishing to minimize its total cost (cleanup cost plus tax bill) would compare the tax cost of discharging a unit of pollution with the cost of controlling or preventing the discharge. As long as the cost of control was less than the tax or charge, the firm would want to prevent the discharge. In fact, it would reduce pollution to the point where its marginal cost of control was just equal to the tax and indirectly equal to the marginal damage the pollution would cause. The properly set tax would cause the firm to undertake on its own accord the optimum amount of pollution control.

The pollution tax or charge strategy has long been attractive to economists because it provides a certain and graduated incentive to firms by making pollution itself a cost of production. And it provides an incentive for innovation and technological change in pollution control. Also, since the polluters are not likely to reduce their discharges to zero, the government would collect revenues.

A system of marketable or tradable discharge permits (TDPs) has essentially the same incentive effects as a tax on pollution. The government would issue a limited number of pollution permits or "tickets." Each ticket would entitle its owner to discharge one unit of pollution during a specific time period. The government could either distribute the tickets free of charge to polluters on some basis or auction them off to the highest bidders. Dischargers could also buy and sell permits among themselves. The cost of purchasing a ticket or forgoing the revenue from selling the ticket to someone else has the same incentive effects as a tax on pollution of the same amount.

Polluters can respond to the higher cost of pollution that a tax or TDP system imposes in a variety of ways. Polluters could install some form of conventional treatment system if the cost of treatment was less than the tax or permit price. But there are perhaps more important technical options as well. Polluters can consider changing to processes that are inherently less polluting. They can recover and recycle materials that otherwise would remain in the waste stream. They can change to inputs that result in less pollution. For example, a paper mill's response to a tax on dioxin in its effluent might be to stop using chlorine as a bleaching agent. Finally, since the firm would have to pay for whatever pollution it did not control, this cost would result in higher prices for its products and fewer units of its products being purchased by consumers. The effects of higher prices and lower quantities demanded would be to reduce the production level of the firm and, other things being equal, to further reduce the amount of pollution being generated.

A system of pollution taxes or TDPs can make a major contribution to achieving cost-effectiveness. If several sources are discharging into the environment, they will be induced to minimize the total cost of achieving any given reduction in pollution. This is because each discharger will control discharges up to the point where its marginal or incremental cost of control is equated to the tax or permit price. If all dischargers face the same tax or price, their marginal costs of pollution control will be equal. This is the condition for cost-effectiveness. Low-cost sources will control relatively more, thus leading to a cost-effective allocation of cleanup responsibilities. There is no reallocation of responsibilities for reducing discharges that will achieve the same total reduction at a lower total cost.

One difficulty with implementing a pollution charge system is knowing what the charge should be. In some cases enough is already known about the costs of control for typical or average polluters so that the appropriate charge could be calculated. Provision should always be made for adjusting the charge if experience reveals that it was initially set too high or too low.

One advantage of the TDP system is that the market determines the price of a permit that is equivalent to the tax in the case of a pollution charge. Another advantage of a system of TDPs in comparison with effluent charges is that it represents a less radical departure from the existing system. Since all sources are presently required to obtain permits specifying the maximum allowable discharges, it would be relatively easy to rewrite permits in a divisible format (ten one-ton-per-day permits instead of one ten-ton-per-day permit) and allow sources to buy or sell them. A more modest step would be to allow two (or more) sources to propose a reallocation of cleanup requirements between them if they found it to their mutual advantage and if there was no degradation of water quality. A source with low incremental costs of control should be willing to increase its cleanup provided another firm compensated it for its increase in pollution control costs. And a source with high pollution control costs would find it cheaper to pay the other source rather than clean up itself. The permit-writing authority should be willing to rewrite the permits for these two sources if it found that water quality would not be lowered.

More Modest Reforms

The Environmental Protection Agency has already found several ways to use economic incentives in a more limited way to introduce greater flexibility into the existing legal framework and to foster cost-effectiveness in meeting existing targets. Two of the most interesting of these are the creation of "bubbles" and pollution control "offsets."

Bubbles

The bubble concept was first applied to multiple-stack sources of air pollution. It was given this name because it treats a collection of smoke stacks or sources within a large factory as if they were encased in a bubble. Pollution control requirements are applied to the aggregate of emissions leaving the bubble rather than to each individual stack or source. EPA has also begun to apply the concept to the control of water pollution.

In a major industrial facility such as an integrated steel mill or petrochemical plant, there may be several separate activities or processes, each of which is subject to a different pollution limit or standard. Many of these activities discharge the same substances, yet the incremental costs of pollution control may be quite different across activities. As a result, the total cost of controlling the aggregate discharge from the plant is often higher than necessary. In such cases plant managers should be allowed to adjust the control levels of different activities if they can lower total control costs, as long as the total amount of a pollutant discharged from the plant does not exceed the aggregate of the effluent limitations for individual processes.

EPA has approved more than one hundred bubble transactions over the past decade.[18] Although accurate data on the realized cost savings from increased cost-effectiveness are not available, it seems likely that aggregate savings have amounted to several billion dollars. Since EPA regulations for governing bubbles sometimes require a net reduction in emissions from the bubble, the net effect on air quality has probably been positive.

Offsets

The so-called offset policy was created in the mid-1970s to resolve a conflict in some regions between achieving federal air-quality standards and allowing economic growth and development. The Clean Air Act of 1970 prohibited the licensing of new air pollution sources if they would interfere with the attainment of federal air-quality standards. Taken literally, this would prohibit any new industrial facilities with air pollution emissions in those parts of the country not in compliance with existing air-quality standards. In response to this dilemma, EPA issued a set of rules that would allow new sources to be licensed in nonattainment areas provided they could show that there would be no net increase in pollution. The offsetting reduction in polluted air would come from reducing emissions from existing sources of pollution in the nonattainment area above and beyond what had already been required—either by installing additional controls on these sources or by shutting them down.

The offset rules give firms desiring to expand or enter a region an incentive to find additional ways to reduce emissions from existing sources in the region. The offsets need not be limited to reductions at other sources owned by the firm planning a new source investment. Firms are free to seek offsets from other existing sources as well, creating an opportunity for existing sources to "sell" emissions reductions to new sources.

In the past decade there were an estimated two thousand offset transactions under EPA rules. About 10 percent were between firms; thus, they represented true market transactions. The remainder were within the firms desiring to expand or create a new source.[19] Since EPA rules require that offsets be executed on a greater than one-for-one basis, the net impact on air quality has probably been positive. The policy also encourages technological innovation to find means of creating offsets and probably encourages older dirty facilities to shut down sooner than they otherwise would.

Economic Incentives and Environmental Policy in the 1990s

Two events in June 1989 make it likely that economic incentives will play a larger role in the environmental policies of the 1990s than they did in the previous decade. The first event was the release on June 12, 1989, of President George Bush's plan for revising the Clean Air Act of 1970. The centerpiece of the president's plan is greater reliance on emissions reduction trading among sources. The plan also provides for increased use of emissions reduction credits and banking for the control of toxic air pollutants.

The second event was the release in the same week of a bipartisan report titled *Project 88, Harnessing Market Forces to Protect Our Environment: Initiatives for the New President.* Cosponsored by Sen. Tim Wirth, D-Colo., and Sen. John Heinz, R-Pa., the report contends that "conventional regulatory policies need to be supplemented by market-based strategies which can foster major improvements in environmental quality by enlisting the innovative capacity of our economy in the development of efficient and equitable solutions." [20] The report urges much greater use of incentive-based systems such as tradable discharge permits and pollution taxes. It also suggests how these incentive systems can be applied to various environmental problems. I will briefly discuss three possible applications: reducing carbon dioxide emissions, reducing pesticides applications, and controlling hazardous wastes.

Reducing CO_2 Emissions: Taxes or TDPs?

Largely because of the burning of fossil fuels and deforestation, the concentration of carbon dioxide (CO_2) in the global atmosphere is steadily increasing. Carbon dioxide and other greenhouse gases inhibit the radiation of thermal energy away from the earth. If present trends in emissions and atmospheric concentrations of CO_2 continue, average temperatures worldwide could increase by several degrees Celsius over the next fifty years. If global warming is to be avoided or at least retarded, global emissions of CO_2 must be held steady if not substantially reduced. Thus, a major policy question facing all nations is how to slow, if not reverse, the rising trend in CO_2 emissions. One possibility is to implement an economic incentive system such as a tax or TDP program.

To fully realize the potential incentive and cost-minimizing effects of such a system, it is necessary to apply the tax or TDP program directly to CO_2. For example, a tax on energy would reduce the utilization of all forms of energy, not just those with the highest carbon content. A tax on CO_2 also would reduce energy use, but the reduction in use would be concentrated in those sources with the highest carbon content.

To implement any program to control carbon dioxide emissions, it is necessary to have information on emissions from all sources or all major categories of sources. Monitoring emissions directly might be expensive. As long as there is no feasible technology for the removal of CO_2 from emissions streams, measurement of the carbon input to the combustion processes would be sufficient to implement a tax or TDP system. If removal of CO_2 from emissions streams should prove feasible, then the tax or TDP could be based on carbon input less any documented CO_2 removed.

One way to implement an economic incentive system would be to tax fossil fuels based on their carbon content. This approach has the advantage of ease of implementation, especially considering the multiplicity of small sources of CO_2 emissions (for example, automobiles, home heating, and home cooking).

Several economic and technical factors will influence the effectiveness of any tax or TDP system in reducing emissions of carbon dioxide. Perhaps the most important are the technological options and costs of controlling CO_2 emissions at the source and the opportunities for shifting to lower carbon or noncarbon sources of energy. One effect of a CO_2 tax would be to tilt the economic scale somewhat toward solar, geothermal, and nuclear sources of energy. The greater the substitution of these alternative sources for fossil fuel combustion, the more effective a CO_2 tax would be in reducing emissions. The more limited the range of options for shifting to other sources or controlling CO_2 emissions, the greater will be the effect of the tax on the prices of final products. Thus, a second important factor in determining the effectiveness of a CO_2 tax is how the demand for these final products is affected by an increase in their prices. If small increases in prices result in relatively large decreases in demand (if demand is *elastic*, in the economist's terminology), the tax will be more effective in reducing CO_2 emissions.

A third important factor is how prices of carbon-containing fuels and the supplies of these fuels respond to the tax. If the current prices of high carbon fuels are substantially greater than the cost of discovering, developing, and extracting them, then a tax on the carbon content will result in a decrease in the price (net of tax) received by the producers without a corresponding increase in the price (inclusive of tax) to the users. Consequently, the incentive to shift to alternative fuels might be quite weak, and it would take a very large tax on carbon content to achieve significant reductions in emissions of carbon dioxide.

Given a policy decision to seek a reduction in CO_2 emissions, the case for preferring an incentive-based system over direct regulation is strong. In terms of incentives, enforcement, cost-effectiveness, and administrative ease, both the tax and TDP system come out ahead of direct regulation. A tax may be somewhat easier to administer than a TDP system, but this advantage is not overwhelming.

The most important consideration in choosing between a tax and TDP system is the different ways in which the consequences of uncertainty are felt. The greater certainty about emissions reductions under a TDP system is not a great advantage since at this time it does not seem to be essential to meet a specific target for emissions reductions. And since very little is known about the economic costs of controlling CO_2 emissions, the uncertainty of the costs and economic impact of a TDP is a significant disadvantage.

This suggests that, at least in the near term, a tax on CO_2 emissions is preferable to a TDP system. A modest tax on CO_2 emissions of, say, one cent per pound might be a good starting point. For example, the complete combustion of the carbon in one gallon of gasoline would produce about twenty pounds of carbon dioxide. So a tax of one cent per pound of CO_2 would add about twenty cents to the price of gasoline. After allowing two to three years for adjustment, the data on fuel use and tax revenues would provide a basis for estimating the reduction in emissions it had achieved and its cost. The tax rate could then be adjusted accordingly.

Pesticides

High rates of application of chemical pesticides in agriculture have resulted in two kinds of environmental problems. First, pesticide residues can adhere to soil particles that erode from the land; these residues can cause ecological problems in downstream lakes and rivers. Second, pesticide residues can leach directly into underlying groundwater aquifers resulting in contaminated water supplies to households.

EPA currently has the power to ban specific pesticides entirely or to ban or otherwise regulate applications on particular crops. The degree of erosion and the potential for pesticide residues to leach into groundwater vary widely across different regions of the country. Also the value of pesticide use varies widely by crop and by region. Thus, any system of direct regulation is likely to be very cost-ineffective in protecting surface and groundwater quality. The Project 88 report suggests placing a tax on the use of certain pesticides to discourage their use and to encourage the development and utilization of environmentally sound agricultural practices. In the absence of specific knowledge about the costs to farmers of reducing their applications of pesticides, it is difficult to know at what level to set a tax for each pesticide in question. If the tax is set too low, too much of the pesticide would be used; if the tax is set too high, the degree of overregulation would impose unnecessary costs on farmers and on society as whole.

A better alternative might be a regionally based system of marketable pesticide application permits (PAPs). Local officials could estimate the maximum allowable applications of each pesticide in the region that are consistent with protecting surface and groundwater quality. Farmers could then bid for PAPs in an auction. Some farmers would find that the auction price was greater than the value to them of using the pesticide, so they would seek out alternative ways of dealing with pest problems.

Assuming adequate monitoring and enforcement, the maximum safe levels of pesticide application would not be exceeded.

Soda Cans and Hazardous Waste

Federal policy on hazardous wastes focuses on regulating disposal practices. The effectiveness of this policy is highly dependent on the ability to monitor and enforce these disposal regulations and to detect and penalize illegal disposal practices such as so-called midnight dumping. Both industry and government have recognized that the problem of safe disposal can be made more manageable by reducing the quantities of hazardous wastes being generated. The high cost of complying with disposal regulations is itself an incentive for industry to engage in source reduction, but it is also an incentive to evade the disposal regulation.

For some types of wastes, a deposit-refund system could provide better incentives to reduce the source of hazardous wastes as well as to dispose of them safely. The system would be similar to the deposits on returnable cans and bottles established in some states. For example, the manufacturer of a solvent that would become a hazardous waste after it is used could be required to pay EPA a deposit of so many dollars per gallon of solvent produced. The amount of the deposit would have to be at least as high as the cost of recycling the solvent or disposing of it safely. Since paying the deposit is, in effect, part of the cost of producing the solvent, the manufacturer would have to raise its price accordingly. This would discourage the use of the solvent, thus encouraging source reduction. The deposit would be refunded to whoever returned one gallon of the solvent to a certified safe disposal facility or to a recycler. Thus, the user of the solvent would find it more profitable to return the solvent than to dispose of it illegally. In this way private incentives and the search for profit are harnessed to the task of environmental protection.[21]

Conclusion

Economic analysis is likely to be increasingly useful in grappling with the environmental problems of the 1990s for at least three reasons. First, as policy makers address the more complex and deeply rooted national and global environmental problems, they are finding that solutions are more and more costly. Thus, it is increasingly important that the public gets its "money's worth" from these policies. This means looking at benefits and comparing them with costs. Therefore, some form of benefit-cost analysis, such as that required by President Reagan's Executive Order 12291, will play a larger role in policy debates and decisions in the future.

Second, the slow progress that has been made over the past twenty years in dealing with conventional air and water pollution problems shows the need to use private initiative more effectively through altering the incentive structure. This means placing greater reliance on pollution charges, tradable discharge permits, and deposit-refund systems. I have suggested three possible applications of incentive-based mechanisms to emerging problems, but the list of potential applications is much longer, as is made clear in the Project 88 report.

Finally, the high aggregate cost of controlling various pollutants and environmental threats makes it imperative to design policies that are cost-effective. Incentive-based mechanisms can play a very important role in achieving pollution control targets at something approaching the minimum possible social cost.

Notes

1. For introductions to the principles of benefit-cost analysis and applications in the realm of environmental policy, see Peter Bohm, *Social Efficiency: A Concise Introduction to Welfare Economics* (New York: Wiley, 1973); Tom Tietenberg, *Environmental and Natural Resource Economics*, 2d ed. (Glenview, Ill.: Scott, Foresman, 1988); and Daniel Swartzman, Richard A. Liroff, and Kevin G. Croke, *Cost-Benefit Analysis and Environmental Regulations: Politics, Ethics, and Methods* (Washington, D.C.: Conservation Foundation, 1982).
2. See, for example, Tietenberg, *Environmental and Natural Resource Economics*, chap. 14.
3. A. Myrick Freeman III, *Air and Water Pollution Control: A Benefit-Cost Assessment* (New York: Wiley, 1982).
4. For a discussion of some of the economic implications of Executive Order 12291, see V. Kerry Smith, ed., *Environmental Policy Under Reagan's Executive Order: The Role of Benefit-Cost Analysis* (Chapel Hill: University of North Carolina Press, 1984).
5. Albert L. Nichols and Richard J. Zeckhauser, "The Perils of Prudence," *Regulation* (November-December 1986): 13-24.
6. U.S. Environmental Protection Agency, *Costs and Benefits of Reducing Lead in Gasoline: Final Regulatory Impact Analysis* (Washington, D.C.: U.S. Environmental Protection Agency, 1985).
7. For a description of how bad economic analysis is used to justify proposals of this sort, see Alan Carlin, "The Grand Canyon Controversy: Or, How Reclamation Justifies the Unjustifiable," in *Pollution, Resources, and the Environment*, ed. Alain C. Enthoven and A. Myrick Freeman III (New York: Norton, 1973).
8. See A. Myrick Freeman III, "The Benefits and Costs of the Dickey-Lincoln Project: A Preliminary Report," unpublished paper, Bowdoin College, Brunswick, Maine, 1974; and A. Myrick Freeman III, "The Benefits and Costs of the Dickey-Lincoln Project: An Interim Update," unpublished paper,

Bowdoin College, Brunswick, Maine, 1978.

9. See Paul R. Portney et al., "L. A. Law: Regulating Air Quality in California's South Coast," *Issues in Science and Technology* 13, no. 4 (1989): 68-73.
10. For more detailed discussions of the major provisions of federal air and water pollution law, see Paul R. Portney "Air Pollution Policy," and A. Myrick Freeman III, "Water Pollution Policy," in *Public Policies for Environmental Protection*, ed. Paul. R. Portney, (Washington, D.C.: Resources for the Future, 1990).
11. See Tietenberg, *Environmental and Natural Resource Economics*, 320-326.
12. Wesley A. Magat, Alan J. Krupnick, and Winston Harrington, *Rules in the Making: A Statistical Analysis of Regulatory Agency Behavior* (Washington, D.C.: Resources for the Future, 1986), Table 6-1.
13. Ibid.
14. See Curtis C. Travis, S. Richter Pack, and Ann Fisher, "Cost-Effectiveness as a Factor in Cancer Risk Management," *Environment International* 13 (1987): 469-474. Martin Bailey has found similarly wide differences in costs per life saved for a wide range of government policies on public health, safety, and environmental protection. The most cost-effective means of reducing premature death was through improved traffic safety at $37,500 per life saved, while reducing occupational exposure to some chemicals had costs in the hundreds of millions per life saved. See Martin J. Bailey, *Reducing Risks to Life: Measurement of the Benefits* (Washington, D.C.: American Enterprise Institute, 1980), Table 4.
15. T. H. Tietenberg, *Emissions Trading: An Exercise in Reforming Pollution Policy* (Washington, D.C.: Resources for the Future, 1985), 38-47.
16. See U.S. General Accounting Office, *Waste Water Dischargers Are Not Complying with EPA Pollution Control Permits* (Washington, D.C.: U.S. General Accounting Office, 1983). This study and other evidence are discussed by Clifford S. Russell in "Monitoring and Enforcement," in *Public Policies for Environmental Protection*, ed. Paul R. Portney. In addition, Winston Harrington's very detailed study of the monitoring and enforcement process in New Mexico suggests that similar problems are frequent in the realm of air pollution. See Winston Harrington, *The Regulatory Approach to Air Quality Management: A Case Study of New Mexico* (Washington, D.C.: Resources for the Future, 1981).
17. Allen V. Kneese and Charles L. Schultze are perhaps the best-known advocates of greater reliance on charges and other economic incentives. See their book *Pollution, Prices, and Public Policy* (Washington, D.C.: Brookings Institution, 1975). See also Frederick R. Anderson et al., *Environmental Improvement Through Economic Incentives* (Baltimore: Johns Hopkins University Press for Resources for the Future, 1977). For a more critical perspective, see Susan Rose-Ackerman, "Market Models for Pollution Control: Their Strengths and Weaknesses," *Public Policy* 25 (1977): 383-406; and Clifford S. Russell, "What Can We Get from Effluent Charges?" *Policy Analysis* 5 (Spring 1979): 155-180.
18. Robert W. Hahn and Gordon L. Hester, "Marketable Permits: Lessons from Theory and Practice," *Ecology Law Quarterly* 16, no. 2 (1989): 361-406.
19. Ibid.

20. *Project 88, Harnessing Market Forces to Protect Our Environment: Initiatives for the New President*, a public policy study sponsored by Sen. Tim Wirth, D-Colo., and Sen. John Heinz, R-Pa., (Washington, D.C.: Project 88, December 1988.) See also Bruce A. Ackerman and Richard B. Stewart, "Reforming Environmental Law: The Democratic Case for Market Incentives," *Columbia Journal of Environmental Law* 13 (1988): 171-199; and Richard B. Stewart, "Controlling Environmental Risks Through Economic Incentives," *Columbia Journal of Environmental Law* 13 (1988): 153-169.
21. See *Project 88*, chap. 7; and Clifford S. Russell, "Economic Incentives in the Management of Hazardous Waste," *Columbia Journal of Environmental Law* 13 (1988): 1101-1119.

8

Risk Assessment: Regulation and Beyond

Richard N. L. Andrews

Environmental regulation in the 1980s was pervaded by the concept of risk, and environmental policy analysis by the concepts and methods of quantitative risk assessment (QRA). Between 1976 and 1980, such assessments were performed on only eight chemicals proposed for regulation; between 1981 and 1985, on fifty-five. By the end of the 1980s, the vocabulary of risk had become the basic language of environmental policy making at the Environmental Protection Agency (EPA), and to varying degrees in other agencies as well.[1] In 1984 EPA administrator William Ruckelshaus officially endorsed "risk assessment and risk management" as the primary framework for EPA decision making; in 1987 a major agency report stated flatly that "the fundamental mission of the Environmental Protection Agency is to reduce risks."[2]

The adoption of this framework of concepts has important implications for the course of U.S. environmental policy. Risk assessment remains controversial, both among scientists and policy makers and in general political debate; even many of its advocates are uneasy that it is often oversold or abused. It may well continue to dominate environmental policy making in the 1990s, with both positive and negative results; or it may be overshadowed by new environmental policy priorities that do not readily fit its vocabulary and methods, leaving it a more modest role in framing those decision issues to which it is well suited. To appraise the long-term significance of risk assessment, therefore, one must first understand how it has come to be so widely used; what it is, and why it is controversial; and the ways in which it is and is not well matched to the environmental issues of the 1990s.

The Regulatory Legacy

U.S. environmental policy up to 1970 included more than seven decades' experience in managing the environment as a natural resource base—lands and forests, minerals, water, fish and wildlife—but almost none in regulating environmental quality. Beginning in 1970, however, U.S. policy emphasis shifted dramatically from environmental management to environmental regulation, and from state and local to national primacy. EPA was created by reorganizing many of the existing regulatory programs into one agency; and Congress embarked on a decade of unprecedented expansion of federal regulatory mandates, enacting more than a dozen major new statutes, each requiring many individual regulatory actions governing particular substances, technologies, and practices.

Risk-Based Regulation

Initially these laws emphasized the use of known technologies and clear statutory directives to reduce the most obvious problems: urban sewage, automotive air pollution, and the half-dozen or so major industrial pollutants of air and water. The Clean Air Act of 1970, for instance, established explicit national ambient air quality standards for six major pollutants, based on health criteria, and set deliberately "technology-forcing" statutory timetables for meeting them. The Federal Water Pollution Control Act Amendments of 1972 similarly required federal permits for all new water pollution sources, and again used technology-based standards—"best practicable" and "best available" technologies—to force improved pollution control throughout each industrial process.

As these measures took effect, however, environmental politics became increasingly intertwined with the fear of cancer, and specifically with the possibility that pesticides and other manufactured chemicals might be important environmental causes of it.[3] The environmental control agenda was broadened and redirected, therefore, to address the far larger domain of chemical hazards as a whole: toxic air and water pollutants, production of toxic substances, pesticides, drinking water contaminants, hazardous wastes, and others. This domain included thousands of compounds, far too many to address explicitly in statutes, most not yet even well studied, and many that had important economic uses despite (or for pesticides, even because of) their toxicity.[4]

To deal with toxic chemicals, therefore, Congress enacted "risk-based" and "risk-balancing" statutes, which required EPA to assess the risks of each substance it proposed to regulate, and then either to protect the public with "margins of safety" against "unreasonable risks" or to make choices that would balance those risks against the substance's economic benefits.

In turn, EPA and other agencies, such as the Occupational Safety and Health Administration and the Consumer Product Safety Commission, had to develop methods for *setting risk priorities* among many possible candidates for regulation; for *justifying particular regulatory decisions*, balancing risks against benefits; and for *approving site decisions,* based on an "acceptable risk" for certifying a cleaned-up hazardous-waste site or permitting a new facility.[5]

The Politics of Accountability

By the late 1970s, EPA and other regulatory agencies also faced increasing pressure for closer political oversight and accountability. From one side, these pressures came from environmental groups frustrated by EPA's slow implementation of regulatory mandates. They took such forms as congressional action to set deadlines, with "hammer clauses" for implementation of each new regulatory mandate, and lawsuits to compel EPA regulation of high-priority substances by agreed deadlines.

From the other side, pressures for closer oversight came from business interests seeking to restrain the scope and pace of regulation. One primary form of such pressure was to increase the burden of analytical requirements that EPA must meet before each regulation could be promulgated. Two important examples were President Reagan's Executive Order 12291, which required "regulatory impact assessments" and review by the Office of Management and Budget (OMB) for all proposed regulations; and a Supreme Court decision in 1980 that held, in effect, that many proposed environmental health standards for chemicals could be invalidated if the agency did not justify them by quantitative risk assessments.[6] These pressures converged in the growth of quantitative risk assessment as a framework for policy analysis.

Risk Assessment and Risk Management

Quantitative risk assessment has been defined as "the process of obtaining quantitative measures of risk levels, where risk refers to the possibility of uncertain, adverse consequences."[7] The term is used in different ways, however, by at least a half dozen professional communities.[8] To engineers, it is a methodology for estimating probabilities of technological failures through "fault-tree" studies: a famous example during the 1970s was the so-called "Rasmussen report" on nuclear reactor safety.[9] To life insurance actuaries, it is a standard practice for estimating life expectancy; to business executives, a procedure for evaluating the financial risks of investments; and to cognitive scientists, a more general psychological process that shapes every individual's perceptions of, and behavior toward, choices that may bring gain or pain.

To toxicologists and epidemiologists, however—and to most EPA staff—risk assessment primarily meant quantitative *health* risk assessment (QHRA). To them, "risk" normally is assumed to mean "the probability of injury, disease, or death under specific circumstances," and risk assessment means "the characterization of the potential adverse health effects of human exposure to environmental hazards." [10] Note that these definitions combine two separate concepts, the concept of hazard (adverse consequence, usually assumed to be a health hazard) and the concept of probability (quantitative measures of possibility or uncertainty). This mixing of two concepts is one cause of the confusion and controversy that surrounds risk assessment. Other approaches are sometimes discussed, but it is the concepts and methods of QHRA that have come to dominate environmental regulatory practice.

One fundamental doctrine of this approach is that risk assessment should be clearly distinguished from risk management. Risk assessment, in this view, is a purely scientific activity based on expert analysis of facts. Risk management is the ensuing decision process in which the scientific conclusions of the risk assessment are weighed among other considerations (such as statutory requirements, costs, public values, and politics). This distinction was advocated by William Lowrance in an influential book on risk in 1976, endorsed by a National Research Council report in 1983, and adopted as EPA policy by administrator William Ruckelshaus. It remains a basic tenet of texts on risk assessment, though Ruckelshaus himself subsequently acknowledged the difficulty of maintaining such a clear distinction in practice.[11]

Risk Assessment

Quantitative health risk assessment has now been refined into a detailed analytical procedure that includes four elements:

- *hazard identification,* in which the analyst gathers information on whether a substance may be a health hazard
- *dose-response assessment,* in which the analyst attempts to describe quantitatively the relationship between the amount of exposure to the substance and the degree of toxic effect
- *exposure assessment,* in which the analyst estimates how many people may actually be exposed to the substance and under what conditions (how much of it, how often, for how long, from what sources)
- *risk characterization,* in which the analyst combines information from the previous steps into an assessment of overall health risk: for example, an added risk that one person in a thousand (or a hundred, or a million) will develop cancer after exposure at the expected levels over a lifetime

Suppose, for instance, that EPA decides to assess the health risks of an organic solvent used to degrease metal parts: a liquid, moderately volatile, that is somewhat soluble in water and degrades slowly in it.[12] The hazard identification step reveals several experimental animal studies between 1940 and 1960, all showing lethal toxicity to the liver at high doses but no toxic effects below an identifiable "threshold" dose; cancer was not studied. One more recent study, however, appears to show that lifetime exposure to much lower doses causes significant increase in liver cancers in both mice and rats. The only human data are on exposed workers, too few to draw statistically valid conclusions (two cases of cancer diagnosed in fewer than two hundred workers, when one case might have been expected). From these data, EPA decides that the solvent is a "possible" (as opposed to probable or definite) human carcinogen.

In dose-response assessment the analyst then uses a mathematical model to predict a plausible "upper-bound" estimate of human cancer risk by extrapolating from the animal studies: from high to low doses, and from laboratory species (rats and mice) to humans. Applying these models to the measured animal data, EPA estimates a "unit cancer risk" (risk for an average lifetime exposure to one milligram per kilogram of body weight per day) of about two in one hundred for lung cancer from inhalation, based on studies of male rats, and about five in one hundred for liver cancer from ingestion, based on studies of male mice.

In exposure assessment the analyst then uses monitoring data and dispersion models to calculate that approximately eighty neighbors may be exposed to about eight ten-thousandths of a milligram per kilogram of body weight per day, and 150 workers to about one thousandth mg./kg. per day; and through gradual groundwater contamination, about 50,000 people may be exposed to one to two thousandths mg./kg. per day in their drinking water after about twenty years.

Finally, the risk characterization combines these calculations into numerical upper-bound estimates of excess lifetime human cancer risk. In this hypothetical case, the result might be eight in one hundred thousand of the general population, one in one thousand nearby residents, and three in a thousand workers (note from the previous paragraph that the actual numbers—of neighbors and workers, at least—are far smaller, but risk assessments are normally expressed in numbers per thousand for consistency's sake.)

These estimates are then to be used by EPA's "risk managers"—that is, the officials responsible for its regulatory decisions—to decide what risks are the highest priority for regulation and what regulatory action (if any) is justified in this particular case.

Risk Management

In current EPA practice, risk management primarily means choosing and justifying regulatory initiatives. EPA does not have an "organic act," a single broad statutory mandate for environmental management. It administers a complex patchwork of separate statutes, each of which addresses a particular set of problems, establishes its own range of authorized management actions (usually regulatory authorities), and specifies its own criteria for making such decisions. Some of the laws direct that health risks be minimized regardless of costs; others that the risks be balanced against costs; and still others that the best available technology be used to minimize risks (allowing some judgment about what technologies are economically "available"), or that new technology be developed to meet a standard.[13]

Whatever these laws may say, in practice EPA and other regulatory agencies actually apply their own rules of thumb, based on risk and cost, to manage health risks. Travis et al. (1987) examined 132 federal regulatory decisions concerning environmental carcinogens from 1976 through 1985 and discovered two clear patterns. Every chemical with an individual cancer risk greater than four chances in one thousand was regulated; and with only one exception, no action was taken to regulate any chemical with an individual risk less than one chance in one million. In the risk range between these two levels, the primary criterion used was cost-effectiveness: risks were regulated if the cost per life saved was less than 2 million dollars, but not if the cost was higher.[14]

These findings strongly suggest that "risk managers" use their own norms to distinguish among *de manifestis* risks (risks so high that agencies will almost always act to reduce them, regardless of cost), *de minimis* risks (risks that they judge too small to be worth consideration, even though they may be serious for highly exposed or susceptible individuals in the population), and a gray area in between in which the primary criterion used is cost-effectiveness. Risk management means regulation, and regulation is directed toward measurably high risks and toward moderate risks with moderate costs for reduction.

Science and Values

Quantitative risk assessment has now been adopted in varying degrees by all the federal environmental and health regulatory agencies. It has also been institutionalized in a professional society (the Society for Risk Analysis), a journal, and a growing professional community of practitioners in government agencies, chemical producer and user industries, consulting firms, universities and research institutes, and advocacy organizations.

Despite its widespread use, however, serious dispute remains as to whether risk assessment is really scientific or merely a recasting of value judgments into scientific jargon. The language of risk assessment is less accessible to the general public and their elected representatives; does it nonetheless provide a more scientifically objective basis for public policy decisions?

Risk Assessment Policy

Risk assessment in practice is permeated by value judgments. One such judgment concerns which substances are selected for risk assessment in the first place. Such judgments in practice are based not only on preliminary evidence of risk but also on publicity, lawsuits, and other political pressures. Another judgment concerns what effects, or "end-points," are considered: most focus on cancer, with little attention as yet to other health hazards (such as toxicity to the reproductive system, the immune system, the central nervous system, or child development processes). Risks to other species, to ecosystems, or to other environmental values are not now incorporated into most QRA procedures, and both the data and the methodology needed to do so are lacking.

In conducting each risk assessment, the analysts' own value judgments come into play whenever they must make assumptions or draw inferences in the absence of objective facts. Such judgments are identified collectively as "risk assessment policy." Hazard identification, for example, relies on evidence from epidemiological studies of human effects, from animal bioassays, from short-term laboratory tests *(in vitro),* or simply from comparison of the compound's molecular structure with other known hazards. In practice, these data are usually few and fragmentary, often collected for different purposes, and of varied quality; the analyst must make numerous judgments about their applicability.

For both dose-response and exposure assessment, analysts must routinely use mathematical models to generate risk estimates. Even the best dose-response models, however, are based on simplified biology and fragmentary data. Scientists must interpolate the dose-response relationship between a small number of observations, extrapolate it to lower doses often far beyond the observed range, and adjust for the many possible differences between species and conditions of exposure. Similarly, in exposure assessment, analysts must make many assumptions about variability in natural dispersion patterns and population movements, about other sources of exposure, and about the susceptibility of those exposed (for instance, healthy adults compared with children or chemically sensitive persons).

Finally, the analyst must synthesize a characterization of overall risk out of the diverse, uncertain, and sometimes conflicting estimates derived from the previous three steps. Such choices include weighing the quality, persuasiveness, and applicability of differing bodies of evidence; deciding how to estimate and adjust for statistical uncertainties; and even choosing which of various possible estimates to present ("best estimate" or "upper bound," for instance).

Inference Guidelines

Given these many unavoidable judgments, the conclusions of health risk assessments inevitably are shaped far more by their assumptions than by objective "facts." Both EPA and other agencies have therefore developed guidance documents called "inference guidelines," which specify what assumptions and rules of thumb are to be used in calculating risks. Such guidelines cannot be scientifically definitive, since the underlying science contains fundamental uncertainties. They are, rather, policy directives, based on a mixture of scientific consensus and political choices about the appropriate level of prudence. The rationale for inference guidelines is that even if absolute risk levels are unknown, better comparative risk decisions can still be made if all risk assessments use a consistent set of methods and assumptions.

EPA published its first interim guidelines for cancer risk assessment in 1976.[15] More detailed guidance was published in 1986, including guidelines for carcinogenicity and mutagenicity risk assessment, for health risk assessment of chemical mixtures and suspect developmental toxicants, and for estimating exposures; proposed guidelines for assessing reproductive risks were published in 1988.[16] Other agencies also proposed guidelines for cancer risk assessment during this period: the National Cancer Advisory Board in 1976; the Interagency Regulatory Liaison Group, the Regulatory Council, and the president's Office of Science and Technology Policy (OSTP) in 1979; the Occupational Safety and Health Administration in 1980; and OSTP again in the 1980s.[17]

These guidelines differed in important respects. The 1982 OSTP draft, for instance, recommended more skeptical evaluation of extrapolation from high to low dosages, reasoning that high dosages introduce artificially toxic effects of their own that would not occur at lower dosages. This position represented one view within the scientific community, but one different from EPA's and consistent with the Reagan administration's goal of less regulation.

A Conservative Bias?

A major reason for differences among the guidelines is an intense and continuing debate—both scientific and political—over whether the regulatory agencies' risk estimates are systematically biased in favor of excessive caution. If each assumption includes some intuitive "safety factor" favoring health protection, for instance, and these factors are then multiplied (as they often must be), the overall safety factor may be far greater than any of them individually. There is a growing conventional wisdom among many risk analysts, especially in the business community but also in EPA, that because of these practices EPA's risk assessments have become excessively cautious, and that they should be revised to reflect only best estimates of risk rather than large margins of safety. In September 1988 EPA decided to rewrite its inference guidelines once again, possibly due to pressure from this conventional wisdom to incorporate less conservative assumptions.[18]

Other risk experts argue, however, that many of these assumptions may not be excessively cautious at all. Human susceptibility and exposure levels can both be as easily underestimated as overestimated, as can the toxicity of a substance itself. A distinguished risk research group in 1988 identified plausible biological reasons showing that existing risk assessment methods—despite all their "safety factors"—may in fact underestimate some risks of low-level exposure. Given scientific uncertainty, moreover, "best estimate" methods cannot themselves avoid value judgments, errors, and biases: they may simply substitute different ones, favoring less prudence toward health protection.[19]

Multiple Risks and Risk Management

The unavoidability of value judgments pervades risk assessment even in its simplest forms, applied as above to the risk of a single result (cancer) from a single substance. Beyond these simplest cases, however, lies the far greater complexity of the decisions that EPA and other agencies must actually make, and the multiplicity of risks involved in such "risk management" decisions.

Imagine, for instance, a relatively common type of issue: EPA must establish requirements for air and water emissions and hazardous-waste storage permits at a new chemical reprocessing and incineration facility. There are many risks to consider in setting such standards: risks of cancer, respiratory ailments, fish mortality, stream eutrophication, crop damage, diminished visibility, and economic hardship to the surrounding community, to list just a few. There may be many beneficial effects as well: reduction of health and ecological damage associated with current methods of waste disposal, economic benefits to the surrounding community, and others.

In principle, risk assessment can estimate the probability of each of these effects individually; but it does not specify which should be considered, does not make them commensurable, and does not provide weights specifying their relative importance. In practice, risk assessment has dealt with these issues by oversimplifying them, focusing on only a few human health effects. This simplification may, however, obscure the more diverse considerations required by more complex decisions.

Risk Assessment and Environmental Decisions

By the end of the 1980s, risk assessment had been established as the primary language of analysis and management at EPA. EPA's statutes did not contain this consistency of discourse, but virtually every EPA administrative decision was couched in terms of how much risk it would reduce: setting budget allocation priorities among programs, justifying individual regulatory proposals, even framing EPA's proposed research program for the 1990s. Why?

Managerial Tool

From the perspective of senior EPA administrators such as Ruckelshaus and his successor Lee Thomas, formal risk assessment offered a powerful new management tool. One of the most intractable problems facing every EPA administrator is the proliferation of uncoordinated statutes, programs, and regulatory mandates, each advocated (and opposed) by powerful constituencies in the glare of the mass media. This fragmentation is exacerbated by innumerable ad hoc restrictions—statutory deadlines and "hammer clauses," court orders and consent decrees, and others—by which these constituencies have sought to force EPA's priorities and decisions toward their preferences.[20]

Risk assessment provided a common denominator—human health risk—by which the administrator could rationalize and defend the administrative decisions he must ultimately make across these many mandates and constituencies. Lacking any unified framework or criteria in statutes, the administrator in effect used risk assessment to *create* such a framework, justified by the common-sense virtues of reasonableness, consistency, and scientific objectivity.

Assistant administrator Milton Russell argued in a 1987 article, for instance, that risk balancing was the only alternative to a much cruder and more fragmented approach, in which priorities were set mainly by historical accident and political influence, and regulatory remedies were limited to requiring specific technologies to clean up individual media (ignoring, for example, the risks that might be increased by moving pollutants from water to land or land to air).[21]

Political Tool

At least as important as its managerial value, however, was the political value of risk assessment. It gave the EPA administrator a powerful new way to control the agenda of environmental regulatory debates on terms favorable to EPA.

An important antecedent to EPA's risk assessment requirements was the earlier requirement of cost-benefit analysis by the Bureau of the Budget (now the Office of Management and Budget), as a framework for evaluating proposed water resource projects. Like environmental regulations today, water resource projects had become subject to highly politicized ad hoc decision making, though usually in the form of pork-barrel lobbying for them rather than media campaigns or lawsuits against them. Like risk assessment, cost-benefit analysis was mentioned but not formalized in the relevant statutes; it was adopted by the executive branch as a means of administrative management and agenda control.[22]

By requiring that each proposed action be justified through a detailed quantitative reasoning process, cost-benefit analysis gave OMB administrators a powerful weapon against both lower-level program advocates and external political forces—Congress and the media as well as businesses and environmentalists—which tended to seek particular decisions regardless of their comparative merits. Like risk assessment, the substantive assumptions and methods of cost-benefit analysis in practice were controversial and often abused. But they provided a common denominator for comparing programs and proposals, a veneer of scientific rationality, and a framework in which the most flagrantly self-interested proposals were more difficult to justify.

By the early 1980s, OMB had obtained vastly broadened authority to impose cost-benefit requirements—renamed "regulatory impact assessments"—on environmental (and other) regulatory proposals as well as water projects. These requirements shifted the terms of debate from health and environmental quality to economics, and thus significantly expanded OMB's influence on the environmental regulatory agenda—and that of the regulated businesses—at the expense of EPA.

Risk assessment made risk rather than dollars the new focus for policy analysis and a criterion by which to compare programs and proposals on terms relevant to EPA's mission and expertise. To be sure, risk assessment was also being used by practitioners in the business community as a weapon *against* aggressive regulation, by lobbying for less cautious inference guidelines.[23] But at least the debate was defined in terms of scientific issues, about which EPA's scientists could argue from strength, and on which the EPA administrator's decisions were normally accorded greater deference than in the broader domains of economics and politics.[24] Whatever its imperfections, therefore, risk assessment allowed EPA to wrap its decisions in the legitimacy and apparent objectivity of science, and in the language of health effects rather than merely economic benefits.

Risk Perception and Communication

While the use of risk assessment strengthened EPA's hand in dealing with OMB, it tended to exacerbate conflict between EPA and the general public. First, most controversies over environmental hazards turned on the question of how much evidence was needed before regulating. Public advocacy groups tend to take the stand, "If in doubt, regulate to protect health," whereas businesses say, "If in doubt, don't regulate until you have proof." From the perspective of the public, quantitative risk assessment tipped such controversies in favor of business by implicitly accepting the view that proof rather than prudence was required to justify regulations and by promoting "paralysis by analysis" in the regulatory process.

Second, the professionalization of risk assessment created a new commonality of perspective among risk "experts," who shared a technical view of risks and disdained the broader concerns of the general public as ignorant, irrational, or self-interested. Expert risk analysts frequently hold strong prejudices that their relatively narrow and specialized methods are not merely one source of relevant information, but the *only* proper basis for risk management decisions; and these value judgments themselves exacerbate public distrust of risk analysis.[25] Why are technical estimates of hypothetical cancer risks any more "real," or any more exclusively the proper basis for policy decisions, than public concerns about unanticipated leaks, spills, or plant malfunctions? About risks to their economic well-being, or about changes in the character of their community associated with industrial-waste disposal? Or for that matter, about the possibility that the estimates made by today's risk analysts may turn out to be wrong?

Most risk experts, moreover, were employed either by businesses or by the regulatory agencies themselves; and while they might disagree about technical details, most shared the attitude that as professionals they understood the issues better than the lay public. The result therefore was to create in effect a new alliance between experts in the agencies and in the regulated industries, and to redefine the issues as matters of expert reason versus the lay public's irrationality. Perhaps understandably, the public in turn tended to distrust both the jargon and the value judgments of risk assessment experts.[26]

Risk analysts have responded to this dilemma by advocating better "risk communication." Most such efforts, however, have been essentially one-way attempts to convince the public that the technical understanding of risks is the correct one. Risk communication seems unlikely to succeed until risk experts accept the legitimacy of public perceptions and concerns that go beyond their own technical definitions of risk and begin to deal with these concerns. They must accept that quantitative risk assessment is merely one useful tool, and not the overall rule, for making environmental decisions.[27]

Toward the 1990s

Risk assessment was an effective response to the environmental agenda of the 1980s, an agenda dominated by EPA's need to set regulatory priorities among large numbers of toxic chemicals and to justify regulatory decisions. It has also been useful in other settings for which space does not permit adequate discussion here: examples include regulation of drugs, cosmetics, and food additives; other consumer products; occupational health hazards; siting of industrial facilities; and the design and management of hazardous technologies. As an especially poignant example, the use of quantitative risk assessment rather than wishful subjective judgments might well have prevented the disastrous explosion of the *Challenger* space shuttle.[28]

The 1990s, however, may well bring substantial evolution in the use of risk assessment, as well as new priorities on the environmental policy agenda for which risk assessment is less useful.

Risk Science and Risk Politics

The issues of science and politics *within* risk assessment remain. EPA optimists envision a trend toward the substitution of real data, backed by scientific consensus, for the cautious assumptions and safety factors that have so far dominated risk assessments.[29] Most observers, however, and even many practitioners, are more skeptical. Beyond a few well-studied substances and health effects, data remain scarce and expensive, basic mechanisms (let alone magnitudes) of toxicity remain uncertain, and exposure patterns and confounding factors will always be too complex to identify with certainty. Interestingly, a study of EPA risk-assessment personnel found that although most of those trained in the physical or social sciences, engineering, and law favored the use of risk assessment in policy making, two-thirds of those trained in biomedical and environmental sciences—presumably those most familiar with its substance—opposed it.[30]

The politics of environmental decision making is unlikely to yield to a new era of expert authority in any case. Political pluralism is deeply rooted in the statutes and procedures of American environmental management, and the emerging direction of these procedures is toward more explicit negotiation processes among all affected parties rather than toward a return to expert authority.[31] A more likely result is that risk assessment will continue to be routinized, refined, and elaborated to incorporate additional health risks. As with cost-benefit analysis before it, however, arguments about the assumptions and inferences in risk assessment will continue to be used as surrogates for arguments about the real issues: whether particular substances or sites will be more tightly regulated, who will bear the risks and costs, and whether such decisions should be made by consensus among experts or through political negotiation.

Risk Disclosure and Liability

The greatest effects of risk assessment in the 1990s, however, may be not in justifying EPA's regulations but in forcing public disclosure and imposing financial liability on the use of toxic chemicals. Whatever its advocates' ideals, one effect of risk-assessment requirements has been to raise the burden of proof on EPA before it can regulate. For all EPA's statutory authorities and efforts for more than nearly two decades, it has actually developed regulations for only a tiny fraction of commercially used substances.

In public disclosure and liability requirements, however, the burden of proof can be reversed, forcing *businesses* to assess and manage the risks. The federal Superfund law of 1980, for example, imposed strict liability for cleanup costs on all generators of hazardous wastes; and the Superfund amendments of 1986 require public disclosure to a "local emergency planning committee" of all significant use and emissions of some 400 toxic chemicals. Both the financial liability and the unwelcome publicity associated with these disclosures provide powerful new incentives for businesses to assess the relative risks of these materials and to substitute less risky ones. In some communities, the local committees themselves are going beyond emergency response planning to negotiate with local businesses ways of reducing their use of toxic chemicals.[32]

California's Proposition 65 goes even further, requiring businesses to put warning labels on all products that contain significant levels of substances that can cause cancer or birth defects (specifically, the amount that can cause a risk of one additional cancer per 100,000 people). By 1989 some 250 chemicals had been listed, and allowable doses were being set for the fifty most widely used ones. In effect, Proposition 65 linked risk assessment to mainstream economic ideology—let the marketplace decide, but with full information—and initial industry horror stories appear to have been replaced by quiet compliance and grudging acceptance on their part.[33]

Finally, environmental groups are waging a national campaign for reduction in the use of toxic chemicals, building on the federal and California laws and others. This campaign will probably be one of the major focal points of environmental politics and policy in the 1990s. The goal of these groups is to reduce the amounts of toxic chemicals used, rather than to debate the fine points of risk assessment; but risk assessment will unavoidably be an important basis for decisions about whether substitute chemicals are less hazardous.

Risks Other Than Health

Lastly, we can expect continuing efforts to extend the concepts and methods of risk assessment to risks other than health. These efforts may or may not be successful, however; more likely they will reveal some of the limitations of risk assessment as an overall language for environmental policy analysis.

EPA's formalized emphasis on health risks has been administratively useful in that it provides a single metric as a basis for comparative evaluation. At the same time, this narrowness artificially excludes large portions of the agency's mission and responsibilities: risks of ecosystem degradation, of pollutant damage to cultural resources and esthetic values, and of other adverse effects on environmental conditions.

A key issue for environmental policy analysis in the 1990s, therefore, is whether EPA's approach to risk assessment can be extended effectively to risks other than health. If it cannot, EPA must either force-fit them into that methodology, limit its attention to those problems that *do* fit the language of risk, or retreat from its effort to define risk reduction as its all-encompassing mission.

A good example of the problem is the idea of ecological risk. The concepts of quantitative health risk assessment are derived from human toxicology and are applicable in principle to health risks to other species. One possible approach to ecological risk assessment, therefore, is to assess risks to particular species as surrogates or "sentinels" for ecosystem health as a whole, such as mussels in estuaries; research on several such possibilities is already under way.

But how does toxicity to any one species translate into risk to an ecosystem as a whole? Is there any single indicator, analogous to mortality, for the health of an ecosystem? Human actions unavoidably cause qualitative changes in the character of ecosystems, some of which may be adverse, some beneficial, and some just different (or beneficial in some respects while simultaneously adverse in others, such as damming a river to increase lake fisheries while destroying stream fisheries).

Ecosystems, in short, are too complex to be described by any single common denominator of risk. Moreover, our environmental policy purposes in ecosystems—preservation, aesthetics, recreation, economic use, and others—are also too diverse to be reduced easily to the language of risk assessment. Risk assessment can be applied to specific toxic hazards to particular species, but it cannot usefully be applied to ecosystems unless good indicators can be defined for the critical attributes of overall ecosystem "health" at the regional or landscape scale. It may even turn out that risk assessment is an inadequate conceptual framework for assessing ecosystem changes as a whole.

Comparative Risk Studies

Quantitative risk assessment is also inadequate for setting priorities among diverse *kinds* of environmental problems. An unusual study by EPA in 1987 compared the relative risks of some thirty-one environmental problems, spanning the full range of EPA's responsibilities and beyond. The study considered four different kinds of risk: cancer, noncancer health risks, ecological effects, and other effects on human welfare (for example, pollution damage to historic structures).

Significantly, this study was not a formal quantitative risk assessment, especially since both data and methodology are lacking for most noncancer risks. Rather, it was based simply on the consensus of perceptions of relative risk offered by some seventy-five EPA senior managers, and on comparisons of those perceptions with opinion poll data on perceptions held by the general public. These perceived risks were then compared with the amount of effort EPA was devoting to each problem.

The study found that the information available to assess risks for virtually any of these problems was surprisingly poor: best for cancer, though even that was spotty, but very poor for hazardous-waste sites, biotechnology, new chemicals, pesticides, ecosystems, and others. It also found that the agency's actual risk-management priorities were more consistent with public opinion concerns than with the problems EPA managers thought most serious (for example, EPA was devoting more effort to the problem of chemical-waste disposal than to indoor air pollution and radon). Third, it found that in all programs except surface water quality, EPA had been more concerned with pollution that affects public health than with the protection of natural habitats and ecosystems. Finally, it found that even with respect to public health hazards, localized hazards cause much higher risks to individuals than overall risk estimates reveal.[34]

This study was an admirably candid step on EPA's part to take stock of the relative importance of its diverse responsibilities; similar assessments have since been conducted in three of EPA's ten regions as well. The study also showed, however, both the opportunities and the difficulties of using risk as a common denominator for all these concerns. On the one hand, it used the idea of relative risk to build consensus about priorities across the patchwork of disparate statutes and programs that EPA must administer. At the same time, however, it accepted subjective managerial judgments, rather than quantitative methodology, as the basis for these priorities; and by doing so, it implicitly redefined risk to include not only quantifiable health hazards but all environmental concerns. A likely result will be to make risk assessment a more general language of political debate about environmental priorities, but to diminish its precision as a more technical procedure for health risk estimation.

Risk Management or Environmental Management?

EPA's experiment with comparative risk assessment thus brings us to the final question, namely how adequately EPA's risk assessment/risk management framework will fit the broader agenda of environmental management issues of the 1990s.

The environmental policy agenda of the 1980s was dominated by the regulation of public health risks from toxic chemicals, for which risk assessment provided a useful (if imperfect) framework for policy analysis. The agenda of the 1990s, however, may be dominated by broader questions of environmental management—waste reduction, global change, and sustainable development, for instance—for which the whole language of "risk," let alone the formalized procedures of quantitative risk assessment, may be more awkward and distracting than helpful.

Waste reduction. EPA's fragmented statutes and programs attempt to protect the environment by regulating each waste stream or destination in isolation. As a result, pollutants often are simply shifted from one place or form to another: from water to land (sludge), land to air (incineration), air to land (incinerator ash), and so forth. In 1989, therefore, EPA adopted a new policy statement emphasizing pollution prevention, by encouraging the reduction of wastes at their sources, rather than merely requiring waste treatment and safe disposal.[35]

Risk assessment provides one source of priorities and evaluation criteria for this task, asking which pollutants we most wish to reduce from the standpoint of health risk, and what alternatives are in fact safer. The real challenges for policy analysis, however, lie elsewhere. How should we define and measure waste reduction? What changes in technology, in economic production processes, and in our behavior and lifestyles would help to achieve it? And what public policy incentives—not just regulations, but economic charges and subsidies, procurement practices, and others—would most encourage it? These questions are no less important than questions of risks, but require different analyses for their resolution.

Global change. Dominating the rising environmental agenda of the 1990s is the issue of global environmental degradation, caused by the material production, consumption, and urbanization of a steadily increasing population, and in particular by increasing fossil fuel combustion. If the emerging scientific and popular consensus is correct, this complex of issues may be the greatest environmental hazard we know of, second only (perhaps) to nuclear warfare.

Is the global environment a matter for quantitative risk assessment? One can describe its degradation as a serious risk in intuitive terms, but it is hard to say what the formalized language and procedures of risk assessment would add to it. The causes are reasonably clear; the magnitudes and probabilities are imperfectly understood but serious enough to command attention; and the goal is not a finely tuned regulation, but a change in the directions of very gross trends. If we defer action until EPA can develop detailed quantitative risk estimates, these trends may progress far beyond our control, if they have not already. Instead of waiting for more quantitative risk assessment, therefore, we should seek, based on prudence rather than proof, at least to slow the trends while continuing to monitor the results.

Sustainable development. Finally, environmental management is not, and can never be, merely a matter of "reducing risks." As René Dubos has so articulately noted, we humans and our environment constantly shape each another, in beneficial and beautiful ways as well as in damaging and ugly ones.[36] To sustain environmental quality therefore requires positive action and creative vision, not merely control of risks. Where in the prevailing language of risk would one find the creative vision of environmental design? Or even the stewardship perspective of environmental conservation? On a more concrete level, where would one place the idea of rehabilitating degraded ecosystems? The vocabulary of risk assessment and risk management is too narrowly oriented toward adverse outcomes, toward health outcomes in particular, and toward regulation to provide an adequate framework for these more complex and creative tasks of environmental management.

These questions require a broader vision and understanding of the human environment—and of the range of policy instruments to be used in its management—than is captured in the conceptual framework of risk assessment. This broader vision was laid out in concept by the recent World Commission on Environment and Development, and a high priority task for the 1990s is to spell out its details and work toward its implementation.[37]

Notes

1. Curtis C. Travis, Samantha A. Richter, Edmund A. C. Crouch, Richard Wilson, and Ernest D. Klema, "Cancer Risk Management: A Review of 132 Federal Regulatory Decisions," *Environmental Science & Technology* 21 (1987): 415-420.
2. Environmental Protection Agency, *Risk Assessment and Risk Management: Framework for Decisionmaking* (Washington, D.C.: Environmental Protection Agency, 1984); *Unfinished Business: A Comparative Assessment of Environmental Problems* (Washington, D.C.: Environmental Protection Agency, 1987), 1.
3. Mark E. Rushefsky, *Making Cancer Policy* (Albany: State University of New York Press, 1986), 74-80.
4. Ibid., 59-84.
5. Milton Russell and Michael Gruber, "Risk Assessment in Environmental Policy-Making," *Science* 236 (April 17, 1987): 286-290.
6. Executive Order No. 12291, February 17, 1981; and *Industrial Union Department, AFL-CIO* v. *American Petroleum Institute,* 448 U.S. 607 (1980). As a legal matter, the extent to which quantitative risk assessment

(QRA) is required must be decided on a statute-by-statute basis; while this decision actually involved a proposed standard by the Occupational Safety and Health Administration for occupational exposure to benzene, it influenced all the regulatory agencies to put increased emphasis on QRA.

7. Vincent Covello and Joshua Menkes, *Risk Assessment and Risk Assessment Methods: The State-of-the-Art* (Washington, D.C.: Division of Policy Research and Analysis, National Science Foundation, 1985), xxiii.
8. For a historical perspective on risk assessment, see Vincent T. Covello and Jeryl Mumpower, "Risk Analysis and Risk Management: A Historical Perspective," *Risk Analysis* 5 (1985): 103-120.
9. Nuclear Regulatory Commission, *Reactor Safety Study: An Assessment of Accident Risks in U.S. Commercial Nuclear Power Plants, WASH-1400,* Report No. NUREG-75/014 (Washington, D.C.: Nuclear Regulatory Commission, 1975).
10. ENVIRON Corporation, *Elements of Toxicology and Chemical Risk Assessment* (Washington, D.C.: ENVIRON Corporation, revised edition July 1988), 9; National Research Council, *Risk Assessment in the Federal Government: Managing the Process* (Washington, D.C.: National Academy Press, 1983), 18.
11. William Lowrance, *Of Acceptable Risk: Science and the Determination of Safety* (Los Altos, Calif.: William Kaufman, 1976); National Research Council, *Risk Assessment in the Federal Government*, 1983; William D. Ruckelshaus, "Science, Risk, and Public Policy," *Science* 221 (September 9, 1983): 1027-1028; ENVIRON, *Elements of Toxicology;* William D. Ruckelshaus, "Risk in a Free Society," *Risk Analysis* 4 (1984): 157-162.
12. Example adapted from EPA, "Workshop on Risk and Decision Making," materials prepared for EPA by Temple, Barker and Sloane Inc. and ENVIRON Corporation, 1986.
13. For a list see Rushefsky, *Making Cancer Policy*, 68-70.
14. Travis et al., "Cancer Risk Management."
15. Environmental Protection Agency, "Health Risk and Economic Impact Assessments of Suspected Carcinogens: Interim Procedures and Guidelines," *Federal Register* 41 (May 25, 1976): 21402-21405.
16. *Federal Register* 51 (September 24, 1986): 33992-34054; *Federal Register* 53 (June 30, 1988): 24836-24869.
17. See Rushefsky, *Making Cancer Policy*, chaps. 3-6.
18. See, for instance, Adam M. Finkel, "Has Risk Assessment Become Too 'Conservative'?" *Resources* (Summer 1989): 11-13; and Terry F. Yosie, "Science and Sociology: The Transition to a Post-Conservative Risk Assessment Era," plenary address to the 1987 annual meeting of the Society for Risk Analysis (Houston, Texas, November 2, 1987). Dr. Yosie was then director of the EPA Science Advisory Board.
19. Finkel, "Has Risk Assessment Become Too 'Conservative'?"; John C. Bailar III, Edmund A. C. Crouch, Rashid Shaikh, and Donna Speigelman, "One-Hit Models of Carcinogenesis: Conservative or Not?" *Risk Analysis* 8 (1988): 485-497.
20. See Bruce A. Ackerman and William T. Hassler, *Clean Coal/Dirty Air* (New Haven, Conn.: Yale University Press, 1981) for a fuller discussion of the

politics of administrative decision-making processes for environmental protection.
21. Russell and Gruber, "Risk Assessment in Environmental Policy-Making."
22. Richard N. L. Andrews, "Economics and Environmental Decisions, Past and Present," in *Environmental Policy Under Reagan's Executive Order*, ed. V. Kerry Smith (Chapel Hill: University of North Carolina Press, 1984).
23. Rushefsky, *Making Cancer Policy*, 92-94; see also *AIHC Recommended Alternatives to OSHA's Generic Carcinogen Proposal* (Scarsdale, N.Y.: American Industrial Health Council, 1978), and Edith Efron, *The Apocalyptics: Cancer and the Big Lie; How Environmental Politics Controls What We Know About Cancer* (New York: Simon and Schuster, 1984).
24. Yosie, "Science and Sociology."
25. Sheldon Krimsky and Alonzo Plough, *Environmental Hazards: Communicating Risks as a Social Process* (Dover, Mass.: Auburn House, 1989).
26. Ibid.; see also Hugh Heclo, "Issue Networks and the Executive Establishment," in *The New American Political System*, ed. Anthony King (Washington, D.C.: American Enterprise Institute, 1978); and EPA, *Unfinished Business*.
27. Krimsky and Plough, *Environmental Hazards*. The "tool versus rule" issue has also been discussed in relation to cost-benefit analysis of regulatory proposals: see Richard N. L. Andrews, "Cost-Benefit Analysis as Regulatory Reform," in *Cost-Benefit Analysis and Environmental Regulations: Politics, Ethics, and Methods*, ed. Daniel Swartzman, Richard A. Liroff, and Kevin G. Croke (Washington, D.C.: Conservation Foundation, 1982).
28. Richard P. Feynman, *What Do You Care What Other People Think?* (New York: Norton, 1988), 177-188, 220-237.
29. Yosie, "Science and Sociology."
30. Robert W. Rycroft, James L. Regens, and Thomas Dietz, "Incorporating Risk Assessment and Benefit-Cost Analysis in Environmental Management," *Risk Analysis* 8 (1988): 415-420.
31. Michael P. Elliott, "The Effect of Differing Assessments of Risk in Hazardous Waste Siting Negotiations," in *Negotiating Hazardous Waste Facility Siting and Permitting Agreements*, ed. Gail Bingham and Timothy Mealey (Washington, D.C.: Conservation Foundation, 1988).
32. Frances M. Lynn, "Citizen Involvement in Using Right-to-Know Information for Emergency Planning and Source Reduction," paper presented at the annual meeting of the Air and Waste Management Association, Anaheim, California, June 25-30, 1989, paper no. 89-44.4.
33. Leslie Roberts, "A Corrosive Fight over California's Toxics Law," *Science* 243 (January 20, 1989): 306-309.
34. EPA, *Unfinished Business*.
35. EPA, "Pollution Prevention Policy Statement," *Federal Register* 54 (January 26, 1989): 3845-3847.
36. René Dubos, *The Wooing of Earth* (New York: Scribner's, 1980).
37. World Commission on Environment and Development, *Our Common Future* (New York: Oxford University Press, 1987); see also chap. 13 by Richard Tobin in this volume.

III. ENVIRONMENTAL DISPUTE RESOLUTION AND POLICY INTEGRATION

9

Environmental Policy in the Courts

Lettie M. Wenner

The logical method and form flatter that longing for certainty and for repose which is in every human mind. But certainty generally is illusion, and repose is not the destiny of man.

Oliver Wendell Holmes
Harvard Law Review 39 (1897)

The Role of Courts in Environmental Policy

In 1803 John Marshall, the chief justice of the United States, established the power of courts to oversee the constitutionality of actions by other branches of government when he declared that it is "the duty of the judicial department to say what the law is." [1] Even before Marshall made this famous pronouncement, state courts and federal courts were helping to formulate and implement public policy through their powers to interpret and enforce laws, and they continue to do so to this day. Nevertheless, some analysts argue that judges are singularly unsuited to make broad policy decisions because of their lack of expertise and the necessity for them to answer individual questions about particular cases.[2] Others caution against the dominance of technical experts and urge the continued use of lay judges to counterbalance the inequities that are certain to arise when there is an unrestrained technocracy controlling policy.[3] There exists constant tension between Americans' desire for substantively "correct" decisions reached by technical experts and for democratic decisions made through public participation and facilitated by the courts' insistence on due process.[4] Like other institutions of government, courts are caught between these two equally important values in the American polity, and they continue to struggle to reconcile them.

In the first section of this chapter I look at how developments in regulatory law have affected court practices. Next I describe criticisms of the courts' authority over technical policies and counterarguments to these criticisms. Two approaches—procedural and substantive—that judges have assumed for undertaking their new enforcement duties are compared, and the use of the courts by interest groups as well as the courts' response to them are investigated. The kind of cases that have been decided and patterns of court outcomes are described in the next section. Finally, I speculate about the issues, such as the importance of cost-benefit analysis, that are likely to be found in environmental cases in the 1990s.

The Common Law: Compensation After Injury

In the decades preceding the explosion of environmental legislation in the 1970s, the only legal control possible over people and organizations that imposed the costs of their economic activities on others came through common law concepts such as trespass, personal injury, and liability for damages caused to other people. In other words, parties injured by polluted air, water, leaking toxic wastes, or other hazards may ask the courts for compensation for the harm imposed on them as a result of a degraded environment. In such cases, however, the burden of proof customarily falls on the plaintiff, who must show that each injury is the fault of a particular polluter. This is extremely difficult to prove, as can be demonstrated by the experiences of thousands of Vietnam veterans who argued that they were damaged by exposure to Agent Orange in the 1970s, or hundreds of heirs of cancer victims who have tried to prove that tobacco smoking caused their relatives' deaths. There are simply too many other variables that may have contributed to the victims' problems for most judges or juries to assign fault for the injuries.

The relatively few victims who successfully prove that the manufacturer of a product, or the operator of a plant that dumps toxic materials into the air, water, or soil, is at fault are often dissatisfied by the outcome. From their perspective, the greatest drawback to the judicial remedy of damages is that nothing is done to change the situation in which the injury occurred. It is often cheaper for the industry creating third-party costs simply to pay damages and continue the harmful behavior. Theoretically, the fear of having to pay damages for injuries done to customers, workers, and innocent bystanders will have a chilling effect on the behavior of industrial firms inclined to manufacture products and dispose of wastes without concern for the effect these activities have on third parties. However, the uncertainty of being sued and the difficulty of establishing proof often diminish the impact of this fear.[5]

An alternative remedy to damage judgments exists in the common law in the form of equity suits that give the courts power to issue an order forcing the party causing the harm to cease doing so. All the difficulties of proof in civil law cases still exist in equity cases, however, and judges are loath to order organizations performing essential services for a community, such as operating a hazardous-waste landfill, to halt operations. The potential damage being done to third parties is often balanced against the economic good that the polluter provides; it is extremely difficult to shut down a business that is providing hundreds of jobs. It is especially difficult for a court to balance the equities in favor of a complainant when it is evident that many different polluters have contributed to a cumulative problem. Just as courts are reluctant to compensate for injuries, so too do they find it difficult to balance interests and restore equity.

Public Law: The Goal of Prevention

The common law of nuisance, trespass, and injury has proved a weak and inconsistent remedy for many problems of environmental degradation, and most proponents of resource conservation and pollution control have turned to public law as an alternative.[6] Rather than depending on the fear of a potential lawsuit after harm has been done, statutory law attempts to prevent the harm from ever occurring. By proscribing certain actions (dumping crude oil into waterways, for example) and prescribing others (for example, treating sewage before release into waterways), lawmakers hope to prevent many injuries to public health and the natural environment. By shifting legal recourse out of the realm of private law (suits between individuals and groups) and into the realm of public law (with the government as a prominent actor) policy makers hope to resolve some of the problems of proof and to redress the imbalance between the two parties in traditional common law cases. Prevention, rather than remediation, is the goal of public law.[7]

The number of statutory environmental laws intended to regulate behavior in the field of natural resource management and environmental protection grew in the 1970s, but this growth did not reduce the courts' role in such policies. Rather, it greatly increased the workload and passed some of the burden of resolving uncertainty to the courts. The proliferation of new statutory laws not only creates the need for an administrative state to enforce them, but also increases the need for courts to interpret them. The discretion of the courts grew as congressional ambiguity about policy intent and bureaucratic uncertainty about regulatory design increased. Regulatory law forced courts to make prospective decisions about the potential for harm rather than retrospective judgments about the causes of demonstrated injuries. It cast judges in entirely new roles as quasi-legislators and quasi-administrators in implementing these new laws.[8] Some commentators believe this to be a dangerous development.

Public Law Critics

Critics argue that judges are singularly unfit for making public policy choices for the people. If scientists and experts are uncertain about environmental and health risks, how likely are judges, untrained in technical matters, to understand them? These critics contend that courts are not qualified to make judgments on policy issues, whether they involve technical problems concerning nuclear power or social problems concerning education or desegregation.[9]

These critics further argue that judges, with their myopic view of individual disputes, are in no position to make broad judgments about public policy that will affect the entire nation. Given the nature of the judicial process in which individual litigants bring their grievances to court and argue their particular case, it is difficult for a judge to understand the complexity of the policy issue or to view the larger societal problems clearly. For example, a judge may agree with an organization that argues that the U.S. Environmental Protection Agency (EPA) must meet a deadline for setting toxic air emission standards specified by Congress in the Clean Air Act. EPA may strain its resources to meet that requirement and withdraw resources from other equally or more important priorities.[10] Thus, the impact of a judicial decision may have a deleterious effect on the totality of an agency's program.

Furthermore, judges must depend on the facts given to them by litigants and their advocates. They have no separate expertise in the area, and they can be misled by one side with an abundance of resources to make its case rather than a preponderance of all the evidence. Thus, the adversarial nature of the judicial process militates against an optimal solution being reached. Rather than find the best technical solution to a problem, courts are inclined to balance the equities of two sides arguing from opposite perspectives and to make compromises that may exacerbate the situation. Ironically, proponents of environmental dispute resolution argue the opposite—namely, that judges always find entirely for one litigant and are unable to reach compromise solutions between two opposing sides (see Chapter 10).

Finally, public law critics argue that courts should refrain from making public policy because they are a nondemocratic, unelected branch of government and hence not responsive to the people. Judges, these critics argue, should only adjudicate private law cases and individual disputes; they should keep out of general policy making, which should be left to the democratically elected representatives of the people or to experts in administrative agencies.

Public Law Upheld

It is possible to counter all of these arguments against the judiciary as public policy maker. First, it is unrealistic to argue that courts are not engaged in policy making when they adjudicate disputes between individuals and organizations in society. The pattern of decisions they make influences the actions of thousands of potential litigants and their legal counsel, who observe what happens in cases in which they have an interest.

Second, in the early twentieth century potential polluters recognized the inability of judges using common law to find for parties injured by the economic activities of others. Without an effective restraint on their behavior, many simply ignored any third-party costs their profit making imposed on society. The legal costs to defend a few personal injury cases were negligible compared with the substantial costs of preventing injuries. In recent years, however, some courts interpreted the law of personal injury to mean that victims of negligence should be handsomely compensated; insurance companies and other corporate defendants now complain about the patterns of court-made policy in this area. These corporate interests have turned to legislative remedies, just as environmental groups earlier asked Congress to address the inequities they perceived. Insurance companies and their corporate clients now urge state legislatures to put a cap on the damages that can be assessed against a defendant to compensate victims in personal injury cases.[11]

Third, judges must grapple with the problems of uncertainty in technical matters not because they wish to usurp the role of other policy makers, but because the latter have been unable to solve the problems themselves. It is difficult, if not impossible, for legislators to foresee all contingencies, and Congress often writes into environmental laws specific authority for courts to oversee administrative regulations. Congress has expressed its skepticism about the ability of administrative agencies to make optimal decisions, and in some laws Congress has provided authority for private citizens to take cases to the courts when they believe the administrative agencies are not fulfilling their function.[12]

This is not to argue that judicial opinions should be substituted for administrative ones. It is just as difficult for judges to determine which expert has the better arguments as it is for agency experts to make decisions about balances to be struck between costs and benefits of regulations. Experts do disagree, whether they be economists arguing about the costs of eliminating toxic pollutants from the air or biologists discussing the impact of acid rainfall on tree growth. The arguments they make can often be predicted by knowing who sponsors the research, as illustrated by the American Tobacco Institute's studies of the effect of nicotine on human lungs.

Fourth, when judges make their decisions, they admittedly do not have the priorities of the individual agencies in mind. Concerned with balancing the equities between the litigants, they are typically unconcerned about where the resources will come from to, say, investigate the impact of toxic emissions or even the cost to industry of meeting the standard. This may compensate, however, for the tendency of some agencies to drag their feet in complying with the language of the law because the political appointees at the top of the organization do not wish to carry out the mandate of Congress. Careerists in the hierarchy of the agency may, in fact, welcome judicial orders that force their superiors to allow them to proceed with their mission of writing regulations and imposing strict limits on emissions. EPA itself may be grateful when a court tells the Office of Management and Budget to cease obstructing EPA's issuance of regulations on the grounds that they are too expensive for industry to afford. Hence, the federal courts may very well serve as the gorilla in the closet that regulatory agencies in every administration need in their competition over which policies should get priority and which missions should be assigned resources to carry them out.[13]

Finally, federal judges are unelected, nonrepresentative officials in the U.S. system of government, but so too are experts in agencies to whom some critics would turn over all discretion in determining the direction of policy. In the courts those who are losing their arguments in the executive branch of government find an alternative forum to which they may bring their case. Courts perform the very important function of checking the tendencies of other branches of government long ago proposed by the Federalist judge John Marshall. They may inject a democratic element into the process by widening participation and countering the tendency to turn over too much authority to the bureaucratic state. They may also correct the tendency of elected policy makers to change the policies of their predecessors at will and overturn legislation through nonenforcement, as the Reagan administration tried to do with environmental policies in the early 1980s.

Court Oversight of Administrative Discretion

Federal judges are well aware of the new role they are being called upon to play in the field of public law and the more specific policy area of environmental law. In the traditional role as neutral arbiter of individual disputes, the judge has finished work when she or he renders a verdict preferring one party's argument over the other; but in the new role of public policy maker, the judge also must oversee how well the responsible agency carries out the court's order. In many cases the judge orders that an agency comply with the letter of the law passed by Congress by writing regulations by a certain date, issuing a permit, or even rethinking the grounds for its previous decision. Sometimes a judge must continue to exercise managerial control over the same case for years.[14]

For the period preceding the court's verdict as well, the judge's role has greatly expanded. Judges today often act as intermediaries who bring opposing parties into their chambers to work out a compromise solution before the case reaches trial. In so doing, judges' discretion and influence over policy are broadened greatly.[15] This informal role of mediator taken on by many judges helps explain the decline in the number of cases that go to trial. Although some four hundred to five hundred environmental cases are filed in federal courts each year, only about two hundred actually are adjudicated. The remainder are settled by the parties and their attorneys, often with judicial encouragement.

There has been considerable debate among the judges themselves about the direction that their oversight of administrative agency decisions should take. One former judge on the U.S. Court of Appeals for the D.C. Circuit, Harold Leventhal, argued that it is the courts' responsibility to guarantee that agencies take a "hard look" at all factors when making their decisions.[16] For agencies whose primary mission is distributing benefits or constructing public works, this hard look should emphasize environmental variables. For agencies engaged in regulating others' behavior in the name of environmental or public health values, judicial review should focus on economic considerations.

To facilitate the judges' ability to adequately review decisions made by technical experts in administrative agencies, Judge Leventhal argued that judges should have access to court-appointed scientific experts to assist them in understanding the conflicting testimony of adversarial expert witnesses. Others have argued that the United States needs, on these knotty technical issues, a specialized federal court with "unbiased" judges trained not only in legal procedures, but also in technical areas.[17] A third suggestion for increasing technical expertise in the process is for creating a "science court" composed of natural scientists to define the common ground among experts over controversies involving scientific phenomena. These panels of expert judges would not be asked to make value judgments, but would rule only on the scientific aspects of the policy.[18] Skeptics, however, doubt that it would be possible to distinguish between issues of scientific fact and value judgments. They also fear that definitive statements from a science court would stifle future debate over the same issues.[19]

Judge Leventhal himself was skeptical of separate specialized courts to try environmental cases. He believed that the selection of judges for such a court would become a political issue within the administration making the appointments. Colleagues of Judge Leventhal (for example, Judge David Bazelon of the D.C. Circuit) were skeptical of his suggestion that experts be assigned to judges to clarify uncertainties about scientific matters. Judge Bazelon's solution was to insist on procedures designed to ensure that all opinions about an issue are incorporated into the agency's decision-making process. Judge Bazelon did not dispute the complexity of the technical problems facing the courts, but he also believed that science and technology are not the exclusive domain of scientists and engineers. He argued that many cases before the courts involve major value choices that may be cloaked in technical questions, but should be open to public scrutiny and multiple-party participation. Rather than cure the problem with separate expert advisers for judges, he preferred that all contending groups have an opportunity to have their rival experts heard before administrative agencies and in court as well.[20]

Interest Group Use of Federal Courts

Judge Bazelon's desire to incorporate a pluralist competition of ideas in the judicial process has been put into practice by many interest groups concerned with environmental policy. The same interests that try to influence Congress to pass and modify environmental laws are usually active in tracking the way agencies carry out these laws. Industries as well as environmental groups actively lobby agencies whenever they set rules and regulations. Not surprisingly, the same protagonists who urged Congress to pass legislation also come before the courts to have the law enforced. Those who were disappointed in the outcomes at either the legislative or executive level have another chance to influence policy in court. Those who succeed in the legislative process rightly view this as only the first step in successful policy influence. Given the ambiguity of many of the policies made by both legislative and administrative actors, the shift to the courts for further debate over the merits of these policies is the obvious next step.[21]

Most environmental litigation is initiated by one of three primary actors. The best known are environmental groups that worked to get environmental protection and natural resource legislation passed and reformed in the 1970s. Examples are the National Audubon Society and the Sierra Club. Subsequently, these groups and newer organizations established in the 1970s, such as the Natural Resources Defense Council and the Environmental Defense Fund, sued government agencies to carry out the mandates they had been given by Congress. During the early 1970s, environmental groups made many of the initial demands on the federal courts to get environmental and natural resource laws enforced, and they were successful to some degree in having their own interpretations of the laws accepted.

More recently, business and property interests have reacted to initial environmental successes by using the same laws to challenge regulatory actions by government.[22] With their superior legal and economic resources, many major corporations have been highly successful in the courts and in some cases have outstripped environmental groups in the number and intensity of demands they have made on federal courts. It was common in the 1980s for both industry and environmental groups to simultaneously sue EPA over the same regulations it had issued for the same pollutants; one litigant claimed the regulations were too strict, while the other argued that they were too lenient.[23]

Government itself has participated on both sides of environmental issues. When challenged by environmental groups, it often represents an economic or development interest normally associated with major corporations; in these cases its arguments favor the development of natural resources and more cost-conscious regulations. When challenged by industry, on the other hand, government often represents an environmental point of view. During the 1980s the government's legal resources were nearly evenly divided in defending its actions against challenges from business and from environmental/conservation groups arguing that the government was, respectively, too strict or too lax in its regulations.

In addition, government agencies developed a considerable agenda of their own, taking on industry and private property owners in order to enforce statutory laws and the conditions of permits, and in order to halt violations of regulations. Most environmental cases could be classified into one of three modal types—environmental groups versus government, industry versus government, and government versus industry—except for those occasional cases in which government appealed against an environmental victory at the trial level.[24]

Changes in Uses of Courts

When Ronald Reagan's presidency began in 1981, it was expected that there would be fewer government enforcement actions and less need for industry to challenge regulations, which were then being made by business-oriented individuals appointed to policy positions in the executive branch. This, however, did not happen. Government prosecutions actually increased in 1981, the year that Anne McGill Gorsuch (Burford) took over as administrator of EPA. One reason for this increase was that most court cases adjudicated in 1981 were initiated earlier, probably during the last year of Jimmy Carter's administration. Careerists in the agency rushed to complete their case preparations before Carter left office, which created a surge of cases clearing the courts in 1981. Later, however, the number of EPA enforcement actions that were sent to the Justice Department dropped precipitously. After Burford was replaced as administrator by William Ruckelshaus and later by Lee Thomas, the number of referrals rose again. By 1987 environmental cases were referred in record numbers.

At least two other reasons may explain the apparent increase in government initiated cases. First, career civil servants, believing in the goals of the statutes they administered, may have tried to compensate for the reduction in staff and resources devoted to the enforcement process. Second, the increase in actual numbers may be deceptive because the number of laws under which government may sue industry increased in the 1980s. That is, referrals from EPA to the Justice Department actually may represent a lower percentage of cases in proportion to the total potential cases. Of the 372 civil cases EPA referred to Justice in 1987, only 86 were Clean Air Act cases and 123 were water pollution cases. The largest number were 143 hazardous-waste cases under laws or regulations that were not enacted until the 1980s.[25]

Industry dramatically increased its demands on the courts throughout the 1970s; individual corporations as well as trade associations hired contingents of lawyers specializing in the new field of environmental law. With Ronald Reagan as its advocate in the White House, industry in the 1980s was expected to reduce its efforts to influence policy in the federal courts, but this did not happen. In fact, industry-initiated cases peaked in 1980 at the trial level and in 1981 at the appellate level, and they fell off in the early years of Reagan's presidency. The dip was temporary, however, for by 1985 business inputs had risen again.[26]

Under many pollution control and conservation laws, it is possible to challenge administrative regulations at the appellate level without first going to trial court. The strategy of industry is that the best defense is a good offense, and it challenges most government regulations before they can take effect. In addition, industry has begun attacking state government regulations, as states have become more active in attempting to control environmental problems that they believe the federal government is neglecting.[27]

Given the pro-industry perspective of the executive branch in the 1980s, it was expected that environmental groups would be more dissatisfied with public policy than industry and would turn increasingly to the courts for redress of their grievances. This did not happen to the degree anticipated, however. Environmental groups began the 1970s by making numerous demands at both trial and appellate court levels, and these did not increase as dramatically as industry's in the late 1970s. There were normal fluctuations over the years, with a notable drop in demands made during the Carter years when environmentalists had substantial access to the White House. By the end of the 1980s environmental groups were again competing with industry for the largest number of inputs to the courts. Limited resources of environmental groups may have created constraints on the number of the cases they could afford to initiate, as compared to the number of potential cases they would have liked to bring.

Changes in Strategy for Environmentalists

Many environmental groups in recent years have changed the kind of cases they initiate, if not the number. They continue to use their traditional method of suing government for regulating too loosely, but they have added a new kind of environmental law case in which the major interests confront one another directly in court rather than suing the government as a surrogate representative of the opposing side. Congress made this possible by writing into several of the environmental laws a provision for private attorneys general. This power enables a private citizen or group to take legal action against a polluter when the appropriate agency fails to do so.

Disappointed in EPA's unwillingness to undertake enforcement actions, environmental groups have sued to force individual industries and plants to conform to the limits written into discharge permits granted them by state and federal officials. For example, in 1985 the Sierra Club sued a furnace company and two oil companies for violating their discharge permits under the Clean Water Act. Similarly, the Students Public Interest Research Group of New Jersey sued various companies (including two chemical corporations, a power company, AT&T Labs, and a thread company) for discharge violations.[28]

In this way environmental groups have been able to pursue directly their disagreements with their chief rival, industry, even when the agencies responsible for enforcing environmental and conservation laws are unwilling to play their pro-environmental role. Conservative critics label these cases "judicial activism," but the initiative clearly comes from the public, not the courts. As long as Congress continues to provide authority for private attorneys general in most of the major pollution control laws, it seems likely that the number of cases will grow in the face of benign neglect by the executive branch of government.

Types of Issues in Federal Courts

The majority of federal cases about the environment fall into seven general categories: National Environmental Policy Act (NEPA) cases in which environmental groups challenge government projects because of their deleterious impact on the environment; pollution control, including both air and water; energy issues; disputes over the use of public trust lands; threats to public health from use of toxic materials such as pesticides as well as from contamination from hazardous wastes; wildlife and wilderness protection; and state issues. The four environmental topics that have consumed most of the time of federal courts have been NEPA, pollution control, energy/public trust, and toxic materials cases, and each of these has established its own pattern of litigation over time.

During the "environmental decade" of the 1970s, many cases concerned NEPA, which requires the federal government to write an environmental impact statement (EIS) before undertaking a government-funded or regulated project, such as highway or dam construction, or permitting the operation of a nuclear reactor. Federal courts started by treating such questions very seriously, insisting that agencies should prove that they indeed had taken Leventhal's "hard look" at all such projects.[29] In addition, district and circuit court judges began fashioning stringent requirements about the kind of procedures that federal agencies must develop in order to ensure that all parties interested in projects have an opportunity to enter the process, in accordance with Judge Bazelon's desire for complete procedural protection.

By the end of the 1970s, however, the Supreme Court had narrowed the scope of NEPA by overturning many of these cases.[30] One NEPA case that generated considerable controversy was *Vermont Yankee* v. *NRDC* (1978), in which the Supreme Court overturned two District of Columbia Circuit Court decisions remanding Nuclear Regulatory Commission (NRC) decisions for inadequate treatment of environmental issues. Judge Bazelon's original D.C. Circuit decision in *Vermont Yankee* would have required NRC to consider additional issues that intervenors wanted to discuss, including conservation of energy and disposal of nuclear wastes, before issuing permits for nuclear plants.[31] Writing for a unanimous Supreme Court, Justice William Rehnquist chastised the D.C. Circuit for interfering with NRC discretion and inserting its own policy preferences for that of an expert commission. After having their decisions overturned by the Supreme Court repeatedly in the 1970s, the federal courts came to treat the writing of environmental impact statements as a paper exercise. They generally ruled in favor of government projects as long as the requirement to write an EIS had been observed. As a consequence, in the 1980s the number of NEPA cases declined dramatically as environmental groups turned their resources to pollution control issues.

Air and water pollution cases have been the most persistent topic in the federal courts' workload. Although air pollution cases constituted a modest 10 percent of environmental cases throughout the 1970s, there were nearly three times as many water pollution cases. When EPA finished writing most of its regulations on clean water and air, court challenges were expected to decline because the law of pollution control had become "settled." This did not happen, but the initiators of many of these kinds of cases did change. Government enforcement actions did go down substantially in the early 1980s, but environmental groups replaced many government actions with their own private attorneys general cases. During the Carter administration, environmental groups initiated only 20 percent of pollution control cases at the trial level, but in the Reagan years they initiated nearly 50 percent of them.

Courts have been somewhat receptive to the claim of environmental groups that they are appropriate private attorneys general to enforce pollution control statutes. When there are ongoing public enforcement actions, or when the pollution has ceased, environmental groups are unlikely to win their cases. But when there is continuing pollution and no evidence of official enforcement at either the state or federal level, the courts are willing to give private attorneys general standing and likely to decide these cases substantively for the environmental groups, even awarding them attorney's fees afterward.

Initially, there were few cases involving energy issues, but the number rose substantially in the mid-1970s because of the energy crisis. Related to energy issues are public trust cases that concern publicly owned lands located primarily in the western United States and the natural resources they contain. Timber and ranching interests as well as mining industries are eager for rapid development of these resources, and conservation groups continually try to slow this process. Although the number of cases declined somewhat in the early 1980s, energy/public trust issues now constitute an important subject for environmental cases. After the 11-million-gallon oil spill by the *Exxon Valdez* in Prince William Sound in March 1989, it appears that conflicts over exploitation of natural resources in the United States are likely to constitute an even larger portion of environmental confrontations in the future. Not only will this accident generate many civil and criminal cases under water pollution statutes, but it will influence arguments about opening up additional Alaskan wilderness areas to oil exploration. These arguments are likely to create much congressional debate in the 1990s, as well as involve the courts again in balancing risks to the environment against benefits to the economy from developing energy resources.

The type of environmental case that experienced the steepest increase in number involves toxic substances and solid-waste problems. It is in these areas of public policy that Congress has most recently legislated. In 1976 it passed the Resource Conservation and Recovery Act to control the disposal of solid wastes, including hazardous wastes. In 1980 Congress passed the Comprehensive Environmental Response, Compensation, and Liability Act (also known as Superfund) to clean up abandoned waste dumps. Whenever a law is first implemented, courts have numerous opportunities to interpret it, given the uncertainty of key actors about what the new law means. After the area of the law becomes routinized, there are fewer reasons to test it in court.

Many of the initial Superfund cases have concerned such procedural and preliminary questions as whether the defendants are entitled to a jury trial, whether and how much notice the government must give before initiating proceedings against a violation, and what the statutory limitations are for recovery of costs.[32] The Superfund legislation provides for recovery of costs from the owners and former users of abandoned waste sites, and many cases have concerned the liability of different owners and users of a site. The question normally is how to divide liability among several corporations that benefited from use of the site in the past. Courts have been willing to assess liability quite broadly on former and present operators, haulers, and users of sites in the 1980s. Some companies have gone bankrupt, and courts have divided over the question of whether costs of cleaning up such sites should take precedence over other debts owed by the same corporation.[33] One corporation often sues another to accept responsibility for its share of the damage, and federal courts have generally agreed that former property owners should share the cleanup costs, except when the owner is a government entity, in which case sovereign immunity has frequently been invoked.[34]

Patterns in Court Outcomes

Given the Reagan administration's opposition to governmental regulation, especially for the sake of environmental and conservation causes, federal court decisions in this policy area were expected to change in the 1980s. When William French Smith and later Edwin Meese headed the Justice Department, candidates for the federal bench were carefully screened for ideological purity. This presumably meant conforming not only with the administration's social policies regarding abortion and church-state relations, but also its philosophy of increasing business discretion in the marketplace and reducing government control over economic behavior. One would expect that as the decade wore on and more Reagan appointees were available to make judicial decisions, fewer environmental victories would be recorded in federal courts. Yet this did not happen.

As is expected in all areas of litigation including cases on the environment, government agencies were more successful than either their industrial or environmental opponents, and this did not change from 1970 through the Reagan era. Industry success has fluctuated over time, but business has tended to have slightly lower success rates than environmental groups except for a brief period at the end of the Carter administration. Industry ended the 1980s with lower scores than did its environmental opponents, despite the increased number of Reagan judges. Environmental groups have experienced some swings in their court success rates; their low spot occurred in 1979, before the Reagan administration took office, and since then they have improved their scores, even exceeding the government's success rate in 1985. Therefore, environmental and conservation groups have not yet lost ground in their efforts to have their demands met by courts, despite Reagan's appointees to the judiciary.[35]

A number of factors may have affected responses of federal judges to environmental cases during the 1980s. Courts are traditional organizations that follow precedents set by their predecessors. Therefore, judges with a pro-business bias may be influenced by pro-environmental precedents and hence rule less often for industry than they would if left entirely to their own preferences. Second, environmental groups may have made stiffer demands on the courts during the Carter years; believing they had an ally in the White House, they may have been willing to risk more in court. Conversely, they may have pulled in their horns in the Reagan era, making less extreme demands on the courts in order not to lose ground. A moderate victory might be viewed as better than total defeat in a hostile environment. Similarly, during a period when business interests were well represented in the executive branch, business might have escalated its demands on the courts. Federal judges are slow to change, and they may not have reacted as favorably as the executive branch.

Regional patterns in federal court decisions have remained constant. The Northeast, Midwest, and West Coast have remained favorably disposed toward environmental litigants since the 1970s.[36] Judges in the Southeast, Southwest, and Rocky Mountains have tended to favor developmental and economic causes. Interest groups, whether economic or environmental, are aware of the forums that are most favorably disposed toward their cause. Whenever they have a choice about where to raise an issue, they take their case to the court most likely to agree with them.[37]

The Supreme Court in the 1970s was less receptive to environmental claims than were the lower federal courts, and this division widened in the 1980s. The lower courts were trained to rule positively on governmental regulations during the 1960s, following the precedents of the liberal Court under Chief Justice Earl Warren. When the Supreme Court began its turn to the right in the early 1980s, the lower courts did not immediately follow its lead, and they now seem out of step in civil rights and economic regulatory cases.

Projections for the 1990s

The Supreme Court today is a more conservative institution than it was in the 1970s. It became more pro-business during the early 1980s under the leadership of Chief Justice Warren Burger, and since 1986, when William Rehnquist became chief justice, it has become even more conservative. It is also a divided court, with some justices vigorously opposed to their colleagues' views with regard to risk assessment and the usefulness of cost-benefit analysis in environmental and other policies (see Chapters 7 and 8).

Two cases in the area of worker protection during the Burger Court illustrate this division. Although not environmental, these cases are closely related to many pollution control and toxic materials cases because they involve questions about the need to balance the costs of keeping contaminants out of the environment against the benefits obtained by avoiding risks to human health or to ecological systems. In 1977 the Occupational Safety and Health Administration (OSHA) set strict standards for workers' exposure to benzene. The American Petroleum Institute immediately challenged the new regulations in the U.S. Court of Appeals for the Fifth Circuit in New Orleans, known for its pro-business point of view. The appeals court agreed with business that the estimated risks to workers were not worth the costs to industry to avoid them. In 1980 the Supreme Court upheld this ruling in a 5-4 decision. A plurality headed by Justice John Paul Stevens and including pro-business Justices Lewis Powell and Potter Stewart, and Chief Justice Burger argued that OSHA had failed to prove that significant benefits, in the form of decreased risks to the health of workers, would accrue from the regulation.[38] It is normally easier to show how much a control technology will cost than it is to demonstrate the level of risk a given contaminant poses for humans or other species.

Justice William Rehnquist agreed with the plurality's ruling, but went further, arguing that the Congress had overdelegated its legislative power (in this case to OSHA), an argument seldom heard in the Supreme Court since the 1930s when a very conservative court overturned numerous New Deal laws regulating the economy. Four dissenters—Justices Thurgood Marshall, William Brennan, Byron White, and Harry Blackmun—wrote stinging rebuttals, accusing their colleagues of usurping the regulatory function to allow industry's costs to override concern for workers' safety.

In 1980 Judge Bazelon in the D.C. Circuit, known for his concern for environmental and health matters, upheld cotton dust standards set by OSHA, and this too was challenged in the Supreme Court. This time the Supreme Court upheld the agency's decision by a 5-3 vote on the grounds that the law (the same law as in the benzene case) did not mandate cost-benefit justification.[39] Three of the majority justices in the benzene standard case (Stewart, Rehnquist, and Burger) became the dissenters in this case. Justice Stevens moved from his position in the previous case and voted in favor of the regulation of cotton dust. The majority opinions written by Justice Brennan and joined by Marshall, Blackmun, White, and Stevens, said that no cost-benefit analysis was necessary since the agency had shown that 25 percent of all workers in the industry suffered from a disease caused by inhalation of cotton fibers. Justice Rehnquist continued to make his argument that Congress had overdelegated its authority to OSHA, and in this he was joined by Justice Burger. (Justice Powell took no part in the case.)

Since 1980 cost-benefit analysis and its companion concept, risk assessment, have become even more important in the public discussion of health and environmental issues. President George Bush in 1989 urged Congress to consider costs to industry in making any changes in the Clean Air Act. Although there have been changes on the Court since the cotton dust decision, these changes are not likely to alter the balance on the Court on this issue. Justices Stewart and Powell were replaced by Justices Sandra Day O'Connor and Anthony Kennedy. Chief Justice Burger's vote has now been replaced by that of Justice Antonin Scalia (who technically replaced Rehnquist on the bench when he became chief justice in 1986). The three new Reagan appointees are equally, if not more, protective of business interests than their predecessors were. Justice Scalia has opposed even well-established antitrust regulations on the grounds that they inhibit free enterprise. Justice O'Connor has expressed her willingness to defer to the technical expertise of agencies such as the Nuclear Regulatory Commission, but it remains to be seen whether she will defer to the judgment of agencies more likely to regulate stringently on technical issues related to the environment.

Only the three oldest justices—Brennan, Marshall, and Blackmun—consistently favor public health values over economic interests. The balance of power in these matters is held by Stevens, a moderate, and White, who appears increasingly influenced by the new conservative majority. Any new justices appointed by President Bush could give a solid majority to the conservatives. Aware of its pro-business climate, environmentalists have made few appeals to the high court in recent years.

One other issue that is likely to find its way to the Supreme Court in the 1990s is state regulation of economic activity, as states try to fill the void left by lack of federal enforcement. Two conservative justices, Rehnquist and O'Connor, have been labeled states' rights judges in the past primarily because of their willingness to allow states to regulate on social issues such as abortion. They are much less supportive of states' desires to regulate economic behavior and have become less so since Justice Scalia joined the Court. In 1987, for example, Rehnquist and O'Connor joined Justice Scalia's opinion that the California Coastal Zone Commission could not force owners of beachfront property to provide public access to the ocean in exchange for a permit to rebuild their houses. The justices based their argument on the Fourteenth Amendment to the U.S. Constitution, which prohibits the taking of property without due process of law.[40] Justices Brennan, Marshall, and Blackmun, who all support a woman's right to an abortion, vigorously dissented from the California case. In the 1990s it can be expected that the Court's conservative majority will solidly oppose any state's regulation of economic behavior, while the liberals will oppose state control of individual behavior. Lower court judges appointed by Reagan and Bush are likely to follow the lead of the conservative majority on the Supreme Court.

The increasingly conservative composition of the judiciary may be offset, however, by countertrends that could affect the role of the courts. First, in revising the Clean Air Act and other major laws in the 1990s, Congress may restrict, or at least clarify, the use of cost-benefit and risk-benefit standards. For example, it could amend Section 111 of the Clean Air Act, which requires economic impact statements for new regulations, to state whether the intent of this section is (a) to require that benefits from risk reduction equal the costs to industry, (b) to allow EPA to set limits at its own discretion without cost-benefit analysis, or (c) to require EPA to set minimum pollutant levels without regard to cost.

Second, there is a more general trend toward negotiated rule making and alternative forms of dispute resolution (see Chapter 10). Many environmental disputes are now settled out of court, with or without judicial supervision. This trend is likely to continue given the high costs of litigation, the Bush administration's encouragement of voluntary mediation, and the increased unwillingness of industry and environmental groups to prolong cleanup controversies.

A final complicating factor is the internationalization of environmental disputes. As more policies are adopted pursuant to international treaties and agreements, the role of U.S. courts in interpreting and administering environmental standards may diminish. However, American courts may face an increasing volume of cases brought by foreign parties who seek to challenge U.S. policies that affect their operations. How the courts will respond to such challenges remains to be seen.

Conclusion

The judicial branch has played a major role in the development and implementation of environmental policies in America. This reflects the unique role of the courts in the U.S. political system and a cultural tendency to turn every dispute into a legal one. It also reflects the scientific complexity of environmental policy, inevitably characterized by conflicting evidence and disputes among experts. The institutional capacities of the courts to rule on technical controversies have been widely questioned, but no consensus on alternative procedures for resolving them has emerged. One lesson of this chapter is that courts have been better able to resolve disputes than they are commonly given credit for. The courts themselves have increasingly encouraged litigants to reach negotiated settlements that can be formalized through consent decrees, but it is not likely that they will be able to avoid making many critical policy decisions in the future. As to the charge that this is undemocratic, it must be remembered that litigation can allow for greater public participation in making policies, as Judge Bazelon advocated. The judicial process represents an important antidote to the tendency to allow a transient majority's policy preferences to rule. The continuing conflict between the need for technical expertise and certainty, on the one hand, and for public participation and democracy, on the other, is not likely to end soon. The courts will continue to strike a balance whenever one principle threatens to overcome the other.

Notes

1. *Marbury* v. *Madison*, 5 U.S. (1 Cranch) 137; 2 L.Ed. 60 (1803).
2. Donald L. Horowitz, *The Courts and Social Policy* (Washington, D.C.: Brookings Institution, 1977); and R. Shep Melnick, *Regulation and the Courts* (Washington, D.C.: Brookings Institution, 1983).
3. Lawrence Tribe, "Policy Science: Analysis or Ideology?" *Philosophy and Public Affairs* 2 (1972): 56; and Joel Yellin, "High Technology and the Courts: Nuclear Power and the Need for Institution Reform," *Harvard Law Review* 94 (1981): 489.
4. Martin Shapiro, "On Predicting the Future of Administrative Law," *Regulation* (May/June 1982): 18-25; and David M. O'Brien, *What Process Is Due?* (New York: Russell Sage Foundation, 1987).
5. Lettie M. Wenner, *One Environment Under Law* (Pacific Palisades, Calif.: Goodyear, 1976), 7-9.
6. Joseph L. Sax, *Defending the Environment* (New York: Knopf, 1971); and Norman J. Landau and Paul D. Rheingold, *The Environmental Law Handbook* (New York: Ballantine, 1971).
7. James Willard Hurst traced the law's development from common law in the nineteenth century through the development of public laws to regulate individual behavior for the common good. See Hurst, *Law and Social Order in the United States* (Ithaca, N.Y.: Cornell University Press, 1977). Also see Norman Vig and Patrick Bruer, "The Courts and Risk Assessment," *Policy Studies Review* 1 (May 1982): 716-727.
8. Among those who applaud this development are Hurst, *Law and Social Order;* and Abram Chayes, "The Role of Judges in Public Law Litigation," *Harvard Law Review* 89 (1976): 1281-1316.
9. Nathan Glazer, "Toward An Imperial Judiciary?" *The Public Interest* 41 (1975): 104-123; and Horowitz, *The Courts and Social Policy.*
10. In *Sierra Club* v. *Gorsuch*, 18 ERC 1549 (1982), a federal district court in California forced EPA to set radioactive nuclides standards, which may have taken attention away from other types of priorities EPA had under the Clean Air Act. See Melnick, *Regulation and the Courts.*
11. The National Legal Center for the Public Interest was founded in 1975 by the corporate defense bar to argue for reducing personal injury awards and to oppose any expansion of public law. *Annual Report* (Washington, D.C.: National Legal Center for the Public Interest, 1987).
12. Abram Chayes, "Foreword: Public Law Litigation and the Burger Court," *Harvard Law Review* 96 (1981): 4-60.

13. In 1986 a federal district court in Washington, D.C., told OMB to stop delaying standards for hazardous-waste disposal. See *EDF* v. *Thomas*, 23 ERC 1922 (1986).
14. See, for example, the Reserve Mining case, which dragged on for seven years. Robert V. Bartlett, *The Reserve Mining Controversy* (Bloomington: Indiana University Press, 1980).
15. Judith Resniak, "Managerial Judges," *Harvard Law Review* 96 (1982): 374.
16. Harold Leventhal, "Environmental Decisionmaking and the Role of the Courts," *University of Pennsylvania Law Review* 122 (1974): 509-555.
17. The Clean Water Act of 1972 went so far as to order the U.S. attorney general to investigate the feasibility of establishing a separate court or court system to try environmental cases. This proposal was rejected by the attorney general in 1973. *Report of the President Acting Through the Attorney General on the Feasibility of Establishing an Environmental Court System* (Washington, D.C.: U.S. Government Printing Office, 1973).
18. The science court's primary spokesperson is Arthur Kantrowitz, chairman of Avco Everett Research. See Arthur Kantrowitz, "Controlling Technology Democratically," *American Scientist* (1975): 505; and Arthur Kantrowitz, "Science Court Experiment," *Trial* 13 (March 1977): 48-49.
19. James A. Martin, "The Proposed 'Science Court,'" *Michigan Law Review* 75 (April/May 1977): 1058-1091; and A. D. Sofaer, "Science Court: Unscientific and Unsound," *Environmental Law* 9 (Fall 1978): 1-27.
20. David L. Bazelon, "Coping with Technology Through the Legal Process," *Cornell Law Review* 62 (1977): 817-832.
21. Lettie M. Wenner, "Interest Group Litigation and Environmental Policy," *Policy Studies Journal* 11 (1983): 671-683.
22. Lettie M. Wenner, *The Environmental Decade in Court* (Bloomington: Indiana University Press, 1982).
23. In 1980 EPA issued consolidated permit regulations that enable an industry to obtain one permit to conform to the Clean Water Act, the Safe Drinking Water Act, the Clean Air Act, and the Resource Conservation and Recovery Act. The Natural Resources Defense Council challenged these regulations as too lenient. Industrial groups (including the Chemical Manufacturers Association, American Iron and Steel Institute, Edison Electric Institute, and the American Petroleum Institute) and individual corporations (including Exxon and Republic Steel) challenged them as too strict. Various groups filed protests in different federal circuit courts. In 1981 the D.C. Circuit took jurisdiction over all of these consolidated cases. See *NRDC* v. *EPA*, 15 ERC 1157 (1981).
24. Data for this analysis come from cases published by the Bureau of National Affairs, which since 1970 has reported environmental cases in its *Environmental Reporter—Cases* (ERC). In addition, environmental cases were searched for in the West Publishing Company's two reporter systems for official federal cases: the *Federal Supplement* (for trial cases) and the *Federal Reporter—2d Series* (for appellate cases). This resulted in a universe of more than 3,000 cases. For a more comprehensive discussion of the coding of these cases, see Lettie M. Wenner, *The Environmental Decade in Court*.

25. B. Dan Wood, "Principals, Bureaucrats, and Responsiveness in Clean Air Act Enforcements," *American Political Science Review* 82 (March 1988): 213-234; and Philip Shabecoff, "EPA Announces '87 Record in Legal Actions on Pollution," *New York Times*, December 8, 1988, 12.
26. In 1986, for example, Phillips Petroleum Company objected to the regulations passed by EPA under the Safe Drinking Water Act concerning the injection of petroleum wastes into deep wells for disposal. See *Phillips Petroleum* v. *EPA*, 25 ERC 1033 (1986).
27. For example, in 1986 the Potomac Electric Company challenged the state of Maryland's hazardous-waste law regulating the method of disposing of polychlorinated biphenyls in the state on the grounds that federal toxic substances regulations should have preempted any state controls. See *Potomac Electric* v. *Sachs*, 24 ERC 1200 (1986); 25 ERC 1215 (1986).
28. *Sierra Club* v. *Hanna Furnace Corp.*, 23 ERC 1910 (1985); *Sierra Club* v. *Kerr-McGee Corp.*, 23 ERC 1685 (1985); *Sierra Club* v. *Union Oil Company of Calif.*, 23 ERC 1487 (1985) and 25 ERC 1801 (1987); *SPIRG* v. *American Cyanamid*, 23 ERC 2044 (1985); *SPIRG* v. *Hercules, Inc.*, 23 ERC 2081 (1986); *SPIRG* v. *Jersey Central Power*, 24 ERC 1627 (1986); *SPIRG* v. *AT&T Laboratories*, 23 ERC 1201 (1985) and 24 ERC 1996 (1986); and *SPIRG* v. *Anchor Thread Company*, 22 ERC 1150 (1984).
29. The high point of the Supreme Court's acceptance of this doctrine came in *Citizens to Preserve Overton Park* v. *Volpe*, 401 U.S. 402 (1971). The Supreme Court in this decision agreed with the lower federal court that the Department of Transportation had exercised too much discretion in deciding to take a public park in order to build a highway under the Federal Aid Highway Act of 1968.
30. In *Kleppe* v. *Sierra Club*, 427 U.S. 391 (1976), the Supreme Court decided that an environmental impact statement (EIS) is not required until there is some final federal action to review. In *Andrus* v. *Sierra Club*, 442 U.S. 347 (1979), the Court continued to narrow the scope of NEPA by agreeing with the executive branch that the budget process was exempt from EIS requirements regardless of its impact on the environment. See James M. Koshland, "The Scope of the Program EIS Requirement: The Need for a Coherent Judicial Approach," *Stanford Law Review* 30 (1978): 767-802. *Andrus* reduced substantially the precedential value of *Calvert Cliffs* v. *AEC* (1972), through which the D.C. Circuit had influenced many agencies to prepare EISs early in order to use those documents in planning. *Kleppe* also reduced the scope of EISs because it allowed the Department of Interior to write environmental impact statements for *each* area to be strip mined without considering the cumulative impact of many strip mining projects in one region.
31. James F. Raymond, "A *Vermont Yankee* in King Burger's Court: Constraints on Judicial Review Under NEPA," *Boston College Environmental Affairs Law Review* 7 (1979): 629-664; Richard Stewart, "*Vermont Yankee* and the Evolution of Administrative Procedure," *Harvard Law Review* 91 (1978): 1805-1845; and Katherine B. Edwards, "NRC Regulations," *Texas Law Review* 58 (1980): 355-391.

32. *U.S.* v. *Charles George Trucking Company,* 24 ERC 1812 (1986); *U.S.* v. *Carolina Transformer Company,* 25 ERC 1644 (1987); and *U.S.* v. *Dickerson,* 24 ERC 1875 (1986).
33. *U.S.* v. *Maryland Bank and Trust,* 24 ERC 1193 (1986); *In Re: Wall Tube and Metal Products,* 24 ERC 2010 (1986).
34. Sovereign immunity can be invoked by state governments, which argue that citizens of a state cannot sue the state itself. *N L Industries* v. *Kaplan,* 24 ERC 2127 (1987); *Sterling* v. *Velsicol Chemical Company,* 24 ERC 2017 (1986); and *City of New York* v. *Exxon Corp.,* 24 ERC 1361 (1986).
35. Lettie M. Wenner, "The Reagan Era in Environmental Litigation" (Paper delivered at the annual meeting of the American Political Science Association, Washington, D.C., 1988).
36. Lettie M. Wenner, "Contextual Influences on Judicial Decision Making," *Western Political Quarterly* 41 (March 1988): 115-134.
37. Thomas O. McGarity, "Multi-Party Forum Shopping for Appellate Review of Administrative Action," *University of Pennsylvania Law Review* 129 (1980): 302-376.
38. *Industrial Union Department AFL-CIO* v. *American Petroleum Institute,* 100 S.C. 244 (1980); and William H. Rodgers, Jr., "Judicial Review of Risk Assessments: The Role of Decision Theory in Unscrambling the Benzene Decision," *Environmental Law* 11 (1981): 301-320.
39. *Textile Manufacturers Institute, Inc.* v. *Donovan,* 425 U.S. 490 (1981).
40. *Nollan* v. *California Coastal Zone Commission,* 107 S.C. 3141 (1987).

10

Environmental Dispute Resolution: The Promise and the Pitfalls

Douglas J. Amy

A hunter in the woods encountered a huge bear. As he took aim, he heard the soothing . . . beguiling voice of his prey: 'Isn't it better to talk than to shoot? What do you want? Let's negotiate.'

Cradling his weapon, the hunter said, 'I want a fur coat.'

'Good,' said the bear agreeably. 'That's negotiable. I only want a full stomach. Let's be reasonable.'

So the two traditional adversaries sat down together and negotiated. After a time, the bear walked away alone. He had his full stomach and the hunter had his fur coat.

—Joey Adams (1983)

One of the most intriguing developments in environmental politics in the 1980s was the increasing interest in environmental dispute resolution (EDR). This new approach to environmental controversies, which emphasizes cooperation and consensus building, seemed at odds with the stormy and confrontational style of environmental politics that typified the Reagan era. During those years, public attention was focused primarily on the intense political conflicts generated by the Reagan administration's dramatic changes in environmental policies and priorities, especially as they were pursued by zealous appointees like James Watt and Anne Gorsuch (later Burford). Even during that time of increasing polarization in environmental politics, the movement promoting cooperative techniques such as environmental mediation was growing quietly but steadily.

As administrator of the Environmental Protection Agency (EPA) in the early 1980s, William Ruckelshaus supported several experiments with environmental dispute resolution in his agency and confidently declared that this innovative process "had almost transcendent importance in the future of our country's dealing with problems like the protection of the environment." [1] Not everyone is this enthusiastic. Indeed, some in the environmental community are decidedly suspicious of EDR, fearing that what is described as cooperation may be more akin to cooptation. Nevertheless, it is clear that this approach has become a political option that will have to be taken seriously by those involved in environmental conflicts. This chapter offers a brief overview of EDR, examines the cases for and against this new approach, explores its deeper political implications, and considers what role it may have in the environmental politics of the 1990s.

History and Use of EDR

Broadly speaking, "environmental dispute resolution" describes any effort to use informal, face-to-face negotiations and consensus building to resolve disputes over environmental issues. In most cases, a neutral mediator brings together the various interests involved in a dispute (business people, environmentalists, citizens, government officials, and so on) and they attempt to fashion a compromise upon which everyone can agree. Environmental dispute resolution generally is offered as an alternative to litigation, an approach commonly used to resolve environmental disputes. In this sense, EDR is part of a larger alternative dispute resolution movement in the United States, a movement that also includes divorce mediation, landlord-tenant mediation, and neighborhood dispute mediation. This larger movement sees itself as a response to the tendency of Americans to overuse the courts as a way of settling disputes (see Chapter 9). The United States, it is argued, has become a "litigation happy" society. As former chief justice Warren Burger put it, Americans have "an almost irrational focus—virtually a mania—on litigation as a way to solve problems." [2] In the environmental area, it is argued that this mania has resulted in overcrowded courts, long delays, exorbitant expenses, and poor environmental decisions. Informal techniques such as environmental mediation are thought to be the solution to these problems.

The first attempts at environmental mediation began in the mid-1970s, when environmental litigation seemed to be growing at an alarming rate. These first efforts were pioneered by Gerald Cormick and Leah Patton of the Office of Environmental Mediation at the University of Washington. After initial successes involving flood control and an interstate highway, interest in this new nonconfrontational approach began to grow.

By 1980, a number of environmental mediation programs had been established around the country, often funded by grants from the Ford Foundation or the Hewlett Foundation. These programs offered mediation services as well as workshops and training courses. Many, such as the Public Disputes Program at the Harvard Law School, also became centers for research. There are now environmental mediation organizations or mediators in fifteen states. This increased availability of mediators led to growth in the number of mediated disputes, which rose from four cases in 1977 to thirty-six cases in 1984. As the following table illustrates, during the period from 1974 to 1984, 182 environmental disputes were handled by mediators or facilitators, with a claimed success rate of 78 percent.[3]

Year	Number of cases
1974	1
1975	2
1976	2
1977	4
1978	11
1979	19
1980	30
1981	19
1982	25
1983	33
1984	36

Source: Gail Bingham, *Resolving Environmental Disputes: A Decade of Experience* (Washington, D.C.: Conservation Foundation, 1986), 29.

In its early years, environmental dispute resolution was used mostly on an ad hoc basis, primarily in unique, site-specific disputes. Between 1974 and 1984, 75 percent of the EDR cases were of this kind.[4] Typically, a local controversy would emerge over a development issue, such as a proposal to build a new shopping center, and after the dispute had dragged on for a period of time someone eventually would think of inviting a mediation organization or mediator to help resolve the conflict. A wide variety of controversies have been addressed in this manner, including disputes over parks and open space, sewage treatment, fishing rights, mine reclamation, airport noise, wetlands protection, timber management, water quality, and hazardous-waste siting. As illustrated in Table 10-1, EDR has been most useful in land-use controversies and natural resource management issues.

In recent years, however, there has been an effort to move away from these ad hoc uses of EDR and to begin to "institutionalize" this process—that is, to build dispute resolution mechanisms into various

Table 10-1 Primary Issues at Stake in Environmental Dispute Resolution Cases, 1974-1984

Issue	Number of cases
Land use	
Parks, landfills, highways, annexation, wetlands protection, hazardous-waste siting, sewage treatment, agricultural land preservation, etc.	86
Natural resource management	
Fishing rights, mining, logging, offshore oil drilling, wilderness, public land management, white water recreation, etc.	33
Water resources	
Water quality, water supply, flood protection, thermal effects	17
Toxics	
Asbestos, pesticides, hazardous materials cleanup, regulation of chemicals under the Toxic Substances Control Act, etc.	16
Energy	
Hydropower, coal conversions, nuclear energy, geothermal energy, regional energy policy, etc.	13
Air quality	
Odor, stationary source emission control, acid rain	13

Source: Gail Bingham, *Resolving Environmental Disputes: A Decade of Experience* (Washington, D.C.: Conservation Foundation, 1986), 32-33.

environmental decision-making processes so that EDR may be used on a regular basis. For example, several states, including Massachusetts, Rhode Island, Texas, Virginia, and Wisconsin, have passed legislation authorizing or even requiring negotiations over disputes involving the siting of solid-waste or hazardous-waste facilities.[5] There is also an effort being put forth to use EDR more often in resolving general policy and regulatory issues, rather than limiting its use to one-time, site-specific issues. For instance, on the federal level, legislation was introduced in Congress in 1988 that would authorize federal agencies like EPA to use mediation as a formal part of their rule-making process.[6] Instead of agency personnel drafting prospective rules and regulations on their own, they would invite representatives of environmental groups, businesses, and other interested organizations to join them in designing a rule that would satisfy all the various interests—and thus attempt to avoid court challenges later on. This approach, known as negotiated rule making or regulatory negotiation, may have a major impact on environmental administration and may become the most common use of EDR in the future.[7]

As environmental dispute resolution has become a more established part of environmental politics, the debate concerning the merits of this approach has increased. While EDR has a number of enthusiastic supporters among environmentalists, business groups, and government officials, it also has its share of vocal critics. It is useful to examine the arguments offered by both sides, not only because they help us understand the advantages and disadvantages of this new approach, but also because these arguments can shed some light on the nature of the divisions that currently exist in the environmental community, and can give us an indication of where the environmental movement may be headed in the 1990s.

The Case for EDR

When advancing the case for EDR, most proponents begin by pointing out the shortcomings of litigation as a method of resolving environmental conflicts. It is often argued that since an ever-increasing number of environmental disputes end up in court, this merely adds to the burden of a seriously overcrowded judicial system. Some proponents maintain that "the courts simply can't handle the load [of new environmental cases]." [8] But court overcrowding is just one of the potential drawbacks of overreliance on litigation to resolve environmental conflicts. Critics of litigation also cite several other serious problems with litigation that make EDR a more attractive alternative.

EDR Is Faster and Cheaper than Litigation

One of the most frequent complaints about litigation is the long delay before a final decision is made. Even in the best of circumstances, litigation tends to take place at a leisurely pace. The crowded court dockets in many jurisdictions often slow the process even more. It is not unusual for environmental cases to take months to come to trial, and the trials themselves can take several months more. The losing parties often file an appeal, or they may initiate more litigation on a different legal issue or in a different jurisdiction. In the end, it may take years to resolve an environmental dispute through litigation.

The Storm King Mountain case in New York State is often cited as an example of how extreme this type of situation can become. The controversy began in 1963 when Consolidated Edison proposed to build a pump storage power plant at the base of Storm King Mountain on the Hudson River. The proposal was vigorously opposed by environmental groups and the ensuing dispute was in and out of the courts and various regulatory agencies for almost seventeen years. It was not until 1979, when a mediator was called in, that a successful compromise agreement put an end to the dispute. The mediation process was a lengthy one—a year and a half—but it succeeded where almost two decades of litigation had failed.[9]

Litigation delays entail a number of disadvantages for those involved in these cases. One major problem is the sheer expense of prolonged court battles. Lawyers' fees and other legal expenses can add up very quickly and become a substantial burden to environmental groups, especially small, local organizations. Such groups may find that litigation depletes funds needed for other important activities, such as public education campaigns. In some cases, the litigation expense may become so prohibitive that it acts as a barrier that prevents some groups from pursuing their interests in court.

Court delays often exact other costs on litigants as well. In the case of developers, inflation may raise construction and capital costs while their projects are delayed; they may also have to carry the costs of partially completed projects. Environmentalists may also be thwarted by delays, especially if environmentally destructive practices are allowed to continue during litigation. For example, it was discovered in the late 1960s that the Reserve Mining Company was dumping large amounts of environmentally hazardous material into Lake Superior; the dumping continued for more than a decade as the company fought the case through various levels of state and federal courts. Environmental interests may also be hurt by long delays in the implementation of important environmental regulations caused by the inevitable court challenges from affected industries. Such challenges are commonplace. It has been estimated that 80 percent of environmental regulatory decisions are appealed in court, either by industries that believe the rules are too stringent or by environmental groups that believe them to be too lax.[10]

These frustrating delays and burdensome costs prompted many to search for alternatives to litigation, and this eventually led them to embrace EDR. For example, in a speech at the 1983 meeting of the Chemical Manufacturers Association, Louis Fernandez, chairman of the board of the Monsanto Company, proclaimed that it was now time for business people, government officials, environmentalists, and concerned citizens to "discard old, combative ways of thinking and acting" and "try cooperation instead of confrontation." This new approach should be embraced, he argued, because "the alternatives of continued bickering, continued pulling and tugging at the regulatory agencies, and finally, continued litigation are simply more expensive than any of us can afford and more time-consuming than the public will tolerate."[11] Thus, for many advocates of environmental dispute resolution, the main attraction of mediation is that it "can provide conflict resolution for environmental disputes less expensively, in terms of time and money, than can litigation."[12]

EDR Resolves the Real Issues in a Dispute

The other major complaint about litigation, besides time and expense, is that it often fails to address and resolve the real issues at stake in environmental conflicts. This may be the strongest argument made by proponents of EDR. The real source of an environmental conflict often cannot serve as the legal basis for a court challenge. Environmentalists are not free to bring a developer to court simply because they disagree with a certain project. They must have specific *legal* grounds on which to challenge the project. But often the only legal grounds available are quite different from the issues that are at the heart of the dispute.

A National Institute for Dispute Resolution study concluded that "lawyers may have to reframe the issues separating the parties to fit a particular legal doctrine, and thus may change the nature of the dispute. As a result, the court is often not able to address the real issues and tailor an appropriate remedy." [13] For example, many of the suits brought by environmentalists must be legally grounded in the National Environmental Policy Act or the Administrative Procedure Act. These acts stipulate certain procedures that developers and government officials must follow. Thus to challenge projects in court, environmental groups must usually do so on procedural grounds, such as the failure of developers to provide an environmental impact statement or their failure to complete an adequate one. While the real substantive issues in the dispute may be quite different—centering on the specific environmental impacts of the project—the only *litigable* issues are the procedural ones.

When the courts focus on legal and procedural issues instead of the substantive issues, the likely result is a decision that fails to resolve the controversy. Even when an environmental group wins a court case challenging an environmental impact statement, the decision usually only forces the developer to complete a new one. What the group really wants, and does not get, is the abandonment or severe modification of the project, and so the battle over the project usually continues.

In contrast, environmental dispute resolution is designed to identify and resolve the real issues at stake in a dispute. Mediation efforts are informal and flexible, and mediators encourage the participants to move beyond the legal questions and address the real sources of the conflict. It is argued that once participants sit down for face-to-face discussions and are able to share information and talk about their concerns, they often find that the real issues in the dispute are quite different from the ones they had imagined. Indeed, they may find that the controversy has been caused largely by miscommunication and misunderstanding and that it is not nearly as formidable as first thought. For instance, the Homestake Mining Company, which owned the rights to a large deposit of uranium ore in the Gunnison National Forest in Colorado, proposed to build a mine there that was one mile long, one-third mile wide, and seven hundred feet deep. Local environmental groups became concerned with the problem of reclamation and vigorously opposed the project. A legal battle went on for four years before a mediation team was called in. Once the parties were able to get together for joint sessions, the environmentalists quickly found that Homestake was willing to negotiate over how to best reclaim the land—not *whether* to reclaim it, as the environmentalists had feared. As a result, after one year of negotiations, the two sides were able to agree on such things as specific standards for mine-site water quality, desired levels of backfilling after the uranium was extracted, and the measures of success for revegetation efforts.

Proponents of mediation argue that many environmental controversies are like this example and that they could be cleared up simply by better communication between the parties. Informal discussions without lawyers or other intermediaries often allow disputants to move beyond misleading preconceptions of the conflict and to undermine their stereotypes of each other; as a result, much of the conflict itself often dissolves as well. As one mediator explains, "At least half of the conflicts we see occur because people did not have access to accurate information, or had no mechanism for talking with the other side (or sides). These 'unnecessary' conflicts could have been avoided if people had had some mechanism for talking candidly with each other." [14]

The uranium mine example illustrates another advantage that EDR has over litigation: it allows for compromise agreements that satisfy the interests of all the parties involved. In contrast, the court process is necessarily an adversarial one and the decisions handed down are of the "win-lose" variety: One party wins and the other loses; one party is found right and the other party is found wrong. As Lawrence Susskind and Jeffrey Cruikshank have observed, "Unfortunately, the courts are often unwilling (and in many instances, unable) to fashion remedies that meet the needs of all sides. Simply put, the court's purpose is to interpret the law, not to reconcile conflicting interests." [15] As a result, court decisions rarely end a conflict. Win-lose decisions merely encourage the losing party to keep pursuing its case through appeals or through other legal actions. In contrast, EDR is explicitly designed to facilitate the search for "win-win" solutions: creative compromises that fulfill the needs of all the parties involved and thus actually resolve the conflict for good.

Creating Win-Win Solutions

For many mediators the creation of these win-win agreements is the key to successful negotiations, and much of the mediation literature focuses on how such agreements can be fostered. It is often pointed out, for example, that win-win solutions are only likely to be found if the parties first abandon their tendency to see their conflict in moral terms: good versus bad, right versus wrong. When disputants assume that they are right and their opponents are wrong, they tend to dig in their heels and reject compromises. Why should they compromise with an opponent who is wrong? For this reason, mediator Gerald Cormick encourages parties to abandon moral definitions of disputes and to see them instead as conflicts of interests. He explains that it is best to see environmental disputes as products of "legitimate differences in priorities among persons with varying perspectives and divergent aspirations. These differences cannot be dealt with in terms of 'right' and 'wrong'—all are 'right' or legitimate concerns."[16]

Obviously it is much more palatable to bargain over one's interests than to compromise one's morality. Once disputants begin to see their conflicts in terms of interests, this clears the way for the creative trade-offs and compromises that constitute the win-win approach. In the case of the Homestake mine, once environmentalists could get beyond their image of the mining company as an immoral despoiler of pristine land, they realized that there was room to bargain over the extent and standards of land reclamation. Roger Fisher and William Ury, two leading theorists in dispute resolution, argue that another crucial step in creating win-win solutions is the realization that while parties in a dispute may have *different* interests, these interests are not necessarily *conflicting* ones.[17] To appreciate this distinction, it is helpful to consider the parable of the two sisters and the orange: Two sisters quarreled over an orange. Each wanted the orange and was unwilling to share it with the other. They argued and yelled and threatened violence. Only after their mother arrived and began asking questions did it become clear that the conflict was quite unnecessary. It turned out that one sister wanted the orange to make orange juice while the other sister wanted only the peel in order to make marmalade. The point is that while the sisters had different interests, those interests were not incompatible, and this allowed for the creation of a compromise that satisfied them both.

Mediators often see environmental disputes as being like the conflict over the orange. Given the initial positions of the disputants, there appears to be a direct conflict between them. But a more careful examination of the basic goals of the two sides reveals that these goals are not necessarily incompatible and that there are grounds for a compromise agreement. In the case of the Homestake mine, it was possible both to have a mine and to adequately reclaim the land. Consider another case: the controversy that developed over a U.S. Forest Service proposal in 1976 to allow logging in the Francis Marion National Forest in South Carolina. Environmentalists opposed the logging on grounds that it would disturb the last known nesting place of the Bachman's Warbler, one of the rarest North American songbirds. The dispute heated up and became entangled in a long, expensive court battle. Finally a mediator was called in. After several months of dialogue, field trips, and research, an agreement was reached that satisfied the basic goals of each side: lumbering would be permitted, but not in the bottom land areas that served as nesting places for the warblers.

Proponents of EDR argue that many environmental disputes are not necessarily zero-sum games where developers and environmentalists only gain at the expense of each other. As Susskind and Cruikshank have observed, "Most public disputes are not of the zero-sum variety, even though they may be framed that way at the outset. All too often, disputants conclude that there is nothing to trade simply because they have not been thinking along those lines." [18] Thus, once a mediator can get disputants to think in this manner, they are likely to find that there indeed are creative compromises that can satisfy the needs of both environmentalists and the business community.

Economic Growth and Environmental Protection

The vision of compatibility between economic and environmental interests is ultimately the most intriguing feature of the EDR movement. Much of the excitement surrounding this alternative approach is based on the promise that both vigorous economic development and stringent environmental protection are possible. This point was stressed by former interior secretary William Clark in a 1983 speech to environmentalists. He maintained that "there is no inherent conflict between our major goals and concerns: environmental, economic, energy, agricultural, social," and that "the greatest mistake environmentalists can make is to forget that housing, agriculture, and industry are also part of the environment." He concluded that "it should be recognized by all concerned that without wise economic development of resources we cannot provide the jobs and products to meet social and environmental goals." [19] Echoing this theme in his book, *Business and the Environment: Toward Common Ground*, Kent Gilbreath argues that the emergence of EDR marks a new stage in environmental politics, where business leaders and environmentalists now acknowledge the legitimacy of each other's concerns and recognize the importance of cooperation.

> In recent years, there has been a conspicuous "reaching out" to one another by the environmental and business communities. The debate between the two groups no longer centers on whether the environment should be protected but rather on how best to do so most efficiently. . . .
>
> A new generation of corporate executives educated in social responsibility now hold[s] the reins. A new generation of environmen-

> tal leaders, whose emphasis is more technocratic and issue oriented, act[s] from the need to work with, not against, the business community.[20]

This, then, is the fundamental political message underlying environmental dispute resolution: If the various sides in these controversies would abandon their adversarial postures and sit down and talk with each other, then they would recognize that cooperative and consensual approaches will allow for creative compromises that often will enable all sides to achieve their basic goals.

The Case Against EDR

At first glance, it is difficult to see why anyone would criticize the environmental dispute resolution approach. Why would anyone be against such desirable things as cooperation, communication, and win-win solutions? Nevertheless, there are critics of this process and they have three general areas of complaint: first, that many of the EDR advocates' criticisms of litigation are exaggerated and inaccurate; second, that EDR may work more to the advantage of business groups than environmentalists; and third, that EDR fosters a distorted understanding of the nature of environmental conflicts.

EDR Is Not Faster or Cheaper

As noted earlier, much of the case *for* EDR is actually a case *against* litigation. But the complaints about litigation may not be nearly as strong as many proponents of EDR purport. Consider, for example, the claim that the courts are becoming overwhelmed with environmental litigation and cannot cope with an ever-increasing caseload. The evidence contradicts this assertion. While there was a sharp rise in the number of environmental cases on the federal level in the early 1970s, research indicates that the volume of environmental litigation leveled off in the mid-1970s and has even declined somewhat since then. The number of suits filed in U.S. district courts under any environmental statute dropped from 519 in 1978 to 456 in 1983.[21]

In addition, it is not clear whether EDR has been faster than litigation. While proponents of EDR usually cite anecdotal evidence of individual environmental court cases that dragged on for years before they were resolved by mediation, there have been no systematic studies that demonstrate that mediation efforts are typically faster than litigation. The best study of this claim was conducted by Gail Bingham of the Conservation Foundation, and even this leading exponent of EDR could find little reliable evidence for this claim. She was forced to conclude that "it is the *threat* of protracted litigation, not the length of the standard case, that creates the popular conception that mediation is faster than litigation."[22]

Similarly, there is little evidence that mediation is cheaper than litigation. Indeed, there is reason to believe that it could often prove more expensive. Mediation is often not a substitute for litigation, but goes on at the same time. Thus, additional expenditures in attorneys' fees or mediators' salaries may be required. Moreover, even when mediation does substitute for litigation, it may be more expensive. As David Doniger of the Natural Resources Defense Council has pointed out, the research required to adequately participate in regulatory negotiation efforts and the time involved in travel and negotiation sessions can often use up much more of an organization's resources than other approaches, such as submitting comments or filing a brief challenging a regulation in court.[23] And while federal provisions often allow environmental groups to recoup attorneys' fees, this option is usually unavailable in mediation efforts.

Problems of Access in EDR

Critics of EDR argue that it does not, in fact, have many of the advantages it claims, and that it has some hidden disadvantages, especially for environmental groups. One such disadvantage centers around the problem of access to mediation efforts. Proponents of EDR portray it as a new form of citizen participation open to all who want to participate, but it is not clear whether such equal access exists in practice. Mediators usually play the pivotal role in deciding who is invited to participate, and they often opt to keep the number as small as possible to facilitate the process of coming to an agreement. Unfortunately, one of the criteria often used to choose participants is power. Powerful groups with the ability to block potential agreements are invited, while less powerful groups are left out. As one mediator explained, "One of the reasons that mediation works is that it is usually limited to people that have some impact on the situation. I don't ask people who don't have clout to participate in the mediation. This is not public participation, this is cloutful people's participation."[24]

The groups that tend to get left out in this approach are the less powerful or less organized citizen and environmental groups, particularly those on the local level. Some have argued that this is exactly what happened in the negotiation efforts used by the Wisconsin state legislature on several environmental issues. These efforts, called the "consensus process," used informal study groups made up of state legislators, administrators, and representatives from various interest groups to fashion environmental legislation. However, a survey of more than seventy participants and observers revealed that less than one-quarter saw the process as being open to all interests. The following comments were typical: "Some with legitimate interests were left out of the process and denied genuine opportunity to participate"; "Groups that have little political power are often systematically left (kept) out of the process"; "In effect, the consensus process disenfranchises some citizens."[25] In a situation such as this, where groups with legitimate interests are left out, the fairness and legitimacy of any agreements coming out of the negotiation process are inevitably undermined.

Imbalance of Power in Mediation Efforts

Even if the problem of unequal access were to be eliminated, the disparities in power that exist among the various participants could also create serious problems in the negotiation process itself. One of the assumptions underlying mediation is that it works best when there is a balance of power among the participants—that such a balance is necessary to ensure fair and equitable agreements. But in practice there are often substantial power imbalances among the parties, and this can give some parties important advantages at the negotiation table.

Power imbalances can take many forms. One is an imbalance in negotiating expertise. Mediators suggest that any intelligent citizen can effectively participate in a negotiation effort. Unlike the courts, with their complicated legal procedures that require extensive legal expertise, mediation is often portrayed as simple and straightforward: One merely sits down and talks directly with one's opponents. In reality, however, negotiating is a highly sophisticated and complicated art, and those who are good at it have spent years mastering a large body of knowledge and the many tricks of the trade. Because of this, there is always the danger that novices can be "taken to the cleaners" by more experienced and wily opponents. In environmental mediation, it is often the environmental and citizens groups, especially local ones, who are the novices. In contrast, business groups usually have access to professional negotiators with years of experience in contract or labor negotiations. As J. Walton Blackburn has pointed out, these inequities in negotiating expertise, coupled with the disarmingly informal atmosphere of many negotiation sessions, may lead some parties to agree to unjust settlements—settlements they would not have accepted in a more adversarial setting.

> The internal dynamics of environmental mediation are completely different [from] the courtroom context. Participants in mediation often develop bonds of trust, understanding and even affection, toward their opponents. The climate of understanding and progress in working toward mutually satisfactory solutions creates subtle pressures to be reasonable and conciliatory. These dynamics may undermine the

> determination of unsophisticated parties to stand their ground on issues. . . . The parties with less experience and sophistication may walk away with an agreement which favors their perspective much less than would have been possible in a more public, adversarial context.[26]

Another form of unequal expertise that may be even more problematic in environmental mediation is scientific and technical expertise. Scientific and technical questions play a crucial role in almost every environmental dispute. The disputes often center on the exact environmental effects of certain pollutants or development activities. This puts a premium on expertise and research, and can give the advantage in negotiations to those groups that can best mobilize those resources. The groups best able to collect and analyze the pertinent data are inevitably in a more powerful position at the bargaining table.

Again, this advantage often goes to business and industry. They typically have the necessary economic resources, the in-house staff, and the outside consultants to produce volumes of research to support their position on a particular dispute. Even more important, industry often has sole access to proprietary technical information about industrial processes to which environmentalists and the government are not privy. The result of this imbalance in expertise is, as one conservationist put it, that "environmentalists who get involved in mediation are certainly outmanned and perhaps even intimidated. It is clearly a mismatch when it comes to being able to counter the industries' side when they have a wealth of information, computer models, and analysts."[27]

In short, despite the appearance of EDR as being a purely informal process where people sit down to talk as equals, in reality it may be no different from other political decision-making processes in which the special interests with the most power and resources have substantial advantages. These imbalances raise important questions about how fair the negotiation process is and whether the resulting decisions are equitable and promote the public interest.[28]

Support for EDR from Questionable Quarters

Another aspect of EDR that makes the environmental community nervous is the nature of the organizations that have supported this approach. Some of the earliest financial backers of EDR were in the business community. Atlantic-Richfield provided the seed money to start Resolve, one of the first centers for environmental dispute resolution. Other corporations, including Dow Chemical, U.S. Steel, and Union Carbide, have invested money in promoting this approach. This corporate endorsement is grist for the mill of critics of EDR. It suggests that this approach is serving the interests of business rather than environmentalists.

If EDR does confer on business groups the advantages discussed above, it would be easy to see why they would be interested in promoting this approach. Perhaps more important, some critics see EDR as part of a corporate campaign to delegitimize environmental activism and to distract environmentalists from the courts, the scene of many important environmental victories. For instance, Samuel Hays suggests that business has supported EDR because the process carries with it an implicit criticism of activists who try to use the courts to protect the environment.

> The idea of environmental mediation was strongly supported by the business community, as well it might be. . . . Its initial point of departure often was a focus on the litigation citizen environmentalists had generated, which was described as excessive. The atmosphere around environmental mediation continued to be one of criticism of citizen action rather than of the business community. On the whole it helped to bolster the corporate drive to discredit public environmental initiatives.[29]

To be fair, it should be noted that the strongest supporters of environmental dispute resolution include not only members of the business community, but also members of the environmental community. However, a careful look at the environmental groups that have endorsed this approach does little to quell the suspicions of critics of EDR. Only a few environmental organizations have been unabashedly enthusiastic about EDR, and they are generally considered to be the most conservative politically. The leading environmental exponent of EDR has been the Conservation Foundation in Washington, D.C. The Conservation Foundation has not only engaged in mediation efforts itself, but has also sponsored conferences and workshops on EDR, and it publishes the leading newsletter on environmental mediation, *Resolve*. The Conservation Foundation has never been a strong activist organization and has always had unusually close ties with business and industry. It is not a public membership organization, and instead has relied heavily on grants from foundations and corporations for its operating funds. In 1984, for example, almost 20 percent of its revenues came from gifts from such corporate sponsors as Atlantic Richfield, Mobil, Conoco, Exxon, Gulf Oil, Shell, Standard Oil, IBM, Monsanto, Du Pont, Crown Zellerbach, General Electric, R. J. Reynolds, Phillip Morris, Weyerhaeuser, Alcoa, Union Carbide, and others. Few other environmental groups rely so heavily on business support, especially from companies with questionable environmental records. These kinds of ties with business have aroused the suspicions of some environmentalists. These critics note that the Conservation Foundation has at various times supported increased environmental deregulation, the use of cost-benefit analysis, and the substitution of incentives rather than penalties in environmental regulations—all positions that have been part of the political agenda of business in the 1980s.[30] Thus the support of EDR from this kind of environmental organization has done little to reassure those who find the process politically questionable.

The Deeper Debate

While supporters and critics of environmental dispute resolution continue to disagree over such things as how cheap it is, whether there are significant power imbalances, and whose interests it serves, it is important to see that these arguments are only one part of the debate. The controversy over EDR is often a surrogate for a much more fundamental debate that is going on in environmental politics and in the environmental movement itself. That debate has to do with conflicting conceptions about the nature of our environmental problems and differing views concerning what environmental politics is all about. These deeper disagreements provide much of the fuel for the debate over EDR.

As previously discussed, EDR carries with it a number of significant assumptions about the nature of environmental problems and environmental politics. EDR assumes that (1) most environmental disputes have little to do with conflicting values or principles; (2) many disputes are the fault of misinformation, mistaken preconceptions, and poor communication; (3) all disputants have equally valid interests and concerns; (4) compromise is usually the best outcome in disputes; and (5) the interests and goals of business and environmentalists are fundamentally compatible. If these assumptions are correct, then it is certainly possible for environmental politics to become a less adversarial activity—to evolve into a largely cooperative search for creative compromises that satisfy all parties.

Many critics of EDR do not share these assumptions, however, and have a quite different view of environmental problems and environmental politics. They see the EDR vision of environmental politics as misleading and dangerously naive. For them, environmental disputes have little to do with miscommunication, but instead are rooted in fundamental conflicts of interest, values, and principles. For example, many environmentalists see environmental issues as having a strong moral dimension.[31] They see environmental destruction and pollution as immoral and unethical and often call for a new environmental ethic to substitute for the domination and abuse of nature they see inherent in the Western worldview. Indeed, the compelling moral dimensions of environmental issues often motivate people to become environmental activists in the first place. Such activists would naturally be suspicious of an approach like EDR, which suggests that they should abandon their moral judgments and acknowledge that the positions of industrial polluters are as legitimate as their own.

This vision of environmental issues as revolving around matters of principle, moral or otherwise, causes environmentalists to question another assumption of EDR: that compromise is always a desirable approach to resolving these disputes. Consider a situation where environmentalists are fighting for a basic principle, such as the protection of wilderness areas from economic development. A negotiated agreement that allows some limited mining of resources in those areas with proper environmental safeguards is not seen by these environmentalists as a "win-win agreement" or a "reasonable compromise." Instead, it is seen as a dangerous capitulation that sets a precedent for further exploitation. As one environmental lawyer has argued, there are simply some issues where if one agrees to negotiate and compromise over them at the very beginning, one has already lost much of the battle.

> There are some cases where the chance to negotiate equals giving up what you're fighting for. There are some absolutes in the world and I think lawyers are just going to have to flat-out fight to preserve them. I disagree that there are always going to be negotiations. There *are* going to be some ultimate decisions, but it should be clearly recognized that there are times when you just can't negotiate, because some things in the world are non-negotiable.[32]

If many environmental issues are of the nonnegotiable type, then it would follow that a more aggressive and adversarial form of environmental politics should be practiced. This vision of environmental politics would embrace litigation, and would celebrate, rather than criticize, the win-lose style of decisions handed down by the courts because this allows for the complete vindication of the environmental position.

Many environmentalists, especially those on the left, would also question the assumption that business and environmental interests are fundamentally compatible. Many see basic contradictions between business and environmental priorities. It is often argued that industries will always be reluctant to incur the extra costs associated with environmental protection because this will cut into profits and undermine the competitiveness of individual firms. In this sense, business has a strong interest in continuing to pollute the environment, and thus will not change this behavior unless forced by legislation, litigation, or regulation.

Other environmentalists have suggested that the principle of an ever-growing economy is also at odds with environmental values—that such an economy will inevitably have to exploit ever-greater amounts of natural resources and produce increasing amounts of pollution. Interestingly, it is not only environmentalists who assume this kind of incompatibility; many in the business community share this assumption. Despite the claims of EDR advocates that business leaders now embrace environmental concerns, there is evidence to the contrary. The business community's all-out political campaign in the 1980s to prevent the passage of new environmental legislation and to roll back enforcement of regulations already enacted could be seen as an indication that many still believe that environmental protection measures are at odds with their interests. In any case, if one believes that there are fundamental contradictions between business and environmental requirements, then one will look skeptically upon the notion that environmental disputes can be resolved simply through better communication.

These differing assumptions about the nature of environmental problems often form the basis for disagreements about the desirability of EDR efforts. When environmentalists criticize specific mediation efforts, their complaints often focus not so much on questions of cost or imbalances of power, but on how mediation and mediators tend to foster a misleading and mistaken understanding of what is at stake in these disputes. It is alleged that the central issues and principles are often ignored or downplayed in an effort to encourage an agreement. For example, in a dispute over a mining operation in northern Wisconsin, one local environmentalist complained that the negotiations tended to ignore the most fundamental questions involved. "None of the fundamental policy issues concerning mining were ever discussed in the [negotiating process]. Attention was diverted from such basic questions as 'Do we need this mine—here and now—and if so why?' to focus on details of after-the-fact mitigation: 'How do we make this mine nice?' "[33] In another case, in a mediation effort in Colorado concerning water use, one observer charged that the effort ignored the most basic and pressing issue: the problem of growth.

> They all got together and one of the first things they decided was that we all have to realize that we're not going to get into the subject of growth, that we're not going to get into the idea of trying to limit diversion because we don't think that more people should be there. . . . But what good environmentalist would sit there and say that we should have as many people as could possibly be stacked in the middle of the desert in Colorado and supply them with all the water they need[?] Growth is part of the environmental problem there. . . . So already from their initial operating principle they narrowed the scope of the issue to the advantage of the development interests and the water exporters and to the disadvantage of the environmentalists.[34]

As examples such as these make clear, the deeper disagreements about the foundations of environmental problems and environmental disputes often separate critics and supporters of EDR. While it is true that it makes the mediator's job easier to assume that there are no basic conflicts of values, principles, or interests in a dispute, for many environmentalists this constitutes a dangerous distortion of what environmental issues are all about.

EDR in the 1990s

Despite its controversial nature, environmental dispute resolution has begun to establish itself as a force on the environmental scene. It remains to be seen, however, just what role it will eventually come to play in environmental politics in the 1990s. Many EDR enthusiasts believe it is the wave of the future and that the 1990s will be the decade of environmental cooperation. Some even predict that by 1995 more environmental disputes will be mediated than litigated.[35] Yet, it is far from clear that this will be the case. There are, in fact, several factors that could work to limit the use of EDR. Many observers believe that this technique is only likely to work in limited circumstances—where certain conditions make it likely that negotiations will be successful. The necessary conditions that are most often mentioned include:

- a balance of power exists between the disputants;
- the dispute does not center on disagreements over basic values or principles;
- no legal precedents or fundamental policy issues are at stake;
- there is no substantial disagreement among the parties as to the relevant facts of the case;
- only a small number of interests or affected parties are involved;
- none of the parties will benefit from delay or stalemate.[36]

Obviously, these kinds of conditions are not likely to exist in many environmental disputes. Most environmental controversies become serious disputes precisely because they *do* involve such things as disagreements over basic values and policies, substantial disagreement over the facts, a large number of affected parties, and so on. Acknowledging this, the dean of environmental mediators, Gerald Cormick, has concluded that the above conditions would only be met in about 10 percent of environmental disputes.[37] Thus, if this technique were to be limited to situations in which it was appropriate, it would seem destined to play only a relatively small role in environmental politics in the 1990s.

There are, however, a number of political forces at work that could increase the use of EDR in the 1990s. First, there is the movement to institutionalize the use of EDR by making it a formal stage in many state and federal decision-making processes. For example, some officials believe that mandatory negotiations may be the best way to approach the "Not In My Back Yard" (NIMBY) type of environmental issue. NIMBY issues typically include such things as where to locate facilities to store nuclear waste or to dispose of hazardous waste—decisions that must be made by officials but that are likely to face vehement local opposition. As EDR proponents have noted, mediation techniques can help government officials to better manage and overcome public opposition.

> Environmental conflict will be less disruptive to agency decision making if officials learn to use conflict management tools like conciliation, facilitation, and mediation. . . . [Conflict management] should not be confused with more requirements for public participation. The key word is *management*. In cases where public groups are fighting with the Federal government, better conflict management means better control of the participation process.[38]

In this vein, several states now encourage or require local areas to negotiate over the siting of new hazardous- and solid-waste disposal facilities. By requiring local towns to engage in these negotiations, government officials hope to defuse the confrontational atmosphere and overcome the opposition of local officials and citizen activists. Not surprisingly, however, many local areas have viewed these negotiation efforts with suspicion and some have refused to take part. Nevertheless, as these NIMBY issues proliferate in the 1990s, we are likely to see increased interest by state and federal governments in using EDR to manage and quell local opposition.

On the federal level, there is also a movement to promote "negotiated rule making"—the effort to incorporate negotiations among government administrators, business groups, and environmentalists into the rule-making process in agencies like EPA. This effort received a large boost with the appointment of William Reilly as head of EPA in the Bush administration. Reilly had been president of the Conservation Foundation, and is a leading proponent of EDR techniques and increased cooperation between environmentalists and business. He is likely to make EDR techniques a central part of his administration. He has pointed with pride to the fact that President Bush has endorsed a policy of "no net loss" of wetlands, a proposal that was developed in a Conservation Foundation forum that brought together environmentalists, industrialists, and developers.[39] Reilly's emphasis on dialogue and negotiation would seem to blend well with President Bush's desire to mend fences with environmentalists and his administration's move toward a more low-key, nonconfrontational style of politics.

Nevertheless, the increasing use of EDR in federal environmental agencies like EPA may not please everyone in the environmental community, especially those who fear that an emphasis on EDR could further weaken the political aggressiveness of EPA. Many environmentalists want EPA to be a strong advocate for environmental values and policies; they do not want it reduced to the role of a "neutral broker" trying to fashion consensus agreements between business and environmentalists. Whatever the outcome, it is clear that Reilly's appointment has been a boost for the EDR movement that will lead to increased use of these techniques, at least in the short term.

Finally, the fate of EDR depends heavily on which direction the environmental movement is headed in the 1990s. Since mediation remains a largely voluntary process, the frequency of its use depends heavily on its degree of support in the environmental community. Many proponents of EDR believe that the environmental movement has reached a new stage, one which recognizes the need to abandon old adversarial approaches and embrace more cooperative ones. As Kent Gilbreath has explained:

> A decade ago the urgent task of awakening people to the dangers posed by a lack of environmental policies may well have required intransigence and direct conflict. Under the circumstances, loud voices may have been the only way to dramatize the issues. Now, having aroused the nation's concern, most environmentalists recognize the need to embrace more constructive and cooperative tactics. . . . Some environmentalists, of course, still see the business community as the enemy, believing the only proper relationship with business is adversarial. Fortunately, uncompromising, adversarial attitudes are waning in the mainstream of the national environmental movement.[40]

If this is an accurate prediction of the future direction of the environmental movement, then it is likely that cooperative techniques such as environmental mediation will indeed come to play a more common part in environmental controversies. However, not all environmentalists agree with this vision of the future of the movement. In fact, the 1980s witnessed the rebirth of a more militant and confrontational approach to environmental issues, led by such grass-roots organizations as Earth First!, Greenpeace, and Citizens Clearinghouse for Hazardous Waste. Some in the environmental community resent that the large, established environmental organizations, such as the Sierra Club, the National Wildlife Federation, and the Environmental Defense Fund, have become increasingly bureaucratic, staff-dominated, and Washington-oriented. As Dick Russell has observed:

> Many local [environmental] groups fear, with some cause, that the well-heeled organizations lobbying in Washington are too ready to compromise with both governmental agencies and corporate polluters. For thousands of men, women and children living hard by toxic waste sites or polluted rivers, the time for deals and the half measures they produce is long past. This is reflected in the growing number of mass demonstrations and even civil disobedience actions by desperate citizens plagued by unsafe air and drinking water.[41]

This growing tension between the establishment and the activist factions in the environmental movement was illustrated vividly in the bitter dispute that erupted over control of Friends of the Earth in 1986. The internal battle came to a head over a proposal to move the organization's headquarters from San Francisco to Washington, D.C. Some members saw this move as symbolizing the "abandonment of gritty grass-roots organizing in favor of glitzy Washington lobbying." [42] Clearly, many of these new environmental militants believe that the true strength of the environmental movement resides in grass-roots organizing and that the movement needs to become revitalized through a new commitment to activism and militancy. If this more activist wing of the environmental movement continues to gain political momentum in the 1990s, it is likely that EDR, with its preference for accommodation, will remain at the periphery of environmental politics.

In any case, it is clear that environmental dispute resolution has now gained a foothold in environmental politics and that it is here to stay, in one form or another. Whether that is a desirable development, and whether this approach should take center stage or be relegated to the wings, will continue to be debated. It will be worthwhile to monitor the future development of EDR, not simply because of the controversy surrounding it, but also because the fate of EDR will give some important clues about the path that environmentalism and environmental politics are likely to take in the 1990s.

Notes

1. William D. Ruckelshaus, "Transcript of Remarks of William Ruckelshaus to the Conservation Foundation's Second National Conference on Environmental Dispute Resolution, October 1, 1984" (Washington, D.C.: Conservation Foundation, 1984), 1.
2. "Debunking Litigation Magic," *Newsweek*, November 21, 1983, 98.
3. Defining just what constitutes a "successful" mediation result is often a difficult task. Usually an effort is considered a success merely if agreement is reached and no attempt is made to evaluate the substance of the agreement. For a discussion of how the 78 percent success-rate figure was derived, see Gail Bingham, *Resolving Environmental Disputes: A Decade of Experience* (Washington, D.C.: Conservation Foundation, 1986), 65-89.
4. Ibid., 32-33.
5. Ibid., 51-54.
6. U.S. Congress. Senate. Committee on Governmental Affairs. *Negotiated Rulemaking Act of 1988*. 100th Cong., 2d sess., 1988. S. 1504.
7. For more material on the theory and practice of negotiated rule making, see Philip J. Harter, "Negotiating Regulations: A Cure for the Malaise?" *Georgetown Law Review* 71 (October 1982): 1-118; Lawrence Susskind and Gerald McMahon, "The Theory and Practice of Negotiated Rulemaking," *Yale Journal of Regulation* 3 (1985): 133-165; Henry H. Perritt, Jr.,

"Negotiated Rulemaking in Practice," *Journal of Policy Analysis and Management* 5 (Spring 1986): 482-495; and Daniel J. Fiorino, "Regulatory Negotiation as a Policy Process," *Public Administration Review* 48, no. 4 (July/August 1988): 764-772.

8. Jay Hair, "Winning Through Mediation," in *Business and the Environment: Toward Common Ground,* 2d ed., ed. Kent Gilbreath (Washington, D.C.: Conservation Foundation, 1984), 529.
9. For more detail on the Storm King Mountain controversy, see Allan Talbot, *Settling Things: Six Case Studies in Environmental Mediation* (Washington, D.C.: Conservation Foundation, 1983), chap. 1.
10. Mark E. Rushefsky, "Reducing Risk Conflict by Regulatory Negotiation: A Preliminary Evaluation" (Paper delivered at the annual meeting of the American Political Science Association, Washington, D.C., August 28-31, 1986), 4.
11. Louis Fernandez, "Let's Try Cooperation Instead of Confrontation," in Gilbreath, *Business and the Environment,* 514, 519.
12. J. Walton Blackburn, "Environmental Mediation as an Alternative to Litigation," *Policy Studies Journal* 16, no. 3 (Spring 1988): 563.
13. National Institute for Dispute Resolution, "Paths to Justice: Major Public Policy Issues of Dispute Resolution" (Washington, D.C.: Department of Justice, 1984), 10.
14. Susan Carpenter quoted in Kai N. Lee, " 'Neutral' Interveners in Environmental Disputes: An Analytic Framework" (Seattle: University of Washington Institute for Environmental Studies, 1982), mimeo, 32.
15. Lawrence Susskind and Jeffrey Cruikshank, *Breaking the Impasse: Consensual Approaches to Resolving Public Disputes* (New York: Basic Books, 1987), 9.
16. Gerald Cormick, "Mediating Environmental Controversies: Perspectives and First Experiences," *Earth Law Journal* 2 (1976): 215.
17. Roger Fisher and William Ury, *Getting to Yes: Negotiating Without Giving In* (Boston: Houghton Mifflin, 1981) esp. chap. 4.
18. Susskind and Cruikshank, *Breaking the Impasse,* 245.
19. Quoted in Douglas J. Amy, *The Politics of Environmental Mediation* (New York: Columbia University Press, 1987), 65.
20. Gilbreath, *Business and the Environment,* 445, 447.
21. Bingham, *Resolving Environmental Disputes,* 133-134.
22. Ibid., xxvi.
23. See David Doniger's comments in *Dispute Resolution Forum,* January 1986, 9.
24. Quoted in Amy, *The Politics of Environmental Mediation,* 134.
25. Quoted in ibid., 136.
26. Blackburn, "Environmental Mediation as an Alternative," 569.
27. James Benson, telephone interview with the author, November 17, 1981.
28. See Fiorino, "Regulatory Negotiation as a Policy Process," 769.
29. Samuel Hays, *Beauty, Health, and Permanence: Environmental Politics in the United States, 1955-1985* (New York: Cambridge University Press, 1987), 417.
30. John Green, "Reilly Given Environmental Portfolio," *In These Times* 13, no.

9 (January 18-24, 1989): 4-5. See also a discussion of the Conservation Foundation in Hays, *Beauty, Health, and Permanence*, 419-422.

31. To say that environmental issues have a strong moral dimension is not to deny that they may involve factual disputes as well. It should be recognized that EDR can encourage the sharing of information and the development of jointly sponsored research; this, in turn, can resolve some of the empirical and scientific disagreements that underlie disputes. See Amy, *The Politics of Environmental Mediation*, 53-57.
32. Quoted in Northern Rockies Action Group, "Selected Transcripts from the NRAG Conference on Negotiations," *NRAG Papers* (Fall 1980): 21.
33. Quoted in Amy, *The Politics of Environmental Mediation*, 191.
34. Quoted in ibid., 191-192.
35. Hair, "Winning Through Mediation," 527.
36. See, for example, Blackburn, "Environmental Mediation as an Alternative," 567.
37. Gerald Cormick, "Environmental Mediation in the U.S.: Experience and Future Directions" (Seattle: Mediation Institute, 1981), mimeo, 17.
38. Peter Clark and Wendy Emrich, quoted in Amy, *The Politics of Environmental Mediation*, 151.
39. Jack Lewis, "A Profile of a New Administrator," *EPA Journal* (March/April 1989): 8.
40. Gilbreath, *Business and the Environment*, 445.
41. Dick Russell, "We Are Losing the War," *The Nation*, March 27, 1989, 403.
42. Paul Rauber, "With Friends Like These. . .," *Mother Jones*, November 1986, 35.

11

Comprehensive Environmental Decision Making: Can It Work?

Robert V. Bartlett

The idea that policy should somehow take account of the environment *comprehensively* is implicit in the modern use of the word *environment* to focus understanding and problem solving. Particularly in the 1960s, numerous writers and thinkers argued that this term could be used to conceptualize the world as a complex interrelated whole, thereby filling a need that had been inadequately served by such terms as *pollution, conservation, natural resources, preservation, public health,* or even *ecology*. Real solutions to problems that were truly environmental were not possible if segmented and fragmented thinking was the basis for decision making. Integrated comprehensive decision making, in which problems would be considered with regard to their interrelated, interconnected totality, was required by the nature of the environment itself. A focus on environment, many argued, would facilitate a restructuring of social, governmental, and academic institutions to deal effectively with environmental problems.

Incisive critiques of public policy processes in the United States and elsewhere have been offered from this perspective.[1] Although the idea of comprehensive environmental decision making has occasionally influenced policy (for example, the National Environmental Policy Act), reforms aimed at making environmental decisions more comprehensive have encountered formidable political obstacles. Most environmental decision making has proceeded by way of segmented and only loosely coordinated, if not conflicting, attacks on specific issues and problems.

The need for comprehensiveness in decision making notwithstanding, devastating criticisms have been directed at the ideal of comprehensive decision making by theorists. These criticisms have made clear the impracticality and undesirability, indeed impossibility, of fully comprehensive decision making. Thus emerges the classic environmental dilemma: What *must* be done *cannot* be done. As an absolute ideal, comprehensive environmental decision making is unrealistic, not doable.

Yet the idea of comprehensive environmental decision making cannot be so easily dismissed, in part because of the persuasiveness of the case made for comprehensiveness. In the 1980s there was a growing realization, particularly with respect to pollution control, that policies addressing pollution in only one medium (air, land, or water) at a time, and only "at the end of the pipe" rather than at the source or at the ultimate destination, were not fully successful and were in some ways compounding the problems. Frequently pollutants were merely shifted from one medium to another rather than controlled or prevented. Regulatory systems were costly, inflexible, and complex, thus making it difficult to identify new problems, set priorities among problems and programs, and coordinate different programs.[2]

During the 1980s, calls for more integrated approaches to controlling pollution were made by environmental policy scholars, Environmental Protection Agency (EPA) officials, international organizations, and the environmental ministries of other nations.[3] EPA had undertaken demonstration projects and small organizational initiatives (such as the Integrated Environmental Management Program and the Pollution Prevention Office) even before the appointment by President George Bush of William Reilly to head the agency. Reilly had been president of the Conservation Foundation before becoming EPA administrator; under Reilly, the foundation had published several studies on comprehensive and integrated pollution control as part of its Options for a New Environmental Policy Project. J. Clarence Davies, executive vice president of the foundation and director of the project on integrated pollution control, followed Reilly to EPA as assistant administrator for policy, planning, and evaluation.

The goal of achieving a greater *degree* of comprehensiveness in environmental policy is likely to be of increasing importance in the 1990s and beyond. Political trends and circumstances are such that initiatives, reforms, demonstrations, and experiments are likely to be proposed and undertaken in the 1990s, at least for pollution control if not environmental policy more broadly. Yet comprehensive environmental decision making is beset with theoretical and practical difficulties that must be confronted in the design and implementation of workable institutions and mechanisms for environmental policy.

Some of these difficulties are well understood, whereas others have barely been addressed in the few analytic studies that have been conducted. Clearly, successful design and implementation of comprehensive environmental decision-making capabilities will have to be based on institutionally rich models of the policy process.[4] A great deal more attention and analytic resources will have to be devoted to understanding the potentialities, limitations, and institutional requirements of alternative conceptions of comprehensiveness. Additional research will be needed to learn from past experience. The short and limited history of comprehensive environmental decision making is more varied, involved, and potentially fruitful than might be suspected.

A Brief History

In a 1963 article where for the first time the term *environment* was linked to the terms *policy* and *administration*, Lynton K. Caldwell had as his central theme the need for environmental policy to be comprehensive. Much of the inadequacy of environmental decision making, he argued, was the fault of the essentially segmental character of policy, "of failing to perceive specific environmental situations in comprehensive environmental terms." The use of *environment* as an integrating concept necessarily implied a different kind of administration, suggesting "an attempt to deal with environments comprehensively, as environments, in contrast to focusing upon their component parts." Thus,

> a policy focus on environment in its fullest practicable sense would make more likely the consideration of all the major elements relevant to an environment-affecting decision. Whatever content is ascribed to the adjective "good," it becomes daily more evident that public administration of the environment will not be "good" if it fails to deal with environmental problems in comprehensive terms.[5]

Clearly, much of the appeal of the term *environment*, for Caldwell and other writers and activists and ultimately for much of the public, was that it was simultaneously a comprehensive and an integrative concept. By using a number of ideas and concepts from the science of ecology and focusing on the environment, it was possible to bring together in a politically potent way a then-diffuse array of emerging and intensifying social concerns—pollution, resource depletion, aesthetics, health, recreation, population growth, economic waste, natural areas preservation, urbanization, and consumer protection, among others. It provided a conceptual lever for arguing that ecological principles should extend to the formulation and execution of all public policies that impinge on the ecological basis of human life. Chief among these ecological principles, or insights, are the complexity of any ecosystem, the interrelatedness of all (including human) ecosystem components, and the necessity of comprehending ecosystems as wholes. Human decisions affect human environments ecologically; any hope of making good environmental decisions is contingent upon understanding and taking into account all the crucial relationships in the whole environment. Assuming that a common-sense balance could readily be found between piecemeal, expedient, fragmented decision making and detailed, all-encompassing, all-knowing decision making, environmental reformers—many of them with scientific backgrounds—argued that the recently perceived environmental crisis demanded new, more rational processes and structures of comprehensive social decision making.

The kinds of reforms suggested and attempted fell into various categories. Some focused on the informational basis of decision making, such as regional or ecosystem modeling, quality of life indicator systems, and environmental impact assessment.[6] Others focused on mechanisms or rules of decision making, such as consultation, permits, disclosure, review, participation, and appeal mechanisms. Perhaps the most prominent category of comprehensiveness reforms, however, was structural reform: formal revision of organizational arrangements for arriving at collective decisions of environmental importance. Reforms might entail creating new organizations or units of organizations, rearranging existing organizations, or, usually, some combination of both.

In addition to persons interested in environmentally comprehensive decision making, among the other politically significant audiences this last category of reforms appealed to were persons and groups concerned with the effective, efficient, controllable operation of government.[7] Illogical organizational structure had long been a traditional explanation of government ineffectiveness, inefficiency, and lack of accountability. The same kind of inadequate structure could now also be blamed, conveniently, for the inadequate response of government to environment problems.

Two distinct reform strategies, often ideologically driven, dominated thinking about comprehensiveness through structural reform. The first involved the hierarchical restructuring of organizations, individually and collectively, to provide a comprehensive scope for decisions—by the establishment of environmental units in existing organizations; by the creation of one or more new planning, advisory, or coordinative organizations; or by the creation of a "super agency" that would be jurisdictionally comprehensive and managerially integrative.[8] The second reform strategy involved achieving comprehensiveness by local or individual empowerment coordinated by social, quasi-market, and mutual adjustment mechanisms, rather than by hierarchical organizational integration. No one individual or unit thus would make comprehensive decisions, but the resulting collective decision or set of decisions should be, according to proponents, comprehensive in scope and quality.[9]

The list of specific efforts that have been made to undertake, or institutionalize, comprehensive environmental decision making is long and richly varied. Elaborate mathematical models have been developed and used to understand better natural and social processes and the consequences and range of interactions among processes. A well-known effort to be broadly comprehensive was the *Global 2000 Report to the President*, which drew upon numerous computer models used by various bureaucracies of the federal government. Particularly since the mid-1970s, much of the politics of the environment has been influenced by, and revolved around, these kinds of sophisticated models. For example, legislative and administrative debates over energy policy, reauthorization of the Clean Air and Water Pollution Control Acts, and the reduction of lead in gasoline were structured by the various models used to explain relationships and predict direct and indirect impacts. Policy on such matters as acid rain, ozone depletion, and global climate change is almost wholly dependent on the level of confidence politicians have in the highly complex models that attempt to predict these phenomena.[10]

The principle of a priori impact assessment has been adopted by several levels of government in the United States, by numerous other nations, and by international agencies. The most well-known types of impact assessment are probably environmental impact assessment and cost-benefit analysis, but cognate approaches such as risk assessment (see Chapter 8), technology assessment, and social impact assessment are highly relevant to the comprehensiveness of environmental decision making.[11]

Many of these have been required by law or by political expectations as a part of environmental decision-making processes. For example, the Nuclear Waste Policy Act of 1982 required extensive and elaborate environmental assessments of potential waste repository sites. The implementation of the 1987 law requiring comprehensive technology and environmental impact assessment of a single site at Yucca Mountain, Nevada, will take several years and cost billions of dollars.[12] The development of Office of Management and Budget regulatory review and cost-benefit analysis also is a mechanism for achieving comprehensiveness—as a kind of surrogate for both hierarchical policy coordination by a "super department" and coordination by economic market mechanisms.

Hundreds, if not thousands, of specific rules are now written into statutes and regulations requiring and pushing the government toward comprehensiveness in its environmental decisions. Statutory charters for some agencies, for example the Bureau of Land Management and the U.S. Forest Service, have been passed or rewritten.[13] Federal, state, and local agencies are required by a large number of statutes and regulations to consider multiple objectives and a wide range of consequences; to inform and consult each other and the public; and to coordinate, streamline, and integrate decision processes.[14] Federal courts impose related standards as part of their review of agency actions to assure that administrative decision making is open, fair, and based on adequate analysis.

As for organizational reform, many agencies have added environmental advisory, planning, or research units to their formal structures.[15] Existing agencies have been reorganized to broaden and balance perspectives. Innumerable interagency committees, both permanent and ad hoc, have been established.[16] Cabinet-level coordinating councils have been tried.[17] Mediating, research, advising, overseeing, and counterbalancing organizations, such as the U.S. Council on Environmental Quality, have been created.[18] New central regulatory agencies have been established, making many environmental programs the responsibility of a single agency. The creation of such far reaching environmental management organizations has been a prominent response among the states and many nations. At the federal level, the most important consequence of this particular reform thrust was the establishment of the Environmental Protection Agency.[19] Internationally, a modest but complex institutional capacity has evolved; the most prominent among many organizations is the United Nations Environment Programme, headquartered in Nairobi, Kenya, with an underfunded research, reporting, coordinating, and catalytic mission (see Chapter 14).

Nevertheless, if the goal was institutionalization, or even demonstration, of comprehensive environmental decision making, the results have been disappointing to many policy scholars. Analytic models, no matter how encompassing and sophisticated, are still inadequate and analytically questionable.[20] Models must be based on simplified information, partial specification of relationships, assumptions that can be questioned or rejected, and knowledge that can change. Thus all models tend to be controversial. Models can be improved, but basic ecological survey and modeling research is so far a low budget priority of all governments, as is interdisciplinary environmental research generally. Indicator and monitoring systems are necessarily value laden (and thus politically vulnerable) and too expensive to be truly comprehensive, even if all the information they might generate could be productively managed.

Rules governing decision processes continue to be circumvented, subverted, or emasculated. Moreover, superficial consideration of only a few broader issues does not make a decision truly comprehensive. Impact assessment systems have been widely misunderstood and underestimated as mechanisms of comprehensive environmental decision making. For example, agency administrative systems seldom provide for using impact assessment information in policy management.[21] Although environmental impact assessment has proven to be a profound and powerful policy strategy, neither it nor other impact assessment approaches promise or deliver full comprehensiveness in environmental decisions.

Interagency committees and cabinet councils have many shortcomings as mechanisms for communication, much less decision making.[22] To be effective, oversight and advisory agencies require authority and resources that rarely have been forthcoming; most, like the Council on Environmental Quality, have never lived up to their original promise for this reason. Often, hierarchical, umbrella, implementing agencies—the

Department of Interior or state-level departments of the environment, for example—have ended up being only inconsequentially integrated, with real power remaining in highly fragmented decision processes. Even EPA, which from the beginning was focused only on pollution problems rather than the environment comprehensively, has always been dominated by its highly specialized and largely autonomous components corresponding to the pollution media being regulated, notably air and water.

Indeed, in a particularly negative assessment, Barry G. Rabe concludes that "the majority of federal and state efforts to better integrate their numerous environmental protection activities have had little impact." [23] Overall, assessments by other analysts have been negative as well.[24]

What explains this apparent failure of the idea of comprehensive environmental decision making? Part of the problem may lie with the critics: By overemphasizing the idea of individual decisions based on analytical comprehensiveness and the hierarchical integration of organizations, they give the false impression that few decisions are in any way comprehensive. The degree of comprehensiveness achieved by environmental impact assessments, for example, is thereby unduly discounted. In addition, evaluation of comprehensive environmental decision making is distorted by variable definitions and confused expectations. The severity of the limits to comprehensiveness are often not fully acknowledged, with reform efforts deprecated accordingly. Indeed, if reasonably defined and reevaluated by appropriate criteria in the shadow of these imposing limits, it may be possible to say that the idea of comprehensive environmental decision making has not failed at all, but has realized modest and informative successes.

The Limits to Comprehensive Environmental Decision Making

Limits to comprehensiveness in environmental decision making seem to be of two broad kinds: pragmatic impediments and constraints imposed by existing institutions, attitudes, and resources; and theoretical limits imposed by the nature of decision making, organization, and rationality.

Practical Political Impediments

The practical obstacles to comprehensiveness are formidable. Efforts to undertake or institutionalize comprehensive environmental decision making are likely to cost money, which may be hard to find in the face of overall budget and economic pressures and the pressing needs of existing environmental programs. Clearly, the case for comprehensive environmental decision making is not widely understood or appreciated by the general public. Such an abstract issue may gradually develop more public support, but it is unlikely to achieve a prominent place on the policy agenda primarily as a consequence of public demand, even in an era of rising environmental concern.

Even if it were to become a much more salient political issue, that would not necessarily imply that the realization of comprehensiveness was imminent or even probable. Fragmentation is a prevailing pattern in public policy for many reasons, not the least of which is the fragmented nature of politics, especially in the United States and in international policy making, but also in more unitary systems. Rarely is there a clear constituency for comprehensive decision making either within government or outside it. By contrast, narrow constituencies supporting narrowly conceived individual policies and decisions abound. Current institutional biases weigh strongly against greater consideration of comprehensiveness in policy making.

Even among policy analysts working in government, in academia, and for environmental and business interest groups, there is little consistent support for a focus on comprehensiveness. The whole emphasis of comprehensiveness runs counter to the modern nature of expertise—not only the expertise of high-level policy analysts, but also that of the day-to-day implementors of policy. Expertise almost always means narrow, specialized, disciplinary expertise; few persons by training, experience, or predilection are prepared to engage in or promote comprehensive environmental decision making. The idea of comprehensive environmental decision making finds little institutional support in the ways universities, science, or the professions generally are structured, or in the ways persons in government or business are employed.

Likewise, comprehensive environmental decision making is not easy to sell even among active environmentalists. Most environmentalists would probably agree in principle that the need for comprehensiveness is compelling, but in reality they are persuaded that immediate substantive interests are better served by achievable reform of the already fragmented status quo, however disjointed and narrowly focused.[25] The consequences of abstract and often untried comprehensive decision-making proposals are necessarily uncertain; what is certain is that political advantage would shift in poorly understood and unpredictable (and thus politically risky) ways. This might, for example, "allow the EPA to be plunged into the 'fetid swamps of uncertainty' and engage in a period of inaction on pollution control across the board." [26] For many environmentalists, reasons can always be found to postpone serious consideration of comprehensive environmental decision making until political circumstances are more propitious.

Comprehensive environmental decision making has never received sustained, focused attention from environmentalists, government analysts, or policy scholars. Little reliable research has addressed the dimensions of the problem, and little evaluative effort has been expended to assess those reforms attempted.

Theoretical Limits

A second set of less obvious but no less important limits to the feasibility of comprehensive environmental decision making is suggested by developments in social scientific theories of rationality, decisions, and organizations. Theorists and researchers have convincingly argued that, outside of artificially simplified situations such as in laboratories or in games, humans do not have the capability for omniscient decision making or objective rationality, even when aided by powerful computers.[27]

Most often presented as an alternative to comprehensive decision making is *incremental* decision making, a pragmatic approach that avoids many of the conceptual and political difficulties of rational decision making. In incremental decision making, analysis is sharply limited to alternatives that differ only incrementally from the status quo, with no pretense that all outcomes or values are being considered; policy is made iteratively, by trial and error, with minimal reliance on theoretical knowledge.[28]

A large body of scholarly research emphasizes that comprehensive decision making is hopelessly idealistic and infeasible for individuals and organizations. Moreover, it might even be politically undesirable in its antidemocratic tendencies.[29] Even if possible, the first set of limits discussed above would come into play: Comprehensive decision-making reform would be costly, difficult to put into effect, and likely to fail, given the breadth and depth of institutional biases against it and the dynamics of institutional change.

Given the history of comprehensive environmental decision-making reforms and the growth in theoretical and practical understanding of the limits of comprehensiveness, it should not be surprising that the whole idea has been widely dismissed, even as a goal, and that it has received little serious attention since the early 1970s. That is not to say that it has received no attention, however; proposals continue to surface and innovative reforms are occasionally implemented.

The arguments made on behalf of the need for comprehensiveness are more compelling now than two decades ago. Whatever the general virtues of incrementalism, for environmental concerns an exclusive reliance on incremental decision making is a severely flawed strategy.[30] Environmental problems are ill-structured problems, poorly addressed by traditional incremental approaches. Using reason to try to put manageable boundaries around a problem, Stahrl W. Edmunds notes, "presumes to solve one problem by focusing on a few variables while unknowingly creating others—and hence, each new solution becomes a new problem that requires still another remedy. Frequently in ecological issues, the end result of these iterative fixes may be worse than the initial condition." [31]

The virtues of incremental decision making derive from a reliance on decomposition, feedback, and trial and error. Characteristic of decisions having significant impact on the environment, however,

> are consequences that are often irreversible and impacts that may be geographically or temporally dispersed or may appear at the end of a long causal sequence. Some environmentally important outcomes will only result if a (usually unknown) threshold is exceeded. Sometimes actions have effects that would be unremarkable if the actions occurred independently in isolation, but are noteworthy as the product of more than one action (that is, cumulative, interactive, and synergistic effects). [32]

By their very nature, environmental concerns require a degree of "thinking big" and a measure of protection against "the tyranny of small decisions." [33]

How insurmountable, then, are the obstacles to comprehensive environmental decision making? An answer seems to depend on just what is meant by the term *comprehensive decision making.*

Conceptual Analysis of "Comprehensive Decision Making"

Whether arguing for or against it, analysts do not agree on a definition of comprehensive decision making. Few, if any, analysts formally define the term before using it. It is not uncommon to be able to identify a multiplicity of meanings by a single author; often, particular meanings may be implied for rhetorical convenience. Some brief examples of how key terms are commonly used or not used will illustrate the problem of semantic confusion and ambiguity and will serve as a beginning point for assessing the prospects for comprehensive environmental decision making.

Decision, by itself, is a problematic term. Does decision refer both to collective decisions and individual decisions? If decisions can be collective, the issues of structure and process are compounded. Analysts may disagree on the boundaries of a decision: Is a decision a choice occurring in an instant, or is it a process requiring a variable amount of time? Who, exactly, actually "makes" collective decisions? Are decisions separable and mutually exclusive phenomena? Are the value and factual inputs to a decision part of the decision? If not, when is a decision made? Does decision always, or ever, mean something different than *judgment* or *conclusion*?

The term *comprehensive* is even more confused in use. Does

comprehensive mean *including all*, or *including everything?* (Often this is the meaning implied when comprehensive decision making is being set up as a straw man to be knocked down.) Are there degrees and types of comprehensiveness? If so, what must be included to meet a criterion of comprehensiveness? How exactly is comprehensiveness to occur—cognitively, organizationally, politically, or some other way? What does it mean—exactly and concretely—to comprise, to include, to embrace, or to contain? Is comprehensiveness a state or a process? What are the temporal boundaries of comprehensiveness? Does comprehensive necessarily imply comprehension (understanding)?

Using *comprehensive* to modify *decision* multiplies the potential for ambiguity and confusion. Sometimes the term *comprehensive decision making* is used to refer to decision making based entirely on comprehensive analysis; other times it is meant to refer to decisions that are comprehensive in the scope of their impact or in the breadth of their regard for values. Decision and analysis become almost hopelessly muddled in the literature on the subject.

Other related concepts are also used in loose and ambiguous ways—sometimes in lieu of, sometimes in conjunction with comprehensive decision making. Notably, *policy, administration*, or *management* are frequently substituted for *decision making*—hardly achieving an improvement in clarity and precision. Also closely linked to the idea of comprehensive decision making, and sometimes substituted for it, are the concepts of *coordination* and *integration*. Many definitions of each can be offered.[34] Integration is often defined as being almost synonymous with coordination. Some analysts, however, distinguish between the two concepts, suggesting that integration, as "the act or process of making whole or entire," entails the structural merging of identities and "obviates the very need for coordination." [35] Other analysts use *integrated* virtually synonymously with *comprehensive* to refer in a rough way to the antithesis of narrow, fragmented, or segmented.[36]

So the term *comprehensive decision making* has a deceptively simple appearance; but rather than a commonly understood meaning we have a tangled semantic swamp. What is to be made of this ambiguity and confusion? Exploring all the implications of the various definitional issues raised here would be a task extending far beyond the modest objectives of this chapter. But a full cataloging of uses of the idea and its related concepts is not necessary in order to derive a few important conclusions.

First, both the practical and theoretical limits to comprehensive decision making are far more restrictive for some meanings than for others. If we have in mind discrete decisions that each deal with everything at once, then clearly comprehensive decision making is impossible. If, on the other hand, we think of decisions as social processes involving many people over time, and of comprehensiveness as referring to greater degrees of consideration of matters of importance, then comprehensive decision making is possible and may be desirable. Second, comprehensive decision-making reforms ought to be evaluated by reasonable standards derived from realistic theoretical conceptions rather than by idealized criteria, based on extreme definitions, that guarantee failure in advance. Third, the prospects for comprehensive decision making should be enhanced by a better understanding of the rich complexity of the concept, which ought to encourage more innovative, well-designed, politically promising policy proposals.

Can It Be Done?

In spite of the formidable difficulties, political and theoretical, of comprehensive environmental decision making, policy opportunities will continue to arise (surprisingly frequently) for creating greater capabilities. New efforts to institutionalize a greater degree of comprehensive environmental decision making will probably succeed when skilled policy entrepreneurs are able to exploit a convergence of the availability of ideas, a constituency for the ideas, and some triggering events that have stimulated a perceived need for innovation.[37] These factors are not fully independent of each other; events help create a constituency, as do ideas—and entrepreneurs are attracted by ideas. If the past three decades are any guide to the future, a constituency for comprehensive environmental decision making will continue to grow in the face of expanding understanding about environmental problems and the inadequacy of existing policies. Unexpected triggering events (for example, oil spills, heat waves, contaminated environments, ozone holes) will continue to be reported with a disturbing frequency. What is less predictable is the availability of ideas and the presence of skilled policy entrepreneurs at the right time and place.

Being ready to help create and take advantage of opportunities will require persons who are concerned with the challenges of environmental policy in the 1990s to move beyond the sterile dead ends of dichotomous thinking that had effectively trapped development of the idea of comprehensive environmental decision making throughout much of the 1970s and 1980s. Before promising policy mechanisms can be designed and adopted, intellectual and policy debate on the subject must rise above such polar assertions as, "because everything is interrelated, comprehensiveness means each decision must be comprehensive," or, "because we cannot deal with everything at once, narrow incrementalism is the only alternative." Although seriously advanced, such assertions are not to be taken seriously in light of both the ambiguity and conceptual richness of the idea of comprehensive decision making and the growing understanding of its complex limitations. What is needed are policy analyses and policy proposals that transcend the stultifying classificatory language of "comprehensive versus incremental" (or "incremental versus nonincremental," or "comprehensive versus noncomprehensive").

Recognizing the complex range of concepts flying under the single flag of comprehensive decision making means recognizing that there are many ways of achieving greater comprehensiveness. This is an exciting prospect for policy designers. It also means recognizing that all governments, all organizations, and all social groups already do grapple, *must* grapple, with the various questions about comprehensive decision making raised in this chapter. By overemphasizing the ideal of basing individual decisions on comprehensive analysis, we create the false impression that currently most decisions are narrow, fragmented, and wholly uncoordinated.[38] Yet an immense range of social choice mechanisms operates every day to coordinate, however inadequately, our many collective choices of environmental significance: price signals, administrative commands, formal rules, shared values, mutual adjustment, negotiation, force, and discussion, among others.[39] Even setting aside the possible contribution of extended analysis, there are many ways to achieve greater comprehensiveness in decision making, ways that invite further comparative evaluation and creative tinkering.

We have a great many places to look for insights and lessons. Not only do we know much less than we should about the policy effects of past efforts to induce comprehensive environmental decision making, whether through administrative reorganizations, policy statements, coordinative mechanisms, integration of legislation, augmentation of analytical capability, or impact assessment requirements (and *all* are under studied), but we have also only begun to study systematically an immense array of evolved traditional arrangements through which people around the world have successfully and comprehensively managed common property resources.[40]

Our knowledge of past experience is sufficient, however, to suggest a number of guiding principles. The problems and challenges of comprehensive environmental decision making are not solvable by integrating all environmental decisions through administrative hierarchies or by basing environmental decision making on comprehensive analysis of all relevant facts. This would be true even if *none* of the practical and theoretical limits to comprehensive decision making, discussed earlier, applied. Global comprehensiveness "also increases the abstracting and synthesis requirement to the point at which the information about the environment may no longer resemble reality." [41]

Fortunately, global comprehensiveness is only sometimes needed for environmental policy, although that need may sometimes be great, as dramatically illustrated by such problems as climate change and ozone depletion. Many serious environmental problems, in terms of causality, major consequences, and scope of possible solutions, are micro-level problems, for which a much greater degree of regional and local, rather than global, comprehensiveness is needed. Solutions to these kinds of problems must be sensitive to time- and place-specific constraints, information, and resources.

Traditional thinking has limited the use of the label "environmental policy" to those policies that directly and explicitly focus on environmental effects (for example, air and water pollution, species extinction, resource depletion, toxic contamination, climate change). But policies that influence the causes of environmental effects (or, all too often, policies that are themselves the causes of environmental degradation—for example, economic development, agriculture, and transportation policies) are also environmental policies, and may in fact be the most significant environmental policies. Thus, in a nontrivial way, *all* problems are environmental problems. In arguing for "shifting the focus to the policy sources," this point is cogently made by the World Commission on Environment and Development (Brundtland commission) in its report, *Our Common Future:*

> Environmental protection and sustainable development must be an integral part of the mandates of all agencies of governments, of international organizations, and of major private-sector institutions. . . . The ability to choose policy paths that are sustainable requires that the ecological dimensions of policy be considered at the same time as the economic, trade, energy, agricultural, industrial, and other dimensions—on the same agendas and in the same national and international institutions.[42]

Thus the goal of comprehensive environmental decision making is in fact a goal of environmentally oriented *general* decision making (the point made by Caldwell in 1963), with all that implies in terms of the practical and theoretical limits discussed earlier. Clearly national and international capabilities for a greater degree of comprehensive decision making can be dramatically improved, and the Brundtland report offers valuable recommendations toward this end. But the very interrelatedness of everything, which is what makes the case for comprehensive decision making so compelling, means that only in the broadest and most general way can environmental policy be comprehensive on a global scale. The ecological, economic, and social uniqueness of most microenvironments, and the more intimate and immediate relations that humans have to these environments, implies that environmental policy in this broad sense of the policy sources—and therefore the idea of routine comprehensive environmental decision making—is most relevant to local and community governance.

Nevertheless, it is important to remember that a greater degree of comprehensiveness can never be the only goal. There is a danger that the quest for comprehensiveness, as Harold Seidman and Robert Gilmour argue with regard to coordination, can become the equivalent of the medieval search for a philosopher's stone that would provide the key to the universe and solve all problems: "If only we can find the right formula for coordination, we can reconcile the irreconcilable, harmonize competing and wholly divergent interests, overcome irrationalities in our government structures, and make hard policy choices to which no one will dissent." [43] Decision making, whether global, national, local, or at an intermediate regional level, may be highly comprehensive without being environmentally beneficial. Examples abound from the planned socialist societies of eastern Europe and Asia.

Comprehensive environmental decision making is commonly understood to refer to decisions concerning the environment; simultaneously there is a strong implication that such decisions will be oriented toward achieving environmental quality. But without attention to the processes and criteria of choice that will determine a decision, or to the system of values by which a decision will be judged, or to the structured biases and inadequacies of institutions and social choice mechanisms, there is no assurance that the resulting decisions will be ecologically rational.[44] Perhaps more important than the Brundtland commission's recommendation for greater comprehensiveness is its call for all agencies, public and private, to be reoriented toward environmental protection—no small goal itself.

A prerequisite of comprehensive environmental decision making is institutionalization of ecological rationality—a rationality "of living systems, an order of relationships among living systems and their environments." [45] Ecological rationality, however, may not be wholly compatible with comprehensive environmental decision making as it is often conceived. Not necessarily implicit in the concept itself, but certainly identifiable in many of the advocates of comprehensive environmental decision making, is a worldview that is instrumental, material, and technocratic, girded by the premises that all things are knowable and all things are controllable by humans and their technology.[46] To this extent comprehensive decision making is a logical product of the rationalization of the world and the dominance of technical and economic rationality in the modern mind. But these assumptions are certainly flawed; all things are not knowable and controllable. And this worldview is itself environmentally problematic. If pursuit of the goal of comprehensive decision making diverts people from recognizing these flaws by promising a kind of administrative-technological policy "fix" of all modern environmental problems, to that extent it is a dangerous idea. Ironically, one of the best ways to make human societies more ecologically rational may be to reduce and limit, where possible, the need for comprehensive decision making.[47] The achievement of ecological rationality in human governance would probably result in a degree and type of comprehensive environmental decision making far different than that envisioned by most theorists and reformers to date.

"Can it be done?" inevitably shades into "Will it be done?" The resilience of the ideal,[48] the past policy experiments that can be studied and built upon, and continuing developments in methodological and technological capabilities suggest that comprehensive environmental decision making will remain a fertile idea that will continue to find expression in policy proposals in the 1990s. New proposals and initiatives may be more thoughtfully and carefully designed, may have broader political support than in the past, and may benefit from propitious political circumstances. Not only has the environment become a dramatically more salient and potent political issue nationally and internationally in the late 1980s, but key Bush administration appointees have been closely identified with policy research and reform proposals for more comprehensive environmental decision making.

Efforts to achieve a greater degree of comprehensiveness in environmental decision making are likely in the 1990s, but, as in the past, only some of these will successfully navigate the political obstacles. Most likely, given the current availability of ideas, existing constituencies, recent triggering events, and the placement of likely entrepreneurs in the Bush administration, are initiatives on integrated multimedia approaches to pollution control.

Internationally, pressure will continue to build to develop institutional mechanisms to address habitat destruction, climate change, and management of global commons in more comprehensive frameworks. In spite of the publicity generated by the Brundtland report, significant shifting of the focus to the policy sources in the 1990s is most likely to occur at the local level—as has already begun in a dramatic way with regard to solid and hazardous wastes.

Truly fundamental, profound reform is possible but not likely in the 1990s, in part because of formidable political obstacles, but also because our knowledge about comprehensive environmental decision making is still in its infancy. Any reforms in this direction, however badly needed, are still speculative experiments. The most salutary development possible in the 1990s would be for the ideas and concepts of comprehensive environmental decision making to receive finally "the attention or cultivation . . . needed to gain analytic strength or . . . sufficient clarity and force to influence policy." [49] Without more research on past comprehensiveness initiatives, without more funding for systems and interdisciplinary analysis generally, especially institutional analysis,[50] and without more serious theoretical attention to the meanings and conceptual implications of comprehensive environmental decision making, those responsible for trying to make environmental policy more comprehensive "cannot really have any idea about what they are doing."[51]

Notes

1. See, for example, William Ophuls, *Ecology and the Politics of Scarcity: Prologue to a Political Theory of the Steady State* (San Francisco: W. H. Freeman, 1977).
2. Frances Irwin, "Introduction to Integrated Pollution Control," in *Integrated Pollution Control in Europe and North America,* ed. Nigel Haigh and Frances Irwin (Washington, D.C.: Conservation Foundation, 1989), 7-9; and Conservation Foundation, "Rationale and Summary," *The Environmental Protection Act,* unpublished second draft (Washington, D.C.: Conservation Foundation, 1988).
3. Irwin, "Introduction to Integrated Pollution Control," 5-6.
4. Giandomenico Majone, "Policy Science," in *Guidance, Control, and Evaluation in the Public Sector,* ed. Franz X. Kaufmann, Giandomenico Majone, and Vincent Ostrom (New York: Walter de Gruyter, 1986), 70.
5. Lynton K. Caldwell, "Environment: A New Focus for Public Policy," *Public Administration Review* 23 (September 1963): 138-139.
6. Peter W. House, *The Quest for Completeness: Comprehensive Analysis in Environmental Management and Planning* (Lexington, Mass.: Lexington Books, 1976).
7. Alfred A. Marcus, *Promise and Performance: Choosing and Implementing an Environmental Policy* (Westport, Conn.: Greenwood Press, 1980).
8. Kem Lowry and Richard A. Carpenter, *Holistic Nature and Fragmented Bureaucracies: A Study of Government Organization for Natural Systems Management* (Honolulu: East-West Center, 1984), 10.
9. Most of the serious normative work by environmental economists emphasizes the potential of economic incentives in a more integrated system of pollution control. The residual management research and proposals produced by Resources for the Future scholars have been among the more comprehensively oriented works. See, for example, Allen V. Kneese and Blair T. Bower, *Environmental Quality and Residuals Management* (Baltimore: Resources for the Future, 1979).
10. Peter W. House and Roger D. Shull, *Regulatory Reform: Politics and the Environment* (Lanham, Md.: Abt Books, 1985).
11. Robert V. Bartlett, "Impact Assessment as a Policy Strategy," in *Policy Through Impact Assessment: Institutionalized Analysis as a Policy Strategy,* ed. Robert V. Bartlett (Westport, Conn.: Greenwood Press, 1989), 1-4; and Alan L. Porter and Frederick A. Rossini, "Why Integrated Impact Assessment? in *Integrated Impact Assessment,* ed. Frederick A. Rossini and Alan L. Porter (Boulder, Colo.: Westview Press, 1983), 3-16.
12. Bruce B. Clary and Michael E. Kraft, "Environmental Assessment, Science, and Policy Failure: The Politics of Nuclear Waste Disposal," in Bartlett, *Policy Through Impact Assessment,* 37-50.

13. The Federal Land Policy and Management Act of 1976 established comprehensive decision making and integrated, coherent management as goals of the Bureau of Land Management; the Forest and Rangeland Renewable Resources Planning Act of 1974 and the National Forest Management Act of 1976 endorsed, refined, and extended an already existing emphasis, both statutory and bureaucratic, on comprehensive decision making by the Forest Service. See Daniel H. Henning and William R. Mangun, *Managing the Environmental Crisis: Incorporating Competing Values in Natural Resource Administration* (Durham, N.C.: Duke University Press, 1989), 106-151.
14. Donald F. Kettl, *The Regulation of American Federalism* (Baltimore: Johns Hopkins University Press, 1987).
15. This is a popular strategy in many other nations as well. See Lowry and Carpenter, *Holistic Nature and Fragmented Bureaucracies*, 10-12.
16. This is perhaps the most common mechanism for bureaucratic coordination. See J. Clarence Davies III and Barbara S. Davies, *The Politics of Pollution*, 2d ed. (Indianapolis: Pegasus, 1975), 120; and Harold Seidman and Robert Gilmour, *Politics, Position, and Power: From the Positive to the Regulatory State*, 4th ed. (New York: Oxford University Press, 1976), 226-236.
17. For example, the following councils were created: under President Nixon, the Environmental Quality Council and the Cabinet Committee on the Environment, later swallowed up by the Domestic Council; under President Reagan, the Cabinet Council on Natural Resources and Environment. See Richard A. Liroff, *A National Policy for the Environment: NEPA and Its Aftermath* (Bloomington: Indiana University Press, 1976), 10-35; and J. Clarence Davies III, "Environmental Institutions and the Reagan Administration," in *Environmental Policy in the 1980s: Reagan's New Agenda*, ed. Norman J. Vig and Michael E. Kraft (Washington, D.C.: CQ Press, 1984), 149.
18. As originally conceived and established, the Council on Environmental Quality also would have had a major research function. This mission was partially transferred to EPA and was never fully realized either there or at CEQ.
19. The EPA model, which locates all pollution regulatory functions in one agency, is different than the so-called super agency model, which also consolidates conservation and development functions into the same agency. See Marcus, *Promise and Performance*, 31-43; and Council of State Governments, *Integration and Coordination of State Environmental Programs* (Lexington, Ky.: Council of State Governments, 1975), 19-23.
20. Donella Meadows, John Richardson, and Gerhart Bruckman, *Groping in the Dark: The First Decade of Global Modeling* (New York: John Wiley, 1982); M. C. McHale, *Ominous Trends and Valid Hopes: A Comparison of Five World Reports* (Minneapolis: Hubert H. Humphrey Institute of Public Affairs, 1981); and Vaclav Smil, *Energy, Food, Environment: Realities, Myths, Options* (New York: Oxford University Press, 1987).
21. See William R. Mangun, "Environmental Impact Assessment as a Tool for Wildlife Policy Management," in Bartlett, *Policy Through Impact Assessment*, 51-61.
22. Davies and Davies, *The Politics of Pollution*, 120-121; and Lowry and

Carpenter, *Holistic Nature and Fragmented Bureaucracies*, 15-16.

23. Barry G. Rabe, *Fragmentation and Integration in State Environmental Management* (Washington, D.C.: Conservation Foundation, 1986), xiv.
24. House, *The Quest for Completeness;* and Joseph M. Petulla, *Environmental Protection in the United States: Industry, Agencies, Environmentalists* (San Francisco: San Francisco Study Center, 1987).
25. "Environmentalists do not want to risk losing hard-won concrete gains for the sake of what may seem abstract integration." Conservation Foundation, *Controlling Cross-Media Pollutants* (Washington, D.C.: Conservation Foundation, 1984), 43. See also Rabe, *Fragmentation and Integration in State Environmental Management*, 127.
26. Statement by Glenn Paulson in Conservation Foundation, *New Perspectives on Pollution Control: Cross-Media Problems* (Washington, D.C.: Conservation Foundation, 1985), 77.
27. Robert V. Bartlett, "Rationality in Administrative Behavior: Simon, Science, and Public Administration," *Public Administration Quarterly* 12 (Fall 1988): 301-314; Herbert A. Simon, *Administrative Behavior*, 3d ed. (New York: Free Press, 1976), 80-81; and Herbert A. Simon, "From Substantive to Procedural Rationality," in *Method and Appraisal in Economics*, ed. Spiro J. Latsis (Cambridge: Cambridge University Press, 1976), 131-135.
28. Charles E. Lindblom, "The Science of Muddling Through," *Public Administration Review* 19 (Spring 1959): 81-86.
29. Aaron Wildavsky, *The Politics of the Budgetary Process*, 2d ed. (Boston: Little, Brown, 1974), 189-194; and Walter F. Baber, "Impact Assessment and Democratic Politics," *Policy Studies Review* 8 (Autumn 1988): 172-178.
30. Ophuls, *Ecology and the Politics of Scarcity*, 191-193.
31. Stahrl W. Edmunds, "Environmental Policy: Bounded Rationality Applied to Unbounded Ecological Problems," in *Environmental Policy Formation*, ed. Dean E. Mann (Lexington, Mass.: Lexington Books, 1981), 192.
32. Robert V. Bartlett, "Rationality and the Logic of the National Environmental Policy Act," *The Environmental Professional* 8 (1986): 107.
33. Alfred E. Kahn, "The Tyranny of Small Decisions," *KYKLOS: International Review for Social Science* 19 (1966): 23-45.
34. Robert V. Bartlett and Walter F. Baber, "Bureaucracy or Analysis: Implications of Impact Assessment for Public Administration," in Bartlett, *Policy Through Impact Assessment*, 143-153. Perhaps the best discussion of coordination issues in environmental policy is in Joseph J. Molnar and David L. Rogers, "Interorganizational Coordination in Environmental Management: Process, Strategy, and Objective," in *Environmental Policy Implementation*, ed. Dean E. Mann (Lexington, Mass.: Lexington Books, 1982), 95-108.
35. Council of State Governments, *Integration and Coordination of State Environmental Programs*, 95.
36. See, for example, Rabe, *Fragmentation and Integration in State Environmental Management*. Other terms, such as *holistic* and *interdisciplinary*, are also used in the environmental policy literature as rough synonyms for comprehensive environmental decision making (see page 143).
37. Rabe, *Fragmentation and Integration in State Environmental Management*, 67-85; and John W. Kingdon, *Agendas, Alternatives, and Public*

Policies (Boston: Little, Brown, 1984).

38. Seidman and Gilmour, *Politics, Position, and Power*, 225.
39. John S. Dryzek, *Rational Ecology: Environment and Political Ecology* (New York: Basil Blackwell, 1987), 63. See also Charles E. Lindblom, "Incrementalism and Environmentalism," in *Managing the Environment* (Washington, D.C.: Environmental Protection Agency, 1973), 84.
40. Geoffrey Cowley, "The Electronic Goddess: Computerizing Bali's Ancient Irrigation Rites," *Newsweek*, March 13, 1989; Elinor Ostrom, "Institutional Arrangements and the Commons Dilemma," in *Rethinking Institutional Analysis and Development: Issues, Alternatives, and Choices*, ed. Vincent Ostrom, David Feeny, and Hartmut Picht (San Francisco: International Center for Economic Growth, 1988), 101-139; and Fenton Martin, *Common Pool Resources and Collective Action: A Bibliography* (Bloomington, Ind.: Indiana University Workshop in Political Theory and Policy Analysis, 1989).
41. Edmunds, "Environmental Policy," 191.
42. World Commission on Environment and Development, *Our Common Future* (New York: Oxford University Press, 1987), 311-313.
43. Seidman and Gilmour, *Politics, Position, and Power*, 219.
44. Dryzek, *Rational Ecology;* Robert V. Bartlett, "Ecological Rationality: Reason and Environmental Policy," *Environmental Ethics* 8 (Fall 1986): 221-239; and Robert V. Bartlett, "Ecological Reason in Administration: Environmental Impact Assessment and Administrative Theory," in *Limiting Leviathan: Environmental Politics and the Administrative State*, ed. Robert Paehlke and Douglas Torgerson (Peterborough, Ontario: Broadview Press, 1990).
45. Bartlett, "Ecological Rationality," 229.
46. David Ehrenfeld, *The Arrogance of Humanism* (New York: Oxford University Press, 1981).
47. Dryzek, *Rational Ecology*, 217-218.
48. Rabe, *Fragmentation and Integration in State Environmental Management*, xv, 153.
49. Ibid., 116.
50. William T. Gormley, Jr., *Taming the Bureaucracy: Muscles, Prayers, and Other Strategies* (Princeton, N.J.: Princeton University Press, 1989); Kaufmann, Majone, and Ostrom, eds., *Guidance, Control, and Evaluation in the Public Sector;* and Ostrom, Feeny, and Picht, eds., *Rethinking Institutional Analysis and Development*.
51. W. D. Kay, "Impact Assessment and Regulating Technological Change: Why the Philosophy of Technology Is a Political Problem," in Bartlett, *Policy Through Impact Assessment*, 121-127.

IV. TOWARD GLOBAL ENVIRONMENTAL POLICY

12

Environmental Policy in Europe and Japan

David Vogel

This chapter provides an overview of the politics of environmental protection at work outside the United States. It places American environmental policy in comparative perspective and then examines such policy in a number of other political settings. It focuses primarily on developments in Great Britain and Japan, tracing the evolution of environmental regulation from the nineteenth century through the end of the 1980s. Recent changes in environmental policies and politics in the Federal Republic of Germany (FRG) and Eastern Europe are also examined. The chapter concludes with a discussion of the increasing globalization of environmental regulations, with particular emphasis on developments in the European Community (EC).

Over the last decade a number of studies have compared environmental policy in the United States with that of other industrial nations.[1] While their scope and focus have varied, each has reached the identical conclusion, namely, that the way in which American environmental regulation is made and enforced is distinctive.[2] No other nation has consistently imposed so many strict requirements on industry, made such extensive use of the courts to enforce compliance, or allowed environmental organizations such extensive opportunity to participate in the policy process. As a result, in no other industrial nation has environmental regulation consistently created as much conflict between industry and government.

The distinctiveness of American environmental policy is in large measure rooted in the American constitutional system. The primary responsibility for the administration of environmental regulation rests with a government's bureaucracy. In the United States, this bureaucratic unit is the Environmental Protection Agency; in Japan it is the Environment Agency; in Great Britain it is the Department of the Environment. With the exception of the United States, these regulatory bureaucracies enjoy substantial autonomy; government officials negotiate with industry without having their decisions second-guessed by either the national legislature or the courts. The result is a style of regulation that contributes to and is based upon substantial cooperation between business and government.

In contrast, the American system of government is based upon the separation of powers principle. This has enabled both the American Congress and the American courts to play a much more influential role in the regulatory process.[3] One result has been a substantial increase in the political effectiveness of the American environmental movement. Environmental organizations have been able to use their influence in Congress and their access to the courts to closely monitor decisions made in the executive branch of government. At the same time, lobbyists from industry have been able to use both the courts and the Congress to seek to defend their economic interests. As a consequence, American regulatory officials—unlike their counterparts in Europe and Japan—enjoy relatively little autonomy. The result is a style of regulation that has created considerable political conflict.[4]

The History of Environmental Regulation in Great Britain and Japan

The political context within which environmental policy is made varies in each nation. These variations are a function of each nation's history, legal system, and political culture.

The Nineteenth Century

The Industrial Revolution exacerbated environmental problems in each nation in which it occurred. As the first nation to industrialize, England was also the first nation to experience a significant deterioration in the quality of its physical environment. To cope with the substantial increase in air pollution caused by the burning of coal, in 1821 Parliament enacted a statute making it easier for individuals to sue the owners of furnaces that were emitting large quantities of particulates (smoke). Unfortunately, this legislation did little to keep the air in much of Britain from becoming steadily dirtier as more and more factories were built. Faced with protests from influential landowners whose crops and livestock had become damaged, Parliament in 1863 enacted legislation establishing the world's first explicit pollution control standard. The Alkali Act required the manufacturers of alkali—a chemical widely used in the manufacture of soap, glass, and textiles—to remove 95 percent of the hydrochloric acid emitted by their factories. To enforce this emissions standard, the British government established the world's first pollution control agency, which they named the Alkali Inspectorate. It was comprised of a chief inspector and three associates, all trained in chemical engineering and with extensive experience in industry. This set a pattern of regulation by experts that has continued in Britain to date.

The British conservation movement also began in the nineteenth century. In 1889 a group of residents of Manchester established the Fur and Feather Group to protest the use of bird feathers in the making of hats. Shortly afterward, several members of the English gentry, upset by the threat to open space posed by rapid industrial and urban expansion, founded the National Trust for Places of Historic Interest and Natural Beauty. Its objective was to acquire land and buildings by either gift or purchase in order to protect them from economic development and thereby ensure the public's continual access to them. The Trust saw itself not simply as a landowning body but as "the national champion of the preservationist cause." [5]

The rapid industrialization of Japan that took place during the latter third of the nineteenth century also created a number of environmental problems in that island nation. In 1877 Ichibei Furukawa, a silk merchant with important government connections, purchased a defunct copper mine in Ashio, a village one hundred miles north of Tokyo. Anticipating the growing demand for copper as electricity began to be introduced into Japan, he invested large sums to expand the mine's capacity. Within two decades, the mine at Ashio was responsible for nearly half of Japan's copper production and had become one of the largest industrial enterprises of its kind in the Far East. However, every time the mine became flooded, the villagers who lived downstream found themselves suffering from copper poisoning. Farmland was made desolate and unproductive. Epidemics killed many domestic animals as well as a number of human beings. Often the human victims of this man-made disaster were left without clothes to wear or food to eat.[6] More than twenty-five villages were affected. The Ashio case became a national scandal when a study traced the poisonings to the mine.

The government was strongly criticized in the newly formed Japanese parliament, known as the Diet, for its refusal to close the mine in spite of its clear threat to the public's health. The central government instructed the local state government to form an arbitration committee to settle the dispute between Furukawa and the afflicted farmers, but the committee awarded the farmers only a small sum. Although the company promised to install equipment to collect the poisonous mineral residues and thus prevent further contamination of the river, its abatement equipment proved ineffective. By the turn of the century, more than 40,000 hectares had become contaminated and the pollution had spread as far as Tokyo. Finally, to put an end to the farmers' protests the government decided to transform Yanaka village, which had been at the center of the opposition to the mine, into a reservoir to absorb future flood waters. The villagers were forced to sell their lands and were forcibly relocated to a remote northern island.

The Postwar Period

This brief account of environmental issues in nineteenth-century Britain and Japan demonstrates that environmental regulation has a long history in both countries. It also suggests some contrasts between the politics of environmental protection in the two nations. During the nineteenth and early twentieth centuries, Britain, in part because it was both more affluent and more democratic, was considerably more responsive to the public's concerns with environmental quality than was Japan. This pattern continued through the late 1960s.

During the postwar decades, the British government steadily expanded the scope of its regulations over both air and water pollution and land use. It enacted legislation establishing a comprehensive system of land-use controls in 1947 and a Nature Conservancy to manage the nation's nature reserves in 1949. In 1956, following an "unusually nasty" fog that had descended over London for four days in 1952 and resulted in 4,000 deaths, Parliament approved the Clean Air act. This legislation represented a major step forward in the control of air pollution in Britain's cities. It granted local governmental officials the right to restrict the burning of coal by both households and factories within their jurisdictions. The number of "smokeless zones" increased rapidly, and average urban ground-level concentrations of smoke declined by 80 percent over the next two decades.

In contrast, during the two decades following the end of World War II, the Japanese government single-mindedly pursued policies aimed at promoting rapid industrial development.[7] Its efforts were extremely effective; by 1968 Japan's Gross National Product (GNP) was the second largest of any capitalist nation. However, Japan had become the world's most polluted industrial nation. Air pollution was so severe in Japan's major cities that many school children were issued masks to protect their health, and a substantial portion of the fish caught in and around Japan could no longer be eaten because of contamination caused by the dumping of industrial wastes into the rivers and sea. Moreover, thousands of Japanese had become visibly deformed and physically impaired as a result of mercury poisoning (Minamata disease), cadmium poisoning (itas-itai disease), and PCB poisoning. Yet the government refused to crack down on industrial pollution because it was afraid of doing anything that might interfere with the nation's rapid economic growth.

The 1960s and 1970s

From the mid-1960s through the mid-1970s, environmental issues became much more salient in nearly every industrial nation. Nearly two decades of unusually rapid economic growth in North America, Western

Europe, and Japan had both severely exacerbated environmental problems in the developed world and increased the public's willingness to help pay the costs of ameliorating them. The world press was suddenly filled with dramatic accounts of environmental disasters, including the wreckage of the oil tanker *Torry Canyon* off the coasts of France and England, massive poisoning of fish by accidental discharges of pesticides into the Rhine River, the explosion of an oil well off the coast of Santa Barbara, California, the washing ashore of eighty-nine drums of dangerous chemicals in southwestern England, and the outbreak of Minamata disease in Japan. Environmental organizations grew in size and became more influential throughout the democratic industrialized world. The governments of nearly every industrialized democracy responded by enacting additional environmental regulations and establishing new agencies to administer them.

In no nation did the politics of environmental protection change as rapidly as in Japan. Thanks to favorable and extensive press coverage, "No social issue in postwar Japan received more media coverage than did the pollution problem during the mid-1960s." [8] The demands of the victims of pollution for compensation were highly publicized, thus enabling them to attract increased public support. While previously Japanese public opinion had tended to regard them as "troublemakers who were putting their own interests before the economic and social well-being of the community," [9] now the public recognized that the level of pollution in Japan had indeed reached crisis proportions. The number of citizens groups formed in Japan to protest environmental pollution increased tenfold between 1970 and 1973. In 1971 local governments received more than 75,000 pollution-related complaints, double the number they had received two years earlier. By 1973, more than 10,000 local disputes about pollution had sprung up throughout Japan.[10] For the first time in the postwar period, Japanese industry found itself on the defensive. Instead of welcoming new industry into their communities, citizens groups began to worry about its environmental impact. The influence and legitimacy of victims groups and their supporters were further strengthened by a series of key court rulings that held that companies were responsible for compensating the individuals who had suffered either financially or otherwise from the pollution emitted by their factories. Even more significantly, Japan's dominant political party, the LDP, experienced a number of setbacks in local elections due to its close identification with the interests of industry.

As a result of this change in the political climate, Japanese environmental policy was dramatically transformed. In 1970 the Japanese Diet passed fourteen major environmental laws. This "pollution Diet," as it came to be known, transformed Japan virtually overnight from the industrial nation that had historically paid the least attention to environmental concerns to one with the world's most ambitious program of pollution control. The automotive emission standards and controls over air pollution established by the Japanese government over the bitter opposition of the business community were the strictest in the world. They were also relatively well enforced. By 1975, Japanese industry was devoting 4.6 percent of its total investment to pollution control—more than any other industrial nation.[11] The comparable figures were 3.4 percent for the United States and 1.7 percent for Great Britain. This amounted to 1 percent of Japan's GNP, as compared to .44 percent for the United States and .29 percent for Great Britain.

Public concern about environmental quality also increased in Great Britain. The membership of the Society for the Promotion of Nature Conservation increased from 35,000 to 75,000 between 1968 and 1972, while the membership of the Royal Society for the Protection of Birds expanded from 41,000 to 108,000 during the same period. By the early 1970s environmental groups had been established in more than one thousand communities. The total membership of the local conservation movement had grown to approximately 300,000, or slightly less than 1 percent of the British population. One journalist observed, "The environmental lobby has succeeded in creating a halo effect for the conservationist cause; today it is a bold politician who risks its disapprobation." Another noted, "The environment as a general issue has risen to a dominant position among political concerns." [12] In her address to the opening of Parliament in 1970, Queen Elizabeth promised that her ministers would "intensify the drive to remedy past damage to the environment and . . . seek to safeguard the beauty of the British countryside and the seashore for the future." [13] The British government subsequently approved a number of new environmental statutes, including the Deposit of Poisonous Waste Act (1972), the Water Act (1974), and the Control of Pollution Act (1974). The Control of Pollution Act marked the first time in Britain that a single piece of legislation had addressed a multiplicity of environmental problems, including waste disposal, water pollution, noise nuisance, and air pollution. It thus represented a "major step forward in the administration of pollution control in the U.K." [14]

Comparing Japanese and British Environmental Regulations

Many of the environmental issues that have surfaced in Japan and Great Britain during the last three decades have been similar. Both nations have experienced considerable conflict over the construction of new airports. Community opposition has frustrated the efforts of the British government to develop a third international airport to serve the London area since 1964; similarly, the unwillingness of a small group of farmers, aided by a group of radical students, to sell their land to the Japanese government has prevented the construction of a second runway at Narita, the international airport serving the Tokyo area.[15] Both nations have also been preoccupied with automobile emissions. In Japan, industry and government battled throughout the 1970s over the rate at which emissions of hydrocarbons should be restricted; a similar controversy surfaced in Britain over the allowable lead content of gasoline.

The problem of hazardous wastes and toxic dumps has been a recurrent environmental issue in both countries as evidence about the health hazards of various dump sites and particular chemicals has periodically come to light. Environmental activists in both nations have placed a major priority on preventing the construction of additional nuclear power plants.

In a number of other respects, the environmental agenda has differed substantially in the two countries. For more than a century, the central preoccupation of environmental policies in Japan has been the threat posed by pollution to human health; it was the mobilization of the victims of various pollution-related diseases—and their successful lawsuits against various companies—that spearheaded the emergence of environmentalism as a major political issue in Japan between the mid-1960s and the mid-1970s. Significantly, Japan is the only major industrial nation to have established an administrative compensation system designed specifically to compensate the victims of toxic-substance pollution. With relatively few exceptions, most of the citizens groups formed during the 1970s were primarily interested in curbing pollution from local sources that appeared to threaten their own health and that of their neighbors.

By contrast, in Britain, as in the United States and the rest of Western Europe, health issues have represented only one dimension of environmentalism. British environmental organizations have also placed a high priority on preserving wildlife—primarily birds—and on protecting the nation's scenic countryside from the effects of industrial expansion, highway construction, and mining. During the 1970s and 1980s, there was considerable controversy over issues such as the protection of the Scottish coastline from the development associated with North Sea oil, mineral exploration in the national parks, and the protection of the hedgerows that dot the English countryside from farmers who wanted to destroy them in order to cultivate their land more efficiently. Whereas Japanese farmers have been among the major supporters of controls over industrial pollution, British farmers have frequently been criticized by conservation groups concerned about the effects of commercial agriculture—including the extensive use of pesticides—on the landscape, wild animals, birds, and flowers.

The differences between Japanese and British environmental policies and politics are due to a number of factors. The importance of conservation issues in Britain and their relative neglect in Japan is, in part, cultural. Western culture has historically placed a relatively high value on the protection of animals and "nature." The British government in particular has played a leading role in seeking to prevent the slaughter of wild birds in Europe, and the British have restricted the import of products made from endangered species.

In contrast, "nature" has generally been regarded more as a threat than as a source of solace in Japan. When the Japanese think of nature they think of the typhoons and earthquakes that have been a recurrent feature of Japanese life, not of undeveloped wilderness areas or the peaceful countryside. Moreover, the Japanese do not give the protection of animals the priority it has in the West. Until recently Japan continued to permit the import of products made from endangered species, such as ivory, whose import had been restricted by almost all other industrial countries. And while Japan has promised to reduce the number of fishing boats that use nets that kill marine mammals, it remains the only major industrial nation that continues to engage in whaling.

There are also important differences between the social base of environmentalism in the two countries. The English landed aristocracy has long been interested in both conservation and pollution-control issues. Much of the British environmental movement retains a strong upper-class flavor. Many of Britain's most prominent environmental organizations are headed by members of the House of Lords and members of the royal family, including most recently Prince Charles. These aristocrats frequently lend their names to the various fund-raising efforts of conservation organizations. By contrast, Japanese environmental organizations tend to draw their primary support from the least affluent and least educated segments of the Japanese population, many of whom live in rural areas; they are interested less in conservation and pollution control for its own sake than in protecting their own health and sources of income.

Contemporary Environmental Politics and Policies

During the 1980s the politics of environmental protection changed substantially in both Japan and Great Britain. While the environment as a political issue has declined in importance in Japan, it has become more visible in Great Britain.

Japanese Environmental Policy

Environmentalism has become much less politically salient in Japan since the mid-1970s. The attention of the media has moved to other issues. At the local level, many of the politicians who had been strong supporters of strict environmental controls during the late 1960s and early 1970s have since been voted out of office. Their successors, members of Japan's conservative political party, the LDP, have been reluctant to antagonize local industry. Likewise, the courts, which formerly had played a critical role in challenging the privileged position enjoyed by Japanese business, have since become much more hesitant to rule in favor of citizen plaintiffs. In addition, the budgets for pollution control by local agencies were reduced during the 1980s. Investment in pollution control by private firms peaked in 1975 and has since steadily declined; in 1981 Japanese firms spent only one-third of the amount they had spent in 1975 (in constant yen).[16]

At the national level, the environmental movement in Japan remains poorly organized and enjoys little political influence, although it does occasionally succeed in halting particular development projects. A mid-1989 survey reported that the Japanese public trails far behind that of other nations in realizing the importance of preserving the environment.[17] The Environment Agency, established in 1971, is still relatively powerless. Environmental organizations have virtually no access to it, and since the mid-1970s it has been much less willing to challenge Japan's powerful business community. For example, thanks to the opposition of business, an environmental assessment bill has remained stalled in the Diet. As a result, Japan is one of the only industrial nations that does not require an environmental impact assessment for government projects.

While Japan was close to the forefront of global pollution-control efforts during the first half of the 1970s, since that time its initiatives have tended to lag behind those of most other industrial nations. Japan has not played a leadership role in responding to the new environmental issues of the 1980s, such as acid rain, ozone depletion, deforestation, or the greenhouse effect. Indeed, it is precisely Japan's seemingly insatiable demand for lumber that has prompted the Brazilian government to open up additional areas of the Amazon to lumbering. More generally, "Despite her enthusiastic pledge of environmental good citizenship at the 1972 Stockholm Conference on the Human Environment, Japan has consistently taken anti-environmental positions in international negotiations." [18] However, in 1986 the Japanese Diet did vote to restrict the production and consumption of freon, which contributes to the destruction of the ozone layer; and in 1988 the Japanese government announced that it would begin regulating the production and importation of chlorofluorocarbons (CFCs) in accordance with the terms of the 1987 Montreal Protocol. (Under the terms of this protocol, signed by forty nations, member nations must reduce the production and use of CFCs by 50 percent by the turn of the century. CFCs are viewed as a major cause of the destruction of the ozone layer.) Two major Japanese industrial firms, NEC and Matsushita, subsequently announced that they planned to completely phase out the use of CFCs by the end of the century.

Moreover, the Japanese government has announced a major program to support research to develop replacements for CFCs, alternative-fuel engines for cars, and more powerful solar batteries.

The Japanese record on pollution control is a mixed one. Japan has made considerable progress in reducing sulfur dioxide emissions; the average annual concentration of sulfur dioxide peaked in 1967 and has declined steadily since. In fact, Japan is a world leader in the development of sulfur oxide control technologies. It employs five times as many scrubbers—devices that remove sulfur and nitrogen oxides from smokestack emissions—as any other industrial nation. Japan also disposes of 50 percent of its toxic wastes by high-temperature incineration, compared to 1 percent in the United States. It also has one of the world's most sophisticated systems for sorting, collecting, and incinerating household wastes, including a separate system for disposing of batteries. Its automotive emission standards, although weakened during the 1970s, remain among the strictest in the world. Nevertheless, while the overall level of air pollutants in Japan is less than in Europe, air pollution in the highly industrialized area around Tokyo remains a public health problem. The steady increase in automobile use has resulted in an increase in the national ambient level of nitrogen oxides during the last two decades. Japan, like much of Western Europe and the United States, also faces a growing acid rain problem. Nearly 10 percent of Japan's major lakes are now acidic.

Japan has made considerable improvements in reducing the concentration of heavy metals and toxic chemicals in rivers and streams. But overall, water quality in Japan has improved very slowly during the last two decades. While the concentration of toxic substances in factory emissions has been reduced, population growth continues to exceed the rate of sewer construction. The continued heavy reliance by Japanese farmers on pesticides remains an important contributor to water pollution; Japan's per acre use of pesticides is the highest in the developed world. More recently, Japan has also begun to face a growing groundwater pollution problem caused by the leakage of toxic organic chemicals used in producing integrated circuits.

The "Greening" of Britain

While the political saliency of environmental concerns and the strength of the environmental movement did not decline as much in Britain between the mid-1970s and mid-1980s as in Japan, the pace of new regulatory initiatives did slow down. Like Japan during the 1950s and through much of the 1960s, Britain during most of the 1980s was preoccupied with improving its economic performance. Moreover, Britain's prime minister, Margaret Thatcher, was generally unsympathetic to the concerns of environmentalists; at one point she described them as "the enemy within."[19] Under her leadership, the British government fought vigorously in the European Community for the least restrictive limits on the production of chlorofluorocarbons, emissions of sulfur (a leading cause of acid rain in Europe), and radiation in food.

In the fall of 1988 the British government's position on environmental regulation changed abruptly. In a major speech before the Royal Society in September 1988, Prime Minister Thatcher declared that protecting "the balance of nature" represented "one of the greatest challenges of the late 20th century," adding that the cost of expensive cleanup actions was "money well and necessarily spent because the health of the economy and the health of our environment are totally dependent upon each other."[20] She emphasized the importance of global environmental problems, including the greenhouse effect, the hole in the ozone layer, and acid rain, and promised that Britain would begin to play a leadership role in devising solutions to these major threats to the biosphere.

The change in Thatcher's position reflected a growing concern about environmental issues on the part of the British public. In 1982, 50 percent of those polled stated that protecting the environment was more important than keeping prices down. By 1985 this figure had increased to 60 percent; in 1988 it stood at 74 percent.[21] Increased concern about the environment was especially strong among conservative Tory voters, many of whom—having shared in the prosperity of the Thatcher years—had now become anxious to preserve the quality of life in the British countryside where they had purchased homes.

The British public had been relatively satisfied with the efforts of the British government to control water and air pollution during the 1960s and 1970s. In fact, the British record was a reasonably impressive one. Between 1958 and 1971 urban ground concentration levels of sulfur dioxide fell by 50 percent; in the same period emissions of smoke from industrial sources declined by 94 percent. London's famous fogs, which were actually caused by the burning of coal, disappeared. Britain's water quality also steadily improved, with the Thames becoming the cleanest tidal river in the world. However, these improvements did not continue through the 1980s. Thanks in part to the recovery of British industry, sulfate emissions began to increase again after 1986 and, on balance, Britain's rivers were dirtier in 1988 than they had been in 1980. In a poll conducted in 1988, 64 percent of the British public described their environment as having been "destroyed to a considerable extent,"[22] while more than half expressed the view that the countryside was changing for the worse.[23]

Environmental Politics in Western Europe

The "greening" of Margaret Thatcher was the most prominent sign of the heightened interest in environmental issues that took place throughout Europe during the second half of the 1980s. One reporter wrote, "Nearly two decades after the first Earth Day, ecology is back in vogue . . . suddenly . . . the environment [has become] a fashionable issue among world leaders." [24] Provoked in part by the accident at the Chernobyl nuclear power plant in the Soviet Union and a massive chemical spill of toxins into the Rhine river—both of which took place in 1986—environmental issues moved rapidly to a prominent position on the political agenda in a number of developed nations. The *Washington Post* observed in December 1988:

> Dead seals in the North Sea, a chemical fire on the Loire, killer algae off the coast of Sweden, contaminated drinking water in Cornwall. A drumbeat of emergencies has intensified the environmental debate this year in Europe, when public concern about pollution has never been higher.[25]

Opinion polls in Sweden revealed that 70 percent of the electorate rated the environment as their top concern. In parliamentary elections in Sweden held in 1988, the newly formed Green party captured twenty seats, becoming the first new party to be represented in the Swedish legislature in seventy years. Almost concurrently, Greens were elected for the first time to two provincial parliaments in Austria; and in France, the Green party received twice as many votes in local elections as it had six years earlier. Most significantly, in the elections to the European Parliament held in June 1989, Europe's Green parties captured an additional seventeen seats, bringing their total representation to thirty-seven and making them among the biggest "winners" of the election.

During the second half of the 1980s, the West European nation with the most politically influential environmental movement was the Federal Republic of Germany. One indication of the political strength of the West German environmental movement was the extent of electoral support for the Green party. Established in 1980 as the FRG's fourth political party, it received 5.6 percent of the votes cast in national elections in 1983, entitling it to twenty-seven seats in the Federal Parliament. Four years later, its national vote total increased to 8.3 percent and the number of its seats to forty-two. But public support for environmental regulation in West Germany has extended far beyond the electoral supporters of the Green party. A poll taken in December 1986 reported that 52 percent of the electorate regarded the environment as the most important issue facing their nation.[26]

While the Green party has been primarily preoccupied with opposing nuclear power (as well as the presence of nuclear weapons on German soil), the most visible environmental issues in West Germany have been the death of the nation's historic "black" forests from acid rain and the pollution of its most important river, the Rhine. To reduce emissions of sulfur dioxide—a major cause of acid rain—West Germany has embarked on Europe's most expensive cleanup program. By mandating the installation of scrubbers on most of its coal-fired power stations, the FRG plans to reduce SO_2 emissions by two-thirds by the mid-1990s. Within the European Community, West Germany has played a leadership role in urging strict antipollution controls on car exhausts, which also contribute to acid rain.

The West German government also has been extremely active in the fight against water pollution. For example, it imposed strict controls on its large and highly profitable chemical industry in order to prevent the accidental discharge of toxic pollutants into the nation's rivers. (Twenty-eight major chemical plants are located on the Rhine.) It also has imposed the tightest controls in Europe on the use of phosphates in detergents. In addition, in 1987 it announced a plan to completely eliminate the burning of waste at sea by 1994. The government estimated that industry's share of the costs of ending the dumping of sewage sludge and the burning of toxic wastes in the North Sea by employing alternative methods of waste disposal would come to more than $11 billion.[27]

It is highly unlikely that the Green parties will ever acquire sufficient electoral strength to become an important part of any European government, but their growing strength has certainly had an important impact on the policies of a number of national governments. In particular, both West German chancellor Helmut Kohl and French president François Mitterrand have become far more responsive to environmental concerns than they otherwise would have been. Equally important, the presence of a large number of Greens in a number of European legislatures, and in the European Parliament, has given the European environmental movement an important political forum. They now have much more ability to participate in the making and implementation of environmental policy than they had in the past.[28]

Environmental Politics in the Communist World

While visible public concern with environmental issues had previously been restricted to the democratic capitalist nations, during the late 1980s environmentalism became part of the political agenda in a number of communist nations for the first time. As part of its policy of *glasnost*, the Soviet government began to admit publicly the magnitude of that nation's environmental problems. The first director of the newly established National Environment Committee, who is a close associate of Mikhail Gorbachev, admitted that "industrial pollution is 10 times greater than safe-health norms in 102 Soviet cities, affecting 50 million people."[29] The Soviet press reported that Lake Ladoga near Leningrad is thought to be terminally polluted and noted that the Aral Sea in Central Asia, once the fourth-largest lake on earth, had shrunk by two-thirds during the last three decades due to drainage for irrigation. Huge areas of the Siberian Far East have been stripped of timber, leaving vast barren tracts that will take generations of tender care to renew.

Equally important, an environmental movement has begun to emerge in the Soviet Union. Ecology groups succeeded in blocking the construction of a bridge that was planned to cut through a nature reserve on the Dnieper island of Khortitsa. Public pressure also persuaded the government to abandon a scheme to reverse the flow of Siberian rivers to help irrigation. Thousands rallied to protest the pollution from a phosphate plant in Estonia and a chemical factory in Kazan, and in opposition to a proposed hydroelectric power plant in Latvia. In the summer of 1988 a human chain more than twenty-two miles long was formed to protest pollution of the Baltic seacoast. More than 300,000 Lithuanians signed petitions demanding international inspection of a local nuclear power plant.

The political liberalization that has taken place in Eastern Europe has also led to an outpouring of public interest in environmental issues in this region of the world. For example, more than sixty national and local environmental organizations have been formed in Poland, the nation with the most severe environmental problems in Eastern Europe. A joint program signed by the Polish government and a number of officially recognized environmental organizations stated, "The threat to human life in Poland as a result of environmental conditions is one of the greatest in the world." [30] According to a study by the Polish National Academy of Science, 11 percent of the nation's land area, containing one-third of its population, was an "environmental disaster area." [31] Ninety-five percent of the river water in Poland is no longer fit for drinking, and half of the nation's lakes have become irreversibly contaminated.

The European Community

The spread of environmentalism throughout a large portion of the industrialized world constitutes one new dimension of the environmentalist upsurge that took place toward the end of the 1980s. A second is the emergence and growing importance of environmental issues that are international in scope. In this context, it is significant that the European Community, whose membership by the 1980s had expanded to twelve nations in western and southern Europe, has begun to play a much more active role in harmonizing environmental regulations among its member states.

European Environmental Issues

There are three factors motivating EC intervention in environmental regulation. First, air and water pollution in Europe do not respect national or political boundaries. River quality in the Netherlands is significantly affected by discharges from factories in France and the Federal Republic of Germany, while pollution levels in the North Sea are shaped by the policies of several nations, especially Great Britain, the FRG, the Netherlands, and Norway. In addition, the winds in Europe move from west to east. Thus, the pollution produced by the burning of coal in Great Britain affects air quality not only in Britain but also in much of northern Europe. As one journalist noted, "Environmental regulations are among the world's toughest in Scandinavia, West Germany and the Netherlands. But that does little good when winds waft Britain's loosely regulated power-plant fumes and their product, acid rain, eastward." [32]

Moreover, the frightening speed at which pollution in one nation can affect the inhabitants of neighboring ones was dramatically demonstrated in 1986; a fire at the warehouse of the Sandoz chemical company in Switzerland created a tide of thirty tons of toxic waste that within ten days had flowed down the Rhine through West Germany, France, and the Netherlands and into the North Sea, causing untold damage along the way, including the destruction of half a million fish in four countries and the disruption of the water supplies of hundreds of towns and cities in West Germany. Not only was this the worst environmental disaster inside Europe in several years, but its political significance was magnified by the fact that it had occurred so soon after the accident in which a nuclear power plant in the Soviet Union had spilled a cloud of radioactivity across half of Europe.

Second, the environmental standards promulgated by each EC member nation significantly affect the international competitiveness of its domestic industry. The existence of twelve separate environmental standards threatened to undermine the efforts of the EC to create a genuine common market in which companies from throughout the EC would compete on a roughly equal basis. Harmonization became particularly important with the approach of 1992—the date by which the EC planned to remove all national barriers to free trade among its member states. As Emile Roco, a Dow Chemical Company government-relations official in Europe and vice chairman of a European industry committee on 1992, put it, "If we're going to open up the borders in 1992, it's desirable to have harmonization so that all play by the same rules." [33]

Finally, the international institutions created by the EC, namely the European Parliament based in Strasbourg, France, and the EC headquarters in Brussels, have proven relatively responsive to pressures from interest groups. Indeed, in a number of cases, environmental organizations and national regulatory officials enjoy more influence over policy makers in Brussels and Strasbourg than they do with their own national governments. Working to strengthen EC environmental standards and regulations enabled many environmental organizations to secure the enactment of stricter regulatory policies than those achieved at the national level. Not surprisingly, this development has caused considerable concern within the European business community, which fears that in the name of "harmonization" the EC will issue regulations so stringent that they will reduce economic growth and trade throughout Europe.

EC Environmental Policy

The European Community first became involved with environmental policy in 1973 when an environmental program was formally adopted by the community's Council of Ministers. The EC's "action plan" stated that "major aspects of environmental policy in individual countries must no longer be planned or implemented in isolation . . . and that national policies should be harmonized within the community." [34] In the course of the next fifteen years, the EC issued more than 120 directives related to the environment. They covered virtually every aspect of environmental policy, including air- and water-quality standards for more than 300 substances; standards for the marketing, use, and labeling of pesticides; and standards for the disposal of toxic wastes. The so-called Sixth Amendment, enacted in 1979, regulated the use and labeling of hundreds of chemicals; the Seveso directive, enacted in 1982 following the accidental release of large quantities of dioxin into the countryside of northern Italy, contains a list of 178 dangerous substances that, when used above certain quantities in a manufacturing process, require detailed safety reports and emergency plans from the manufacturer.

Notwithstanding this flurry of activity, for the most part the rules and standards promulgated by the EC had relatively little effect on national regulatory policies. In many cases, the regulations simply codified existing national standards. And in cases where they went beyond what particular governments had already required, they were often ignored. For example, in 1978 EC regulations required each member state to identify and protect important fish habitats. But only four countries responded—and they avoided additional cleanup costs by designating only lakes and rivers that already met EC water-quality standards for fish. All told, Italy has been in violation of approximately forty directives, and Greece and the FRG have not complied with more than twenty-five. On occasion, the EC has successfully sued national governments in the European Court, but the court's rulings have not been enforced.

During the latter part of the 1980s, largely as a result of increased public concern about the environment on the part of the European public, the EC finally began to have an impact. Significantly, an amendment in 1987 to the Treaty of Rome granted the Commission of the European Communities its first explicit authority over the environment. That same year, the Council of Ministers approved the EC's fourth environmental action program, which raised environmental policy to a central position in the formulation and execution of all other EC policies. In a landmark decision in September 1988, the European Court ruled that environmental protection can take priority over trade under Common Market treaties. One environmentalist observed, "Thirty years after the treaty (that founded the EC) we have the recognition that environmental policy is an essential element of the community." [35] Nonetheless, the European Court has limited power to force member states to implement EC directives.

The Effectiveness of EC Regulations

EC environmental regulations have recently become more effective because they have become more focused.[36] Instead of seeking to duplicate existing national laws, the EC has begun to concentrate its efforts on areas in which there is a genuine need for international cooperation. For example, in 1987 the EC issued a directive requiring its member states to scrutinize the impact of major construction projects—which often can affect more than one nation—before they are begun. In a similar vein, the EC issued a directive requiring member states to notify one another whenever a cargo of highly toxic material crosses a national boundary. It also played an important role in securing an international agreement to limit the dumping of wastes into the North Sea.

One of the most important recent European Community initiatives has been to strengthen the regulation of the production of chemicals whose use is impairing the ozone layer. In March 1989, in what the *New York Times* described as "an unexpectedly strong move," the twelve member states of the EC agreed to cut the production of chlorofluorocarbons by 85 percent as soon as possible, and to eliminate them entirely by the end of the century.[37] (EC members are currently responsible for slightly more than one-third of worldwide chlorofluorocarbon production.) This step went considerably beyond an agreement reached in Montreal in 1987 by thirty-one nations, including the Common Market countries and the United States, that had called for a 50 percent reduction in the production of these chemicals by the end of the century. This new consensus was made possible in large measure by a major shift in the position of the British government.

In addition, after more than a decade of bitter wrangling, the EC finally agreed in 1989 on a pollution control standard for small engine vehicles that will require them by 1992 to meet emission control standards similar to those currently in effect in the United States. Unlike in the United States, where catalytic converters have been required for more than fifteen years, companies will be able to meet the new EC standards by installing either lean-burn engines or catalytic converters.[38] On the other hand, the EC remains divided over the use of lead-free gasoline. It is widely available in those nations that have imposed relatively strict automobile emission standards, namely West Germany, the Netherlands, Belgium, and Denmark, but not commonly available in Great Britain, France, Italy, and Spain, which have not. But in response to increased consumer demand for "clean" cars, a growing proportion of the motor vehicles produced in Europe are being equipped to run on unleaded fuel. In any event, under the terms of this decision the use of catalytic converters will be mandatory for all large cars throughout Europe by 1994.

Equally important, after five years of negotiations, the EC finally agreed in 1988 on a program to cut back on sulfur emissions, the major cause of the acid rain that has affected lakes and forests throughout much of northern Europe. Significantly, Great Britain, Western Europe's biggest producer of sulfur oxides—nearly 60 percent of the sulfur dioxide emitted by Britain is "exported" to the east, primarily to Sweden and Norway—finally agreed to install scrubbers on each of its coal-burning power plants. Britain's Central Electricity Generating Board had bitterly resisted this move for nearly two decades. It is projected that this step will reduce Britain's sulfur emissions 14 percent by 1997.[39]

The Future of European Community Regulation

In 1988 a British barrister predicted that the EC's new environmental program "will ultimately have the most far reaching impact on Europe and . . . will probably affect the lives of its individual citizens in a more fundamental way than the economic, fiscal and technical measures proposed under the 1992 legislation." [40] It is clear that the EC will play an increasingly important role in shaping the environmental policies of each European government. But the overall impact of its increased authority will remain mixed since different national governments continue to have very different political and economic priorities. In some cases, EC regulations will constitute a "floor" forcing stricter environmental standards on member states with the least commitment to environmental protection, who generally tend to be the least affluent. In other cases, EC initiatives will become a "ceiling," preventing those nations willing and able to impose stricter pollution control standards on industry from doing so. What can be predicated with confidence is that as a result of the increased pressure to "harmonize" environmental regulations in Europe, environmental politics will become more contentious—both within and among the national governments.

Conclusion

The globalization of environmentalism represents one of the most significant political developments of the 1980s. Not only has the number of countries whose governments have become concerned with environmental issues substantially increased, but governments throughout the world have become increasingly aware of the international dimensions of environmental regulation. The efforts of governments to harmonize and coordinate their environmental policies with those of other nations have been especially advanced in the nations of Western Europe, for geographic as well as political reasons. But this movement has by no means been confined to this region of the world.

The United States was one of thirty-one nations that signed an agreement in 1987 to reduce the production of chlorofluorocarbons 50 percent by the turn of the century. A year later, the United States joined with twenty-four other industrial nations in signing an international protocol to freeze the rate of emission of nitrogen oxides. The latter represented the first binding commitment of the United States to Canada to limit America's "export" of acid rain to its northern neighbor. And while, unlike in Europe and the United States, the Japanese environmental movement remains politically weak, the Japanese government is finding itself under growing international pressure to do more to address global environmental problems such as the destruction of the ozone layer and of the world's rain forests.[41]

While the way in which each industrial nation goes about making and enforcing environmental regulations will differ no less in the future than it has in the past, national regulatory standards appear to be converging. In addition, America's rule-oriented approach to environmental regulation is becoming more widely adopted outside the United States; the regulatory policies and procedures of the European Community resemble those of the United States more closely than they do any nation in Western Europe. This does not automatically make environmental regulation more effective, since the American approach to regulation has, on balance, proven no more or less effective than that adopted by other industrial nations. (In most cases, American standards *are* stricter, but their enforcement has been highly uneven.)

We can expect the politics of environmental regulation to become more contentious, particularly in Western Europe, as America's adversarial style of regulation spreads to other countries. However, in the final analysis, the actual willingness of any nation to commit substantial additional resources to improving the quality of both the national and global environment will continue to be shaped primarily by both the relative strength of its economy and the priorities of its citizenry. As long as these continue to vary, so will each nation's commitment to protecting the health of its citizens and the viability of the biosphere.

Notes

1. For a comprehensive overview of this literature see David Vogel, "The Comparative Study of Environmental Policy: A Review of the Literature," in *Comparative Policy Research: Learning From Experience*, ed. Meinolf Dierkes, Hans Weiler, and Ariane Berthoin Antal (Brookfield, Vt.: Gower, 1987), 99-170.
2. For a comparison of environmental regulation in Japan and the United States, see Susan Pharr and Joseph Badaracco, Jr., "Coping with Crisis: Environmental Regulation," in *America Versus Japan*, ed. Thomas McCraw (Boston: Harvard Business School Press, 1986), 229-260; for a comparison of British and American environmental policy, see David Vogel, *National Styles of Regulation: Environmental Policy in Great Britain and the United States* (Ithaca, N.Y.: Cornell University Press, 1986); for an examination of the regulation of chemicals in the United States, West Germany, France, and Great Britain, see Ronald Brickman, Shelia Jasanoff, and Thomas Illgen, *Chemical Regulation and Cancer: A Cross-National Study of Policy and Politics* (Ithaca, N.Y.: Program on Science, Technology, and Society, 1982).
3. For an excellent study of the role of the American courts in pollution control policy, see R. Shep Melnick, *Regulation and the Courts: The Case of the Clean Air Act* (Washington, D.C.: Brookings Institution, 1983).
4. See Eugene Bardach and Robert Kagen, *Going by the Book: The Problem of Regulatory Unreasonableness* (Philadelphia: Temple University Press, 1982).
5. Vogel, *National Styles of Regulation*, 34.
6. Norrie Huddle and Michael Reich, *Island of Dreams* (Cambridge, Mass.: Schenkman, 1987), 29.
7. For a wide-ranging and highly critical assessment of Japanese environmental regulation, see Huddle and Reich, *Island of Dreams*.
8. Pharr and Badaracco, "Coping with Crisis," 241.
9. Ibid.
10. Ellis Krauss and Bradford Simock, "Citizens Movements: The Growth and Impact of Environmental Protest in Japan," in *Political Opposition and Local Politics in Japan*, ed. Kurt Steiner, Ellis Krauss, and Scott Flanagan (Princeton, N.J.: Princeton University Press, 1980), 187. For more on citizen protests in Japan, see Margaret McKean, *Environmental Protest and Citizen Politics in Japan* (Berkeley: University of California Press, 1981).
11. Barry Eichengreen, "International Competition in U.S. Basic Industries," in *The United States in the World Economy*, ed. Martin Feldstein (Chicago: University of Chicago Press, 1988), 330.
12. Quoted in Vogel, *National Styles of Regulation*, 43.
13. Quoted in ibid.

14. Ibid.
15. For a gripping account of the latter controversy, see David Apter and Nagayo Sawa, *Against the State: Politics and Social Protest in Japan* (Cambridge, Mass.: Harvard University Press, 1964).
16. Saburo Ikeda, "Risk Management Practices in Japan," in *Risk Management in the U.S. and Japan: A Comparative Perspective* (Nashville: Vanderbilt University, 1984), 27.
17. "Poll Finds Japanese Lack Environmental Concern," *Japan Times*, May 10, 1989.
18. Huddle and Reich, *Island of Dreams*, 10.
19. Robin Herman, "An Ecological Epiphany," *Washington Post National Weekly Edition*, December 5-11, 1988, 19.
20. Ibid.
21. Ibid.
22. Richard Hudson, "Europeans Are Learning That Pollution Must Be Attacked in a Coordinated Way," *Wall Street Journal*, November 1, 1988, A26.
23. "Green Fingers," *Economist*, September 10, 1988, 71.
24. Matthew Vita, "The Greening of International Affairs," *San Francisco Chronicle*, April 12, 1989, Briefing, 1.
25. Herman, "An Ecological Epiphany," 19.
26. Richard Kirkland, Jr., "Environmental Anxiety Goes Global," *Fortune*, November 21, 1988, 118. See also "Germany Slows Burning at Sea," *Chemical Week*, November 25, 1987, 16; and David Marsh, "West Germany Tightens Guidelines," *Financial Times*, July 15, 1988, ix.
27. Eric Sjogren, "Who Will Clean Up Europe's Pollution?" *Management Today*, January 1987, 19.
28. For a survey of Green politics in Europe, see Ferdinand Müller Rommel, ed., *New Politics in Western Europe: The Rise and Success of Green Parties and Alternative Lists* (Boulder, Colo.: Westview Press, 1989).
29. Jeff Trimble, "Perestroika vs. a Growing Wasteland," *U.S. News and World Report*, December 5, 1988, 44.
30. Quoted in Jackson Diehl, "Choking on Their Own Development," *Washington Post National Weekly Edition*, May 29-June 4, 1989, 9.
31. Quoted in ibid.
32. Ibid.
33. Hudson, "Europeans Are Learning," A26.
34. Vogel, *National Styles of Regulation*, 102.
35. Quoted in ibid.
36. For an overview of EC environmental regulation, see Nigel Haigh, *EEC Environmental Policy and Britain* (London: Environmental Data Services, 1984); and Nigel Haigh, *The Coordination of Standards for Chemicals in the Environment* (London: Institute for European Environmental Policy, 1988).
37. Craig Whitney, "12 European Nations to Ban Chemicals That Harm Ozone," *New York Times*, March 2, 1989, 1.
38. Kevin Done, "A Two-Speed Europe on Exhaust Fumes," *Financial Times*, July 18, 1988, 11.
39. "A Twist of Lime in a Cocktail of Troubles," *The Economist*, May 27, 1989, 85.

40. Andrew Geddes, "1992 and the Environment—Sovereignty Well Lost?" *New Law Journal* (1988): 826.
41. "Charging Japan with Crimes Against the Earth," *Business Week*, October 8, 1989, 108, 112.

13

Environment, Population, and Development in the Third World

Richard J. Tobin

Environmental problems occasionally make life in the United States unpleasant and inconvenient, but most Americans contribute to or willingly tolerate this unpleasantness in exchange for the benefits, comforts, and lifestyles associated with a developed, industrialized economy. Most Europeans, Japanese, and Australians share similar lifestyles, so it is not unexpected that they too take modern amenities for granted.

When lifestyles are viewed from a broader perspective, however, much changes. Consider, for example, what life is like for the majority of the world's population. In the late 1980s, America's Gross National Product per capita exceeded $350 per week, but nearly 60 percent of the world's population lived in countries where per capita incomes were less than $20 per week. In India and China, the weekly average in 1987 was less than $6. In Ethiopia, the world's most impoverished country, annual per capita income was about seven-tenths of 1 percent of that in the United States.

Low incomes are not the only problem facing many of the world's inhabitants. In some Third World countries, women, often illiterate with no formal education, will marry as young as age thirteen or fourteen. During their child-bearing years, these women will deliver as many as six or seven babies, about half without the benefits or presence of trained medical personnel. This absence is not without consequences. As the United Nations Children's Fund (UNICEF) notes, the risk of dying because of pregnancy or childbirth is up to 150 times higher in the world's poorest countries than it is in Europe or the United States.[1]

Many of the world's children also are at risk. About 1.3 percent of all

---

The author would like to acknowledge assistance from Yeoh Yeok Kim of the U.N. Fund for Population Activities in Kuala Lumpur, Malaysia, and from Tan Poo-Chang of the University of Malaya.

American infants die before the age of five; in many Asian and African countries, as many as 20 to 30 percent do. *Every day* approximately forty thousand children under five die in the Third World from diseases that rarely kill Americans. Most of the deaths are due to one or more of these six causes: tetanus, measles, malaria, diarrhea, whooping cough, or acute respiratory infections.[2]

Of the Third World children that survive their earliest years, some will have brain damage because their pregnant mothers had no iodine in their diets; others will go blind from lack of proper vitamins. Many will face a life of poverty, never to taste clean water, visit a doctor, enter a classroom, or eat nutritious food regularly or sufficiently. To the extent that shelter is available, it will be rudimentary, usually without electricity or proper sanitary facilities. Because their surroundings have been abused or poorly managed, millions of those in the Third World will also become victims of floods, famine, water-borne diseases, infestation of pests, exceedingly harmful levels of air and water pollution, or desertification.

As these children grow older, many will find that their countries do not have or cannot provide the resources to ensure them a reasonable standard of living. Yet all around them are countries with living standards well beyond their comprehension. The average American uses about thirty-five times more energy and consumes about 60 percent more calories per day, far in excess of minimum daily requirements, than does the average Indian. The Indian might wonder why Americans consume a disproportionate share of the world's resources when he has so little.

In short, life in the Third World provides an entirely different array of problems than those encountered in developed nations. These nations are responding to the benefits and consequences of development, whereas the Third World must cope with widespread poverty and the relative lack of economic development. Yet the problems of both developed and developing nations often cause environmental degradation. Those without property, for example, may be tempted to denude tropical forests for land to farm. Alternately, pressures for development often force countries to overexploit their base of environmental resources.

All of this leads to the key question addressed in this chapter: What are the prospects that the world's poorest countries, with most of the world's population, can improve their lot through sustainable development? According to the World Commission on Environment and Development, sustainable development requires meeting essential needs of the present generation for food, clothing, shelter, jobs, and health without "compromising the ability of future generations to meet their own needs." To achieve this goal, the commission emphasizes the need to stimulate higher levels of economic growth without inflicting irreparable damage on the environment.[3]

Whose responsibility is it to bring about sustainable development?

One view is that richer nations have a moral obligation to assist less fortunate ones. If the former do not meet this obligation, not only will millions in the Third World suffer, but the consequences will be felt in the developed countries as well. Others assert that the poorer nations must accept responsibility for their own fate; outside efforts to help them only worsen the problem and lead to an unhealthy dependence. For example, biologist Garrett Hardin insists that it is wrong to provide food to famine-stricken nations because they have exceeded their environment's carrying capacity. In Hardin's words, "if you give food and save lives and thus increase the number of people, you increase suffering and ultimately increase the loss of life." [4]

The richer nations, whichever position they take, will have some effect on the Third World. It is thus useful to consider how U.S. actions influence the quest for sustainable development. To a large extent, two related factors affect this quest. The first is a country's population; the second is a country's capacity to support its population.

Population Growth: Cure or Culprit?

One of the more controversial elements in the journey toward sustainable development is population growth. Depending on one's perspective, the world is either vastly overpopulated or capable of supporting as many as thirty times its current population (about 5.3 billion in 1990 and increasing at an annual rate of about 1.7 percent).[5] Many of the less developed nations are growing faster than are the industrialized nations (see Table 13-1). Nearly three-quarters of the world's population live outside the more developed regions. If current growth rates continue, the proportion of those in the Third World will increase even more. Between 1990 and 2025, more than 95 percent of the world's population increase will occur in less developed regions, exactly where the people can least afford such a surge.

Africa is particularly prone to high rates of population growth. At more than 4 percent per year, Kenya and the Côte d'Ivoire are among the world's fastest growing countries. The continent has another twenty-three countries that are increasing their populations at 3 percent or more per year. At this rate these nations double their populations every twenty-four years and experience a twentyfold increase every century. Of the dozen countries that have birth rates of at least fifty per thousand, all are in Africa. Fertility rates measure the number of children an average woman has during her lifetime. Thirty-six of the forty-five countries with fertility rates at six or above are in Africa. By comparison, the birth rate in the United States is approximately fifteen per thousand, and its fertility rate is less than two.

High rates of population growth are not necessarily undesirable, and

Table 13-1 Estimated World Populations and Average Annual Growth Rates

Region or country	Population (millions) 1990	2000	2025	Population growth rate (percentage) 1985-1990	Number of years to double population size
World total	5,287	6,251	8,467	1.7	42.0
Developed regions	1,205	1,262	1,352	0.5	144.0
U.S.A.	249	266	301	0.8	90.0
U.S.S.R.	288	308	351	0.8	90.0
Less developed regions	4,078	4,989	7,114	2.1	34.3
China	1,135	1,286	1,493	1.4	51.0
India	853	1,043	1,446	2.1	34.3
Bangladesh	116	151	235	2.7	26.7
Africa	647	872	1,581	3.0	24.0
Côte d'Ivoire	13	19	40	4.1	17.6
Kenya	25	38	78	4.2	17.1
Mexico	88	107	150	2.2	32.7
Brazil	150	179	246	2.1	34.3

Source: Compiled from data included in United Nations Department of International Economic and Social Affairs, *United Nations World Population Chart, 1988* (New York: United Nations, 1988).

criticisms of high rates often bring rebuke. In the early 1970s, for example, when the United States and other developed countries urged less developed countries to stem their growth, more often than not the latter responded with hostility. To pleas that it initiate family planning programs, China complained that they represented capitalist efforts to subjugate the Third World. China viewed a larger population as desirable because it contributed to increases in domestic production.[6]

African delegates to a conference on population in 1973 reported that many of their countries prize high levels of fertility and resent foreigners lecturing them about population growth. Pointing to the vast natural resources and low population density of Africa, the delegates insisted that it could accommodate a much larger population and that the continent's anticipated economic growth would easily satisfy the needs of a growing population. The Africans also offered an alternative view of the world situation that criticized the West's profligate waste of scarce resources. Developed nations, the delegates believed, wanted to resolve shortages of world resources, not by restricting their own use or reducing their own populations, but by restricting Third World growth so that more resources would be available to the West.[7]

By the late 1970s and early 1980s, many developing countries no longer viewed high population growth as desirable. They found themselves with a large number of young, dependent children; increasing rates of unemployment; a cancerous and unchecked growth of urban areas; and a general inability to provide for the social and economic demands of ever larger populations. Many developing countries also realized that if their living standards were to improve, their economic growth would have to exceed their rate of population increase.

Although many countries altered their attitudes about population growth, they soon realized the enormity of the task. The prevailing theory of demographic transition suggests that societies go through three stages. In the first stage, in premodern societies, birth rates and death rates are high, so populations remain stable or increase at low rates. In the second stage, death rates are lower and populations grow more rapidly because of vaccines, better health care, and more nutritious foods. As countries begin to reap the benefits of economic growth, they enter the third stage. Infant mortality declines, but so does the desire or need to have large families. Population growth slows considerably.

This model explains what occurred in the United States and in many European countries: As standards of living increased, birth rates declined. The model's weakness is that it assumes economic growth; in the absence of such growth, many nations are caught in a "demographic trap." [8] They get stuck in the second stage. This is the predicament of many developing countries today. In some of these countries the situation is even worse. Their populations are growing faster than their economies, and living standards are declining. According to UNICEF, average incomes dropped by as much as 10 to 25 percent in most of Africa and much of Latin America in the 1980s. The immediate prospects for improvement are not bright. The World Bank predicts that many African and Latin American nations will face even lower average incomes in the 1990s.[9]

These declines create a cruel paradox. Larger populations produce increased demands for health and educational services; deteriorating economies make it more difficult to provide the services. Evidence for the latter is found in governmental budgets. In the African nation of Zaire, the national government devoted slightly more than 15 percent of its expenditures to education in 1972; by 1986, education's share of the budget was less than 1 percent. Uganda spent more than 5 percent of its budget on health in 1972, but less than half of this in 1987.[10]

Economic decline is not the only barrier to reducing population growth, but in the absence of sufficient levels of economic growth, large families are either imperative or difficult to avoid. With economic futures so uncertain, children provide families with additional labor, sometimes as early as age seven or eight. Children also provide a source of income security for their parents during illnesses or retirement. In addition, since infant mortality is high, having many children is necessary to ensure the survival of at least a few.

Abortions and contraceptives can contribute to lower growth rates, but these approaches may not be followed because of the social and religious objections of the people. Consider the example of the Philippines. Its population increased by more than 250 percent between the mid-1940s and the mid-1970s. Demographers estimated the growth rate to be just under 3 percent in the mid-1980s. If this rate continued, they argued, the Philippines would be unable to improve its standard of living. Recommendations that contraceptives be provided to all Filipino men and women of reproductive age were condemned by the Catholic Bishops Conference, which called contraceptives "dehumanising and ethically objectionable." [11] The Philippines is overwhelmingly Catholic, so the Church's objections have nearly paralyzed the country's response to its high growth rates.

Another barrier to slower growth can be found in the opportunity to lower death rates significantly. In some Asian and African countries the average life expectancy at birth is less than forty-five years (compared with seventy-five in the United States and seventy-eight in Japan). If these Asians and Africans had access to the medicines, vaccines, and nutritious foods readily available in the developed nations, then death rates would drop substantially. Life expectancies might be extended by fifteen years or more.

Indeed, there is good reason to expect death rates to decline. Over the past fifteen years the United Nations and other development agencies have attempted to reduce infant mortality by immunizing children against potentially fatal illnesses and by making available inexpensive cures for diarrhea, the single largest cause of death among children under five.[12] These programs have met with considerable success and more is anticipated. The consequence of this success, matched with higher birth rates, is that at least ten low-income countries, all in Africa, will experience even faster growth in the 1990s than they did in the 1960s, 1970s, and 1980s. Reduced infant mortality rates should also reduce fertility rates, but the change will be gradual and millions of children will be born in the meantime.

Given these problems, the success of developing countries such as Cuba, Sri Lanka, South Korea, and Thailand in lowering their population growth rates is all the more remarkable. Thailand reduced its growth rate by half in fifteen years. As *Time* reported in early 1989, the Thais have used both humor and showmanship to achieve this reduction. A private association distributes condoms at movie theaters and traffic jams, sponsors condom-blowing contests, and organizes a special cops-and-rubbers program each New Year's Eve. The association also offers free vasectomies on the king's birthday; for those who cannot wait, the normal charge is $20.[13]

Perhaps the best known but most controversial population control programs are in India and China. India's family planning program started in the early 1950s as a low-key educational effort that achieved only modest success. The government changed course from volunteerism to compulsion in the mid-1970s. The minimum age for marriage was increased, and India's states were encouraged to select their own methods to reduce growth.

Several states chose coercion. Parents with two or more children were expected to have themselves sterilized. To ensure compliance, states threatened to withhold salaries or to dismiss people from their government jobs. Public officials were likewise threatened with sanctions if they did not provide enough people for sterilization.[14] One result was a massive program of forced sterilization that caused considerable political turmoil. Although the program was eventually relaxed, India was able to cut its birth and fertility rates by almost 30 percent between 1965 and the late 1980s. Even with these declines, however, India's growth rate is still sufficiently high that it might become the world's most populated country, with more than 1,500,000,000 people, by the middle of the next century.

India may gain this distinction because of what is happening in China. Sharply reversing its earlier position in the late 1970s, the Chinese government conceded that too rapid population growth was leading to shortages of jobs, housing, and consumer goods, and further frustrating efforts to modernize its economy.[15] To reduce the country's population growth rate, the government now discourages early marriages. Beginning in 1979, it also adopted a one-child-per-family policy. The government gives one-child families monthly subsidies, free education for their child, preference for housing and health care, and higher pensions upon retirement. Families that choose to have more than one child are deprived of these benefits and penalized financially if they had previously agreed to have only one child.

The controversial element of the program involves the government's monitoring of women's menstrual cycles; allegations of forced abortions and sterilizations, some occurring as late as the last three months of pregnancy; and even female infanticide in some rural areas. Chinese officials admit that abortions have occasionally been forced on some unwilling women. These officials quickly add, however, that such practices represent aberrations, not accepted guidelines, and that they violate the government's birth control policies.

In its initial years the program in China successfully lowered annual rates of population growth by 50 percent—from 2.2 percent in the 1970s to only 1.1 percent by 1985. Perhaps because of this success the program has encountered considerable resistance and, in some areas, outright disregard. Consequently, the government has relaxed its restrictions and exempted certain families, particularly in rural areas, from the one-child policy. These policy changes led to a 20 percent increase in the birth rate between 1985 and 1987, and China soon announced that it had abandoned its goal of a population of 1.2 billion by 2000.[16] Abandoning this goal does not mean that China has forsaken its entire population control strategy. Renewed concern about population growth in the late 1980s caused the Chinese government to reassess the effectiveness of its programs. If these programs fail and current birth rates continue, China's population could approach 2 billion by the middle of the next century.

The position of the U.S. government toward China's population control efforts has not been consistent. For many years the American government viewed rapidly growing populations as a threat to the Third World's development. The United States backed its rhetoric with money; it was the single largest donor to international population control programs. Then during Ronald Reagan's presidency, the official U.S. position changed dramatically. In mid-1984, the U.S. government declared that it would no longer provide support to private organizations that condone abortion as a form of population control.[17]

A few weeks later at the United Nations International Conference on Population in Mexico City, the Americans stressed that large populations are a problem only when they are not used productively to enhance economic growth. The solution to the lack of such growth is not government intervention, the U.S. delegation asserted, but individual initiatives and the spread of capitalist, free-market economies; economic growth provides a "natural mechanism for slowing population growth." [18] This view led to a decision to reduce U.S. support for population control activities. Due to the United Nations' support of China's population program, the United States announced that it would not contribute to the United Nations Fund for Population Activities after 1985.

Part of the U.S. change was attributed to the administration's opposition to abortion and its belief that larger populations can be advantageous. Some proponents of larger populations claim that they enhance political power, contribute to economic growth, encourage innovation, stimulate agricultural and economic production, and increase prospects that more geniuses will be available to solve human problems.[19]

These views are not limited to a few academics. Several developing countries want to increase their populations. Among them are Bolivia, Iraq, Madagascar, Malawi, Malaysia, Mozambique, North Korea, Zaire, and ironically, the Côte d'Ivoire, already one of the fastest growing countries in the world. Government demographers had once projected that Malaysia's population would eventually stabilize at about 30 to 40 million people, or about two to two and one-half times its population in 1985. Insisting that a larger population would provide a bigger domestic market and more industrial growth, the government announced a population goal of 70 million by 2100.[20]

Clearly, the appropriateness of different population sizes is debatable. There is no clear answer to whether growth by itself is good or bad. The important issue is a country's carrying capacity. Can it ensure its population a reasonable standard of living?

Providing Food and Fuel for Growing Populations

Sustainable development requires that environmental resources not be overtaxed so that they are available for future generations. As Lester Brown points out, however, when populations exceed sustainable yields of their forests, aquifers, and croplands, "they begin directly or indirectly to consume the resource base itself" and gradually destroy it.[21] The eventual result is an irreversible collapse of biological and environmental support systems. Is there any evidence that these systems are now being strained?

The first place to look is in the area of food production. Nations can grow their own food, import it, or, as most nations do, rely on both options. In terms of growing food, the earth is richly endowed with agricultural potential and production. Millions of acres of arable land remain to be cultivated, and farmers now produce enough food to satisfy the daily caloric and protein needs of a world population exceeding 10 billion, far more than are already alive.[22] These data suggest the ready availability of food as well as a potential for even larger levels of production. This good news must be balanced with the sobering realization that nearly a billion people in the developing world today do not have enough food to survive.

As with economic growth, the amount of food available in a country must increase at least as fast as the rate of population growth; otherwise per capita consumption will decline. If existing levels of caloric intake are already inadequate, then food production (and imports) must increase faster than population growth in order to meet minimum caloric needs. Assisted by the expanded use of irrigation, pesticides, and fertilizers, many developing countries, particularly in Asia, dramatically increased their food production over the past two or three decades. Asia's three largest countries—India, China, and Indonesia—are no longer heavily dependent on imports. Between 1965 and 1986, China and Indonesia were able to increase their population's average daily caloric supply by more than 35 percent.[23] In fact, the average citizen in both countries now consumes about 10 percent more calories than the minimum daily requirement.

Despite these and a few other notable successes, much of the developing world is in the midst of a long-term agricultural crisis. Of the fifty poorest countries (three-quarters of which are in Africa), thirty-seven actually produced less food per person in the mid-1980s than they had fifteen years earlier. Not surprisingly, in twenty of the thirty-seven countries daily caloric consumption decreased, in some cases by as much as 20 to 30 percent. The remaining thirteen countries experienced modest to sizable increases in per capita production, but seven were still unable to meet minimum subsistence levels in 1985. In many developing countries the average daily caloric consumption, already below subsistence levels in 1965, declined still further by 1986, as agricultural productivity per capita plunged by as much as 30 to 40 percent in some places (see Table 13-2).[24]

Of course, some people consume more and others less than the average caloric intake in each country. The result is that in many countries that exceed average caloric requirements, some people are on the brink of starvation. In Senegal, Syria, Liberia, Morocco, and the Dominican Republic, the average citizen consumes more than the required number of calories each day, but at least 25 percent of the children in these countries suffer from mild to severe malnutrition.[25]

In many of these countries the low levels of production can be attributed to inefficient farming practices: lack of irrigation, pesticides, and fertilizers and in some instances corruption or incompetence. Zaire exemplifies several of these problems. According to the United Nations Food and Agriculture Organization (FAO), Zaire is "land abundant." With a low level of agricultural inputs (in other words, with traditional farming practices), Zaire was capable of producing almost twelve times as much food as it needed in 1975, according to FAO calculations. With a higher level of inputs, the country could feed all Africans several times over. In spite of this potential, Zaire's increase in food production between 1980 and 1987 lagged behind its population growth. This was not at all unusual. Among the ten "land abundant" African countries, none increased its agricultural production faster than their populations over this time period.[26]

If current agricultural practices are continued, more than half of the 117 developing countries studied by the FAO will not be able to provide minimum levels of nutrition by the turn of the century. If, however, their agricultural practices are significantly improved to include complete mechanization and other high-technology approaches, then ninety-eight of the countries could feed themselves by 2000.[27]

It is theoretically possible to expand agricultural outputs, as the FAO found, but its calculations did not incorporate practical limitations. No consideration was given to whether money would be available to purchase the higher level of inputs.[28] The calculations also assumed that all land that could be cultivated would be cultivated; no cropland would be lost to degradation; no livestock would be allowed to graze on land that had the potential to grow food; and no nonfood crops, such as tea, coffee, or cotton, would be grown! The study also assumed that only minimum

Table 13-2 Daily Caloric Intake and Changes in Agricultural Production in Selected Countries

Country	Daily caloric supply per capita — Years: 1965	1986	Index of total agricultural production per capita (1969-1971=100) — Years: 1985-1987
Mozambique	1,979	1,595	58
Ethiopia	1,824	1,749	75
Tanzania	1,832	2,192	76
Kenya	2,289	2,060	89
Bangladesh	1,972	1,927	88
China	1,926	2,630	150
India	2,111	2,238	110
Japan	2,687	2,864	92
Canada	3,212	3,462	119
United States	3,224	3,645	110

Sources: World Bank, *World Development Report, 1989* (New York: Oxford University Press, 1989); United Nations Food and Agriculture Organization, *The State of Food and Agriculture, 1982* (Rome: Food and Agriculture Organization, 1983); and United Nations Food and Agriculture Organization, *The State of Food and Agriculture, 1987-88* (Rome: Food and Agriculture Organization, 1988).

nutrition levels would be satisfied and that production could be distributed appropriately. In short, the current-practice scenario is likely to offer a better indication of the state of agricultural production over the near term.

This scenario is a discouraging one. In many countries there is not enough arable land to support existing populations, and some developing countries have already reached or exceeded the sustainable limits of production. In 1975, Kenya had the agricultural potential to support less than 30 percent of its population. With its anticipated growth, Kenya will be able to provide for an even smaller share of its population, at least with continued low levels of agricultural inputs. Many other Asian and African countries face similar predicaments. Their populations are already overexploiting their environment's carrying capacity, and they are using their land beyond its capacity to sustain agricultural production.[29] Unless changes are made soon, production will eventually decline and millions of acres of land will become barren.

Food imports offer a possible solution to deficiencies in domestic production, but here, too, many developing countries encounter problems. In order to finance imports, countries need foreign exchange, usually acquired through their own exports or from loans. Few developing countries have industrial products or professional services to export, so they must rely on minerals, natural resources (such as timber or petroleum), or cash crops (such as tea, sugar, coffee, cocoa, and rubber).

Economic recessions and declining demand in the developed world caused prices for many of these commodities to drop precipitously in the 1980s, and the total value of Third World exports likewise dropped. To remedy this problem, many Third World countries have attempted to increase production, but this often means less attention to production for domestic consumption and increased pressures on land and forests. Many developing nations "are cutting down forests, overusing fertilizers, and exhausting groundwater supplies in efforts to produce cash crops." [30]

There are opportunities to increase exports, but agricultural policies in the developed world often prevent or discourage expanded activity in the Third World. Billions of dollars of agricultural subsidies are given to farmers in Europe and North America each year. A frequent result is overproduction and surpluses in the developed world. In turn, these surpluses discourage imports from the Third World, further reduce prices, and remove incentives to expand production. These subsidies cost developing countries about $26 billion a year in lost markets.[31] Protectionist trade policies in the developed nations similarly prevent access to many markets.

At one time developing countries could depend on loans from private banks or foreign governments to help finance imports. Now, however, many developing countries are burdened with massive debts, which totaled about $1.3 trillion in late 1988. This debt often cannot be repaid because of faltering economies. Failures to make interest payments are common, and banks are increasingly hesitant to lend more money.

Developing countries that attempt to repay their debts find that interest payments alone take a huge share of their earnings from imports, in some cases as much as 40 to 50 percent. Consider as well the change in the flow of money from the late 1970s to the late 1980s. In the earlier period about $40 billion in net aid per year was transferred to the Third World. Ten years later the flow of resources had actually reversed. Developing countries' payments of principal and interest exceeded the value of new loans and foreign aid by more than $30 billion in 1988.[32] Many Third World countries have asked that their repayments be rescheduled or that their debts be forgiven. Many banks have been forced to accept the former; most have rejected the latter. In sum, at a time when many countries are not able to grow enough food, they also find that they cannot afford to import the shortfall, particularly when droughts and poor harvests in exporting countries cause prices to rise.

Shortages in the Third World are not limited to food. Rather than rely on electricity or natural gas, as is common in developed countries, about 2 billion people in the Third World depend on wood or other traditional fuels for heating and cooking. In much of the world, however, fuelwood is in short supply, and efforts to acquire it are time consuming and environmentally destructive. One estimate suggests that a typical household in some parts of east Africa spends as many as three hundred days per year searching for and collecting wood. Despite such efforts, the FAO believes that about 100 million people, half in Africa, are unable to meet their daily minimum needs for fuelwood. Another 1 billion, mostly in Asia, are able to satisfy their needs, but only through overexploitation of existing resources.[33]

Destruction of Tropical Forests

Shortages of fuelwood are indicative of a much larger and potentially catastrophic problem—namely, the destruction of tropical rain forests. The rain forests of Africa, South America, and Southeast Asia are treasure chests of incomparable biological diversity. These forests provide irreplaceable habitats for as much as 80 percent of the world's species of plants and animals, most of which remain to be discovered and described scientifically. Among the species already investigated, many contribute to human well-being. For example, an estimated one-quarter of the prescription drugs used in the United States have their origins in tropical plants. Viable forests also stabilize soils, reduce the impact and incidence of floods, and regulate local climates, watersheds, and river systems.[34] In addition, increasing concern about the effect of excessive levels of carbon dioxide in the atmosphere (the greenhouse effect) underscores the global importance of tropical forests. Through photosynthesis, trees and other plants remove carbon dioxide from the atmosphere and convert it into oxygen. In short, the functions that tropical forests perform are so ecologically priceless that some might argue that these forests should be protected as inviolable sanctuaries. However desirable such protection might be, what often occurs is exactly the opposite. Tropical rain forests, contends biologist Paul Ehrlich, "are the major ecosystems now under the most determined assault by humanity."[35]

At the beginning of this century, tropical forests covered approximately 10 percent of the earth's surface, or about 5.8 million square miles. The deforestation of recent decades has diminished this area by about one-third. Estimates of current rates of deforestation vary, but some experts believe that the pace of destruction is accelerating, with a total loss of about 2 percent of all tropical forests each year. In some areas the pace is much quicker, as nations seemingly rush to destroy their biological heritage and the earth's life-support systems. If current rates of deforestation continue unabated, only a few areas of forest will remain untouched. Humans will have destroyed a natural palliative for the greenhouse effect and condemned to extinction perhaps half of all species now known to exist.

Causes and Solutions

Solutions to the problem of tropical deforestation depend on the root cause. One view blames poverty and the pressures associated with growing populations and shifting cultivators. Landless peasants, so the argument goes, invade tropical forests and denude them for fuelwood or to grow crops with which to survive.[36] Frequent clearing of new areas is necessary because tropical soils are often thin, relatively infertile, and lack sufficient nutrients. In other words, these areas are ill suited for sustained agricultural production. As one researcher explains, "Deprived of its protective cover [a tropical forest] becomes an ugly wasteland—huge expanses of coarse scrub, unusable grassland and lateritic hardpan." [37]

In spite of this knowledge, some governments actively encourage resettlement schemes that require extensive deforestation. In Brazil, which has about 30 percent of the tropical forests in the world, the government has opened the Amazon region in the name of land reform. The results have been spectacular. After the government built several highways into the interior and offered free land to attract settlers, the population of some Amazonian states soared by as much as one-hundred fold between the mid-1960s and the late 1980s. Thousands of square miles of forest—about the size of Maryland—are cleared each year to accommodate the new arrivals and to provide them with permanent settlements.

Indonesia's transmigration program moves people from the densely populated island of Java to sparsely populated, but heavily forested outer islands. Other forested land is being cleared to increase the acreage alloted to cocoa, rubber, palm oil, and other cash crops intended for export. So thorough is the overall destruction, that "Brazil and Indonesia might be regarded as waging the equivalent of thermonuclear war upon their own territories." [38] Both are "winning" the war. If they continue what they are now doing, Brazil and Indonesia will be without any rain forests in the early years of the next century.

Another explanation for deforestation places primary blame on commercial logging intended to satisfy demands for tropical hardwoods in developed countries.[39] Whether strapped for foreign exchange, forced to repay loans from foreign banks, or subjected to domestic pressure to develop their economies, governments in the developing world frequently regard the resources of tropical forests as sources of ready income. Exports of wood now produce about $8 billion in annual revenues for the Third World, and some countries impose few limits in their rush to the bank. In the mid-1980s, Southeast Asia contained about 25 percent of all tropical forests, but the region accounted for nearly 80 percent of the value of all exports of tropical hardwoods.

If tropical forests were managed in an environmentally sustainable manner, the flow of income and benefits to local populations could continue indefinitely. In fact, however, few tropical forests are so managed, and many countries are now becoming victims of past greed and too-rapid exploitation. About three dozen countries were net exporters of tropical hardwoods in 1988, but fewer than ten of these countries will have enough wood to export at the end of the 1990s.[40] Some countries, such as Nigeria and Thailand, have already shifted from being net exporters to net importers.

The consequences of deforestation are not only economic. Nearly 1 billion people are "periodically disrupted by flooding, fuelwood shortages, soil and water degradation and reduced agricultural production caused directly or indirectly by the loss of tropical-forest cover." [41] In late 1988 separate floods devastated much of Bangladesh and southern Thailand. In seeking explanations, officials in the two countries pointed to severe deforestation that had contributed to soil erosion and exacerbated the flooding. Unfortunately, floods would become regular occurrences, these officials predicted, because of deforestation.

Recognizing the causes and consequences of deforestation is not enough to bring about a solution. Commercial logging is profitable, and few governments in the Third World are equipped to manage their forests properly. Governments in developing countries often let logging concerns harvest trees in designated areas under certain conditions. All too frequently, however, the conditions are inadequate or not well enforced because there are too few forest guards. In the western Amazon, according to one account, a single guard has responsibility for an area as large as France! [42] Paltry wages for guards also create opportunities for corruption, and not only among low-level employees. The director general of Thailand's forestry department was once suspended because he had granted a private firm illegal access to a government-owned forest reserve.

Penalties can be imposed on those who violate the conditions, but violators are rarely apprehended. When they are, the fine is often less than the profits associated with the violation. Some countries require companies with concessions to post bonds, which are returned once the companies complete mandatory reforestation projects. Here again, however, the amounts involved are generally so low that many companies would rather forfeit their bonds than reforest.[43] Moreover, concessions are typically granted for brief periods that discourage reforestation. When a logging company receives a twenty-year concession, granting it a right to cut for twenty years, no incentive exists to replant trees for someone else's benefit because many trees take forty to fifty years to reach maturity. One estimate suggests that for every one hundred acres of tropical forests that are cleared, only about one acre is reforested and managed in an environmentally sound manner.[44]

Lack of political will offers still another explanation of poor management practices. Logging concessions are sometimes granted to government officials. In the Malaysian state of Sarawak, one of the largest concession holders is the state's environment minister. In the neighboring state of Sabah, where logging is even more intensive, a former governor is a major holder of concessions. The bulk of Indonesia's concessions have been given to former military officers and high-ranking public officials in lieu of, or in addition to, pensions.

An Alternative View of the Problem

As the pace of tropical deforestation has quickened, so have international pressures on developing countries to halt or mitigate it. In response, Third World leaders quickly emphasize how ironic it is that developed countries, whose consumption of tropical woods is increasing, are simultaneously calling for a reduction of logging and shifting cultivation in developing countries. Furthermore, the major cause of the greenhouse effect is the carbon emissions from the burning of fossil fuels in Japan, Europe, and the United States. Europeans and Americans take the lead in condemning deforestation (because forested areas offer a way to mitigate the consequences of the greenhouse effect), but those in the Third World can offer a different view of the situation. Why should poor countries, they ask, assume responsibility for environmental problems that rich countries have created and then have seemingly ignored, despite their economic, scientific, and technological abilities to solve the problems?

The developing countries point to Europe's destruction of its forests during the industrial revolution and the widespread cutting in the United States in the nineteenth century. Why then should developing countries be held to a different standard than the developed ones? Just as Europe and the United States decided how and when to extract their resources, developing countries insist that they should be allowed to determine their own patterns of consumption. The Brazilian government has a standard reply to its critics: The Amazon is Brazil's, and it is the right of Brazilians to decide what to do with it.[45] One observer, examining the situation in Indonesia, cast the problem somewhat differently. He wondered how Third World bureaucracies can overcome domestic pressures for economic development. He raised this question after hearing the views of an Indonesian involved with logging. As the Indonesian businessman declared, "[W]e are a profit-oriented company, and if that means destroying the environment within the legal limit, then we will do it."[46]

Fortunately, such a view is not universally shared, and there is evidence of change in some developing countries. Thailand imposed a nationwide ban on logging in early 1989, despite projections that the ban would cause thousands of people to lose their jobs. Ghana, Côte d'Ivoire, and the Philippines similarly announced restrictions on logging in the late 1980s. These are well-intentioned efforts, but in each instance the restrictions were imposed well after they could do much good.

International collaboration between wood-producing and wood-consuming nations offers one hope in the battle against deforestation. To date, however, such collaboration has a pitiful record. The U.N.-sponsored International Tropical Timber Organization (ITTO), formed in 1985, was on the brink of collapse just a few years later.[47] Several importing nations had refused to pay their full dues, Japanese importers boycotted ITTO's meetings, and the organization could claim few accomplishments other than its tenuous survival.

Will tropical forests survive? The outlook is dim. There is no shortage of possible solutions. What is lacking is a consensus about which of these solutions will best meet the essential needs of the poor, the reasonable objectives of timber-exporting and timber-importing nations, and the inflexible imperatives of ecological stability. All of these concerns ensure that deforestation and the related issue of the loss of biological diversity will receive increasing attention in the 1990s and beyond.

Conflicting Signals from the Developed World

Improvements in the policies of many Third World countries are surely necessary. Yet, as already noted, industrialized countries sometimes cause or contribute to environmental problems that afflict the Third World. Two brief examples illustrate the point.

The cost of complying with environmental laws in developed countries has led some companies to look to Asia or Africa for sites to dispose of hazardous wastes. Indeed, the transport of such wastes became a booming business in the 1980s, and some developed countries considered Africa to be "little more than a dumping ground for undesirable industrial leftovers." [48] Many receiving nations do not know about the dumping; others, desperate for foreign exchange, willingly accept toxic materials even when they do not have adequate treatment facilities.

Some multinational corporations have established factories in Third World countries in order to avoid restrictive environmental laws elsewhere. In other instances these corporations have exported products that ran afoul of consumer, safety, or environmental laws in their home countries. Products banned or restricted in Europe or the United States are commonly found in the Third World. The pesticide ethylene dibromide (EDB) is a relevant example. The U.S. Environmental Protection Agency (EPA) limited the use of EDB on grains, fruits, and vegetables in the United States in the mid-1980s, but American companies continued to export it legally. Although EPA deemed the pesticide's use to be inappropriate, another federal agency, the Agency for International Development, was subsidizing EDB's use in developing countries. In turn, some of these countries exported EDB-fumigated foods to the United States.

The practice of exporting harmful products to the Third World sends conflicting signals to the recipients. Similarly confusing signals are evident when the Third World examines the state of the environment in those rich countries preaching the merits of sustainable development. The use of chlorofluorocarbons in these countries' refrigerators, spray cans, and styrofoam containers is depleting the ozone layer. In most of the developed world the causes and consequences of acid precipitation remain unattended, and just a handful of countries are primarily responsible for the global greenhouse effect.

A summer visitor to Europe in the early 1990s will find many of its most desirable beaches fouled beyond use and the northern Adriatic Sea nearly dead because of chemical pollution. Seventy percent of the cities on the Mediterranean are dumping unprocessed sewage into the sea, and some European countries are refusing to stop dumping sludge into the North Sea.[49] A Third World visitor to the United States might be impressed with the number and stringency of its environmental laws but would quickly notice considerable disparity between promises and performance. The Clean Air Act Amendments of 1977 pledged that Americans would not breathe unhealthy air in the late 1980s. In the summer of 1988, however, measurements of ozone were among the highest ever recorded in many American cities.

Throughout the 1980s EPA continued to add to its list of abandoned hazardous-waste sites that require immediate remedial attention. While EPA was adding, the Forest Service was subtracting. Commercial logging in the national forests reached record levels in 1988, but the Forest Service still found it necessary to increase allowable cutting for future years.[50] Much of the timber is shipped to Japan in a quest to balance America's trade deficit.

Causes for Optimism?

Although there is cause for concern about the prospects for sustainable development in the Third World, the situation is neither entirely bleak nor beyond hope. Many developing countries are gradually reducing their rate of population growth and are far more appreciative of its linkage to development and environmental quality than they used to be. A survey of policies in developing countries also reveals a growing awareness of the inseparable relation between a healthy environment and economic development. Countries that once favored development over environmental protection now recognize that pollution and neglect of the environment are no longer preconditions for economic development. Specific bureaus or departments with responsibility for environmental issues are now commonly found in the governments of the Third World. Many of these bureaus still have rudimentary skills and expertise, but their creation represents an important first step. Likewise, environmental impact assessments are now common requirements for development projects in many developing countries.

At the international level, multilateral lending institutions such as the World Bank, the Asian Development Bank, and the Inter-American Development Bank are increasingly sensitive to the need to mitigate damage to the environment and are incorporating concern for sustainable development into their development activities. Several of these banks now refuse to fund projects that irreparably damage the environment. Moreover, the World Bank has established an Environment Department with a specific mandate to focus on tropical deforestation, the loss of biological diversity, and the environmental problems of sub-Saharan Africa. The bank has also agreed to work with several countries with severe environmental problems whose governments are committed to improving their management of natural resources.

The international community is demonstrating a new recognition of the earth's ecological interconnectedness. At the request of the U.N. General Assembly, the World Commission on Environment and Development was established in 1983 and asked to formulate long-term environmental strategies for achieving sustainable development. In its report, *Our Common Future*, the commission forcefully emphasized that although environmental degradation is an issue of survival for developing nations, failure to address the degradation satisfactorily will guarantee unparalleled and undesirable global consequences from which no nation will escape.[51] This report's release in 1987 provided at least some of the reason for the increased international attention to environmental issues in the late 1980s, which manifested itself most noticeably at the economic summit meeting of the world's leading industrial powers in Paris in mid-1989. The need for international collaboration to protect the earth's environment was a major topic of discussion at the meeting.

During the late 1980s, three important international environmental agreements were approved. The first addressed the release of carbon emissions into the atmosphere; the second, chlorofluorocarbons and the depletion of the ozone layer; and the third, the shipment of toxic wastes across international boundaries. Regarding the third agreement, representatives from more than one hundred countries drafted a treaty restricting transboundary shipments of hazardous wastes. According to the agreement, shipments are prohibited unless waste exporters notify and receive consent from receiving nations. Furthermore, the treaty imposes an obligation on shipping and receiving nations to dispose of the wastes in an environmentally sound manner.[52]

However promising, these institutional changes and agreements will not be sufficient to protect the environment without concerted and effective international action. The population, development, and environmental problems of the Third World dwarf those of the developed world and are not amenable to immediate resolution, but immediate action is imperative. To meet their daily needs for food and fuel, millions of people are steadily destroying their biological and environmental support systems at unprecedented rates. Driven by poverty and the need to survive, they have become ravenous souls on an earth approaching the limits of its tolerance and resilience. Whether this situation will change depends on the ability of Third World residents, not only to reap the benefits of sustained economic growth, but also to meet the demands of current populations while using their natural resources in a way that accommodates the needs of future generations. Unless the developing nations are able to do so soon, their future will determine ours as well.

Notes

1. United Nations Children's Fund (UNICEF), *State of the World's Children, 1989* (New York: Oxford University Press, 1989), 42.
2. Ibid., 37.
3. World Commission on Environment and Development, *Our Common Future* (London: Oxford University Press, 1987), 8, 43.
4. John N. Wilford, "A Tough-Minded Ecologist Comes to Defense of Malthus," *New York Times*, June 30, 1987, C3.
5. See U.N. Department of International Economic and Social Affairs, *United Nations World Population Chart, 1988* (New York: United Nations, 1988); Colin Clark, *Population Growth and Land Use*, 2d ed. (London: Macmillan, 1977), 153 ("the world's potential agricultural and forest land could supply the needs of 157 billion people"); Paul and Anne Ehrlich, *Extinction* (New York: Random House, 1981), 243 (starting a gradual decline of the human population is "obviously essential").
6. Richard Bernstein, "World's Surging Birthrate Tops the Mexico City Agenda," *New York Times*, July 29, 1984, sec. 4, 3.
7. "African Seminar on Population Policy," in National Academy of Sciences (NAS), *In Search of Population Policy: Views from the Developing World* (Washington, D.C.: NAS, 1974), 57-60; and United Nations Food and Agriculture Organization (FAO), *The State of Food and Agriculture, 1983* (Rome: FAO, 1984), 66.
8. Lester R. Brown, "Analyzing the Demographic Trap," in *State of the World, 1987*, ed. Lester R. Brown (New York: Norton, 1987), 20.
9. UNICEF, *Children, 1989*, 1, 20.
10. World Bank, *World Development Report, 1989* (New York: Oxford Univer-

sity Press, 1989).

11. James Clad, "Genesis of Despair," *Far Eastern Economic Review*, October 20, 1988, 24-25.
12. UNICEF, *Children, 1989*, 8-9.
13. "The Good News: Thailand Controls a Baby Boom," *Time*, Asian international ed., January 2, 1989, 37.
14. K. Srinivasan, "Population Policy and Programme," in U.N. Economic and Social Commission for Asia and the Pacific, *Population of India* (New York: United Nations, 1982), 161.
15. U.N. Department of International Economic and Social Affairs, *World Population Policies*, vol. 1 (New York: United Nations, 1987), 127-129.
16. Marshall Green, "Is China Easing Up on Birth Control?" *New York Times*, April 23, 1986, A25; and "The Mewling That They'll Miss," *Economist*, August 13, 1988, 27.
17. Richard J. Meislin, "Population Parley to Open in Mexico Today," *New York Times*, August 6, 1984, A7.
18. "Statement by U.S. Delegate to the Conference on Population in Mexico City," *New York Times*, August 9, 1984, A8.
19. Chief among these advocates is Julian Simon. See Julian Simon, *The Ultimate Resource* (Princeton, N.J.: Princeton University Press, 1981). For a response to some of Simon's positions, see U.N. Fund for Population Activities, *State of the World Population, 1987* (New York: United Nations, 1987), 6-8.
20. U.N. Department of International Economic and Social Affairs, *Case Studies in Population Policy: Malaysia* (New York: United Nations, 1987), 34-39.
21. Brown, *State of the World*, 21.
22. U.N. Environment Programme, *The State of the Environment, 1987* (Nairobi: United Nations, 1987), 47.
23. World Bank, *World Development Report, 1989*, 218. Indonesia's gains were in jeopardy in the late 1980s because of stagnant production and increasing demand. See "A Battle for Self-Sufficiency," *Asiaweek*, December 2, 1988, 63.
24. These figures are based on the average index of food production per capita found in World Bank, *World Development Report, 1983* (New York: Oxford University Press, 1983), 158; and World Bank, *World Development Report, 1988*, 234.
25. UNICEF, *Children, 1989*, 96-97.
26. United Nations Food and Agriculture Organization, *Potential Population-Supporting Capacities of Lands in the Developing World* (Rome: FAO, 1982), 137.
27. Ibid., 49.
28. Brown, *State of the World*, 24. The criticisms of the study are from Brown's analysis of the FAO report.
29. United Nations Food and Agriculture Organization, *The State of Food and Agriculture, 1983*, 66.
30. "Will the Planet Pay the Price for Third World Debt?" *Business Week*, October 24, 1988, 88.
31. Anthony Rowley, "Harvest of Ill Will," *Far Eastern Economic Review*, January 12, 1989, 51.

32. U.N. Department of International Economic and Social Affairs, *World Economic Survey, 1989: Current Trends and Policies in the World Economy* (New York: United Nations, 1989), 62.
33. National Academy of Sciences, *Population Growth and Economic Development: Policy Questions* (Washington, D.C.: NAS, 1986), 31; and United Nations Food and Agriculture Organization, Committee on Food Development in the Tropics, *Tropical Forest Action Plan* (Rome: FAO, 1985), 2, 47.
34. "The Vanishing Jungle: Ecologists Make Friends with Economists," *Economist*, October 15, 1988, 25.
35. Ehrlich and Ehrlich, *Extinction*, 160.
36. United Nations Food and Agriculture Organization, *Tropical Forest Action Plan*, 2.
37. "Vanishing Jungle," *Economist*, 26.
38. Nicholas Guppy, "Tropical Deforestation: A Global View," *Foreign Affairs* 62 (Spring 1984): 943.
39. Ibid., 931.
40. "Vanishing Jungle," *Economist*, 26.
41. This view of the World Resources Institute is quoted in Margaret Scott, "The Disappearing Forests," *Far Eastern Economic Review*, January 12, 1989, 34.
42. "How Brazil Subsidises the Destruction of the Amazon," *Economist*, March 18, 1989, 79.
43. Michael Richardson, "Indonesia Wonders if Timber Boom Will Backfire," *International Herald Tribune*, September 5, 1988, 1.
44. Scott, "Disappearing Forests," 35.
45. "A Murder in the Forest," *Economist*, January 7, 1989, 36.
46. Michael Vatikiotis, "Tug-of-War over Trees," *Far Eastern Economic Review*, January 12, 1989, 41.
47. Margaret Scott, "Unequal to the Task," *Far Eastern Economic Review*, January 12, 1989, 38.
48. "Who Gets the Garbage?" *Time*, Asian international ed., July 4, 1988, 24; and "The Global Poison Trade," *Newsweek*, Pacific ed., November 7, 1988, 8.
49. Steven Greenhouse, "Rising Tide of Pollution Fouls Europe's Beaches," *International Herald Tribune*, August 9, 1988, 1.
50. Tom Wicker, "Forests: America, Too, Is Stripping," *International Herald Tribune*, March 23, 1989, 6.
51. World Commission, *Our Common Future*.
52. Steven Greenhouse, "Conference Backs Curbs on Export of Toxic Waste," *New York Times*, March 23, 1989, A1.

14

International Environmental Politics: America's Response to Global Imperatives

Lynton K. Caldwell

The global interdependence of man's airs [and waters] and climates is such that local decisions are simply inadequate. Even the sum of all local separate decisions, wisely made, may not be a sufficient safeguard. . . . Man's global interdependence begins to require, in these fields, a new capacity for global decision making and global care.

—Barbara Ward and René Dubos
Only One Earth (1972)

The international environmental policies of the United States during the 1990s are likely to differ substantially from those prevailing in the 1980s. It is possible, even probable, that the nation will recover the lead in international environmental politics it once possessed but largely relinquished during the 1980s. Reasons for this belief have evolved both inside and outside the United States but stem especially from the country's need to respond to external events. During the last decade of the twentieth century Americans will be confronted by a number of environmental issues that will challenge prevailing assumptions regarding the uses of economic and military power. Planetary environmental developments occurring beyond America's borders are now perceived, or anticipated, to be beyond national control. The concept of national sovereignty is of declining significance in a world that increasingly faces environmental problems affecting people everywhere. The fates of the first, second, and third worlds are interlinked through the biosphere.

The first section of this chapter summarizes some recent global ecologic disasters and responses and the new geophysical imperatives they imply for the future. Discussed next are the effects of these trends and events on public awareness and on the policy perspectives of national leaders and governments and the recent flurry of international environmental activity. An agenda for America's response to several of the more pressing global environmental issues is presented in the second half of the chapter, followed by a discussion of the political and institutional potentials for carrying it out and some concluding reflections.

New Geophysical Imperatives

From the mid-1960s to the mid-1970s environmental issues found a place on national and international agendas. The United Nations Environment Programme was launched, and almost every major national government established some type of environmental department or ministry. From the mid-1970s to the mid-1980s governments generally appeared uncertain about how seriously their environmental commitments should be taken. Public opinion surveys indicated continuing popular support for environmental protection and quality of life policies.[1] Nevertheless, many politicians believed that economic growth and development planning should have priority. In the late 1980s, however, a series of environmental events and scientific findings brought environmental policy to the top of the political agenda in both domestic and international affairs.

The cover of *Time*'s first issue in 1989 became a sign of the times. Breaking from its customary "Man of the Year" portrait, *Time* featured the earth as "Planet of the Year." The media were clearly taking a global perspective. In its November 21, 1988, issue, *Fortune* declared that "environmental anxiety goes global." On Sunday, December 25, 1988, a full page in the *New York Times* was headlined: "Suddenly, the World Itself Is World Issue." The *Times's* environmental reporter, Philip Shabecoff, noted that "the environment moves to the center of geopolitics." Scholarly affirmation of these observations was found in a book entitled *Environmental Diplomacy: The Management and Resolution of Transfrontier Environmental Problems.*[2] At the 1989 meeting of the International Studies Association in London, I presented a well-received paper, "The New Geopolitics: International Imperatives of Environmental Science." The American Assembly, which at its seventy-fifth meeting in November 1988 focused on "U.S. Global Interests in the 1990s," identified population and environmental problems as the two major near-term "global imperatives." And, finally, the "biosphere dwarfs other issues," wrote David Suzuki in the *Toronto Globe and Mail* of June 10, 1989. These sample indicators suggested that a critical threshold in world politics had been reached and that the United States and other major governments were considering how it should be crossed.

The new geopolitics differs from its antecedents in that instead of using strategies to advance national economic and military interests, it is a response to geophysical developments on the earth that impact all nations and are beyond the reach of national political or military power. Changes in climate, ocean levels, solar radiation, and genetic diversity occurring on unprecedented scales present challenges not yet faced by modern society. Diplomats cannot argue or bargain with geophysical impacts. Preventive and adaptive strategies are needed to cope with these changes, and positive results often depend on the cooperation of nearly all nations.

Because of far-flung enterprises, investments, and strategic interests overseas, there has been increased vulnerability in the United States to disruptive environmental events occurring elsewhere on the globe. Growing resentment at home and abroad regarding exported technology associated with industrial accidents and ecological deterioration have placed America's investments and reputation in jeopardy. Both human-caused and natural catastrophic events have affected people's perceptions of security and induced apprehension regarding future dangers. Environmental disasters at Bhopal in India (poison gas leak in 1984), at Chernobyl in the Soviet Union (radioactive explosion in 1986), and at Seveso, Italy, and Basel, Switzerland (toxic chemical spills in 1976 and 1986) were widely publicized and drew attention to the possibility of a comparable event in the United States, an apprehension soon realized with the great *Exxon Valdez* oil spill in Alaska in 1989.[3] These and other environmental catastrophes have aroused public awareness of potential hazards to health, safety, and the environment, and have raised popular receptivity to alarms concerning more pervasive issues such as stratospheric ozone depletion, the greenhouse effect, and acidic deposition. Events in 1988 and 1989, widely reported by the press and television, gave rise to this growing concern. Among these were controversies over the transport and disposal of toxic chemicals, spills of oil and toxic chemicals at sea and in rivers, and the fouling of marine beaches in the United States and Europe. In the United States the drought of 1988 and the great fires in Yellowstone Park gave popular credence to theories of a global greenhouse effect.

Disturbing developments in the atmosphere, oceans, and on land have been the consequences of human activity regarded as essential to human welfare. These developments have given rise to policy issues that are characteristically interconnected, planetary in their ultimate effects, and inconsistent with traditional economic, legal, and political assumptions. For example, questions on what to do about acid rain, the thinning ozone layer, global climate change, and long-range transmission of atmospheric contaminants involve interrelated considerations of the sources and uses of energy, technologies of manufacturing and transportation, economic development, domestic water supply, food production, and population policy, among others. All deal with human behavior in relation to the atmosphere, oceans, inland waters, soils, and biota. The difference between these and previous international environmental issues is that the more recent impacts cannot be addressed successfully by unilateral national action. They have moved heads of state, including Margaret Thatcher in Great Britain, Mikhail Gorbachev in the Soviet Union, Helmut Kohl in the Federal Republic of Germany, François Mitterrand in France, and candidates George Bush and Michael Dukakis in the 1988 U.S. presidential election to reveal a sudden and previously unnoticeable concern about the state of the environment. The politicians have at last caught up with the opinion polls. Effective publicity by nongovernmental organizations played an indispensable role in mobilizing and focusing public attention on environmental matters. These organizations (of which the World Wildlife Fund, the International Union for Conservation of Nature and Natural Resources, Greenpeace, the Sierra Club, and various other environmental coalitions are representative) multiplied in both number and membership during the deceptively recessive period of the late 1970s and early 1980s. Ironically, the environmental insensitivity of governments in both the United States and Soviet Union activated public protest and induced policy changes in 1989 under presidents Bush and Gorbachev.

Thus, the upsurge in environmental awareness in 1988 and 1989 resulted from an accelerating process of social learning, triggered by the convergence of events into a popular concern that politics could no longer discount. The perceived impact of implacable geophysical forces was changing world politics, and, hence, national politics in ways that could be as potentially irreversible as the geophysical environmental threats that nations were now belatedly seeking to forestall. To avoid irreversible environmental change, timely and persistent human effort mediated by government was required. Geopolitics had been internationalized.

A New Policy Perspective

Although the environmental disasters of the late 1980s aroused apprehension, their most important effect was to confirm and intensify public concerns developing over two decades. An emerging environmental consciousness has become more global since Christmas Eve of 1968 when humans first viewed their home planet from NASA's *Apollo 8* in outer space. This picture of the whole earth in space has become not only a powerful symbol for space exploration but, more significantly, a "logo" for the biosphere and the only planet on which life is known to exist. Initiation of large scale global environmental research by the International Council of Scientific Unions and United Nations Specialized Agencies, and collaboration between American and Soviet scientists on environmental problems, have expanded perceptions of environmental issues and the possibilities for global cooperation.[4]

By the late 1980s many Americans had come to accept the international and even planetary scope of major environmental problems. They could no longer assume that their environmental problems were unique, or could be solved by unilateral action. Collaborative efforts by American, Canadian, Scandinavian, and Soviet governments in the Arctic region (in relation to polar bears, whales, and oil spills) implied a geopolitics of cooperation rather than confrontation. Translating this limited incidental cooperation into a general conventional procedure required time, but the process was already evident. International cooperation was needed to cope with transnational developments, as it had been necessary earlier to ensure the survival of the Pribilov fur seal herd in the North Pacific and to protect migratory birds in North America. If nation states could cooperate on a broader range of environmental issues, the prospects for worldwide cooperation would be enhanced. Such cooperation is already evident in matters of trade and economics, communications, health, crime, and population dynamics. Predictions that a politics of the planet earth would ultimately emerge may also be approaching fulfillment.[5]

The ultimate consequence of this development could be a reorientation of the international commitments of the United States, notably its national defense policies and foreign policies of geographical containment, import/export policies, and international aid and development strategies.

The Globalization of Policy

Nineteen eighty-eight was a "milestone" year, as national commitments made decades earlier appeared to be reaching practical realization. How soon and how far *action* will implement *rhetoric*—and at what cost—cannot be reasonably predicted. Yet it is highly probable that a threshold has been crossed. The true nature of the environmental question, and its interrelationship with almost every major area of international politics—food, energy, trade, population, and defense—is beginning to be understood. There must be some explanation for the sudden rise of environmental issues to the top of political agendas in the United States, Western Europe, and, surprisingly, the Soviet Union.

Indeed, it was Soviet president Gorbachev who, in his December 1988 address to the General Assembly of the United Nations, expressed this realization of the global nature of public policy in language that his predecessors surely would have regarded as revolutionary. He stated that ". . . the scientific and technological revolution has turned many economic, food, energy, environmental, information, and population problems, which only recently we treated as national or regional, into global problems."[6] Similar views have been implicit in statements by President Bush, British Prime Minister Thatcher, French President Mitterrand, and West German Chancellor Helmut Kohl. At the conclusion of their economic summit of July 1989, these and other leaders of seven industrial democracies made an unprecedented commitment to cooperate in the protection of the global environment.[7] Although such statements of concern have been made previously by chiefs of state without significant follow-up, events in 1988 and 1989 suggest that this situation is different.

The difference may be explained by growing popular reaction to credible scientific findings and the previously noted series of environmental events and disasters. The accidental release of lethal gas from the Union Carbide plant at Bhopal, India, and the resulting loss of more than three thousand lives, shocked Americans into questioning the possibility that a similar event might occur in America. In fact, toxic emissions were found to have escaped from Union Carbide plants in the United States—though on a much smaller scale and without loss of life. But the Bhopal event did not only result in international litigation regarding the liability of Union Carbide and, implicitly, other American firms abroad; it also raised important economic questions about the international transfer of technologies involving potential hazards. International investment and export policies were also involved. The multidimensional nature of environmental issues was dramatized in a way that could be understood even at high levels of industry and finance, not previously noted for environmental concern.

The disaster at Chernobyl strongly reinforced antinuclear apprehensions everywhere.[8] The international implications of the released radioactive gases were overtly evident in the European countries affected and covertly evident in American politics. In 1988 and 1989, controversy escalated over the safety of nuclear weapons facilities supervised by the U.S. Department of Energy (DOE). The nuclear facility in Fernald, Ohio, was cited for radium contamination of water and uranium contamination of air. Also indicative of antinuclear sentiments were the forced close-down of the Savannah River plutonium facility; opposition to start-up of nuclear reactors on Long Island, New York, and in Seabrook, New Hampshire; resistance to DOE plans for nuclear waste repositories in Nevada and New Mexico; and action by governors in Colorado and Idaho to block transport or deposit of nuclear wastes. These events revealed a distrust of federal policies and pronouncements on environmental safety.[9]

Coincident with these events was a heightening of public environmental awareness caused by the burgeoning problem of waste disposal, especially of hazardous wastes. Failure of governments in a growing number of countries and communities to address this problem effectively became even more evident in (1) the running out of disposal sites, (2) controversy over hazardous-waste incineration, (3) failed attempts to ship garbage and hazardous waste from developed to Third World countries, (4) the fouling of beaches on the American Atlantic coast and in Europe by noxious trash, including hospital waste, (5) indiscriminate dumping of waste at sea, and finally (6) transboundary contamination of water supplies, including groundwater.

No single event accounted for the upsurge of environmental concern. Many were local in immediate effect but added collectively to the growing national consciousness. Many others were widely publicized by the press and television and raised new questions related to defense and foreign policies. For example, federal neglect and violation of health and safety standards at the Rocky Flats Arsenal near Denver, Colorado, and other weapons plants, aroused widespread public anger.[10] Concurrently, the U.S. Forest Service came under attack for cutting down the virgin Tongass rain forest in southeastern Alaska to make below-cost sales to Japan at the same time that American environmental organizations and some governmental agencies were trying to persuade Brazil to cease destruction of its tropical rain forest.[11] During no previous period had so many global environmental issues received a comparable amount of publicity.

If there was one issue that stood out, it was the threat to the earth's atmosphere by geophysical changes induced by legitimate but uninformed and misguided human activities. This threat was subsumed under the heading of global climate change but encompassed several interconnected developments originating in industrialized societies. Principal among these were (1) the greenhouse or global warming effect, (2) disintegration of the stratospheric ozone layer, (3) acid rain, and, increasingly, (4) transboundary movement of other airborne contaminants, including dust, that affect air quality.[12]

Although differences existed among scientists regarding the timing and details of these trends, there was widespread agreement on their possible long-term effects. Actions to forestall the projected outcomes, however, would require massive changes in the technologies of energy production, manufacturing, transportation, and agriculture. Thus, rejection of these prognoses and resistance to remedial actions were to be expected. The disadvantaged interests and their allies in politics and administration have undertaken to discount or delay action on grounds that alarms are premature, evidence is uncertain, remedies will be costly, and more research is needed. In early 1989 the U.S. Office of Management and Budget even attempted to "edit" testimony by NASA scientist James Hansen regarding the probability of global climate change.[13]

The drought and exceptional heat in the summer of 1988 won numerous converts to the greenhouse hypothesis.[14] Although most climatologists did not believe that the long, hot, dry summer in North America was caused by the changing composition of the atmosphere, the news media were more speculative. Regardless of its cause, the extraordinary weather focused public attention on the scientific evidence for global climate change.[15] Indeed, the subject became almost obligatory on the conference agendas of scientific, civic, and educational organizations and stimulated a major advance in social learning. Whatever the validity of the scientific explanations, it became evident that any policy to forestall human-induced global climate change would have to be global in scope. Persuading all nations to collaborate would be a mammoth political and diplomatic task.

The global ozone issue attracted slightly less public attention, perhaps because its manifestations were not as disconcerting. The scientific evidence was more certain, and the remedy much less complex than in the case of the greenhouse phenomenon. Moreover, the decay of the ozone layer was attributable to measurable emissions of certain gases into the atmosphere—notably chlorofluorcarbons (CFCs). The remedy was more manageable because production of these compounds was concentrated in a few industrial countries, principally the United States, and substitutes for many of their uses could be found. A series of international meetings and conferences in Vienna (March 1985), Montreal (September 1987), London (March 1989), and Helsinki (May 1989) made the phaseout of CFCs a subject of international agreement, in which the United States played a positive role—although with reservations regarding the speed of remedial action.[16] At Helsinki eighty nations favored an earlier phaseout of ozone-attacking chemicals than had been previously proposed, and the industrial countries agreed to help the poorer countries meet this goal.[17]

These developments led logically to proposals for a Law of the Air treaty, paralleling the still inoperative Law of the Sea treaty. On March 11, 1989, representatives of twenty-four countries met at a conference in The Hague to discuss protection of the atmosphere. Cosponsored by the Netherlands, France, and Norway, the conference adopted a declaration calling for "new" international authority, either by strengthening existing institutions or by creating new institutions.[18]

An Agenda for America's Response

That America has the scientific and technical potential to respond effectively to environmental problems is demonstrable, and research capabilities are present for addressing those questions for which science does not yet have adequate answers. The fundamental question has less often been "how" than "when." Although a substantial majority of Americans show high levels of environmental concern, their commitment is stronger in principle than in practical response when issues involve personal inconvenience or economic disadvantage. This ambivalence has been reflected thus far in the evasive ambiguity of many public officials on environmental issues.

In its November 30, 1988, issue, the *New York Times* identified six major areas of environmental challenge that would confront the Bush administration: air, water, waste, pesticides, land, and global problems. In fact, a more valid listing of challenges would reflect the interconnectedness of environmental problems and their relationship to the nation's economic life. Three critical categories from a longer list of issues have been selected for discussion: energy, chemical contamination, and sustainable agriculture. All of the challenging domestic issues have global implications, and a brief survey of the following environmental problems will indicate why.

Energy

The production and use of energy in the United States is a major contributor to global environmental problems. The combustion of fossil fuels is a principal factor in the pollution of air, water, and land and poses threats to health and safety. Hydrocarbon fuels (coal, oil, and natural gas) are also nonrenewable, and their localized accessibility around the earth creates international problems of dependency, trade, finance, and politics.[19] Nuclear energy presents a different set of problems. Even water power as an energy source not only has environmental effects, but involves major economic and political questions when obtained from international rivers and distributed across national boundaries.

The practical options for energy in relation to national and international environmental impacts are: (1) conservation, (2) conversion, (3) research, and (4) control. These options are implicit in many of the proposed amendments to the Clean Air Act.[20] Acknowledging that these measures would be costly, and would require major changes in industry and transportation, President Bush in 1989 called for a 50 percent reduction in sulfur dioxide emissions by the year 2000, thus reversing the unwillingness of the government to sign the Sulfur Protocol to the Convention on Long-Range Transboundary Air Pollution of 1979; the United States previously had been a signatory to the treaty, but not the protocol.[21] After years of political stalemate, real action to remedy this environmental problem seemed possible. But to achieve clean air goals, major changes in energy production and use would be necessary. Through conservation measures, energy demands could be reduced; conversion to more efficient uses of energy would assist conservation; and conversion to less polluting energy sources would improve the environment. Research on alternative energy sources is, in any case, a practical necessity if future deprivation is to be avoided. All of these options can be pursued simultaneously, setting a good example for nations that have not already taken this course. But American policies for energy have always been heavily infused with special interest politics. Whether the threat of global climate change will move Congress to effectively support national and international preventive measures is yet uncertain. Nevertheless, President Bush has promised to call an international meeting in 1990 to address the global warming issue.[22]

Chemical Contamination

Although the residuals of energy production are major environmental contaminants, industrial chemistry has also produced thousands of compounds of which many have toxic effects. These toxic substances enter into the air, soil, and water, usually as industrial wastes. In 1989 the Environmental Protection Agency reported that at least three hundred toxic chemicals were being emitted in stack gases from American industries.[23] Accidents have increasingly accounted for serious damage; hardly a week has passed in recent years without report of some hazardous chemical spill from tanker trucks or railway tank cars. Explosions and chemical fires both in the United States and abroad have been regular features on television.

The continuing export of chemical products barred by law from sale in the United States is one matter calling for more responsible policy choice. A rather weak, last-minute order by President Carter (Executive Order 12264 of January 15, 1981) requiring exporters to inform foreign governments regarding the hazardous potentials of products (for example, pesticides and pharmaceuticals) was promptly cancelled by President Reagan as an unwarranted infringement on free markets and the right of foreign governments to control their own import policies.

The export of toxic and other wastes to Third World countries is another example of the inconsistencies between national and international policies of the United States. The international flow of toxic chemicals, noxious wastes, and other hazardous materials has become an environmental issue demanding early and effective action. On December 17, 1981, the General Assembly of the United Nations adopted by a 146-1 vote a resolution on Protection Against Products Harmful to Health and Environment. The United States alone declined to support the resolution.[24] During the ensuing decade, world opinion moved toward more positive measures for controlling commerce in hazardous materials. Yet as of 1989, the United States was still resisting restrictions on American exports. Meeting in Basel, Switzerland, from March 20 to 22, 1989, representatives from 116 countries agreed in principle on a treaty to regulate and limit the transboundary shipment of hazardous wastes. Although only 34 countries, excluding the United States, signed the treaty at Basel, the ultimate consummation of a generally acceptable treaty seems probable.[25] The prospect for positive results is obstructed by the apparent fact that effective remedies ultimately can be achieved only by stopping the contamination at its source. In many cases this means stopping production of dangerous substances or finding ways to assure they are rendered harmless.

Ridding the world of hazardous chemicals will be difficult and protracted. Most of the products are perceived to serve desirable human purposes. Finding benign substitutes requires time, money, and increased commitment to research and development. Containment of the chemical emissions contributing to acid deposition and depletion of the stratospheric ozone layer is necessary for both domestic and foreign policy considerations. The U.S. government is already committed to a phased reduction of chlorofluorocarbons, but President Bush has hedged this option with the proviso that a suitable substitute for CFCs be found. Thus, it seems that immediate economic priorities continue to override more fundamental environmental considerations.

But economic priorities can also parallel and reinforce environmental considerations. For example, resistance to the export of toxic wastes, and the growing costs and shrinking space for waste disposal, have stimulated the search for new methods of detoxification, recycling, and biodegradation. International technology transfer is benefiting American businesses and communities, as lessons are being learned from European experience in this area.[26]

Sustainable Agriculture

Probably few people would identify agriculture as an environmental problem of international dimension, yet today it is possibly the greatest threat to natural ecosystems and biological variety and diversity throughout the world. Americans are overly optimistic in the belief that their nation can continue indefinitely to feed the world. Green-revolution-style agriculture practiced at home and propagated abroad by the United States is popularly seen as a spectacular success. In truth, it carries serious ecological, economic, and sociological consequences that cannot be discounted. For example, heavy applications of artificial fertilizers, herbicides, pesticides, and water are required to produce this type of agriculture's greatly increased crop yields. But the yields can be sustained only by costly chemical infusions that leave residuals in soil, surface water, and groundwater—and are sometimes carried into the atmosphere.[27] Irrigation, unless carefully controlled, can have a deleterious effect upon soils, and its runoff contains pollutants that include toxic chemicals and salts. Moreover, this industrialized agriculture is powered by oil, which is unevenly distributed and nonrenewable. Thus, industrial agriculture has destroyed environmental quality and social stability over much of the United States and abroad.[28]

Pushed by international economic development programs, many countries have abandoned food production for local consumption in favor of export commodities—for example, cotton, soy beans, and sugar. When droughts, floods, or civil disturbance reduce the amount or accessibility of food, hunger and starvation follow. In recent years the United States has sent food relief to many countries in which famine is becoming chronic. The immediate need to alleviate suffering precludes giving time and attention to underlying causes, and often elicits contradictory responses from developed countries. Paradoxically, while the United States has encouraged the growing of foreign exchange producing cash crops for export in developing countries, it has obstructed their export to its own nation through the subsidized production of cotton, sugar, and other crops.

Developments in plant genetics and biotechnology have introduced a new element into America's international relationships. American corporations benefiting from international agreements that protect investments by plant breeders have exported genetically engineered plant germ plasm under patent. International development programs have promoted use of these new species, but two adverse effects have followed. First, the new artificial strains tend to drive out the native species, with resulting genetic loss. Preservation of the native biotypes is considered important to the future of biology and plant genetics. Second, farmers adopting the new imported species become captive not only to the owner of the plant patents, but also to the necessity of buying the fertilizers and pesticides needed for their propagation. Thus, American export of patented seeds may contradict the U.S. government's policy on preservation of genetic variety and diversity in the biosphere.[29]

The need to export American farm products for both international trade balance and famine relief, and the political power of subsidized agriculture, result in practices that may not be sustainable over the long run in the United States or abroad. But the intermixture of economics, politics, and agriculture makes any significant change in American policy difficult. The alternative of supporting sustainable agriculture at home and abroad is advocated by a few ecologically oriented private organizations and was strongly endorsed by the World Commission on Environment and Development (the Bruntland commission).[30] But the dominant political and economic forces support with only minor modification the perpetuation of a vulnerable, costly, and ecologically damaging—albeit presently highly productive—agricultural system.

Some Additional Issues

There are additional issues of environmental significance that will require policy decisions during the ensuing decade. Among them are the future of Antarctica, America's stand on the proposed Law of the Sea treaty, and a comprehensive agreement for restoration and maintenance of the Great Lakes-Saint Lawrence Basin ecosystem. Finally, it must be realized that basic to nearly every environmental problem is the multiplication, concentration, and dispersal of human populations.

The environmental future of Antarctica is of interest to American scientists who have conducted research in meteorology, geology, and ecology there. A multinational consultative committee presently makes decisions regarding permissible activities in Antarctica, but expectations for mineral development render its future as a protected scientific reserve uncertain.[31] Scientists and environmentalists believe that preservation of the geophysical and ecological conditions of Antarctica under international control ought to be the American policy position. There has been pressure, however, within both the United States and other countries, for the exploration of minerals in Antarctica.[32] In 1988 a draft minerals convention was adopted by the consultative committee, but its ratification was subsequently rejected by Australia and France. The Reagan administration leaned toward development, but the Bush administration appears to favor environmentally protective mineral development.

The Law of the Sea treaty would provide a codified international law for the oceans. The near future of the treaty is uncertain because leading maritime nations, including the United States, have refused to ratify it. In principle, however, there seems to be international agreement that a binding law is needed. It appears probable that such a treaty will be consummated before the end of the 1990s, and that a parallel Law of the Air treaty will be in some stage of negotiation.[33]

The future of joint Canadian-American responsibilities for the Great Lakes-Saint Lawrence Basin ecosystem is of great practical importance to both countries. The Water Quality Agreements of 1972 and 1978, and the protocol of 1987, presented a broad but incomplete and, in some respects, inconsistent framework for bilateral cooperation.[34] In 1985 the Great Lakes state governors, along with the premiers of Ontario and Quebec, issued a Charter for the Great Lakes, primarily directed toward the issue of diverting water from the basin.[35] Subsequently, the issue of fluctuating lake levels led to the two federal governments requesting from the International Joint Commission a comprehensive study of the problem. Meanwhile, problems of toxic contamination were discovered to be more extensive, complex, and difficult than had been previously assumed. These, among other factors (including shipping, recreation, Native American rights, shoreline development, and fisheries), led a growing number of people to conclude that a more comprehensive and coherent coordinating system was required to implement even existing commitments. The 1988 Free Trade Agreement between Canada and the United States may facilitate negotiation of a Great Lakes-Saint Lawrence Basin ecosystem agreement.

The explosive growth of the human population has become an environmental problem of major proportion. Rapid population growth has imperiled the quality of land, water, air, and living conditions. It has increased the impact of technology on food production, disposal of wastes, and preservation of forests and wildlife, in addition to having adverse sociological effects. During the Reagan years, the United States, reversing earlier policies, not only withdrew government support for international population planning through United Nations agencies, but its official representatives sought to persuade other governments that numbers presented no problem that economic growth could not cure. In November 1989, Bush continued Reagan's policy by vetoing the FY 1990 Foreign Aid Appropriations bill that provided funds for United Nations family planning programs.

Political and Institutional Capabilities

The foregoing issues have been selected from a larger number of environmental problems having both domestic and international implications. It becomes increasingly evident that humanity has reached such numbers and is making such heavy demands upon space and natural resources that the entire planetary biosphere and human society itself are being impacted adversely. There are still localized environmental problems and solutions; in some sense all environmental problems are localized. But from now on they are inevitably linked globally although the connections may be indirect and obscure. Governments and people need to understand the World Commission on Environment and Development's declaration that the future of the world is "our common future." Even George Bush and Mikhail Gorbachev appear to agree that no nation or people can isolate itself from changes now being made in the planetary biosphere.

In this area of politics, as in others, the influence of America is greatest when it is evident in practice. To set an example could be the primary contribution of the United States to the solution of world environmental problems. But foreign aid and assistance, primarily through international organizations such as the United Nations Environment Programme, and expanded research on critical global environmental problems are also needed. Finally, the United States has the capabilities for training people from other countries in various aspects of environmental management and protection. Relative to the need, little of this is presently being done.

The U.S. government has thus far shown no interest or support for the Bruntland Commission report. *Our Common Future* reflected neither the philosophy nor the priorities of the Reagan administration. In contrast, it has been taken very seriously in Canada and Australia—the countries most closely resembling the United States—as well as in Europe. To be sure, the report is a point of departure rather than a blueprint for the future, but it indicates the direction in which nations must move to achieve their common interests.

If we contemplate the changes in the world political order since 1945, it seems difficult to believe that changes of comparable magnitude will not occur in the future. Despite its uncertainties and paradoxes, science is becoming an ever more reliable informant on environmental cause-effect relationships. In the cases of the stratospheric ozone layer, global climate change, and acid precipitation, scientific evidence, although never absolute, is persuading governments to accept informed responsibility for the future. Religion is now joining science in a combination that should possess unusual political power. The New Road Movement, initiated by the World Wildlife Fund at Assisi, Italy, in 1986, and Pope John Paul's first papal statement devoted to the global ecological crisis, brings ecumenical power to realizing many of the objectives presented in *Our Common Future*.[36]

Even military policies have been touched by this new awareness of global environmental dangers and national interdependence. On May 29, 1989, the *New York Times* declared that "traditional definitions of national security are shaken by global environmental threats." [37] Earlier in 1989, a session on national security and environment was sponsored at the annual meeting of the American Association for the Advancement of Science. And ever alert to changing currents of thought, Mikhail Gorbachev proposed in his December 1988 address to the United Nations that the Soviet Union and the United States jointly construct and operate a space station to monitor environmental changes on earth.[38]

If the world in general, and the United States in particular, musters the political will to cope realistically with the environmental problems that modern society has generated, the question of institutional capability must still be answered. Two obstacles must be overcome. The first is the dominance of traditional economic and military assumptions built into the legal and bureaucratic structures of national governments in both the East and West. Dominant thought in modern society, and thus public policy, is only beginning to take account of the interrelatedness of the many human impacts upon the earth. Governments are still structured on the belief that their various functions can be separated into independent categories without much provision for policy coordination. The U.S. National Environmental Policy Act of 1969 confers limited powers of surveillance on the Council for Environmental Quality that could assist policy coordination in the executive branch.[39] The Office of Management and Budget is the principal coordinating agent for the president, but its evaluative criteria have always been almost exclusively economic.

Since 1989, however, several agencies have taken new responsibility for global climate policy and related issues. The State Department has given increased priority to environmental affairs; Secretary of State James Baker's first speech after taking office was to the Working Group of the Intergovernmental Panel on Climate Change, a multilateral body established in 1988 to prepare a "framework agreement" within which all nations may address global warming and related issues in the 1990s. The Bureau of Oceans and International Environmental and Scientific Affairs, thus far an obscure entity in the State Department, has emerged as the lead agency for conducting negotiations on this agreement, scheduled for completion and signing at the United Nations in late 1990.[40]

Other agencies are also increasing their capabilities for international environmental policy making. The Environmental Protection Agency has upgraded its international staff under a new assistant administrator, and the Department of Energy is also creating a new global climate office despite (or perhaps because of) its skepticism about any controls on energy use. Meanwhile, a scientific body—the Committee on Earth Sciences of the Federal Coordinating Council for Science, Engineering, and Technology, under the president's Office of Science and Technology Policy—is coordinating research and technical studies necessary for further international agreements.[41] Finally, the Council on Environmental Quality is seeking to restore its advisory role in international affairs. Whether these institutional developments will result in greater coordination and policy-making effectiveness, or continuing conflicts and turf battles, remains to be seen, but it appears that the Bush administration is making a serious effort to reestablish American leadership in this field.

Unfortunately, in most countries with environmental departments or ministries, the environmental agencies tend to be politically subordinate to others—usually ministries of agriculture, commerce, economic development, energy, or defense. It is therefore not surprising that the international structure of environmental policy is not presently suited to coordinated action on environmental issues.[42] Although the General Assembly of the United Nations has given high priority to environmental declarations, the United Nations Environment Programme has very limited ability to influence policies of the United Nations specialized agencies (for example, FAO, WHO, WMO, and UNESCO). Problems of national and international policy implementation, coordination, and reconciliation will thus require much greater attention in the future.

Conclusion

National and international policies on major environmental issues have become inseparable. Governments are increasingly pressured to respond to values regarding health, safety, and environment shared by people internationally. The trends in all industrial democracies are similar. On June 27, 1989, the U.S. Department of Energy announced that its reordering of priorities will give much greater emphasis to environmental, health, and safety measures in defense-related establishments.

This is indicative, one can hope, of a growing expectation in America that considerations of national security will no longer sufficiently justify disregard of environmental values.[43]

History may not be the best indicator of what may happen in the future regarding national and international environmental affairs. Present circumstances have no historical precedent, and the dangers that humans have inadvertently provoked cannot be removed by mere political or legal fiat. When the penalties of environmental dereliction become less acceptable than their remedial costs (already a visible trend), fundamental changes in policies and institutions will follow. For some environmental developments these changes may come too late to prevent irreversible consequences. Contrary to modern myth, ours is a world of limits as well as opportunities. Public wisdom lies in a selective advance of opportunities without incurring the penalties of overshooting these limits.[44] This requires a new kind of politics for which no nation can as yet claim experience.

Notes

1. Lester W. Milbrath, "Environmental Values and Beliefs of the General Public and Leaders in the United States, England and Germany," in *Environmental Policy Formation: The Impact of Values, Ideology, and Standards*, ed. Dean E. Mann (Lexington, Mass.: Lexington Books, 1981), 41-46; Ronald Inglehart, *Ecological Issues* (Ann Arbor, Mich.: InterUniversity Consortium for Political and Social Research, 1983); and Inglehart, *The Silent Revolution: Changing Values and Political Styles Among Western Publics* (Princeton, N.J.: Princeton University Press, 1977).
2. John Carroll, ed., *Environmental Diplomacy: The Management and Resolution of Transfrontier Environmental Problems* (Cambridge: Cambridge University Press, 1988).
3. For summary accounts see *Keesing's Contemporary Archives: Record of World Events*, Seveso: June 1979, 29688, October 1983, 32475, and March 1986, 34270; Bhopal: March 1985, 33467-33468; Chernobyl: June 1986, 34460-34462. For the Rhine River see *Facts on File*, November 7, 1986, 845G1, November 14, 1986, 858E1, and December 31, 1987, 89B2; and for the *Exxon Valdez* see *Keesing's Record of World Events*, March 1989, 36541, 36606.
4. Barbara Ward and René Dubos, *Only One Earth: The Care and Maintenance of a Small Planet* (New York: Norton, 1972). See also Norman Myers and Dorothy Myers, "How the Global Community Can Respond to International Environmental Problems," *Ambio* 12 (1983): 20-26.
5. Howard Sprout and Margaret Sprout, *Toward a Politics of the Planet Earth* (New York: Van Nostrand Reinhold, 1971).
6. United Nations, *U.N. Chronicle*, 26 (March 1989): 33.
7. James M. Markham, "Greening of European Politicians Spreads as Peril to

Ecology Grows," *New York Times,* April 12, 1989; and Markham, "Key Sections of the Paris Communiqué by the Group of Seven," *New York Times,* July 17, 1989. See also Philip Shabecoff, "U.S. to Press for Joint Effort on Environment at Summit," *New York Times,* July 6, 1989; and Markham, "Paris Group Urges 'Decisive' Action for Environment," *New York Times,* July 17, 1989.

8. Christopher Flavin, *Reassessing Nuclear Power: The Fallout from Chernobyl,* Worldwatch Paper 75 (Washington, D.C.: Worldwatch Institute, 1987); and Joseph Jaffe, "Chernobyl Clouds German Thinking and Besets the Greens," *Wall Street Journal,* May 28, 1989, 31.
9. Matthew L. Wald, "Governors Assail U.S. Effort to Clean Up Nuclear Waste," *New York Times,* May 6, 1989.
10. On public and official response to nuclear pollution, see "Atomic Energy," *Facts on File,* June 9, 1989, 419-420.
11. Timothy Egan, "Federally Subsidized Lumbering Is Questioned," *New York Times,* May 29, 1989.
12. On global climate change, see Thomas F. Malone and J. G. Roederer, eds., *Global Change: Proceedings of a Symposium Sponsored by the International Council of Scientific Unions* (Cambridge: Cambridge University Press, 1985). For less technical treatment, see N. J. Rosenberg et al., eds., *Greenhouse Warming: Abatement and Adaptation* (Washington, D.C.: Resources for the Future, 1989).
13. Philip Shabecoff, "Scientist Says U.S. Agency Altered His Testimony on Global Warming," *New York Times,* May 8, 1989. For coverage of the scientific issues involved, see Richard A. Kerr, "Hansen vs. the World on the Greenhouse Threat," *Science* 244 (June 2, 1989): 1041-1043. For the changing U.S. official position on a treaty, see "U.S. Détente on 'Greenhouse' Treaty," *Facts on File,* May 26, 1989, 376.
14. Sharon Begley with Mary Hager, "Feeling the Heat on the Greenhouse," *Newsweek,* May 22, 1989, 71-80.
15. There is voluminous literature on the greenhouse effect and global climate change. See especially Environmental Protection Agency, *The Potential Effects of Global Climate Change on the United States,* draft report to Congress (Washington, D.C.: Environmental Protection Agency, October 1988); the special issue of *Science* on "Issues in Atmospheric Sciences," February 10, 1989; the special issue of *Scientific American* on "Managing Planet Earth," September 1989; and Stephen H. Schneider, *Global Warming: Are We Entering the Greenhouse Century?* (San Francisco: Sierra Club Books, 1989).
16. For the English language text of the Vienna and Montreal agreements, see *International Legal Materials* 26 (1987): "Vienna Convention for the Protection of the Ozone Layer," 1516-1540, and "Montreal Protocol on Substance that Depletes the Ozone Layer," 1541-1561. See also M. K. Tolba, "The Ozone Agreement and Beyond," *Environmental Conservation* 14 (Winter 1987): 287-290.
17. Craig R. Whitney, "80 Nations Favor Ban to Help Ozone," *New York Times,* May 3, 1989; and Whitney, "Industrial Countries to Aid Poorer Nations on Ozone," *New York Times,* May 6, 1989.

18. *Keesing's Record of World Events* (March 1989), 36540.
19. John Gever et al., *Beyond Oil: The Threat to Food and Fuel in the Coming Decades* (Cambridge, Mass.: Ballinger, 1986). See also U.S. Congress. Senate. Committee on Energy and Natural Resources. *The Geopolitics of Oil.* 96th Cong., 2d sess., December 1980. Staff Report; and James Z. Pugash and Gina Despres, Executive summary in *Science* 210 (December 19, 1980): 1324-1327.
20. *Inside E.P.A. Weekly Report,* June 16, 1989, 1, 7. See also "Bush Unveils Clean Air Plan," *Facts on File,* June 16, 1989, 441.
21. "Convention on Long-Range Transboundary Air Pollution," *Acid News* (May 1989), special issue for International Air Pollution Week. For the texts of these agreements, see *International Environmental Reporter, Reference File—Treaties:* "Convention on Long-Range Transboundary Air Pollution" (entered into force March 16, 1983) 21: 3001-3005; "Protocol on the Reduction of Sulfur Emissions or Their Transboundary Fluxes by at Least 30 Percent" (entered into force September 2, 1987) 21: 3021-3022; and "1988 Protocol to the 1979 Convention on Long-Range Transboundary Air Pollution Concerning the Control of Emissions of Nitrogen Oxides or Their Transboundary Fluxes," 21: 3041-3050.
22. See Philip Shabecoff, "Bush Will Call Meeting About Global Warming," *New York Times,* May 10, 1989; and Allan R. Gold, "Bush Seeks Talks on World Warming," *New York Times,* December 6, 1989, 7.
23. Philip Shabecoff, "Industrial Pollution Called Startling," *New York Times,* April 13, 1989.
24. Libby Bassett, "U.N. Votes to Protect People from Harmful Imports," *World Environment Report* 9 (January 15, 1983): 1-2. See also U.S. Congress. House. Committee on Foreign Affairs. Subcommittee on International Policy and Trade. *Hearings on the Export of Hazardous Products.* 92d Cong. 2d sess., June 5, 12, and September 9, 1980. Public opinion was divided on the issue at the time. Industrial and trade groups opposed U.S. cooperation in restricting the export of toxic and hazardous products, but international regulations were supported by public health and environmental groups. By the end of the 1980s, however, it appeared highly probable that the U.S. official position would move toward some form of international cooperation during the 1990s.
25. Steven Greenhouse, "U.N. Conference Supports Curbs on Exporting of Hazardous Waste: 34 Nations Sign Pact and U.S. Plans to Review It," *New York Times,* March 25, 1989. See also *Keesing's Record of World Events,* News Digest (March 1986): 36541. For background on the toxic waste shipments issues, see *Keesing's Record of World Events* (October 1988): 36250-36252; and, for texts of the agreement, see "1989 Basel Convention on the Control of Transboundary Movements of Hazardous Wastes and Their Disposal," *International Environmental Reporter, Reference File—Treaties* 21: 3701-3712.
26. Bruce W. Piasecki and Gary A. Davis, *America's Future in Toxic Waste Management: Lessons from Europe* (Westport, Conn.: Greenwood Press, 1987).
27. *Water Pollution by Fertilizers and Pesticides* (Paris: Organization for Economic Cooperation and Development, 1986).

28. Kenneth A. Dahlberg, *Beyond the Green Revolution: The Ecology and Politics of Global Agricultural Development* (New York: Plenum Press, 1979).
29. Jack R. Kloppenberg, ed., *Seeds and Sovereignty: The Use and Control of Plant Genetic Resources* (Durham, N.C.: Duke University Press, 1988).
30. World Commission on Environment and Development, *Our Common Future* (New York: Oxford University Press, 1987).
31. Jeffrey D. Myhre, *The Antarctic Treaty System: Politics, Law, and Diplomacy* (Boulder, Colo.: Westview Press, 1986); Gilliam D. Triggs, *The Antarctic Treaty Regime* (Cambridge: Cambridge University Press, 1987); M. J. Peterson, *Managing the Frozen South: The Creation and Evolution of the Antarctic Treaty System* (Berkeley: University of California Press, 1988).
32. William E. Westermeyer, *The Politics of Mineral Resource Development in Antarctica: Alternative Regimes for the Future* (Boulder, Colo.: Westview Press, 1984); and Francisco Orrego Vicuña, *Antarctic Mineral Exploration: The Emerging Legal Framework* (Cambridge: Cambridge University Press, 1988).
33. James K. Sebenius, *Negotiating the Law of the Sea* (Cambridge, Mass.: Harvard University Press, 1984); and Jacques G. Richardson, *Managing the Ocean: Resources, Research, Law* (Mt. Airy, Md.: Lommond Publications, 1985).
34. Lynton K. Caldwell, ed., *Perspectives on Ecosystem Management for the Great Lakes: A Reader* (Albany, N.Y.: SUNY Press, 1988).
35. Ibid., Appendix C, 359-361.
36. World Wildlife Fund, *The New Road: Bulletin of the W.W.F. Network on Conservation and Religion* (Gland, Switzerland: World Wildlife Fund International, 1986); and Clyde Haberman, "John Paul Rebukes Lands That Foster Environment Crisis," *New York Times*, December 6, 1989, 7.
37. Philip Shabecoff, "Environment: Traditional Definitions of National Security Are Shaken by Global Environmental Threats," *New York Times*, May 29, 1989. See also Sen. Al Gore, "The Global Environment: A National Security Issue," keynote address to the National Academy of Sciences Forum on Global Climate Change, May 1, 1989; and Jessica Tuchman Matthews, "Redefining Security," *Foreign Affairs* 68 (Spring 1989): 162-177.
38. United Nations, *U.N. Chronicle* 26 (March 1989): 33.
39. Lynton K. Caldwell, *Science and the National Environmental Policy Act: Redirecting Policy Through Procedural Reform* (University, Ala.: University of Alabama Press, 1982).
40. Baker's speech is reprinted in "Secretary Addresses Panel on Global Climate Change," *Department of State Bulletin* (April 1989): 13-16. On the global warming negotiations and the role of the State Department and other agencies, see Rochelle L. Stanfield, "Greenhouse Diplomacy," *National Journal*, March 4, 1989; and Jessica Tuchman Mathews, "Tackling the Institutional Barriers," *EPA Journal*, issue on "Protecting the Earth: Are Our Institutions Up to It?" (July/August 1989): 11-14.
41. Committee on Earth Sciences, Federal Coordinating Council for Science, Engineering, and Technology, *Our Changing Planet: A U.S. Stragegy for Global Change Research* (Washington, D.C.: Office of Science and Technol-

ogy Policy, 1989).

42. Lynton K. Caldwell, *International Environmental Policy* (Durham, N.C.: Duke University Press, 1984), 63-72, 82-100; and Caldwell, "The Structure of International Environmental Policy," *Journal of Public and International Affairs* 5 (Winter 1984): 1-15.
43. Matthew Wald, "Energy Chief Says Top Aides Lack Skills to Run U.S. Bomb Complex," *New York Times*, June 28, 1989.
44. William Catton, *Overshoot: The Ecological Basis of Revolutionary Change* (Urbana: University of Illinois Press, 1980). See also Donella H. Meadows et al., *The Limits to Growth* (New York: Universe Books, 1972); and Council on Environmental Quality and Department of State, *The Global 2000 Report to the President* (Washington, D.C.: U.S. Government Printing Office, 1980).

V. ETHICS, VALUES, AND THE FUTURE OF ENVIRONMENTAL POLITICS

15

Moral Outrage and the Progress of Environmental Policy: What Do We Tell the Next Generation About How to Care for the Earth?

Geoffrey Wandesforde-Smith

Without outrage, Aldo Leopold [American forester, preservationist, 1886-1948] will be left without a legacy, for the land ethic will suffer the worst kind of failure, the failure to try. Instead of cool analysis, we should embrace a politics of outrage, fury, indignation, wrath, deep umbrage, resentment, exasperation, rancor, and passion which wells up, if we let it, when we see the [earth] destroyed.

Charles Little
"Has the Land Ethic Failed in America?
An Essay on the Legacy of Aldo Leopold" (1986)

As the century draws to a close and as my son prepares to go to college to become, I hope, among other things, a reader of this volume, rows of books portending the destruction of the earth fill the shelves of my office. Many of the titles are deceptively bland: *World Resources, 1988-89, State of the World, 1989, State of the Environment: A View Toward the Nineties.*[1] These titles reveal little of the ominous contents—tales and tables that chronicle the loss of the world's life and habitats. It's almost as if the authors wanted to proclaim a sense of impending crisis, of time running out, and of a desperate search for answers, without really seeming to be critical, hurried, or desperate.

Because of television and press coverage, the alarming subjects covered by these books are quickly becoming familiar—depletion of the ozone layer, changing of the climate, deforestation of the tropics, and

---

The author dedicates this chapter to his son, Alistair, and acknowledges the assistance of Cynthia Ayala, the 1988-89 Mesple Scholar in the Department of Political Science, University of California, Davis.

extinction of animal and plant species on land and in the oceans. The endangerment of the earth and of the life it sustains was *Time* magazine's cover story of the year on January 2, 1989.

I find myself wondering what my son's generation knows about these environmental problems. What do they think they ought to do about them? What advice should they have from people like me, who are presumably older and wiser? What obligations do I have to them, and they to me, if the behavior of my generation and theirs threatens to destroy the resources of the planet and, thus, its habitability? Many of the books in my office and many distinguished environmental seers are strangely silent about the principles that can and should be adopted to justify greater human restraint in using natural resources.

In the first section of this chapter, I share my concerns about the way people are encouraged to think about these questions and especially about the wisdom of treating the earth as if it were only a political economy of scarce resources. Such cool analysis slights the expression of outrage about serious moral and ethical issues. It clouds the contribution a politics of moral outrage can make in a world of moral pluralism—a world full of "earth ethics" and other ethics.[2] Outrage is, I argue, a driving force for change.

The second section reviews the historical association between moral outrage and progress in environmental policy. At the turn of the century, the moral outrage of the Progressives at the waste of resources and the righteous indignation of John Muir at the desecration of Yosemite had very different ethical foundations, but both were important precursors of the policy and institutional reforms of Progressive era conservation. This section examines the politics of land use as well as the dark side of outrage as a force for change—namely, its potential to alter established expectations about property, and to call into question the existing distribution of power. History shows that American political institutions, though periodically destabilized by the politics of outrage, have proven remarkably resilient and adaptive.

The concluding section of the chapter considers the ethical dilemmas of environmental policy making, both global and domestic, in the 1990s, and asks whether they will put new and more intense strains on the body politic.[3]

Moral Pluralism and the Politics of Outrage

Except for the enormous outpouring of disgust at the ethics and actions of Interior Secretary James Watt, outrage was rarely expressed or demonstrated on environmental issues in the 1980s. It surfaced in relation to abortion, for example, and other issues on the conservative agenda of the Reagan years. Some young people took part in the strategies and tactics of direct political action that were deployed by deeply committed activists on both sides of such issues. In other words, they put their principles to the test of action.

In general, however, the moral education of this generation of young people on environmental issues stems from what they have learned at home and at school rather than from political engagement. Does this make it impossible for them to understand how the expression and political exploitation of moral outrage in the 1960s was indispensable to the creation of the modern environmental movement and much of the present corpus of environmental law? I think not, but it does make it difficult.

David Brower was a key figure in environmental politics in the 1960s. He had an inexhaustible willingness to brand as morally outrageous his fellow Americans' treatment of the environment. And this outrage, which he expressed with verve and energy well into the 1980s, had major political impacts, both within the environmental movement and in society at large. But Brower may seem as remote and unreal a figure to many of the younger readers of this book as does John Muir, another moral crusader for the environment who railed against the desecration of his world with great effect until his death in 1914.[4] Unfortunately, analysis as a precursor of policy making is rarely supplemented today by the respect for moral discourse and the commitment to moral action that Muir and Brower exemplified.[5] Analysis is always partial. It can tell us some of the things we want and need to know. But, in Charles Little's apt phrase, it trivializes environmental policy making in important ways.

The prolific literature of resource and environmental economics makes a persuasive case for thinking and acting in relation to the earth as if it were a political economy of scarce resources. But ethical conflicts over the fundamental values that might lead men and women to avoid ecological catastrophes have no place in this discourse.[6] Economists, the archdruids of this gospel, tell people that they can secure happiness for themselves and their posterity by becoming managers—by learning how to make and live with trade-offs, by mastering the art of balancing the benefits and costs of environmental protection, by making the environmental bottom line cost-effective, by applying themselves, in short, to the economic management of scarcity.[7]

Notice that a morality underlies this world view, a set of moral as well as economic principles to restrain and guide behavior. At its core is the primacy and welfare of the human individual and a belief in the hypothetical justice that can be attained under an abstract ethic of compensation.[8] Notice also that the economist's commonsense ethic and explanation of the methods by which it is to be applied to environmental policy choices neither anticipate nor require that moral outrage be a driving force for change.

Economists rarely express outrage. On the contrary, their language is deliberately chosen to have exactly the opposite effect. Their advice to policy makers omits the expression of outrage as a necessary, legitimate, and constructive part of participation in decision making, even on behalf of economic values. And since economists give no thought or mention to any morality except their own, the possibility that other people might reasonably express outrage in the policy process at the morals of economists is left entirely unconsidered.

Economists have nothing to say about how people should confront each other in the policy process when moral views on the care of the earth differ from those underlying modern welfare economics. They are silent, for example, on what might become of efficiency or cost-effectiveness, two of their prime criteria for good policy choices, when this happens. Is it ethical, and can it be conducive to the care of the earth, to compromise efficiency in making decisions? Is there a noneconomic basis that should be used to evaluate an environmental policy choice that is plainly inefficient from an economist's point of view?

Other awkward but important questions are left unanswered. What would acceptance of the economist's calculus of consent mean when factors like the strength of moral convictions have to be taken into account? Must they be priced? Can they be priced? Should they be priced? Can they be compared across and within generations? Can they be traded by policy makers? And, if not, can they be squared in some other way with the goal of efficiency?

These questions are far from being fresh and original. Answers to them have been well rehearsed in the past ten years, partly in response to the renaissance recently enjoyed by cost-benefit thinking.[9] But in this chapter I want to establish the radically different premise that there exist in the world many moralities. They include, certainly, optimizing the welfare of the human individual, but they also extend to the many varieties of environmental ethics so usefully catalogued in *The Rights of Nature* by Roderick Nash.

Given this condition of moral pluralism, ethical dilemmas and political conflicts are inevitable in environmental policy making. They will sometimes be deep, deafening, and divisive. To pretend otherwise is to take refuge in a safe but ethically singular world of cool analysis. When the care of the earth and *all* the people on it is in question, that course seems to me to be neither realistic nor responsible.

Moral dilemmas are vital to environmental policy making. When the direct engagement of people with different ethics is kept alive and nurtured in the environmental policy process, the implications of these different ethics are argued about over and over again. This is what the politics of moral outrage accomplishes. Out of these experiences come important lessons about how people should deal with each other and with the earth, lessons that are unteachable and untaught by treating the earth as if it were only a political economy of scarce resources.[10]

Indeed, there is a clear and long-standing association in America between major new developments in resource and environmental policy, on the one hand, and expressions of moral outrage, on the other hand. In this history there are clear signs of a dark side to moral outrage as a driving force for change. It threatens political stability and established expectations.[11] To date, however, the descent into chaos has been averted.

The Politics of Outrage and American Land

Decisions about land illustrate better than many other examples the moral dilemmas of environmental policy choices and the history of the politics of outrage to which they give rise. An important reason for this is the special place that land and land ownership have always had in the definition of what America means, and what it means to be an American. It is a place worth exploring because it is a point where ethics of efficiency, equity, ecology, and esthetics come together. It is often depicted by contemporary analysts as a place where diverse ethics will have trouble coexisting, but the evidence of history supports a more pluralistic view.[12]

American Values and the American Land

"For three hundred years," writes Lynton K. Caldwell, "American popular culture has strongly linked land ownership with individual personal freedom—especially freedom from the exactions of government." [13] Land and the freedom to use it have also been widely perceived as keys to the creation of wealth and thus to the success of capitalism. But it has been wealth realized in the short run, without regard for the long-term productivity of the land itself and the resources it sustains. Much has been done to public and private land in the name of efficiency. Much less has been done so far in the service of equity, ecology, and esthetics.

The pursuit of basic, indeed characteristically American, values like individual freedom and wealth has exacted a heavy price on the land. Long ago this called into question the legal system of rights and obligations that permitted, indeed promoted, the private possession and use of land as if it were just a commodity. Hence, over the course of this century, public land ownership and government intervention in the land market have gained acceptance and legitimacy. Yet we cannot conclude with any confidence that "the liberal consensus supporting only limited government intervention in land markets has been shattered." [14] In fact, the rights of private landowners are far from being dismantled. Moreover, even in preponderantly urban, modern America many people who own no land "still wear psychologically the coonskin caps of land hungry pioneers and the rose tinted glasses of speculators." [15] This sentimental attachment even of the landless to the value of land as a symbol of freedom and wealth dies hard.

The real importance, then, of the special relationship between land and American beliefs and values is that arguments about rights, ownership, and use "are inherently political for they involve the essential purposes of the liberal democratic state." [16] To what extent should the state and the private sector be required to restrain their use of land? And what values, what moral visions of the state and of its relationship to human welfare, should guide this restraint—those represented by the ethic of efficiency, or of equity, or of ecology, or of esthetics? These ethical questions are inextricably intertwined in the case of land with questions concerning what ethics and whose ethics should guide relationships between generations.

Land, Outrage, and the Choice of Ethics

Each ethic that might guide land policy making has the potential to provoke a politics of moral outrage. And this confrontation over ethical choices is a good thing. It creates new meanings for our ethics. It is unfortunate, then, that the expression of this outrage sometimes occurs side by side with the rejection of other ethics. Two illustrations from contemporary analysts are useful.

Caldwell is outraged that so many people still cling to the economist's ethic of efficiency. Concepts of land rights and ownership that are consistent with the efficiency ethic encourage people to see their relationship to the land as little more than a set of economic opportunities confirmed by law. This precludes the better human relationship to the earth shown to be necessary and possible by the growth of environmental knowledge, and that, too, is outrageous.

Thus, like many others, Caldwell is drawn to a form of practical politics that firmly subordinates the ethic of efficiency and that rejects what he calls the commitment to undifferentiated growth that has long prevailed almost everywhere. He sees very little point in devoting scarce political time and energy to land-use regulation (which, of course, is designed to correct imperfections in the efficient market allocation of resources, not replace it). The strategy for major change must begin instead with a massive transformation of the human values associated with land, after which any ethic other than ecological stewardship would be both unthinkable and redundant. Thus, the politics of outrage is reduced to large-scale campaigns of public education aimed at remaking ecological paradigms, the implicit perceptions people have of the world and their relationship to it.

In Caldwell's causal universe these belief systems determine attitudes, preferences, and behaviors regarding land. One of them is more correct, more appropriate, more ethical than the others. Making the law express that sense of rights, wrongs, and obligations regarding the land—through a National Land Use Policy Act, for example—is the key to progress in environmental policy.

The politics of outrage is also consistent with a more catholic view of land ethics and public policy. Charles Little describes a variety of public and private uses of land that are outrageous at first sight:

> The despoliation of land—[Aldo] Leopold's word—cannot be gainsaid. Everywhere, *everywhere*, the rate of despoliation increases: stripmine gashes, kudzu-covered junkyards, billboards, antennae sprouting like asparagus, Stygian milltowns, "condomania" on the coastlines from Jersey to the Keys; asphalted National Parks, Forests, Recreation Areas, Wildlife Refuges, Monuments, Historic Places that make up the leisure world trailer hook-up that is America; the so-called grey suburbs of Archie Bunkerland in the rustbelt, the ticky-tacky of 'the Valley,' the sad swaybacked shotgun houses of the southern fields, empty now, occupants fled before giant machines that crawl monstrously on the land like battle tanks; the farmbelt fields washing down to become shoals in the Mississippi, farmsteads deserted, a handful of dust in the high plains; the outer city high-rises commingling with the cows, and in one place near my home a new office building with primrose colored windows that looks for all the world as if it were filled with pink cold cream.[17]

On the face of it, this recitation of outrage reads like the preface to a political argument for the elevation of esthetics above other ethics or criteria for good land-use policy. Little states bluntly, however, that "there can be no hierarchy among the three criteria of [ethical land-use decision making] ecology, equity, esthetics." [18] He explains that,

> In our unsuccessful efforts to codify the land ethic in policy—such as for development planning, the stewardship of resource lands, and the protection of critical environmental areas—we have proposed two criteria for establishing the terms of ethical land-use decision making: ecology and equity. In the case of the first of these, we can identify an unethical decision through ecological analysis, such as a decision to clear a forest in a way that would destabilize the ecological balance between plants and animals. In the case of the second, equity, we can identify an unethical decision through socio-economic analysis, such as inappropriately consolidating land for stripmining and consequently depriving individuals of their rights to ownership, safety, and economic use of land.[19]

To these criteria Little adds esthetics and gives it pride of place. He thinks it is a criterion many people can understand and use to evaluate land-use decisions. It has enormous political leverage.

The clarity of the linkage here between moral outrage and the practical politics of environmental policy reform is, I submit, remarkable. Caldwell thinks a massive moral conversion, based on an equally universal educational effort, needs to precede effective political action. Little is more of a populist, inclined to trust the ethical and esthetic sensibilities of the public. These sensibilities, he maintains, are not merely matters of individual taste, but are sufficiently collective to sustain public policy. He just wants ordinary people to act more often and more boldly in defense of the full range of their land values.

In vivid contrast to the stubbornly apolitical vision of resource economists, the central message of Caldwell and Little is that a strategy of mobilization, not cool economic analysis, is the key to success. And both assume that once policy is made to start rolling in the right direction, progress is ensured. In these theories of change, a clear, working, democratic majority will think alike and act in concert; the righteous and their superior land ethics will, therefore, not just rule the world but save it.

Perhaps there is something to be said for choosing one's ethics as cleanly as this. Perhaps it is wise first to choose and inculcate an ecological ethic and the land values that go with it, and then let equity, efficiency, and esthetics tag along behind as best they can. This is, essentially, Caldwell's course. Little chooses a strategy that emphasizes esthetics more than other values, but he wants all values represented. Either way, however, the initial choice is clean and, once it is made, there is no turning back. There are no doubts or ambiguities. No one in the vanguard of change ever flags or loses faith.[20] There is no opposition worthy of the name. No chaos. No counter-revolution. The future, if I may put it in the simplest possible terms, conquers the past by virtue of the ethical purity of its vision.

The Politics of Outrage and the History of Land Policy

These future-oriented conceptions of the politics of outrage present ethical choices about land use in starkly simple terms. But the ethics of efficiency, equity, and esthetics during the past hundred years did not lead to simple choices but to outrage at Americans' treatment of natural resources and the environment. More recently, ecological ethics have done the same.

Choices among ethics have been messy, not clean. Multiple ethics coexist uneasily in the minds of policy makers and in the policies they have chosen. A single ethic has never gained such an ascendancy over the others as to justify the conclusion that its competitors have been relegated to insignificance. Every ethic, therefore, has the capacity to generate outrage, to release political energy, to provoke institutional innovation and restructuring, and to prod policy change, though each is unlikely to be backed by equal skill and resources.

Although there is no sure way to predict what contingent factors will be associated with a future politics of outrage, history holds some fascinating clues. Rather than repeat here the entire analysis of environmental historians in recent years,[21] I will briefly describe only two crucial periods.

The Progressive Era. The first is the formative period in the Progressive Era, which by all accounts opened a new chapter in the history of the American environment.[22] Prior to 1900, the people of the United States and their governments went earnestly about the task of transforming the natural world. Two policies typified the many avenues by which government sought to release the energy driving this transformation.[23]

One was the policy favoring disposal of the public lands. Under this rubric the federal government gave away or sold at token prices much unused land to private owners, on the assumption that the creative energies of settlers and land grantees would put the land and its resources to immediate economic use. The other was the law of capture by which courts treated resources such as oil and gas as if they were migratory wild animals. The ownership of these resources, implying a right of unrestrained exploitation, went to the person who captured them and applied energy and capital to their use. In both cases law and policy rewarded people who took the initiative to make unclaimed nature economically valuable.

As Clayton Koppes carefully notes, no evaluation of the past should denigrate the real achievements of millions of American capitalists, large and small, who lived by these ethics. But by the late 1800s the costs of their undertaking had produced anxiety, tension, doubts, fears, and, I would add, outrage about "irreparable harm to the environment . . . and irreversible damage to the country's scenic splendor." [24] The conservation movement took its distinctive political form in response to these sentiments. As Koppes explains,

> Three ideas were dominant in Progressive Era conservation thinking—efficiency, equity, and esthetics. The efficiency school wanted to manage natural resources by applying modern engineering and managerial techniques, in contrast to the haphazard, short-run practices of the past. Advocates of equity wanted to [e]nsure that the benefits of natural resources development, such as federal irrigation projects, were widely distributed rather than concentrated in a few hands. Supporters of esthetics campaigned to preserve great scenic wonders free from ruinous development.[25]

The distinctive political form of conservation during this period did not arise, however, from the clean choices Progressives made among these ethics. In fact, an ability to see the merits of all three was common to most leaders of the movement. John Muir struggled for many years to accommodate the boundless indignation he felt at the esthetic and biological desecration of Yosemite to the more scientific, practical, and efficient thinking that underlay Gifford Pinchot's approach to managing the national forests. Both men reacted passionately to violations of the ethic each held most dear, but neither presumed that his opponent's ethics were without redeeming value.[26]

It should be no surprise to learn, therefore, that the enactment of Progressive conservation programs reflected compromises struck in the face of a residual ambiguity about ethics. The Forest Service, the Bureau of Reclamation, and the National Park Service are often portrayed as the institutional embodiments, respectively, of efficiency, equity, and esthetics. The mandate of each agency actually embodied contradictions implicit in Progressive conservation and Progressive conservationists. To cite just one classic case, Congress instructed the National Park Service both to preserve the parks unimpaired for the enjoyment of future generations and to see to it that they could be visited and enjoyed in the present.[27]

Progressive reforms were attempts to introduce efficiency, equity, and esthetics into the existing structure of American capitalism, to improve it and make it work better. Thus, the reforms of Progressive conservation were only a minor threat to established expectations, such as those enjoyed by private property owners. The really distinctive features of Progressive conservation programs were their halfway measures, their built-in ironies, and their pursuit of dreams that proved to be flawed in practice.

The Progressives could have taken radical steps (for example, state control of resources or even state production of hydroelectricity from impounded water, which was tried in the United States in some localities and in other capitalist societies).[28] These more radical measures would have required a much more intense political confrontation between advocates of efficiency, equity, and esthetics and, consequently, a more radical resolution of the dilemmas involved in choosing among these ethics. But this was difficult to accomplish as long as Progressive conservation tried politically to embrace all three. More far-reaching changes would have to wait until later, when the Great Depression "discredited the business-oriented policies of the 1920s and dealt advocates of bold governmental action a strong hand."[29]

Add to this the poor political organization of Progressive conservation, especially its equity and esthetic interests, and another useful clue about the politics of outrage in this period emerges. It is that the political means to capitalize on the magnificently eloquent and visionary outrage of a John Muir had yet to be created and refined. The first to organize effectively at the national level were those interested in the efficiency ethic.[30] Moreover, they had access to the president, exemplified in Gifford Pinchot's relationship to Theodore Roosevelt, that others found hard to match.

Progressive conservation had pretensions to be a mass movement in which all of its ethical concerns would be supported and sustained by scientific management, by an active and informed citizenry, and by a rich and vigorous base of interest groups. But these conditions were not fulfilled. It was for these reasons, as well as the internal contradictions among the ethics it contained, that Progressive conservation posed only a modest threat to the existing distribution of power.[31]

The Modern Environmental Movement. Keeping these clues to the conditions associated with Progressive conservation in mind, consider now the most recent outbreak of outrage in American environmental politics, which I am old enough to remember firsthand. This great environmental brouhaha occurred during the late 1960s. It had a literature, even a common parlance, in which fearful and angry words like *eco-catastrophe*, *eco-suicide*, and *terracide* appeared alongside calls for large-scale social, economic, and political transformation. In some quarters there were calls for legal and policy change that was revolutionary by previous American standards.[32]

Then, as now, ecological experts and environmental policy analysts believed man's treatment of the earth could only be described as shortsighted and counterproductive. The symptoms were national pollution problems and other assaults upon the quality of life perceived to be more than just uncomfortable or inconvenient. Issues of beauty, health, and permanence, as Samuel Hays so neatly labels them, pale in comparison to those now associated with global ecological concerns, but they seemed real and urgent at the time.[33]

Americans were deeply disturbed that waste and careless use of resources had sullied their postwar dream of peace and prosperity. Economic growth was not supposed to yield these outcomes. Development theorists, who were then very fashionable advocates of efficiency, predicted surpluses enough to permit a widespread distribution of the good things in life and to avoid what they were fond of calling disequilibria.[34] The latter was a euphemism for unemployment and various other temporary economic dislocations, including the failure of the market to capture, price, and eliminate the unrestrained use of the environment as a waste sink.

As the environmental side effects of growth visibly worsened, however, the dream of plenty became harder and harder for Americans to believe. The economic expectations of millions became tarnished. That was annoying, perhaps, but not outrageous. It was only when people began to assess the benefits of postwar expansion in relation to the costs that outrage surfaced. The range of human values actually sustained by economic growth was questioned. If growth was accompanied by irreversible and irretrievable resource losses, was the ecological snuff worth the economic candle? This was an ecological concern. Would resources run out before almost everyone got a fair share of the good things in life? This was an efficiency and equity concern. Would national parks and monuments in general and something as magnificent as the Grand Canyon in particular have to be sacrificed on the altar of growth? This was an esthetic concern.[35]

Fear and anger and outrage grew in large measure because they were cultivated by conservation groups with new leaders. David Brower, a leader of the Sierra Club who later founded Friends of the Earth, is the archetypal example, but there were many others. They built on the internal reforms in many national conservation groups before and after World War II. They took advantage of a rich infrastructure of state and local groups and refined the art of building national coalitions among them. They became amazingly adept at using powerful techniques of communication and mobilization, usually with few conventional resources. They substituted charisma, passion, fervor, eloquence, and commitment for money, staff, and analytical finesse.

Had these developments been enough to persuade many Americans to take political action in support of a broadening ethic of economic self-interest, the politics of outrage in the 1960s would have been amplified far beyond anything imaginable in the Progressive Era. Established expectations of property and existing distributions of power would have been that much more severely shaken, but probably would not have had their foundations questioned.

Beyond the sources of outrage just described, however, were more disturbing and more powerful concerns. To ecologists and environmental scientists, the heedless pursuit of material affluence by large and growing human populations around the world was insidiously undermining basic life-support systems on the planet. This apocalyptic vision took firm hold symbolically when pictures of the earth were sent back from space. The sight of home floating quite alone in a dark, starry void emphasized that people had nowhere else to go. It fed the perception that the plight of all at home was interconnected.

Ever-increasing levels of affluence for more and more people could destroy this home, and do so with alarming speed as technology progressed. In the end the development of the earth and its resources would not be materially satisfying, spiritually rewarding, or morally uplifting. Rather, in a shockingly ultimate sense, it would be morally corrupt, leading to the extinction of all human expectations.

This prospect was outrageous in ways that went quite beyond an ethics of self-interest triggered by tarnished economic dreams. And believing this prospect to be likely or at least conceivable on the basis of reasonable assumptions, many people were morally outraged by it.

In the late 1960s and early 1970s this outrage about the destruction of life on earth spread at lightning speed and on an unprecedented scale. The mass communications technology that brought the symbol of the outrage back from space also sent direct messages about its outrageous meaning to more people than ever before. Moreover, in this high-tech age the people were educated as never before to understand the implications of new ecological knowledge.[36]

One implication was that efficiency, equity, ecological, and esthetic concerns could be conceptually interrelated in new ways. This could have great political effect because the tendency since the Progressive Era and the New Deal had been to give each of these concerns separate organizational expression as a focus for public policy. The possibilities inherent in tying them together encouraged conservationists such as David Brower to link domestic pollution and quality of life issues with a larger and more systematic planetary agenda, and to imagine that an environmental movement would greatly enhance the political leverage of previously disparate constituencies for change.

These theoretical insights were the key to making ecology a politically subversive science.[37] They did not demand that ecological ethics be put above all others in policy making. They did, however, require policy makers to confront the ethical dilemmas of making choices in ways that gave ecology a new voice. Reconsidering the ethical bases for choice was bound to give efficiency, equity, and esthetics new meaning in public policy debates, and that is precisely what occurred.

The same education that taught people how to link their standard of living and their economic expectations to the state of the earth also taught them how to respond politically. They knew to step forward and act directly in support of an alternate mix of values because there was mounting criticism of the ability of interest group liberalism, or democratic pluralism, to implement an idealized but broadly shared conception of long-term public interest.[38] And people did step forward in very large numbers to participate directly, whether as individuals or through public interest groups, in pressing new values and new interests on policy makers.

The Legacy of Outrage

Thus, in the United States and initially to a lesser extent in other postindustrial nations, the immediate legacy of widespread outrage was the release of enormous political energy. This stimulated organization and mobilization around a wealth of environmental issues. Many of these were specific, local land-use issues linked only loosely to large and portentous principles of ecology at the level of political rhetoric and ideology. The remote chance that they would trigger an eco-catastrophe was far less important than the credibility given to radical proposals for change by framing the issues in these terms. The issues were, in turn, given legitimacy and influence by the spread of environmentalists' attitudes, copiously documented by public opinion polls and survey research.

In cities, counties, and states this politics of outrage sometimes played itself out more than thirty years ago without attracting national attention. Nevertheless, the result was a "quiet revolution in land use control." [39] Instead of asking, as in the past, whether the institution of private property could be reformed to serve the resource management purposes of public policy, people questioned the institution itself. The threat this posed to established local property expectations lasted well into the 1970s and 1980s, and it had political repercussions that are still felt today.

In other instances local and regional concerns escalated into national issues, with the result that Congress wrote public land policies of major new proportions into law. "In retrospect," wrote George Cameron Coggins and Charles Wilkinson,

> it is apparent that a time of unparalleled change and ferment in federal land and resources law began about 1964. . . . Congress suddenly commanded long-advocated planning, inventorying, and other modern management techniques. Wildlife protection achieved an unanticipated degree of priority in a few short years. The Bureau of Land Management finally received a statutory mission in the sweeping Federal Land Policy and Management Act of 1976. Thoroughgoing reform came to the Forest Service, the oldest federal land agency, in the National Forest Management Act of 1976. The Alaska National Interest Lands Conservation Act of 1980 allocated more than 100 million federal acres in Alaska to various conservation systems. Excluding Alaska, Congress conferred wilderness status on more than 20 million acres between the mid-1970s and the mid-1980s.[40]

A characteristic feature of much of this new federal legislation was a redistribution of power. Federal agencies were required to consider environmental interests and ecological principles in their decisions. Changes were made even though their full effects were unforeseeable at the time and could not be known for many years. They were a bold shot in the dark by policy makers.[41]

Overall, the modern environmental movement was remarkably successful at getting land and resource policies changed with little behind this feat except the theory and practice of the politics of outrage. It would be naive to conclude, however, that significant new balances in resource policy were bound to be struck in the 1980s merely because a carefully cultivated and orchestrated politics of outrage secured legislative changes in the 1960s and 1970s.

In the aftermath of such changes, Coggins and Wilkinson write, "it is likely, at least in the short term, that the new organic acts will engender considerable litigation, in turn creating bodies of common law, leading to corrective legislative action." [42] The meaning of the policy changes associated with outrage is determined, in other words, by a process of continuing political ferment, which begins again even as the ink on new laws is drying.

Indeed, to suppose otherwise is to imagine that the meaning of policy change can be fixed and usefully understood by looking back at the language in which a court or a legislature first expressed it, as the meaning of policy analysis might be understood by looking back at the original assumptions of the analysts. But it is a grave error to confuse the process of politics, where commitments to action and the ongoing clash of contending interests actually create the political meaning of policy, with the endless process of analysis, which often has only a tenuous link to action and thus may breed political detachment and disinterest.

The first lesson to learn from the legacy of outrage, then, is that its meaning is always open to interpretation and reinterpretation. The process is never-ending and anyone can take part. The key to shaping outcomes is to stay involved.

The second lesson is that the American political system is tailor-made not only to permit and facilitate such involvement but also to withstand repeated, vigorous confrontations between people with very different ethical views. The other key to shaping outcomes and building on a legacy of reform is to master the intricacies of this amazingly resilient system, and to learn how to use it in a myriad of creative and imaginative ways as skillful political entrepreneurs. Despite what is said in the conventional wisdom and in far too many textbooks, the political system is part of the solution, not part of the problem.[43]

New Ethics for a New Age? The Politics of Outrage in the 1990s

The reform potential of outrage is much greater now than was imaginable in the Progressive Era or even as recently as twenty years ago. State and national environmental groups are extremely sophisticated in their use of the mass media and public opinion. They have excellent legislative lobbying skills. Their use of the courts is unmatched in effectiveness in postwar American politics, with the possible exception of civil rights groups. They have boosted their ability to perform credible policy analyses. And they have retained high levels of public support and confidence for more than twenty years. Nevertheless, it would be arrogant and impractical for the American environmental movement to take on the global agenda single-handedly. Counterparts in other countries around the world are needed.[44] Although international cooperation among national environmental groups is increasing, it barely reaches the level of sustained professionalism that will be required.

On balance, the state of the environmental movement in the United States gives reason to expect vital and vigorous environmental politics in the 1990s, even assuming that the global issues will be relatively intractable compared with those already addressed. It will take, however, renewed moral outrage and renewed grass-roots support to revitalize the professional, corporate image that U.S. environmental groups have cultivated in recent years.[45]

The great success achieved by the politics of outrage has been achieved within a democratic political system and set of institutions. The tactics of public interest entrepreneurship in America will be difficult to transfer to other regimes—for example, to the Byzantine and often fragile political environments that surround many international agencies and to countries with little economic wealth.[46]

In the future, what will be the U.S. political context in which a politics of outrage might play itself out? The modern environmental movement took shape in the United States at a time of relative economic prosperity. If the world economy experiences sustained recession during the next decade, progress on the global agenda will be hindered. The plain truth is that gains from efficiency are needed to help pay for gains in addressing esthetic, equity, and ecological concerns. These values are interdependent and can be made mutually reinforcing.[47]

In the 1960s and 1970s the role of scientists in environmental policy debate was institutionalized, but only after they had taken a major part in the moral discourse criticizing the ethical balance in policy making and had acted in informal political contexts as leading citizens and educators of public opinion.[48] Scientists still need to play political and educational roles for the newer and less familiar global issues of the 1990s. If they do not, the credibility and legitimacy of a new politics of outrage will be substantially eroded.

Another significant factor in recent U.S. politics has been control of Congress by the Democratic party. Major policy changes have come from all three branches of government—from strictly congressional initiatives, from policy competition between Congress and a Republican president, and from prodding by the courts of both the other branches. The greatest gains have clearly come, however, when the Democratic party has simultaneously had control of Congress, the White House, and judicial appointments. Although the environment as a political issue has had strong bipartisan appeal, its equity and esthetic elements have made it, and keep it, a better issue for the Democrats than for the Republicans, who have always put efficiency and economic growth above these other values.

Political parties in the United States and other countries recognize a global agenda of environmental issues and are working on national and international policy proposals in response. In some foreign countries (in Eastern and Western Europe, for example), the growing grass-roots politics of the environment may feed into the party system through minor or separate Green parties, rather than through the major parties. This can happen for constitutional reasons or because the major parties are ideologically insensitive.[49] This weakens the process whereby parties with the potential to form legislative majorities develop and move forward with reform agendas, unless the demands of coalition building force the pace. In the United States, by contrast, the major parties are much more directly and immediately affected by grass-roots pressure, which quickly modifies the terms on which national majorities are sought in elections. The United States, notwithstanding all of its imperfections, is still the place where outrage about global issues is most likely to erupt and where the most promising political leadership able to exploit this outrage in pursuit of a global agenda is likely to emerge.

The influence of these background factors on the efflorescence of outrage, significant though it is, must be weighted by the power of ideas. As Brower and his contemporaries clearly demonstrated, fresh intellectual ferment about the causes and consequences of environmental problems is essential. The most important source of this ferment is the progress of science and the development of new information about global conditions and trends. New scientific appreciations of environmental conditions and trends must be evaluated, however, before their implications for action and public policy become clear. The intellectual ferment here is moral and ethical, rather than scientific, and is occurring on two fronts. The first concerns human beings; the second, all life.

Seen from the human perspective, the question of what social obligations are imposed by the destruction of, say, tropical forests probably will produce a different answer if it is asked of a Brazilian settler in the Amazon than if it is put to an American chairman of the board of a hamburger franchise. But both are likely to say that, since people are much more important than trees, their obligation—indeed their right—is to see that the trees and the land and the other resources of the forest are used efficiently and that each gets a fair share of the human value thus created.

Each is also likely to be outraged at the other's definition of efficiency and equity, and how to achieve them. And if either has a well-developed sensibility to the esthetic values of the forest, there will be further grounds for conflict between them. In the 1990s there will be lots of scope for ferment within an ethical tradition that seeks to maximize individual, inalienable human rights. Indeed, there may well be profound and possibly violent disagreements over whether, how, and when to limit individual freedoms in the use of imperiled resources.[50]

But no matter how these conflicts are resolved, the use of resources will continue at some adjusted rate until the use becomes obsolete, or a substitute is found, or the resource is all used up, or what is left is withdrawn from use and put in a preserve. Within the ethical community shared by the settler and the board chairman, any and all of those outcomes are conceivable and could be judged desirable. The whole earth suffers for the good of its human parts.

There is the further prospect of conflict stemming from more radical ethical premises. On this second front the ferment stems from the assertion that people have rights and duties with respect to all other living things, not just other persons. The social obligation here is to maximize biocentric well-being because people have a duty to respect nature for its own sake and to act accordingly, in large part but not entirely by leaving nature alone.[51]

From this wider perspective, the questions posed by the destruction of tropical forests do not lead to differences that can be resolved within an existing ethical community. They are questions that imply drastic reductions in resource consumption, perhaps in many cases complete cessation, in order that nonhuman species can be left free to pursue their own fate. They are the questions of people who think it right to accomplish these changes by replacing the existing ethical community with a new one. They are asked by people who, in Roderick Nash's words, see "the green world (nature, environment, land or earth) oppressed by the same exploitive, hierarchical values and institutions that once denied rights to slaves and continue to oppress many women, racial minorities, and laborers of all colors." [52] The issue here is liberation.

It is very difficult to appraise the extent to which earth ethics such as these will take hold among people in the United States and elsewhere in the world. Certainly, many people are likely to find such ethics in their pure form unattractive and unacceptable. Others will embrace them, however. More might be persuaded to do so if they see an alternative to traditional Western anthropocentric ethics, which allow domination of the earth by only one species and which, if they keep being relied upon to resolve the everyday dilemmas of policy making, will only make matters worse.

I think that over time those who are in pursuit of an environmental liberation ethic will find allies among those who come to politics primarily because their ethical sensibilities are outraged by shopping malls and toxic dumps. I think these people will begin to redress inequities in the distribution of wealth and power in the world and will find political leverage in mounting public outrage at the human costs of global resource inequalities and degradation.

Efficiency will be squeezed by this pincer movement, much as it was in the 1930s and again in the 1960s. It will be a hard squeeze because the stakes and the costs of inaction are both high. I doubt that it will be hard enough, however, to drive efficiency from the lexicon of policy-making ethics or to plunge resilient institutions into chaos. The forces of efficiency are too deeply embedded in our culture. However, new meanings will be sought and found for efficiency and all the other values.[53] As this process unfolds, I hope my son and the other young men and women of his generation will have figured out what acceptable meanings they can help to create, which they prefer, and how to get them written into the law of the land. If not, they will have to put up with the meanings other people create and live in a world marked by the consequences.

Notes

1. See World Resources Institute and International Institute for Environment and Development, *World Resources, 1988-89* (New York: Basic Books, 1988); Worldwatch Institute, *State of the World, 1989* (New York: Norton, 1989); Conservation Foundation, *State of the Environment: A View Toward the Nineties* (Washington, D.C.: Conservation Foundation, 1987); Neil Sampson and Dwight Hair, eds., in cooperation with the American Forestry Association, *Natural Resources for the Twenty-First Century* (Washington, D.C.: Island Press, 1989); World Commission on Environment and Development, *Our Common Future* (New York: Oxford University Press, 1987); and U.S. Council on Environmental Quality and Department of State, *The Global 2000 Report to the President: Entering the Twenty-First Century*, vol. 1 (New York: Penguin Books, 1982).
2. Christopher Stone, *Earth and Other Ethics: The Case for Moral Pluralism* (New York: Harper & Row, 1987). I give fair warning that this chapter is neither a commentary on ethics in general nor a detailed study of a limited set of problems in environmental ethics. I distinguish between ethics of efficiency, equity, ecology, and esthetics because, like recent historians, I find these distinctions useful and because all four of these elements in environmental ethics have been built explicitly into public policy since the end of the nineteenth century. See Clayton Koppes, "Efficiency/Equity/Esthetics: Towards a Reinterpretation of American Conservation," *Environmental Review* 11 (Summer 1987): 127-146. My focus is on the political leverage that comes when people perceive that one or more of these ethics has been violated, and they express outrage. For a comparable but narrower focus, see Edward Carmines and James Stimson, *Issue Evolution: Race and the Transformation of American Politics* (Princeton, N.J.: Princeton University Press, 1989). This book is of special interest because of the striking analogy between the civil rights and environmental movements in Roderick Nash, *The Rights of Nature* (Madison: University of Wisconsin Press, 1989).
3. For a general review of the ethical dilemmas of policy making, see Rosemarie

Tong, *Ethics in Policy Analysis* (Englewood Cliffs, N.J.: Prentice-Hall, 1986); Allen Buchanan, *Ethics, Efficiency, and the Market* (Totowa, N.J.: Rowman & Littlefield, 1988); and Alan Wolfe, *Whose Keeper? Social Science and Moral Obligation* (Berkeley: University of California Press, 1989). The ethics of intergenerational equity are of special relevance to my essay. See Edith Brown Weiss, "The Planetary Trust: Conservation and Intergenerational Equity," *Ecology Law Quarterly* 11 (1984): 495-581.

4. On Brower, see Bill Devall, "David Brower," *Environmental Review* 9 (Fall 1985): 238-253. On Muir, see Stephen Fox, *John Muir and His Legacy: The American Conservation Movement* (Boston: Little, Brown, 1981).
5. On the relationship between changing scientific analysis and changes in environmental policy with respect to moral discourse, see Arthur McEvoy, *The Fisherman's Problem: Ecology and Law in the History of California's Fisheries, 1850-1980* (Cambridge: Cambridge University Press, 1986).
6. Mark Sagoff, *The Economy of the Earth: Philosophy, Law and the Environment* (Cambridge: Cambridge University Press, 1988) contains the major papers of an ethical dialogue with the economic literature Sagoff has sustained since the early 1980s. For a penetrating portrait of the ethical underbelly of welfare economics, see Steven Kelman, *What Price Incentives? Economists and the Environment* (Boston: Auburn House, 1981). My favorite, recent, and delightfully down-to-earth treatment is Daniel Farber, "From Plastic Trees to Arrow's Theorem," *University of Illinois Law Review* 1986: 337-360.
7. I recall with this phrase the classic characterization of Brower as the archdruid of environmentalism in John McPhee, *Encounters with the Archdruid* (New York: Farrar, Straus & Giroux, 1971). As a reminder that not all economists are practicing members of the priesthood, it is still worth reading Ezra Mishan, *The Costs of Economic Growth* (Harmondsworth: Penguin Books, 1967).
8. Sagoff, *The Economy of the Earth*, chaps. 4 and 5.
9. Michael Reagan, *Regulation: The Politics of Policy* (Boston: Little, Brown, 1987), chaps. 5 and 6 is a useful general introduction. See also V. Kerry Smith, ed., *Environmental Policy Under Reagan's Executive Order: The Role of Benefit-Cost Analysis* (Chapel Hill: University of North Carolina Press, 1984).
10. This thesis was suggested by my reading of Carol Rose, "Crystals and Mud in Property Law," *Stanford Law Review* 40 (February 1988): 577-610.
11. To understand how the dark side manifests itself in relation to the private property interests in land and water resources, see Joseph Sax, "Liberating the Public Trust Doctrine from its Historical Shackles," *U.C. Davis Law Review* 14 (Winter 1980): 185-194. The economist's recognition of and response to the threat are described in Richard Epstein, "The Public Trust Doctrine," in *Public Choice and Constitutional Economics*, ed. James Gwartney and Richard Wagner (Greenwich, Conn.: JAI Press, 1988), 315-333.
12. See, for example, Daniel Mandelker, *Environment and Equity: A Regulatory Challenge* (New York: McGraw-Hill, 1981), and the much less conventional view in Sidney Plotkin, *Keep Out: The Struggle for Land Use Control* (Berkeley: University of California Press, 1987), chaps. 2 and 3. For a global

perspective see Piers Blaikie and Harold Brookfield, *Land Degradation and Society* (London: Methuen, 1987); and Anthony Chisholm and Robert Dumsday, eds., *Land Degradation: Problems and Policies* (Cambridge: Cambridge University Press, 1987).

13. Lynton K. Caldwell, "Land and the Law: Problems in Legal Philosophy," *University of Illinois Law Review* (1986): 320.
14. Elliot Feldman and Michael Goldberg, *Land Rites and Wrongs: The Management, Regulation and Use of Land in Canada and the United States* (Cambridge, Mass.: Lincoln Institute of Land Policy, 1987), 6.
15. Caldwell, "Land and the Law," 320.
16. Feldman and Goldberg, *Land Rites and Wrongs*, 281.
17. Charles Little, "Has the Land Ethic Failed in America? An Essay on the Legacy of Aldo Leopold," *University of Illinois Law Review* (1986): 315.
18. Ibid., 317.
19. Ibid.
20. The environmental attitudes and beliefs of those in the vanguard of change are the subject of Lester Milbrath, *Environmentalists: Vanguard for a New Society* (Albany: State University of New York Press, 1984).
21. For a superb introduction see Donald Worster, *The Ends of the Earth: Perspectives on Modern Environmental History* (Cambridge: Cambridge University Press, 1988).
22. The classic account is Samuel Hays, *Conservation and the Gospel of Efficiency: The Progressive Conservation Movement, 1890-1920* (Cambridge, Mass.: Harvard University Press, 1959).
23. The release of energy analogy was developed to explain economic change by James Willard Hurst, *Law and Economic Growth: The Legal History of the Lumber Industry in Wisconsin, 1836-1915* (Cambridge, Mass.: Harvard University Press, 1964). This chapter extends the use to political change.
24. Clayton Koppes, "Efficiency, Equity, Esthetics: Shifting Themes in American Conservation," in Worster, *The Ends of the Earth*, 233. This is a revision of Koppes's 1987 essay, "Efficiency/Equity/Esthetics: Towards a Reinterpretation of American Conservation."
25. Ibid., 233-234.
26. On the relationship between Muir and Pinchot, and the outrage of each, see Fox, *John Muir and His Legacy*, chap. 4; and Roderick Nash, *Wilderness and the American Mind*, 3d. ed. (New Haven, Conn.: Yale University Press, 1982), chaps. 8 and 10. A paperback edition of Fox's book is published as *The American Conservation Movement: John Muir and His Legacy* (Madison: University of Wisconsin Press, 1985).
27. Ronald Foresta, *America's National Parks and Their Keepers* (Washington, D.C.: Resources for the Future, 1984), chap. 2.
28. Koppes, "Efficiency, Equity, Esthetics: Shifting Themes," 236.
29. Ibid., 239.
30. Hays, *Conservation and the Gospel of Efficiency*, chaps. 7 to 9.
31. Grant McConnell, "Prologue: Environment and the Quality of Political Life," in *Congress and the Environment*, ed. Richard Cooley and Geoffrey Wandesforde-Smith (Seattle: University of Washington Press, 1970), 3-15.
32. The literature and radicalism of the period can be recalled from Charles O.

Jones, "From Gold to Garbage: A Bibliographic Essay on Politics and the Environment," *American Political Science Review* 66 (June 1972): 588-595; and William Ophuls, *Ecology and the Politics of Scarcity: Prologue to a Political Theory of the Steady State* (San Francisco: Freeman, 1977).

33. Samuel Hays, *Beauty, Health, and Permanence: Environmental Politics in the United States, 1955-1985* (Cambridge: Cambridge University Press, 1987).
34. Charles Kindelberger and Bruce Herrick, *Economic Development*, 3d. ed. (New York: McGraw-Hill, 1977); and Gerald Meier, *Leading Issues in Economic Development*, 5th. ed. (Oxford: Oxford University Press, 1989).
35. All three concerns are clearly articulated in Henry Jarrett, ed., *Environmental Quality in a Growing Economy* (Baltimore: Johns Hopkins University Press, 1966). The significance of the fight to save the Grand Canyon from inundation is best explained in Nash, *Wilderness and the American Mind*, chap. 12.
36. Milbrath, *Environmentalists;* Andrew McFarland, *Public Interest Lobbies* (Washington, D.C.: American Enterprise Institute, 1976); and Ronald Inglehart, *The Silent Revolution: Changing Values and Political Styles Among Western Publics* (Princeton, N.J.: Princeton University Press, 1977).
37. Donald Worster, *Nature's Economy: A History of Ecological Ideas* (Cambridge: Cambridge University Press, 1985), dates the subversion from the nineteenth century. See also Paul Shepard and Daniel McKinley, eds., *The Subversive Science: Essays Toward an Ecology of Man* (Boston: Houghton Mifflin, 1969); and Anna Bramwell, *Ecology in the Twentieth Century: A History* (New Haven, Conn.: Yale University Press, 1989).
38. McFarland, *Public Interest Lobbies*, 4-43; and Jeffrey Berry, *The Interest Group Society*, 2d ed. (Boston: Scott, Foresman, 1989), chap. 1.
39. Fred Bosselman and David Callies, *The Quiet Revolution in Land Use Control* (Washington, D.C.: U.S. Government Printing Office, 1972).
40. George Cameron Coggins and Charles Wilkinson, *Federal Public Land and Resources Law*, 2d ed. (Mineola, N.Y.: Foundation Press, 1987), 8-9.
41. Paul Culhane, *Public Lands Politics: Interest Group Influence on the Forest Service and the Bureau of Land Management* (Baltimore: Johns Hopkins University Press, 1981); and Jeanne Nienaber Clarke and Daniel McCool, *Staking Out the Terrain: Power Differentials Among Natural Resource Management Agencies* (Albany: State University of New York Press, 1985).
42. Coggins and Wilkinson, *Federal Public Land and Resources Law*, 9-10.
43. See, for example, Daniel Chiras, *Environmental Science: A Framework for Decision Making*, 2d ed. (Menlo Park, Calif.: Benjamin/Cummings, 1988), chaps. 21 and 22; and G. Tyler Miller, *Living in the Environment: An Introduction to Environmental Science*, 5th ed. (Belmont, Calif.: Wadsworth, 1988), chaps. 25 and 26.
44. See Lisa Fernandez, "Private Conservation Groups on the Rise in Latin America and the Caribbean," *Conservation Foundation Letter*, no. 1 (Washington, D.C.: Conservation Foundation, 1989); and Lynton Caldwell, *International Environmental Policy: Emergence and Dimensions* (Durham, N.C.: Duke University Press, 1984).
45. Geoffrey Wandesforde-Smith, "Learning from Experience, Planning for the

Future: Beyond the Parable (and Paradox?) of Environmentalists as Pin-Striped Pantheists," *Ecology Law Quarterly* 13 (1986): 715-758.

46. For superb case studies of these difficulties, see R. Michael M'Gonigle, "The 'Economizing' of Ecology: Why Big, Rare Whales Still Die," *Ecology Law Quarterly* 9 (1980): 119-237; and David Kay and Harold Jacobson, eds., *Environmental Protection: The International Dimension* (Totowa, N.J.: Allenheld, Osmun, 1983).
47. Sagoff, *The Economy of the Earth*, chap. 9.
48. See the portraits of Aldo Leopold, Rachel Carson, and Barry Commoner in Douglas Strong, *Dreamers and Defenders: American Conservationists* (Lincoln: University of Nebraska Press, 1988). The role of science and scientists is a main concern of Thomas Dunlap, *Saving America's Wildlife* (Princeton, N.J.: Princeton University Press, 1988).
49. Charlene Spretnak and Fritjof Capra, *Green Politics*, rev. ed. (Santa Fe, N.M.: Bear and Co., 1986); and Raymond Dominick, "The Roots of the Green Movement in the United States and West Germany," *Environmental Review* 12 (Fall 1988): 1-30.
50. Kristin Shrader-Frechette, "Environmental Ethics and Global Imperatives," in *The Global Possible: Resources, Development, and the New Century*, ed. Robert Repetto (New Haven, Conn.: Yale University Press, 1986), 97-127.
51. Paul Taylor, *Respect for Nature: A Theory of Environmental Ethics* (Princeton, N.J.: Princeton University Press, 1986).
52. Nash, *The Rights of Nature*, 212.
53. This search leads to a new economics of balance and a new politics of participation in R. Michael M'Gonigle, "The Tribune and the Tribe: Toward a Natural Law of the Market/Legal State," *Ecology Law Quarterly* 13 (1986): 233-310. More conventional approaches to forging new meanings emerge from the unconventional focus of Richard Gaskins, *Environmental Accidents: Personal Injury and Public Responsibility* (Philadelphia: Temple University Press, 1989).

16

Environmental Values and Democracy: The Challenge of the Next Century

Robert C. Paehlke

Earth Day—April 22, 1970—was a more seminal political event than was realized at the time. Gradually, though sometimes haltingly, environmental issues have become first-order political concerns. Indeed, by the late 1980s environmental protection was viewed by many as being as important to our collective well-being as national security, economic prosperity, social justice, and even democracy itself. Some would go even further and argue that if and when trade-offs between first-order values must be made, protecting the environment should be "first among equals," a transcendent priority.

This chapter will consider some of the broader implications of the political ascendancy of environmental protection. It will emphasize the new relationship between environmental protection and the other first-order values: social justice (equity), economic prosperity, national security, and democracy. It will argue that while this ascendancy is welcome, it is probably dangerous to grant any important value a transcendent status. In fact, many of our present-day environmental problems have resulted as outgrowths of the status accorded to either economic prosperity or national security, or both. In contrast, one basic flaw of Marxist theory has been the overriding status given to the long-term pursuit of socioeconomic equity.

Perhaps the most fundamental conclusion in this chapter is that in examining the relationships between environmental protection and each of the four other values, democracy is the guiding value, both as an end and as a means. Environmental protection, in particular, will be most effectively achieved through the maintenance of, indeed the continuing enhancement of, democratic practice.

This assertion flies in the face of the claims and concerns of many environmental and political analysts. Environmentalists frequently asserted in the 1970s that increased scarcity, rooted in resource shortages and ecological limits, would inevitably plague humankind.[1] This scarcity, the result of ecological limits, was viewed by William Ophuls and Robert Heilbroner, for example, as carrying a lamentable threat to political democracy.[2] Some analysts argued that democracy limits society's ability to contend with scarcity and, in effect, redistribute economic decline. Ted Robert Gurr concluded that "bureaucratic-authoritarian states should be better able than democracies to tolerate the stresses of future ecological crises."[3]

However, in noting the failings of democratic societies in the face of scarcity, and as pessimistic as he was about the future prospects of democracy, Gurr's analysis also provides an important basis for hope regarding the future. "The greater the relative increases in scarcity," he observed, "and the more rapid its onset, the greater are its negative political consequences."[4] Therefore, some of these negative political effects could be deflected by early political responses to scarcity. Gurr's view was based, in part, on his pessimism about the ineffectiveness of early responses to environmental problems and resource limitations. The ascendancy of environmental concern in recent years bodes well for the future.

Needless to say, all aspects of environmental politics in North America in the 1980s do not inspire optimism. There were few new environmental policy initiatives during the Reagan years. However, there arose a new momentum for environmental protection, both in terms of public attitudes and in terms of organizational strength. In addition, important flaws in the more pessimistic analyses of the relationship between environmental realities and democratic theory became evident; these will be elaborated on in the conclusion. But before assessing these issues, I first consider the complex relationships among first-order political values. The importance of environmental protection in the politics of the 1990s can be understood best in terms of the ways in which it intersects with the forces of social justice, economic prosperity, national security, and political democracy. First, I will briefly set out the character and place of environmental values themselves.

Environmental Values and Political Decision Making

Historians as well as philosophers have observed that the contemporary environmental movement is based on a transformation of human social values. Historian Samuel Hays noted that new values, rooted in postwar advances in prosperity and educational levels, have emerged in virtually all industrial societies.[5] Others have claimed that recent value shifts run deeper than those which sustained the conservation movement. Philosopher George Sessions has concluded that the ecological "revolution" is fundamentally religious and philosophical and involves "a radical critique of the basic assumptions of modern western society." [6]

Using opinion survey instruments, Ronald Inglehart and other social scientists have measured related shifts in popular attitudes, postulating a "silent revolution" that entails the spread of "post-materialist" values.[7] Riley Dunlap, Lester Milbrath, and others have identified a "new environmental paradigm." [8] Whatever name one attaches to the change, the environmental movement is the political manifestation of a significant shift in societal values.

But what values comprise the essential core of an environmental perspective? In an earlier work, I set out a list of thirteen values; others have developed similar lists.[9] Such lists can be distilled to four core items: (1) a minimization of the negative impacts of human economic activities on ecosystems and habitat, (2) the establishment of sustainable patterns of resource use, (3) the minimization of negative impacts on human health, and (4) the maximization of ecological diversity. However, values at this level of generality are not adequate guides to policy making.

Environmental objectives must compete with other values, but they also conflict with each other. For example, high-yield, yet sustainable forests may lack the diversity that would otherwise provide habitats for many animal species. Similarly, even the act of protecting human health, and thereby ensuring that human population will rise, virtually guarantees the diminution of nonhuman habitat. Such dilemmas do not absolve us of the task of sorting out difficult value questions; indeed, the authoritative allocation of values is the primary function of politics. Political analysts and political practitioners alike should be cautious about leaving such questions unanswered in their rush to pursue narrow, technical solutions.

What, then, are the political implications of core environmental values? Environmental values can be seen as new issues, recently thrust onto the political stage—a stage already and forever too full. The internal contradictions noted above are thus likely to be modest compared to the inevitable clashes between environmental objectives and other first-order political values. However, these clashes, together with possibilities for mutuality, compromise, and coalition-building, portend the future of environmental politics and policy. As will be shown, there are substantial opportunities for advancing several, if not all, of these important values concurrently.

Each of the other first-order political values has an attendant political constituency: investors, corporations, and trade unions promote economic growth; defense industries and the military make the case for national security; the poor, urban politicians, organized minorities, trade unions, churches, and others advance the cause of social justice and equity. Environmental politics, however, is a politics of a different sort in that it is less dominated by material self-interest.

This is not to say that economic growth, national security, or social justice do not have principled adherents. Many who work hard to advance these values have little or nothing to gain materially from variations in outcome. Nor is it to say that those who promote environmental causes do not have economic stakes in environmental protection. For example, Alaskan fishermen clearly have a stake in avoiding another oil spill, such as the one from the *Exxon Valdez*. In addition, many who are involved in environmental siting decisions are there to defend the value of their property. These convergences of values notwithstanding, many environmental advocates oppose pollution because they value health over wealth and understand that environmental objectives often imply significant personal economic costs.

This distinctive political character of environmentalism has several important effects. First, an environmental advocate in one setting may become an environmental opponent under different circumstances (for example, fishermen may promote overfishing). Second, regardless of economic status, all human beings must eat, breathe, and drink. For these reasons and others, it is more difficult for policy makers to reject claims to environmental protection than to reject, for example, claims to social justice. Having a less-focused constituency, however, can have political costs. Indeed, most political scientists would argue that without an economically interested attentive public, fewer political and organizational resources are available.

This diffusion of interest in environmentalism is not without important political advantages. Because environmentalists elect to be advocates on behalf of future generations and other species, not just themselves, they frequently occupy the political high ground. Many proponents of environmental values have undergone a fundamental revision in worldview; thus, they may well pursue their goals both on and off the job. Finally, environmental objectives may be scientifically understood and defended in a way that few other sociopolitical issues can be. In future political disputes involving clashes with those who place a relatively higher priority on social justice, national security, or economic prosperity, it is far from certain that environmental advocates will lose.

It is on this point, among others, that I argue against pessimism regarding the prospects for early and effective environmental protection. First-order values and environmental protection are not mutually exclusive, nor necessarily in conflict. Democracy is threatened principally by political inaction in the short term, which might well lead to insurmountable problems in the longer term. The prospects for effective environmental politics in the 1990s become clear on closer examination of the relationships between core environmental values and each of the other first-order values.

Environmental Protection and Social Justice

As environmental politics has come to comprise a widening portion of the political agenda, there has been some unease that environmental objectives are sometimes achieved at the expense of socioeconomic equity. In the past, environmentalism was seen as predominantly a white, middle-class concern. In this view, money spent on pollution abatement was money *not* spent on inner-city schools; further, environmental protection cost jobs, especially blue-collar jobs. Environmentalists were seen by some as placing unreasonable importance on wilderness—the seemingly legendary places many cannot afford to visit.

What is surprising, then, is how small the differences are in the acceptance of environmental values by class, race, or any other demographic measure.[10] In addition, in terms of economic and social realities (rather than perceptions), the advancement of environmental objectives might improve the everyday lives of ordinary people more than many would expect. This is important not only for its own sake, but also for the health of democracy as well. Gurr and other critics ground their fears for democracy by positing that in scarcity situations, "economically advantaged groups are better able to use market forces and political influence to maintain their positions," and therefore social inequalities will increase.[11] This, in turn, implies fundamental risks for democracy. For example, political and economic power are further concentrated and crime and anomic behavior may well increase. However, this concern says little about the actual relationship between social justice objectives and environmental protection.

Environmental objectives intersect with social justice or equity objectives most significantly in three ways: (1) employment opportunities; (2) consumer opportunities as conditioned, for example, by inflation; and (3) relative health impacts. It is likely, although it has not been demonstrated, that those who are not economically advantaged would rank the importance of the three in this order. Overall, health objectives are very important politically, but they can be seen as something of a luxury in some circumstances.

Employment opportunities are affected by environmental decisions in at least three ways. First, environmental protection expenditures affect international competitiveness at the level of the manufacturer and the nation. Second, specific environmental protection decisions can directly create jobs or result in job losses. For example, not cutting a given stand of virgin timber may cost an export contract; conversely, new abatement regulations may create jobs in the installation and operation of pollution abatement devices. Third, while quantitative employment effects are important, so too are the character, quality, and location of employment gains and losses.

Surprisingly, there is no single comprehensive study of the employment impacts of environmental protection, though much is known on this subject. This issue may be the most politically significant of all the possible conflicts between environmental objectives and other values, since the loss of jobs to protect environmental quality is frequently raised by industry. Ironically, the opposite may be true. The overall net effect of enhanced environmental protection may result in more, rather than fewer, employment opportunities. It has been asserted that the threat of environmental job losses due to environmental protection is more bluff and blackmail than reality.[12] Moreover, since European and Japanese environmental standards are comparable to North American standards, recent declines in North American competitiveness cannot be blamed simply on the cost of environmental protection. Environmental Protection Agency regulations, for example, have created more direct jobs than they have cost.[13] Pollution abatement is employment intensive, and job losses generally are the result of a combination of factors.

Many types of environmental protection initiatives reduce unemployment. For example, recycling generates large numbers of jobs, whereas the extraction of concentrated virgin (nonrecycled) materials is not labor intensive in comparison. So-called bottle bills, which require that containers be refilled, have a net job-creating outcome. Jobs lost in bottling plants are gained in retail stores, trucking companies, warehouses, and bottle-washing facilities. Energy conservation usually requires more jobs than would have been created in energy production had the conservation effort not been undertaken.[14] This is especially true when energy supplies are imported, but still applies when they are not. Enhanced public transportation use, which results in less pollution than private auto use, also generates net employment.[15]

Another dimension of this debate involves the broader question of total economic mix. Nonmanufacturing employment, particularly in services such as health care or education, is labor intensive and involves only minimal environmental impact. When these sectors expand as a proportion of an economy, both unemployment and environmental damage decline.

Environmental protection fares less well when the quality and location of employment opportunities are considered. Replacing employment on energy megaprojects with jobs in energy conservation or recycling is a case in point. High-paying, highly skilled, often unionized jobs may be replaced with lower-skilled, lower-paying jobs, albeit more of them. But while this effect is in one sense the opposite of what Gurr feared, only present jobs are defended politically. Organized labor will only protect existing jobs; jobs that do not yet exist rarely have organized defenders. Thus, environmentalists are sometimes pitted against organized labor, while those who might gain employment from environmental initiatives are frequently left out of the debate.

However, even these generalizations distort the complexity of socioeconomic and political realities. Public transportation jobs are frequently unionized and high paying. The manufacture and installation of pollution abatement equipment requires highly skilled workers. Employment in teaching and health care is not without appeal. But these are probably exceptions. From the perspective of the poor, it is precisely the low-skill, urban-centered jobs that environmental protection can generate that are needed.

Will the cost of environmental protection induce inflation and thereby partially offset these potential social equity gains? One very important dimension of the effects of inflation on the poor has to do with energy prices. Many environmentalists believe that energy prices should continue to rise in the 1990s.[16] However, this begs an important question regarding the less-advantaged segments of society. The percentage of income that one spends on energy is inversely proportional to total income.[17] Any increase in energy costs finds the poor losing ground in purchasing power. Thus, an environmentally oriented energy policy that is neutral in domestic equity terms requires an offset, such as energy efficiency subsidies for the less advantaged.

Many forms of environmental protection are costly, especially when they involve enhanced employment opportunities. But fuller employment, even if achieved directly through reduced work time at constant hourly wages, would carry savings to partially offset costs. There would be reduced costs for unemployment insurance and welfare, a broadened income tax base, and, possibly, reduced costs for police protection and health care. Overall, an environmentally based full-employment policy would provide continuing support for both social justice and political democracy. Both political participation and sociopolitical efficacy are to some extent rooted in employment opportunity.

Some means of achieving environmental protection might help to restrain inflation. These would include: (1) a greater dependence on energy from renewable sources, (2) the downsizing of governmental and corporate vehicle fleets, (3) an emphasis on hazardous-waste reduction over hazardous-waste cleanup, (4) a reduction of packaging on consumer products, and (5) the substitution of communication for transportation, such as in the energy efficient use of conference calls rather than meetings, or fax rather than courier service. While pollution abatement may be inflationary, there is no certainty that it could not be achieved within bounds that could be offset or controlled. In contrast, there is no denying that an economy that depends solely on nonrenewable, environmentally problematic energy sources is virtually assured of inflationary surges at some time in the future. Thus, regarding both employment and inflation, it is too easy to see environmental protection as being in competition with the economic needs of the less advantaged. The realities are far more complex.

Finally, are environmental health impacts evenly felt by rich and poor? Everyone eats, breathes, and drinks, but, for example, many infants now consume "organic" baby food—at double to triple the cost of ordinary brands. Hazardous-waste sites are disproportionately found in poor and/or black neighborhoods. Neither incinerators nor landfills often find their way into the best urban neighborhoods. Air-quality distribution varies within urban locations, sometimes to the disadvantage of the less well-off. Health risk also varies considerably by occupation. There is some evidence that shows that the lowest-paying occupations do not carry the highest risks; nor, for that matter, do the highest-paying (professional, sales, and managerial) jobs. All and all, the better-off segments are probably at least marginally advantaged in terms of current environmental impacts. If this generalization is accurate, then the poor would gain more if there were an across-the-board environmental cleanup; they would lose more in health terms if there were not.

There are indications that environmental advocacy is no longer the exclusive preserve of the white middle class. There are now organizations that have an active interest in the environmental concerns of the urban and rural poor.[18] There have been several recent environmental issues that have mobilized the poor and helped to build small bridges across racial barriers. Nonetheless, at the organizational and membership levels, the environmental movement as a whole remains predominantly white.

While environmental protection policies *can* be implemented at the expense of the poor, they can also be achieved either neutrally or to the advantage of the less well-off. The distributional effects of environmental protection probably depend in large part on *which* socioeconomic groups are mobilized politically in defense of the environment. More importantly, whether adequate protection is achieved also depends on political mobilization and the forms it takes in the future. The 1980s saw ground lost on the environmental front, or at least a slowed rate of gain. They also saw an overall decline in political involvement, especially among the less advantaged sectors of society. Apathy and cynicism carry with them real risks for the quality of democracy. Hence an environmental politics of expanding scope will not exclude the concerns of the less advantaged. Environmental politics at the close of the 1980s entailed much political activism, but there are clear limits to the political capabilities of an environmental movement that does not activate citizens from all segments of society. If there are stringent times ahead, democracy itself must be enhanced and strengthened. The measure of democracy lies in both the political participation and the socioeconomic opportunities of less-advantaged groups.

Successful politics in the United States has always been majoritarian politics—a politics that avoids the exclusion of organized segments of society. Thus, while a successful environmental movement will likely lean to the moderate left of center, it likely cannot lean much further to the left. It will of necessity articulate an imaginative politics that does not continuously affront significant entrenched economic interests. The review here suggests that environmental policies can be designed that have appropriately moderate effects in distributional terms. A politically moderate environmentalism for the 1990s might also stress the role of entrepreneurship and the use of effective market-based policy instruments.

Environmental Realities and Economic Growth

Gurr, Ophuls, and Heilbroner all envisioned a linkage between environmental damage and economic scarcity, and between economic scarcity and declining democratic prospects. Ophuls and Heilbroner each carefully reviewed a wide range of sustainability issues and concluded with a lament for democracy. They considered energy availability, agricultural capabilities, resource availability, pollution, population growth, and other environmental impacts. "Once relative abundance and wealth of opportunity are no longer available to mitigate the harsh political dynamics of scarcity," Ophuls wrote, "the pressures favoring greater inequality, oppression, and conflict will build up so that the return of scarcity portends the revival of age-old political evils, for our descendants if not for ourselves. In short, the golden age of individualism, liberty and democracy is all but over." [19] Heilbroner went further in imagining what would follow: "a social order that will blend a 'religious' orientation and a 'military' discipline." [20]

But to what extent does economic growth—or at least the present level of prosperity—depend on the availability of resources? There are many possible alternative futures. *Our Common Future* (the Brundtland commission report to the United Nations) concludes that economic growth must and can continue.[21] Admittedly, some environmentalists see this as perhaps too optimistic, but in 1966 economist Kenneth Boulding drew a distinction that is critical here. He contrasted economic output with what he called energy and material throughputs.[22] Economic activity can, in fact, increase while the total amount of energy and materials used declines. Both environmental damage and resource shortfalls are a function of energy and materials use, not of economic activity per se.

Needless to say, an economy with relatively limitless energy and materials would likely grow faster than one without. However, the crucial point is that there is decidedly not a one-to-one relationship between resource use and economic activity. Most materials in an economy can be used and reused: Metals, paper, glass, plastic, chemicals, and agricultural wastes are technically recyclable. Moreover, many high-technology products require little additional material and energy, such as the microchip, fiber optics, biotechnologies, hand-held calculators, and portable compact disc players (fabulous sound reproduction, minimal materials and energy). Consider as well, as we did previously in relation to employment opportunities, the growing role of human services, including education, the arts, and entertainment, within all modern economies. In fact, energy and materials use per unit of Gross National Product (GNP) have been in almost continuous gradual decline for a century or more. The oil price hikes of the 1970s perhaps slowed economic growth, but also induced a further increase in the efficiency of energy and materials use in relation to total economic activity.

Why is this important? It means that it may be possible that a widespread sense of extreme stringency can be avoided, even if energy and materials use must be curtailed. The changes involved will be neither automatic nor easy. But while our economies will change radically over the coming century, they will not necessarily shrink in terms of the total value of goods and services. This is particularly true if governments and corporations deliberately accelerate the necessary changes. Perhaps the most critical step in the process of change lies within the realm of individual consumption habits and preferences. We cannot assume that these habits are fixed and immutable. On the contrary, market-based change is generally more rapid than political change. In light of recent events, there is also a real possibility that the large share of GNP now devoted to military procurement can soon be scaled down, freeing existing economic capacity for other uses.

Environmental Protection, National Security, and World Peace

Our Common Future has placed the linkage between environmental protection and world peace front and center. This report is descended from the *World Conservation Strategy* (1980), and as well from Olaf Palme's *Common Security: A Blueprint for Survival* (1982) and Willy Brandt's *World Armament and World Hunger* (1985).[23] These latter two documents have had a wide impact, particularly in Western Europe. Palme's report emphasized a conception of security that went beyond Cold War thinking; Brandt's articulated the relationship between global poverty and global arms expenditures.

The Brundtland report added environmental considerations to this complex mix. For a document drafted within international diplomatic circles, *Our Common Future* is surprisingly candid. Regarding peace and security it argues:

> The deepening and widening environmental crisis presents a threat to national security—and even survival—that may be greater than well-

> armed ill-disposed neighbors and unfriendly alliances. . . . The arms race—in all parts of the world—preempts resources that might be used more productively to diminish the security threats created by environmental conflict and the resentments that are fueled by widespread poverty.[24]

Both environmental damage and arms expenditures are seen as important threats to global and national security, with arms expenditures actually undermining security in terms of opportunity costs. The changes underway in the Soviet Union and Eastern Europe thereby have direct implications for environmental protection; any opportunity to reduce military spending is an opportunity for international cooperation on global environmental protection.

The global future is necessarily a common future. Multilateral cooperation, as in the reconstruction after World War II, is again necessary. "The challenge of finding sustainable development paths," the authors write, "ought to provide the impetus—indeed the imperative—for a renewed search for multilateral solutions and a restructured international system of co-operation."[25] This new cooperation could begin with an altered approach to the international debt crisis. Many indebted nations presently overuse fragile soils and clear their forests to sell enough commodities to service their debts. The commission views this reality as shortsighted—economically, politically, and environmentally. *Our Common Future* thus emphasizes the three-way linkage between peace concerns, development, and environmental damage. "Environmental stress," it states, "is both a cause and an effect of political tension and military conflict. Nations have often fought to assert or resist control over raw materials, energy supplies . . . and other key environmental resources. Such conflicts are likely to increase as these resources become scarcer and competition for them increases."[26]

Thus, just as future scarcity was seen to be a potential threat to democracy, it is also seen as a fundamental threat to world peace. Just as the scarcity threat to democracy could be realized in an increase in domestic inequality, the threat to peace could be realized in a further growth in international inequities. But there are at least three grounds for hope in both cases. First, as previously noted, future scarcity is a possibility, but by no means a certainty. Second, it is possible that both domestic and international inequities can be reduced now to avoid future risks to both democracy and peace. Third (and this is why *Our Common Future* is so important), there is a potential source of funds to help alleviate both inequity and environmental risks. The report clearly favors global cooperation to redirect a significant proportion of global military expenditures to those purposes.

Real security thus requires a transfer of funds from military expenditure to sustainable development. Global military expenditures are equivalent to $1,000 per year for each of the world's poorest 1 billion humans—an amount far beyond their present income. Simply returning military spending to the proportion of global GNP it represented just prior to 1960 would provide an income of $225 annually for each of those persons. Effectively investing this latter amount ($225 billion annually) in sustainable agriculture, reforestation, wetlands restoration, habitat protection, and renewable energy could dramatically transform prospects in Asia, Africa, and Latin America. Alternatively, this expenditure could eliminate North-South global debt in a few years. Or, less grandly, a 0.1 percent tax on global military expenditures could provide family planning globally; a 0.3 percent tax could achieve global literacy; a 0.6 percent tax would fully fund current proposals to alleviate global desertification and deforestation. What is missing are the political and institutional mechanisms to introduce and manage such shifts.

These ideas are hardly new. President Eisenhower, in a speech late in his career, said that "every gun that is made, every warship launched, every rocket fired represents, in the final analysis, a theft from those who hunger and who are not fed, who are cold and are not clothed." [27] The 1980s saw such assertions assume an environmental dimension. In 1980 Amory Lovins used the phrase "the demilitarization of the security concept." [28] This notion was shortly thereafter developed with considerable effect by Lester R. Brown, who argued that the "extensive deterioration of natural support systems and the declining economic conditions evident in much of the Third World pose threats to national and international security that now rival the traditional military ones." [29]

One of the ecologically rooted security threats that Brown noted was transborder migration resulting from desertification and/or crop failure. Areas in northern Africa have been politically destabilized in this manner. In addition, many economies in the developing world were badly shaken by the oil price shocks of the 1970s. Global insecurity is further increased by the magnitude of international debt. Economic instability induces military expenditures by entrenched elites. In Brown's view, this instability threatens both international security and democracy. He pointed out that "the austerity and associated economic shrinkage that [were] agreed to in exchange for rescheduled loans are worsening economic and social conditions." He believes that the "belt-tightening may eventually lead to political unrest," and thereby jeopardize the future of democracy in some societies.[30]

Environmental Protection and Democratic Theory

Another view regarding democracy is possible here. While democracy may (or may not) be vulnerable to greater scarcity within poorer economies, it may be the most effective means of handling such limitations within wealthier societies. John Passmore, writing around the same time as Ophuls and Heilbroner, noted that "the view that ecological problems are more likely to be solved in an authoritarian than in a liberal democratic society rests on the implausible assumption that the authoritarian state would be ruled by ecologist-kings. In practice there is more hope of action in democratic societies." [31]

This perspective is valid for at least three reasons: (1) authoritarian rulers are unlikely to be sensitive to or informed about ecological matters; (2) authoritarian regimes are not necessarily good at inducing positive behavior, especially in the long term; and (3) democracy provides a good climate for social and economic mobilization and even, if necessary, for developing an acceptance of shared hardship. The changes in the Soviet Union and Eastern Europe in the late 1980s lend some contemporary support to these conclusions. Pollution is widespread in those regions and it is increasingly clear that neither environmental protection nor economic growth were maximized in the old authoritarian regimes.

There is also something amiss in Passmore's observation in terms of the contemporary situation. Not all who fear for democracy in a world of scarcity and ecological destruction envision benign (or not so benign) ecologist-kings. Authoritarianism, or quasi-authoritarianism, could be imposed with precisely the opposite intentions. Such regimes might face environmentally undesirable economic activities on unwilling localities. They might distort or suppress scientific findings, or protect the economic or ecological well-being of one locality at the expense of another. Such regimes might well not even intend to solve ecological problems—a frightening vision, but indeed a vision made more plausible the longer global change is delayed.

There are at least five reasons to be more optimistic than were Gurr, Ophuls, and Heilbroner. First, the environmental movement has consistently helped to strengthen democratic practice in important ways. Second, as previously discussed, enhanced domestic economic equity is in many ways compatible with environmental protection, where population levels have not yet outstripped ecological underpinnings. Third, at higher levels of economic development "sustainable" becomes as important as "development"; a reasonable balance between the two may be more easily attained politically. Fourth, as discussed earlier, "postindustrial" forms of economic activity are probably less damaging to the environment than are basic industrial forms. Fifth, greater technological sophistication results in improved environmental monitoring and in "decoupling" economic activity and environmental damage by means of "technical fixes." I will conclude with a further elaboration of the first two items in this list.

Conclusion

Most North American environmental legislation in the 1970s and 1980s contained a significant mechanism for public participation. These institutional innovations have strengthened democracy and helped it adapt to new issues. More than that, environmental organizations have consistently worked to open administrative processes and industrial society itself to expanded public scrutiny.[32] Such scrutiny is the essence of democratic practice. In the early days of environmentalism (the 1960s), openness was seen as a means of avoiding the administrative "capture" to which earlier conservation bureaucracies were prone.[33] More recent legislative initiatives, including workplace and community right-to-know legislation, have gone beyond this and can be taken much further.

Rather than merely opening up governmental decision making, these newer initiatives have taken matters that were once private and opened them to public observation. The movement, use, and storage of hazardous materials are now subject to both democratic and market decision-making processes. For example, Title III of the Superfund Amendments and Reauthorization Act of 1986 requires that industrial toxic emissions be made a matter of public record. Workplace right-to-know legislation in some Canadian provinces mandates that industrial workers be informed about the exposures they encounter. Many Canadian industrial workers have also attained administrative protection of their right to refuse unsafe work. Community right-to-know laws in many U.S. jurisdictions have provided information regarding the use, storage, and transport of hazardous substances.[34] Firemen and other emergency workers, residents, and environmentalists alike have learned from this. The state of California has gone the furthest in requiring notification regarding all carcinogens, be they gasoline additives or supermarket product ingredients. Most such right-to-know measures can help mobilize public opinion and activate people both as consumers and as democratic citizens.

Environmental decision making, as Bartlett observed in Chapter 11, has often involved comprehensiveness as a goal. This, too, has important implications for democratic institutions. Comprehensiveness is by definition integrating, and can undermine the ordinary bureaucratic division of labor. In so doing it shifts decision making out of specialized agencies and into central agencies, the courts, and/or the democratic process itself. Virtually every agency at every level of government has had to integrate environmental issues into its decision-making processes. Even the Defense Department is currently undergoing administrative re-organization related to environmental matters. Should there not now be a cabinet-level presence for environmental protection?

It may well be the case that in the 1990s environmental decisions will increasingly test the mobilizing capacities of democratic systems. It would appear that several of the newer environmental issues will require solutions that are less "regulatory" in character. The new forms of change will require both organizational and behavioral changes, rather than the regulatory coercion of a few economic actors. For example, both recycling and the wider use of public transportation involve behavioral changes. Behavioral changes involving whole communities are less effectively monitored and enforced than promoted and encouraged. The regulatory mode is inappropriate in altering individual consumer and workplace behavior (as opposed to workplace equipment). These new changes require a citizen majority willing to accept and/or participate in such changes. Democracies and democratically managed markets in combination can mobilize educated citizens. So, too can authoritarian-bureaucratic systems under some circumstances. But the recent experience of the Soviet Union would suggest that there are limits to the mobilizational capacities of such systems at advanced levels of economic development. Those who are pessimistic about democracy on ecological grounds have not seen this, nor have they understood that educated populations simply will not be mobilized by regimes they have not chosen as we have seen in Eastern Europe.

Just as industry willingness and cooperation is necessary for effective regulatory compliance, citizen willingness is necessary for nonregulatory compliance. But neither will advance very far in the 1990s without balanced progress. Citizens will not change their behavior unless they perceive that industry is doing what it can. Educated citizens will not participate effectively in collective efforts unless they have been party to decisions regarding priorities. Industry will feel less singled out only if it is not alone in bearing costs. Thus, an effective pluralist democratic system is the best source of balanced, participatory initiatives. Active involvement by individual citizens and private organizations requires a sense of mutual effort. Political science research shows that a sense of political efficacy is necessary. It is here that democracy, at its most effective, may prove absolutely essential to the achievement of environmental protection. Cynicism and indifference will undermine any collective ability to protect environmental life support systems.

Thus, one cannot be content with present levels of democratic participation. Democracy itself must be enhanced to effectively deal with environmental problems as they exist today and as they may exist in the future. One means of doing this is to expand the environmental powers and roles of municipal and regional governments. A second is to introduce an environmental role within all governmental subdivisions, at all levels. The environmental mandate should not necessarily be concentrated within a single agency. Agencies not traditionally involved with environmental matters, including procurement offices, could be ordering ceramic dishes and organic food for the cafeteria, reducing chemical spray programs in parks, downsizing the fleet of vehicles, and ordering recycled paper. Other divisions should be taking other appropriate initiatives. All should have citizen-based environmental advisory committees. Third, environmentalists, as well as others, must realize that a political democracy will not likely run very far ahead of a nation's commitment to economic equity and social justice. Gurr saw a threat to democracy from the potential equity effects of environmental scarcity. While Gurr is accurate in his assessment of the relationship between equity and democracy, this dangerous outcome can be avoided.

In an effective democracy the economic security of the less advantaged cannot be perceived as the price for environmental protection. Environmental activists must be more sensitive to the widespread fear of job loss and displacement. Citizens active in environmental politics must be sensitive to the difference between locally unwanted facilities that are environmentally necessary and carefully and those that are not. The fate of environmental protection and the quality of democracy will be very much intertwined in the 1990s.

In the 1990s global society will move nearer to the end of the oil era. This era has been environmentally destructive in many ways, from urban air quality and oil tanker spills to suburban sprawl into quality farmland. There is reason to think that some of the replacements for oil will be no less environmentally problematic, however. Transitions of this order of magnitude require the mobilizing capabilities of genuinely effective democratic institutions. In the 1990s governments must learn to prevent environmental problems rather than react to environmental crises. Leadership, in both the public and private sectors, is clearly necessary.

There is no longer much doubt that human activities pose multiple threats to the habitat of most other species on the planet. Doubts remain whether future human numbers are sustainable at present or higher amenity levels in the long term. (See Tobin's discussion in Chapter 13.) This is not, however, the same thing as saying that the human species is in grave and immediate danger. The greater threat to human survival is nuclear weapons. Environmental dangers have reached such complexity and magnitude that they now intersect with questions of social justice, world peace, and global economic development. The simultaneous handling of all requires both intelligence and enhanced democratic institutions.

One great hope coming out of the 1980s is that nations are moving rapidly toward greater democracy. In these realms there are more wisps of hope than anything like certain knowledge. But the changes within the Soviet Union and Eastern Europe, for example, are also changes not unmindful of global environmental problems.[35] It may be the case that only changed relations between the superpowers will permit simultaneous progress on global environmental and economic development needs. Such an effort will require near universal international cooperation on a scale humans have only rarely achieved previously. It will also require enormous economic and financial resources. It is now possible to at least imagine that such cooperation might be possible and how such resources may some day become available.

Notes

1. See the work of Thomas R. Malthus, W. Stanley Jeavons, and others discussed in Robert C. Paehlke, *Environmentalism and the Future of Progressive Politics* (New Haven, Conn.: Yale University Press, 1989), chap. 3. See also Donella H. Meadows, et al, *The Limits to Growth* (New York: Universe Books, 1972); and William R. Catton, Jr., *Overshoot: The Ecological Basis of Revolutionary Change* (Urbana: University of Illinois Press, 1980).
2. See in particular William Ophuls, *Ecology and the Politics of Scarcity* (San Francisco: W. H. Freeman, 1977); Robert L. Heilbroner, *An Inquiry into the Human Prospect* (New York: Norton, 1974); and Ted Robert Gurr, "On the Political Consequences of Scarcity and Economic Decline," *International Studies Quarterly* 29 (1985): 51-75.
3. Gurr, "On the Political Consequences of Scarcity," 70.
4. Ibid., 54.
5. Samuel P. Hays, "From Conservation to Environment: Environmental Politics in the United States Since World War Two," *Environmental Review* 6 (Fall 1982): 20.
6. George Sessions, "The Deep Ecology Movement: A Review," *Environmental Review* 11 (Summer 1987): 107.
7. Ronald Inglehart, *The Silent Revolution: Changing Values and Political Styles Among Western Publics* (Princeton, N.J.: Princeton University Press, 1977).
8. Riley E. Dunlap and K. Van Liere, "The New Environmental Paradigm," *The Journal of Environmental Education* 9, no. 4 (1978): 10-19; and Lester W. Milbrath, *Environmentalists: Vanguard for a New Society* (Albany: SUNY Press, 1984).
9. See Paehlke, *Environmentalism and the Future of Progressive Politics*, chap. 6.
10. Milbrath, *Environmentalists*, 74-78.
11. Gurr, "On the Political Consequences of Scarcity," 58.
12. Richard Kazis and Richard L. Grossman, *Fear at Work* (New York: Pilgrim Press, 1982).
13. Several relevant studies are cited in Frederick H. Buttel, Charles C. Geisler, and Irving W. Wiswall, eds., *Labor and the Environment* (Westport, Conn.: Greenwood Press, 1984). See, in particular, their annotations 016, 017, 040, 050, 064, 105, and 159.
14. Regarding recycling and refillable containers and employment, see William U. Chandler, *Materials Recycling: The Virtue of Necessity* (Washington, D.C.: Worldwatch Institute, 1984); and Charles M. Gudger and Jack C.

Bailes, *The Economic Impact of Oregon's Bottle Bill* (Corvallis: Oregon State University Press, 1974). Regarding energy conservation and employment see, for example, sources annotated in Buttel, Geisler, and Wiswall, eds., *Labor and the Environment*.

15. Bruce Hannon and F. Puleo, *Transferring from Urban Cars to Buses: The Energy and Employment Impacts* (Urbana: University of Illinois, Center for Advanced Computation, 1974).
16. Christopher Flavin, Denis Hayes, and Jim MacKenzie, *The Oil Rollercoster* (Washington, D.C.: Fund for Renewable Energy and the Environment, 1987).
17. See Lester Thurow, *The Zero-Sum Society* (New York: Basic Books, 1977), 7.
18. See, for example, Louis Blumberg and Robert Gottlieb, "The New Environmentalists: Saying No to Mass Burn," *Environmental Action* 20 (January/February 1989): 28-30.
19. Ophuls, *Ecology and the Politics of Scarcity*, 145.
20. Heilbroner, *An Inquiry into the Human Prospect*, 161.
21. World Commission on Environment and Development, *Our Common Future* (New York: Oxford University Press, 1987).
22. See Kenneth Boulding, "The Economics of the Coming Spaceship Earth," in *Economics, Ecology, Ethics*, ed. Herman E. Daly (San Francisco: W. H. Freeman, 1980), 253-263.
23. International Union for Conservation of Nature and Natural Resources (IUCN), *World Conservation Strategy* (Gland, Switzerland: IUCN, 1980). Independent Commission on Disarmament and Security Issues (Olaf Palme, chairman), *Common Security: A Blueprint for Survival* (New York: Simon and Schuster, 1982); and Willy Brandt, *World Armament and World Hunger* (London: Victor Gollancz Ltd., 1986).
24. World Commission on Environment and Development, *Our Common Future*, 6-7.
25. Ibid., x.
26. Ibid., 290.
27. Quoted in ibid., 297.
28. Amory B. Lovins and L. Hunter Lovins, *Energy/War: Breaking the Nuclear Link* (New York: Harper and Row, 1980), 153.
29. Lester R. Brown, "Redefining National Security," *State of the World 1986*, ed. Lester R. Brown (New York: Norton, 1986), 204.
30. Ibid., 206.
31. John Passmore, *Man's Responsibility for Nature* (London: Duckworth, 1974), 183.
32. For a broad consideration of environmentalism and administration, including the issue of openness, see Robert Paehlke and Douglas Torgerson, eds., *Managing Leviathan: Environmental Politics and the Administrative State* (Peterborough, Ontario: Broadview Press, 1990).
33. See, for example, Grant McConnell, "The Conservation Movement—Past and Present," *Western Political Quarterly* 7 (1954): 470-471.
34. The broad issue of participation and the right to know is discussed in Susan G. Hadden, *A Citizen's Right to Know: Risk Communication and Public Policy* (Boulder, Colo.: Westview Press, 1989).

35. See, for example, Zia Nuriev, *Renewal of Land Resources* (Moscow: Novosti Press Agency Publishing House, 1985); Igor Petryanov-Sokolov, *Nature Knows No Borders* (Moscow: Novosti Press Agency Publishing House, 1987); and Nikita Moisseyev, *Man, Nature, and the Future of Civilization* (Moscow: Novosti Press Agency Publishing House, 1987). Recently, a willingness to link environmental and peace issues has found a place in speeches by more noted Soviet leaders, including Mikhail Gorbachev's December 1988 speech to the United Nations.

17

Conclusion: Toward a New Environmental Agenda

Norman J. Vig and Michael E. Kraft

> The global environment cannot be separated from political, economic, and moral issues. Environmental concerns must permeate all decisions, from consumer choices through national budgets to international agreements. We must learn to accept the fact that environmental considerations are part of the unified management of our planet. This is our ethical challenge. This is our practical challenge—a challenge we all must take.
>
> Gro Harlem Brundtland
> Former prime minister, Norway

When the 44th General Assembly of the United Nations convened in New York on September 19, 1989, environmental issues were at the top of its agenda. Petitions signed by more than three million people from sixty countries were presented calling upon the United Nations to declare an international emergency caused by the destruction of the world's rain forests. The same day, at a scientific conference held at the Smithsonian Institution in Washington, experts warned of threats to the earth's ecosystems and called for drastic preventive actions. Only a week earlier, the *New Yorker* had carried a long excerpt from a new book entitled, *The End of Nature.*[1] Yet these dire warnings seemed to evoke little response from official Washington. In Congress, the first skirmishes were being fought over amendments to the Clean Air Act, but few expected final legislation before the 1990 session. Meanwhile, President Bush was traveling in the West, urging people to plant trees as a solution to air pollution problems.

One may have a right to be skeptical, perhaps even outraged, as Geoffrey Wandesforde-Smith suggests in Chapter 15, by the failure of political leaders and governments to address the global ecological crisis more seriously. Yet, as much of this volume indicates, there are reasons for greater optimism in the 1990s. Both in the United States and abroad, in countries from Australia to Brazil and the Soviet Union, public awareness of environmental problems has reached a new plateau. What Lester Brown refers to as a new "perceptual threshold" has been attained, and is beginning to affect the way people everywhere think about their place in the biosphere.[2]

Indeed, the first worldwide public opinion survey on the environment, conducted by Louis Harris and Associates for the United Nations Environment Programme and released in May 1989, provided striking evidence that people in developing countries as well as industrial nations are concerned that environmental quality is deteriorating and requires urgent attention. "Very large majorities—between 75 and 100 percent of both the public and the leaders in all 14 countries [covered by the survey]—agreed on the need for stronger action by their governments, stronger action by international organizations such as the United Nations, and stronger laws to contain industrial pollution."[3]

This new global awareness reflects the end of the postwar era in which world attention was focused primarily on two issues: the military rivalry between East and West and the quest for higher rates of economic growth. While these issues have scarcely disappeared, by the mid-1980s they had begun to recede in priority as Western economies stabilized and fundamental changes began in the Soviet Union and Eastern Europe. A series of summit meetings, arms-control agreements, and political reforms dramatically reduced tensions between the United States and the Soviet Union, while the European Community launched a drive for full economic union in 1992. Meanwhile, what Lynton Caldwell in Chapter 14 terms "new geophysical imperatives" began to emerge—pressures from mounting strains on the earth's atmosphere and living systems caused by human disruptions. The cumulative weight of scientific evidence on such matters as ozone depletion, acid rain, climate change, deforestation, and species extinction began to impose itself on world agendas, spurring calls for new forms of human restraint and international cooperation. As suggested in Chapter 1, various long- and short-term political currents appear to be converging again toward environmental activism in this decade.

What will the new agenda look like? This chapter pulls together some of the themes of this book as they bear on the future of environmental policy. In the first section, we discuss the need to rethink the nature of the policy problems themselves, and to broaden and deepen our *concept* of the environmental agenda. Second, we ask what new policy *goals and approaches* may be needed in the 1990s. How should environmental regulation be reformed, and what other alternatives are there for achieving environmental goals? Third, we ask what new *institutional capacities* may be needed in government to carry out these changes. Do we have the structures and resources needed to implement better policies? Fourth, we discuss the opportunities for new kinds of *political action* on behalf of the environment. What can we do? And finally, we ask how are we to *govern* our planetary future?

Broadening and Deepening the Agenda

Sheer quantitative expansion is the most obvious change in the environmental agenda. As environmental research progresses and monitoring techniques improve, we become aware of more threats to human health and ecological systems. This is particularly evident in the area of chemical contamination. The air and water pollution legislation of the early 1970s singled out only a handful of the most apparent industrial byproducts for statutory controls. Most toxic and hazardous wastes and pollutants, including chemical carcinogens, were left to later policies that provided for regulation through cumbersome, case-by-case procedures. As a result, only a few organic chemicals and heavy metals, such as PCBs, lead, and mercury, actually have been regulated under these statutes. Yet in the 1980s evidence of chemical contamination has shown up everywhere, in the form of thousands of toxic-waste dumps, spreading groundwater pollution, uncontrolled toxic air emissions, and acidified lakes and forests. These second generation problems were soon superseded by still a third order of dangers affecting the entire atmosphere and biosphere of the earth. New scientific evidence, much of it gathered by sensory aircraft and satellites, on the extent of the ozone hole over Antarctica, the rate at which rain forests are being burned in the Amazon, and the buildup of carbon dioxide and other greenhouse gases in the atmosphere, has created a truly global environmental agenda.

This globalization amounts to a qualitative as well as quantitative change in perceptions. For the first time it is widely recognized that we are as dependent on other peoples' use of resources as they are on ours. Some of the most severe environmental challenges are perceived to lie in the developing Third World and polluted communist world, though much of the technical and financial assistance to head off future catastrophes in these areas must come from the wealthy nations of the first world. These nations, including the United States, account for a disproportionate share of the world's pollution and resource depletion to date. In the late 1980s the United States, with less than 5 percent of the world's population, emitted about 15 percent of its sulfur dioxide, 25 percent of all nitrogen oxides, and 25 percent of the carbon dioxide, and manufactured about 30 percent of all chlorofluorocarbons (CFCs).[4] As India, China, and other countries have argued in the case of CFCs, the United States cannot expect the rest of the world to refrain from ecologically destructive behavior if it cannot discipline itself.

The third element in rethinking the environmental agenda involves deepening our understanding of its linkages to virtually every other issue, as Gro Harlem Brundtland has suggested. We must recognize, for example, that economic growth and development can no longer be contemplated without ecological safeguards. The concept of sustainable development holds that economic growth and environmental preservation are complementary rather than antagonistic endeavors; that is, we can no longer achieve one without the other.[5] We must think of eliminating poverty and stabilizing population growth by raising living standards as the best policy for preventing destruction of the remaining forests and wildlife habitats of the Third World (see Chapter 13). And Prime Minister Margaret Thatcher has called for reducing greenhouse gas emissions, stating that "even though this kind of action may cost a lot, I believe it to be money well and necessarily spent because the health of the economy and the health of the environment are totally dependent upon each other."[6]

Fourth, our concept of national security must be revised to include ecological stability and human improvement. Population growth that exceeds the carrying capacity of the land, contamination of drinking water supplies and irrigation systems, or drought, famine, and flooding caused by rapid climate change can hardly avoid setting off large-scale social disruption and political instability in the future that will threaten the peace of more fortunate nations. Our international alliances, trading patterns, and sources of critical raw materials could all be in jeopardy in a world of increasingly scarce resources.[7] Even our own social cohesion and national spirit will rest on finding solutions to these problems. We must thus begin the task of converting resources devoted purely to military ends to purposes that will stabilize the world in other ways.

An immediate conclusion to be drawn is that our *research and development (R&D) agenda must be rapidly expanded to address the new environmental problematique*. One of the most anomalous results of environmental policies in the 1980s is that the research budget of the Environmental Protection Agency (EPA) was cut by about 20 percent (in constant dollars) at a time when evidence of environmental degradation was pouring in from all quarters (see Appendix 4). While all federal *nondefense* R&D was declining by 24 percent from 1980 to 1988, *defense* R&D increased by 83 percent (in constant dollars).[8]

EPA's FY 1989 research budget of $389 million was only about one percent of the Department of Defense's R&D budget ($41.6 billion)—indeed, it was less than the cost of a single Stealth bomber or MX missile. We estimate *total* federal government support for environmentally related R&D at no more than $2 billion.[9] Thus, even doubling our current federal environmental research effort would still leave ten times more funding for military R&D—arguably a gross imbalance in light of changing East-West relations and emerging ecological imperatives. One proposal, put forward by Sen. Al Gore, D-Tenn., calls for the United States to launch a "Strategic Environment Initiative" comparable to the military Strategic Defense Initiative (SDI).[10] Such a program could invigorate and draw together previously unconnected research programs and stimulate development across a broad range of new technologies necessary for sustainable growth.

The Bush administration has recognized the need for greater research efforts in some areas. For example, for FY 1990 it requested a 43 percent increase (from $134 million to $191 million) in funding for a coordinated research program on global warming and ozone depletion.[11] But a great deal more research will also be needed to assess risks, set priorities, and find solutions to such pervasive problems as hazardous-waste disposal, urban air pollution, and groundwater contamination. Little improvement in the effectiveness of public policy is likely without much more applied R&D of this kind.

New Goals and Approaches

Modest progress has been made in cleaning up the air and many rivers and lakes under the environmental legislation of the 1970s. These laws set firm deadlines for pollution reduction and required EPA to issue detailed technical guidelines or standards for each type of pollution source. Regulations were to be legally enforceable in the federal courts, with substantial fines and penalities for noncompliance. It was hoped that the federal government could thereby force all polluting industries to adopt state-of-the-art pollution control technology and, indeed, that new generations of control technology would be "forced" by stricter regulations on all new factories, power plants, and vehicles.

This concept of standards and enforcement, or "command and control" regulation, was perhaps necessary to establish the legal responsibility of industry, municipalities, and other generators of pollution for the damage they were imposing on society. The process of developing technical standards, negotiating permits, and litigating specific requirements in the courts has also been a protracted learning experience for all parties involved. Yet what seems rational in principle has often turned out to be irrational in practice because of particularities in individual situations or perversities in the incentives created by legal rules. For example, it has often been cheaper to go to court to avoid compliance than to purchase and install expensive equipment, or simply to keep old, polluting plants in operation rather than build new, more efficient ones for which standards are higher. As A. Myrick Freeman argues in Chapter 7, many aspects of our current regulatory regime are economically irrational and counterproductive. More effective pollution control could be achieved at considerably less cost if clear economic incentives to reduce pollution were built into our regulatory system.

Another lesson of experience is that too much of our regulatory effort has been put into controlling pollution after it occurs (usually by removing it at the "end of the pipe") rather than into preventing its generation in the first place. The idea that pollution problems can be "fixed" without changing basic industrial processes or technologies (such as the internal combustion engine) was prevalent when most environmental legislation was written. It is now recognized that pollution control must be moved "upstream" to the design and operation of technology itself; that is, *pollution prevention* or reduction and elimination at the source must guide future environmental policy. In fact, an Office of Pollution Prevention was established within EPA in late 1988, which officials in the Bush administration assert has top priority. However, EPA also relies heavily on the development of a private waste disposal industry to handle growing volumes of waste for profit, suggesting a possible conflict of interest.[12]

On the other hand, the recognition that economic market forces can be powerful agents for reducing pollution has gradually gained acceptance in this country and abroad.[13] Most obvious, perhaps, is the impact that fuel prices have had on energy conservation. Energy consumption per capita and per unit of output fell dramatically in the late 1970s and early 1980s as oil prices peaked; the reduced demand in turn contributed to collapsing oil prices and rising fuel consumption in the late 1980s.[14] The same principle can apply to the control of chemical and other pollutants. For example, the skyrocketing cost of hazardous-waste disposal and the rapid exhaustion of landfill space are forcing many industries to cut toxic-waste generation and stimulating the development of solid-waste recycling programs throughout the country. By the late 1980s there was a growing consensus that price signals must be employed to stimulate behavioral changes that are necessary for pollution abatement across a broad range of human activities.

But market incentive systems must be carefully designed to achieve their purpose and to consider other values. For example, the principle that "the polluter must pay" means that most of the environmental costs of production will ultimately be passed on to the consumer, often in ways that hurt low-income people the most. Basic considerations of social justice demand that those who already possess a disproportionate share of resources bear the heaviest burdens in cleaning up the environment. As Freeman notes in Chapter 7, market theory allows for compensation to offset distributional inequities resulting from internalizing costs. Yet we have not made much progress in developing concrete proposals for addressing equity issues in the context of environmental regulation.

Greater reliance on economic incentives also does not mean that the fate of environmental resources will simply be turned over to consumptive market demand. In contrast to the pure market principle that private ownership is always the best defense against wasteful exploitation of scarce resources, the new consensus holds that society (that is, government) must set the basic *goals* for environmental protection, but then allow greater use of market forces to determine the most efficient *means* of achieving these goals. Put another way, economic incentives can "leverage" government regulation by working with, rather than against, market forces.[15] This may include granting certain "pollution property rights" that can be traded among firms to achieve the least costly combination of controls. Such a system would provide an ongoing incentive to reduce pollution further as emission rights become increasingly scarce and expensive. President Bush's plan for revising the Clean Air Act is the first serious attempt to embody these principles in legislation.

Reliance on market incentives of this kind will not be feasible, however, in many areas of environmental protection. It cannot be applied, for example, in situations presenting imminent health hazards from highly toxic chemicals, or in protection of unique amenities such as wilderness forests and endangered species. We are doubtful that marketization and privatization of many public resources can be accepted on moral grounds, since it cannot be demonstrated that individuals living in the present are the best judges of how their decisions affect ecosystem stability or the welfare of future generations. No individual or market has the ability or the right to discount the ecological future.

Nevertheless, there are many opportunities to make current environmental policies more flexible and efficient. One way is to concentrate available regulatory resources on the most pressing problems, that is, to set priorities. Cost-benefit analysis can help to focus efforts in areas that produce the largest payoffs in environmental improvement for the least expenditure of money. But it is also necessary to develop criteria for defining the most serious problems. Congress has attempted to do this through legislation, often in response to public fears and concerns. It is also rational, however, to determine specific regulatory priorities based on scientific evidence. Hence, EPA has increasingly relied on risk assessment methods; indeed, it has come to define its mission as being one of "risk reduction" rather than elimination of pollution. However, as its own internal analysis has shown, public and legislative assessments of risk, and consequently its own operating priorities, differ substantially from those determined by scientific experts.[16] As Richard Andrews argues in Chapter 8, this presents a profound social dilemma, especially since the quantitative risk assessment procedures advocated by experts incorporate their own political biases. Regulatory practice in the 1990s must find ways to balance scientific analysis of health risks against popular risk perceptions and preferences, and to improve qualitative risk evaluation of threats to other species and ecological systems for which there is no common metric.

Another problem is the separate statutory basis for protecting each pollution medium—air, water, and land—and EPA's lack of any congressional charter to engage in comprehensive environmental regulation (see Appendix 1). For years now, the Conservation Foundation has argued that this segmented approach ignores "cross-media pollution"—that is, the circulation of pollutants from one medium to the others—with the result that controlling one form of pollution often merely shifts pollutants to another. The Foundation (which EPA administrator William Reilly formerly headed) thus proposed consolidating most of the separate laws into a single new environmental statute giving EPA much greater flexibility to act under a common risk standard.[17] Although efforts to develop a truly comprehensive environmental policy of this kind may be doomed to failure, as Robert Bartlett suggests in Chapter 11, a strong case can be made for better coordination of policies both within EPA and across agencies (see discussion below).

No federal agency can take responsibility for solving all environmental problems. An important change that occurred in the 1980s is a greater delegation of authority to the states, often resulting in initiatives going well beyond federal controls (see Chapter 3). For example, California's new air pollution standards are considerably more stringent than federal requirements, and other states are leading the way in recycling and other programs.[18] In the absence of federal standards, state and local governments may increasingly adopt controls over such things as plastic packaging, toxic materials handling, and toxic air emissions. The "community right-to-know" provisions written into the Superfund Amendments and Reauthorization Act of 1986 now provide local citizens with more information on such hazards.[19] Indeed, community watchdog organizations and consumer or citizen education campaigns are often more effective than government regulators in pressuring companies and developers to clean up their act. If that fails, citizens may sue polluters to force compliance under the "private attorney general" provisions of several statutes, as explained by Lettie Wenner in Chapter 9.

Not all pollution control need be coercive, however. Nonadversarial mechanisms, such as local citizen dialogue, informal bargaining, and voluntary mediation, have become increasingly important as alternative forms of environmental dispute resolution. Such methods may be useful, for example, in avoiding polarized "NIMBY" disputes over hazardous-waste facilities siting (see Chapter 6). When there is basic agreement on goals, mutually acceptable means to achieve them (including financial compensation) can often be devised. However, as Douglas Amy warns in Chapter 10, such forums can exclude or compromise important environmental considerations if care is not taken to include all stakeholders and values.

A newer approach that is likely to become more important in the 1990s involves corporate ethics campaigns to convince companies to alter their practices. In the wake of the *Exxon Valdez* oil spill, a coalition of environmental groups, religious organizations, and pension fund managers controlling more than $100 billion in corporate assets drafted a ten-point code of environmental conduct called the "Valdez Principles" that companies will be asked to endorse.[20] The principles include commitments to protection of the biosphere, sustainable use of resources, reduction and recycling of wastes, and reduced use of energy, and require full disclosure of health and safety hazards to workers and the public and appointment of an environmentalist to the company's board of directors. Future proxy resolutions and other shareholder actions are likely to put increasing pressure on companies to adopt such principles. An advantage of this approach is that it can affect the policies of multinational corporations in other parts of the world, as in the case of the earlier "Sullivan Principles" regulating corporate conduct in South Africa.

Another method for exerting economic leverage on companies is through consumer education campaigns and product boycotts. In Britain, a new "green guide" for shoppers has recently been published to encourage purchase of environmentally benign products. "Green shopping" is likely to become more popular in the 1990s, particularly if entrepreneurs and advertisers see it as a lucrative marketing strategy (as healthful foods and life styles are now extensively advertised). Special investment funds are also being created to attract environmentally conscious investors to "green" companies. On the other side, companies that have especially poor environmental records or that actively oppose environmental preservation may find growing resistance to their products from the public.

Many other new methods will of course be needed to address global environmental problems. Traditionally, nations have only reluctantly made treaties and agreements that restrict their use of domestic or international "common property" resources. However, since 1960 some 200 multilateral agreements on resource conservation and environmental protection have been signed. Especially since the Stockholm Conference of 1972, the United Nations has actively promoted the signing of environmental conventions and protocols to establish common goals and ongoing negotiating structures to promote international environmental cooperation.[21] Among the most notable of such frameworks are the Convention on International Trade in Endangered Species of Wild Fauna and Flora (CITES), which was signed in 1973 and has recently been extended to further protect elephants, the Vienna Convention to Protect the Ozone Layer (1985), and the subsequent Montreal Protocol (1987), which called for a 50 percent reduction in CFC production by the end of the century. At a further conference held in London in March 1989, many nations agreed to accelerate this schedule, while another important agreement limiting international transfer of hazardous wastes was reached in Basel, Switzerland, that same month.[22]

The Montreal Protocol, now signed by more than forty nations, is widely viewed as a model for further multinational agreements to protect the biosphere. An Intergovernmental Panel on Climate Change was set up in 1988 under the auspices of the World Meteorological Organization and United Nations Environment Programme to develop a "framework" convention to facilitate negotiations on global warming and related issues by late 1990. Since the United States is chairing the panel's Response Strategies Working Group, the Bush administration has a golden opportunity to take the lead on global environmental issues.[23]

Other notable international innovations of the 1980s include actions by the World Bank and other financial institutions to impose environmental criteria on loans to developing nations; and agreements among international banks, environmental organizations, and debtor countries to write off debt in return for conservation programs. Several of these "debt for nature" swaps have been carried out in Bolivia, Ecuador, and Costa Rica.[24] The World Bank, United Nations Development Programme, and other organizations have also launched international programs to protect tropical forests and prevent desertification. President Bush has recently announced that the U.S. Peace Corps will be reoriented to carry out environmental projects.[25]

Perhaps the most important thing the United States could do is to reduce its own fossil fuel consumption. U.S. per capita energy consumption is still nearly twice that of Japan and Europe and seven times the world average. The World Conference on the Changing Atmosphere held in Toronto, Canada, in 1988 called for a 20-percent reduction of worldwide carbon dioxide emissions by the year 2005.[26] More recently, a group of twenty-four senators asked President Bush to support legislation to force industry to reduce CO_2 levels by 20 percent by the year 2000. The Bush administration argued that more research is needed before policy options are determined, in part because new evidence casts doubt on some earlier global warming projections. Thus, at an international conference in the Netherlands in November 1989, the United States (along with Japan and the Soviet Union) refused to endorse any specific targets or timetables for reduction of CO_2 emissions. However, the following month, President Bush proposed that a conference be held in Washington in the fall of 1990 to begin negotiating a treaty on global warming.[27]

Institutional Capacities and Needs

Doing more research and adopting new approaches and policies will not be enough in the 1990s. The institutions that implement these policies will also have to be strengthened. In some cases this means restoring to full strength and funding existing institutions that were weakened in the 1980s. The two obvious examples are the Environmental Protection Agency and the Council on Environmental Quality (CEQ). As indicated in Chapter 1, EPA's budget in constant dollars was no higher in 1989 than a decade earlier. Although the Superfund cleanup effort has grown substantially, this program has been criticized from all sides for slow progress and poor management. Other mandated programs, such as those requiring pretreatment of industrial wastes dumped into municipal sewage systems and control of toxic air pollutants, have lagged years behind schedule due in part to inadequate funds and staffs. Morale remains low in many parts of EPA despite renewed vigor and enthusiasm at the top under William Reilly. Around Washington, EPA is regarded as a rather shabby outpost in a distant part of town, staffed with a lot of disgruntled employees. To change this image and infuse new life into the agency, a major influx of money, personnel, and political support from both the White House and Capitol Hill will be needed in coming years. While the Bush administration has given the administrator moral and political support, it has thus far promised only incremental staff and budgetary increases.

The Council on Environmental Quality is an even more spectacular example of institutional neglect—or destruction. Established under the National Environmental Policy Act of 1969, CEQ played an important role in developing the environmental impact assessment process throughout government and in gathering and disseminating statistical information on environmental conditions and needs (published in large, annual *Environmental Quality* reports). The CEQ chairmen during the Nixon, Ford, and Carter administrations were strong environmental advocates advising the president on both national and international environmental affairs. All this ended under President Reagan, who, after trying to abolish the Council (he could not because it was established by Congress), cut its budget and staff by 85 percent (see Appendices 3 and 5).

The outlook appears much better for the 1990s. President Bush has appointed a strong CEQ chairman, Michael Deland, whose mission is to restore what he calls a "moribund" agency. CEQ's funding and staff were doubled in the final budget for FY 1990, and a further doubling has been promised next year (to a total staff of forty). Deland has been given an office adjoining the White House, where he has regular access to the president and his staff. The other two seats on the Council are unlikely to be filled, as Deland seeks a strong personal advisory role more comparable to that, for example, of the president's science adviser.[28]

President Bush clearly needs better advice on scientific affairs than Ronald Reagan had, and there is evidence that he recognizes the necessity for such support. The Office of Science and Technology Policy under its new chairman, science adviser D. Allan Bromley, is taking a more active role on nonmilitary projects and needs. The staff of the Council of Economic Advisers also contains economists interested in environmental matters, and at least one staff member of the Domestic Policy Council (DPC) in the White House specializes in environmental policy. The DPC has established a top-level working group chaired by Bromley to advise the president on global climate issues as the administration moves toward an international convention on global warming (see previous section).

Nevertheless, there are deep divisions within the Bush administration over environmental policy. The president's most important coordinating agency, the Office of Management and Budget (OMB), remains split over virtually every environmental initiative. Other agencies, such as the interior, agriculture, and energy departments, are also deeply divided between new commitments to the environment and their traditional development missions.[29]

As argued in Chapter 2, whether these institutional improvements will be adequate to the task remains very much dependent on strong presidential leadership. In our view, the importance, complexity, and ubiquity of environmental problems will require further enhancement of policy-making capabilities in the future, perhaps in some body equivalent to the National Security Council. In the meantime, EPA should be raised to cabinet status to give it greater authority in dealing with other departments (such as energy, interior, and agriculture). Alternatively, an environmental "czar" or cabinet-level counselor (possibly also head of CEQ) could be made responsible for coordinating all federal environmental policies.

Various proposals have also been put forward for strengthening international institutions to address global climate, pollution, and sustainable development issues. Further conventions or treaties are needed on such matters as atmospheric pollution, protection of biodiversity, and use of chemical pesticides. But much more financial and organizational support is also needed at the international level if global programs are to prove effective, particularly in poor Third World countries. The World Resources Institute estimates that "saving the environment in the developing world will cost $20 to $50 billion a year." [30] Yet the current budget of the United Nations Environment Programme is a miserly $30 *million* per year—less than one cent per world citizen. The leaders of the seven major industrial nations pledged to increase this amount at their first "green" economic summit meeting in Paris in July 1989, but made no firm commitments.[31] New international facilities for collecting and channeling funds to implement international environmental programs are thus urgently needed. One proposal is for a global "greenhouse tax" on carbon dioxide emissions and other sources of global warming that would be used to support a World Atmosphere Fund or Global Environmental Trust Fund.[32]

Several European nations have argued that a new international agency is needed to make and enforce global environmental policies. Although this is not likely in the near future, stronger policy cooperation is necessary. At present there is little coordination among different multilateral agencies and programs, between public and private conservation efforts, and between international and domestic environmental policy making. Africa alone is served by 82 international donors and 1,700 private organizations; without greater focus much of their effort may be wasted.[33]

Domestic policies that affect the international environment also need to be coordinated with foreign policy making within individual countries; indeed, domestic and foreign environmental policies can no longer be separated.[34] Senator Gore and a bipartisan group of nine other senators have proposed one approach to this problem: a World Environmental Policy Act to provide a more integrated environmental framework for American economic, trade, scientific, and other policies. The bill would replace the existing Council on Environmental Quality with a new Council on World Environmental Policy, chaired by the EPA administrator "to formulate and recommend national and international policies to promote the improvement of the quality of the world environment." It also calls for appointment of an ambassador-at-large for the environment to represent the United States in negotiations on global environmental issues.[35]

Renewing Political Action

Perhaps the most significant change in the environmental politics of the 1990s is that environmental protection has moved from the margins into the mainstream of national political life. As such, environmental protection has become a "valence" issue; that is, an issue characterized by consensual agreement on broad values or goals, but with differences over who is better qualified to achieve them and over the proper means for doing so. According to one pollster, "protection of the environment, in fact, has become . . . a basic American value—with no consequential voting bloc opposed to it." [36] It is difficult to find an elected politician in either Europe or the United States who does not profess to be an environmentalist. The danger is, of course, that a politician's reliance on environmental symbolism is not the same as commitment to substantive policy measures, and can obscure the fact that there are still deep political divisions over specific environmental policies. The problem is to make environmentalism a "defining" issue that affects who gets elected and what positions they take on a wide range of issues that impact the environment.

Nevertheless, the political climate seems more propitious for environmental reform than at any time since 1970. Aside from a more sympathetic president in the White House, leadership changes in the U.S. Congress make policy innovation much more likely in the 1990s than in the 1980s. The replacement of Senate majority leader Robert Byrd of West Virginia by Sen. George Mitchell of Maine has removed a major obstacle to revision of the Clean Air Act and other policies related to coal use. The rise of a number of other Democratic environmental policy entrepreneurs in the Senate, such as Al Gore of Tennessee, Tim Wirth of Colorado, and Max Baucus of Montana, together with Republican environmentalists, such as John Chafee of Rhode Island and John Heinz of Pennsylvania, has restored the Senate to the leading role it played in drafting the environmental legislation of the 1970s (see Chapter 5).

Opinion polls indicate that public support for environmental protection reached an all-time high in 1989, and that environmental organizations were rapidly growing in membership at the end of the decade (see Chapter 4). Polls in other countries also show environmental concerns soaring to the top of the list. Members of Green parties have been elected to legislative bodies in West Germany, France, Italy, Austria, Luxembourg, Switzerland, Sweden, Belgium, Finland, and Portugal, and were the largest gainers in the June 1989 elections to the European Parliament.[37] Indeed, upon visiting Europe shortly before the latter election, President Bush is reported to have compared the green movement to a "freight train."

We have a large environmental movement in the United States, both in the form of local grass-roots organizations and national lobbies and think tanks in Washington. The major organizations have made an increasing effort to develop a coherent national agenda, as in their *Blueprint for the Environment*, which was submitted to President Bush after his election in 1988.[38] Efforts are also being made to create an American Green party, but it is not yet large enough to affect elections beyond a few localities.[39] Political strategies that emphasize broad coalitions are most likely to succeed, as suggested by Robert Paehlke in the previous chapter. The danger is that the environmental movement itself will fragment. There is a widening philosophical gulf between the more radical "deep ecology" movement and the older, established environmental and conservation groups that concentrate on lobbying in Washington.[40] As environmental problems intensify, this division is likely to increase unless greater efforts are made to address it.

All these developments suggest enormous opportunities for environmental activism and leadership in the coming decade. Local, state, national, and international organizations, both public and private, are likely to expand their environmental activities. Such opportunities will include: scientific research, such as toxicological analysis and ecological impact assessment; design of new energy conservation, recycling, organic farming, and pollution control programs; political organization, canvassing, and lobbying; environmental education, journalism, and communication; travel, study, and work in developing countries; and creative business and financial ventures to provide alternative products and sources of capital for sustainable technologies. In virtually every field and profession there will be new environmental contributions to be made. Indeed, every institution, including colleges and universities, will need its own environmental policy.

Governing the Future

It has been stated that for the first time in evolutionary history human beings have achieved a greater measure of influence over the future of their planet than evolution itself. If this is so, we have no alternative but to decide what kind of future we want. One option of course is inaction or "business as usual." But there is a growing belief throughout the world that the result would eventually be catastrophic because our present course of development is not ecologically sustainable. At the same time, most environmentalists believe that it is not too late to make the changes needed to head off future disasters. The present generation bears this unique burden of responsibility for the future.

A different pattern of human behavior will be needed to succeed. It will require shifting from the present reactive mode, by which collective action is taken only when severe problems or crises occur, to a much more proactive orientation in which preventive measures are taken on the basis of careful anticipation and foresight. This is particularly true in regard to disturbances of the large global balances that will affect climate change and overall ecological stability.

According to Stephen Schneider, a respected climatologist at the National Center for Atmospheric Research, there are three general strategies that can be followed in regard to severe environmental threats, such as global warming: *technological countermeasures*, *adaptation*, and *prevention*.[41] Until now we have relied heavily on the first strategy to control pollution: adding on corrective technology to contain or neutralize the effects of pollution generation. This solution is often preferred by engineers. It seems unlikely, however, that we will be able to engineer solutions to massive toxic contamination of the air, land, and water (including oceans and groundwater) in the future—nor is it likely that technological countermeasures will be effective in controlling global warming if we persist in burning fossil fuels rich in carbon.

Adaptation may thus be an easier course: devising strategies that "seek to adjust society to environmental changes without attempting to counteract or prevent those changes."[42] In the case of global warming, people can simply get used to higher temperatures, move to higher altitudes or cooler regions, plant more shade trees, and diversify their food supplies. Less polluting materials and technologies can gradually be substituted for existing systems as negative effects are felt and prices rise. This approach is generally supported by economists.

Schneider also discusses a strategy of "active adaptation," which could be considered a separate approach. Under this strategy, efforts are made to anticipate and prepare for future problems by building greater "resiliency" into our systems. For example, research to develop and test new crop strains can be accelerated; certain scarce resources can be stored or held in reserve for future need; dikes can be built to protect against coastal flooding; and mechanisms can be developed for promoting international cooperation and for compensating losses from climate change. Unfortunately, many species cannot adapt rapidly enough to survive climate change at the projected rates, which are tens of times faster than natural rates of change.[43]

The third strategy, that of prevention, implies a more proactive effort: stopping or reversing current activities and trends that are likely to produce greater ecological change in the future. For example, it calls for the immediate curtailment of fossil fuel burning and CFC production to prevent accumulation of greenhouse gases. Environmentalists usually favor this strategy as a matter of principle. However, it is evident that prevention is the most difficult course to follow since it requires alterations in human behavior and technology over a relatively short time that are likely to be economically costly, scientifically uncertain, and politically unpopular. Yet Schneider and many other climate experts argue that enough is known about the potential consequences of present technologies to begin investing in "planetary insurance."

The necessary adjustments can be made in a series of logical steps. For example, James Gustave Speth, president of the World Resources Institute, has suggested that we need to plan for three technological transitions:

> Transition 1 is the shift away from the era of fossil fuels toward an era of energy efficiency and renewable energy. . . .
>
> Transition 2 is the move from an era of capital- and materials-intensive, "high-throughput" technologies to an era of new technologies, soft and hard, that do not generate much pollution because they use raw materials very efficiently, rely on inputs that have low environmental costs, recover and recycle materials, and are hence more "closed.". . .
>
> Transition 3 is the change to a future in which societies actually apply our most sophisticated technology-assessment capabilities and our best science to "design with nature.". . .[44]

It will not be easy to build a consensus for such changes in pluralistic societies such as our own. Despite support in principle for environmental protection (as indicated, for example, in public opinion polls), most people are resistant to lifestyle changes or specific measures that cause inconvenience or cost money. The limits of popular tolerance for such changes are only now beginning to be tested in places like southern California, where restrictions are being planned on the use of automobiles and many gasoline appliances.[45]

Yet in many states and communities stringent controls have been adopted by referenda or other popular majorities. As changes are accepted in one community or industry, they become easier to implement in others. The raising of environmental consciousness is a cumulative long-term process, as we have argued in the first chapter of this book. Moreover, the transition to the twenty-first century is likely to catalyze awareness of the future at all levels and reenforce the environmental "paradigm shift" that is already occurring.[46] In Robert Paehlke's terms, environmental protection is taking its place as a "first-order" value along with economic growth, social justice, national security, and democracy itself (Chapter 16).

Human experience suggests that open, democratic societies are more conducive to change than closed, authoritarian ones that pursue a narrow range of goals. Pluralism and flexibility in governance, as well as in economic activities, permit widespread experimentation and social change when challenges arise. Popular mobilization that results from voluntary cooperation tends to outlast coerced obedience, as we have learned from two world wars and other tragedies of the twentieth century. If we extend and deepen our democratic commitment to nature, we can create a better world in the next century.

Notes

1. Ted Morello, "Environment Tops UN Agenda," *Christian Science Monitor*, September 19, 1989, 4; "All Things Considered" (PBS broadcast), September 19, 1989; and Bill McKibben, "The End of Nature," *The New Yorker*, September 11, 1989, 47-105.
2. Lester R. Brown, Christopher Flavin, and Sandra Postel, "A World at Risk," in *State of the World 1989*, ed. Lester R. Brown et al. (Washington, D.C.: Worldwatch Institute, 1989), 5-8. See also Mostafa Kamal Tolba, *Evolving Environmental Perceptions: From Stockholm to Nairobi* (London: Butterworths, 1988).
3. United Nations Environment Programme, "Sweeping United Nations Survey on the Environment Reflects Worldwide Concern for Impending Disaster," press release, May 9, 1989, 1.
4. World Resources Institute, *The Crucial Decade: The 1990s and the Global Environmental Challenge* (Washington, D.C.: World Resources Institute, January 1989), 1.

5. World Commission on Environment and Development, *Our Common Future* (New York: Oxford University Press, 1987); Jim MacNeill, "Strategies for Sustainable Economic Development," *Scientific American* 261 (September 1989): 154-165; and "Growth Can Be Green," *The Economist,* August 26, 1989, 12-13.
6. Quoted in Stephen H. Schneider, *Global Warming: Are We Entering the Greenhouse Century?* (San Francisco: Sierra Club Books, 1989), 280.
7. Ted Robert Gurr, "On the Political Consequences of Scarcity and Economic Decline," *International Studies Quarterly* 29 (1985): 51-75. See also Jessica Tuchman Matthews, "Redefining Security," *Foreign Affairs* 68 (Spring 1989): 162-177; Norman Myers, "Environment and Security," *Foreign Policy* 74 (Spring 1989): 23-41; and Michael Renner, "National Security: The Economic and Environmental Dimensions," *Worldwatch Paper* 89 (Washington, D.C.: Worldwatch Institute, 1989).
8. Albert H. Teich and Kathleen M. Gramp, *R&D in the 1980s: A Special Report* (Washington, D.C.: American Association for the Advancement of Science, September 1988), 7.
9. Estimated by the authors from *AAAS Report XIV: Research and Development FY 1990* (Washington, D.C.: American Association for the Advancement of Science, 1989); this estimate includes selected research programs funded by the National Science Foundation, Department of Energy, National Aeronautics and Space Administration, Department of Agriculture, and Environmental Protection Agency. On EPA's research priorities and the need for more R&D funding, see Alvin L. Alm, "The Need to Think Ahead," *EPA Journal* 14 (November-December 1988): 25-26. In 1986 the United States spent less on energy R&D per unit of Gross National Product than any major member of the Organization for Economic Cooperation and Development; see Christopher Flavin, "Creating a Sustainable Energy Future," in *State of the World 1988,* ed. Lester R. Brown et al. (Washington, D.C.: Worldwatch Institute, 1988), 36.
10. "The Global Environment: A National Security Issue," keynote address by Sen. Al Gore, National Academy of Sciences, Forum on Global Change, Washington, D.C., May 1, 1989.
11. Philip J. Hilts, "7 Agencies Joining in Climate Watch," *New York Times,* September 1, 1989, 9.
12. Jerry Kotas, "Pollution Prevention: Getting a Higher Priority," *EPA Journal* 14 (November-December 1988): 30-31; and Margaret E. Kriz, "An Ounce of Prevention," *National Journal,* August 19, 1989, 2093-2096. On the last point, see Jim McNeill, "Protective Instincts at the EPA," *In These Times,* October 11, 1989, 8-9.
13. See, for example, Robert N. Stavins, "Harnessing Market Forces to Protect the Environment," *Environment* 31 (January-February 1989): 4-7ff; *Project 88: Harnessing Market Forces to Protect Our Environment: Initiatives for the New President,* a public policy study sponsored by Sen. Tim Wirth, D-Colo., and Sen. John Heinz, R-Pa. (Washington, D.C.: Project 88, December 1988); and Organization for Economic Cooperation and Development, *The Application of Economic Instruments for Environmental Protection* (Paris: OECD, 1989).

14. "Energy efficiency, a comparison of energy used with the amount of goods and services produced, increased 24 percent between 1976 and 1986, but after the price of oil collapsed in 1986, efficiency stopped growing." Matthew D. Wald, "U.S. Progress in Energy Efficiency Is Halting," *New York Times*, February 27, 1989, 1.
15. William K. Reilly, "The Greening of EPA," *EPA Journal* 15 (July-August 1989): 8-10; and William D. Ruckelshaus, "Toward a Sustainable World," *Scientific American* 261 (September 1989): 166-174.
16. Environmental Protection Agency, *Unfinished Business: A Comparative Assessment of Environmental Problems* (Washington, D.C.: Environmental Protection Agency, 1987). See the discussion in Chapter 8 of this book.
17. See Francis H. Irwin, "Could There Be a Better Law?" *EPA Journal* 15 (July-August 1989): 20-23; and Michael Gruber, "Are Today's Institutional Tools Up to the Task?" *EPA Journal* 14 (November-December 1988): 2-6.
18. See, for example, Matthew L. Wald, "Recharting War on Smog," *New York Times*, October 10, 1989, 1.
19. Susan G. Hadden, *A Citizen's Right to Know: Risk Communication and Public Policy* (Boulder, Colo.: Westview Press, 1989).
20. Barnaby J. Feder, "Group Sets Corporate Code on Environmental Conduct," *New York Times*, September 8, 1989, 25. See also Daniel F. Cuff, "Exxon Puts Scientist on Board," *New York Times*, August 31, 1989, 25.
21. John McCormick, *Reclaiming Paradise: The Global Environmental Movement* (Bloomington: Indiana University Press, 1989), 174-179.
22. Craig R. Whitney, "Talks on Ozone End in Britain Without Fixing Chemical Ban," *New York Times*, March 8, 1989, 8; and Steven Greenhouse, "Conference Backs Curbs on Export of Toxic Waste," *New York Times*, March 23, 1989, 1. See also Jane Perlez, "Global Trade in Ivory Is Banned to Protect the African Elephant," *New York Times*, October 17, 1989, 1.
23. Rochelle L. Stanfield, "Greenhouse Diplomacy," *National Journal*, March 4, 1989, 510-513.
24. "Debt-for-Nature Swaps," *National Journal*, August 5, 1989, 2006.
25. Todd Martens, "Ending Tropical Deforestation: What Is the Proper Role of the World Bank?" *Harvard Environmental Law Review* 13 (1989): 485-515; and Maureen Dowd, "Bush, in Visit to West, Prods Congress on Key Bills," *New York Times*, September 19, 1989, 14.
26. Peter Usher, "Special Report: World Conference on the Changing Atmosphere: Implications for Global Security," *Environment* 31 (January 1989): 25-27. See also Schneider, *Global Warming*, 271-274; and Matthew L. Wald, "Environment Dominates 91-Nation Energy Talks," *New York Times*, September 21, 1989, D1.
27. Thomas C. Hayes, "Parley Told of Political Cost of Valdez Spill," *New York Times*, November 14, 1989, 37; William K. Stevens, "Skeptics Are Challenging Dire Greenhouse Views," *New York Times*, December 13, 1989, 1; and Paul Montgomery, "U.S., Japan and Soviets Block Pollution Pact," *New York Times*, November 8, 1989, 13.
28. Michael Weisskopf, "Reviving a Presidential Panel," *Washington Post National Weekly Edition*, August 21, 1989, 34; and personal interviews with Michael Deland and David Struhs.

29. For example, Secretary of Agriculture Clayton Yeutter recently warned: "The environmental advocacy groups are exceptionally well organized ... they will have volumes of proposals.... Some of those proposals will not be reasonable based on past history, and those of us interested in agriculture ought to battle them with vigor [and] make sure the environmental pendulum doesn't swing too far." Quoted in Sharon Schmickle, "Environmental Issues Emerging: Ag Secretary Tells Farmers to Battle Extreme Proposals," Minneapolis *Star Tribune,* September 26, 1989, 3B. See also Michael Weisskopf, "White House Split on Ozone Problem," *Washington Post,* June 10, 1989, 1; and Allan R. Gold, "Bush Proposal for Clean Air Is Dealt a Blow," *New York Times,* October 12, 1989, 1.
30. Rochelle L. Stanfield, "Saving the World," *National Journal,* September 30, 1989, 2432.
31. Marshall Ingwerson, "Environment Is First on Agenda," *Christian Science Monitor,* July 14, 1989, 1; James M. Markham, "Paris Group Urges 'Decisive Action' for Environment," *New York Times,* July 17, 1989, 1; and "Key Sections of the Paris Communiqué by the Group of Seven," *New York Times,* July 17, 1989, 5, point 48. However, President Bush's FY 1990 budget proposal would actually *cut* the U.S. contribution to the United Nations Environment Programme from $9.5 million to $8 million; see Stanfield, "Greenhouse Diplomacy," 510.
32. Marshall Ingwerson, "World Bank Takes Steps to Help Environment," *Christian Science Monitor,* September 22, 1989, 7.
33. Ruckelshaus, "Toward a Sustainable World," 174.
34. Philip Shabecoff, "The Environment as a Diplomatic Issue," *New York Times,* December 25, 1987. See also William B. Wood et al., "Ecopolitics in the Global Greenhouse," *Environment* 31 (September 1989): 12-17, 32-34; and Glenn Garelik, "A New Item on the Agenda," *Time,* October 23, 1989, 60-62.
35. U.S. Congress. Senate. Committee on Environment and Public Works. *World Environmental Policy Act of 1989.* 101st Cong., 1st sess., 1989. S. 201.
36. Quote from Linda C. Lake in Ronald Brownstein, "Testing the Limits," *National Journal,* July 29, 1989, 1916. See also "The Politics of Posterity" (special survey of the environment), *The Economist,* September 2, 1989, esp. 3-5.
37. Gladwin Hill, "A Management Job for the Human Race," *EPA Journal* 15 (July-August 1989): 5; Ferdinand Müller-Rommel, ed., *New Politics in Western Europe: The Rise and Success of Green Parties and Alternate Lists* (Boulder, Colo.: Westview Press, 1989); and Julian Baum, "European Parliament Shifts to Left," *Christian Science Monitor,* June 20, 1989, 4.
38. Later published as *Blueprint for the Environment,* T Allan Comp, ed. (Salt Lake City: Howe Brothers, 1989).
39. Jay Walljasper, "Can Green Politics Take Root in the U.S.?" *Utne Reader,* September-October 1989, 140-143.
40. See, for example, Kirkpatrick Sale, "The Cutting Edge: Deep Ecology and Its Critics," *The Nation,* May 14, 1988, 670-675; and Dick Russell, " 'We Are All Losing the War,' " *The Nation,* March 27, 1989, 403-408.
41. Schneider, *Global Warming,* 249ff.

42. Ibid., 253.
43. Ibid., chap. 3.
44. James Gustave Speth, "Environmental Pollution: A Long-Term Perspective," in *Earth 88: Changing Geographic Perspectives* (Washington, D.C.: National Geographic Society, 1988), 278-279. See also Christopher Flavin, *Slowing Global Warming: A Worldwide Strategy*, Worldwide Paper 91 (Washington, D.C.: Worldwatch Institute, October 1989).
45. Brownstein, "Testing the Limits."
46. On the concept of an environmental "paradigm shift" and its implications for the future, see Lester W. Milbrath, *Environmentalists: Vanguard for a New Society* (Albany: SUNY Press, 1984), and *Envisioning a Sustainable Society: Learning Our Way Out* (Albany: SUNY Press, 1989).

APPENDIX

Appendix 1 Major Federal Laws on the Environment, 1969-1989

Legislation	Implementing agency	Key provisions
	Nixon administration	
National Environmental Policy Act of 1969, PL 91-190	All federal agencies	Declared a national policy to "encourage productive and enjoyable harmony between man and his environment"; required environmental impact statements; created Council on Environmental Quality.
Resources Recovery Act of 1970, PL 91-512	Health, Education, and Welfare Department (later the Environmental Protection Agency)	Set up a program of demonstration and construction grants for innovative solid-waste management systems; provided technical and financial assistance to state and local agencies in developing resource recovery and waste disposal systems.
Clean Air Act Amendments of 1970, PL 91-604	Environmental Protection Agency (EPA)	Required administrator to set national primary and secondary air quality standards and certain emission limits; required states to develop implementation plans by specific dates; required reductions in automobile emissions.
Federal Water Pollution Control Act (Clean Water Act) Amendments of 1972, PL 92-500	EPA	Set national water quality goals; established pollutant discharge permit system; increased federal grants to states to construct waste treatment plants.
Federal Environmental Pesticides Control Act of 1972, PL 92-516 (amended the Federal Insecticide, Fungicide, and Rodenticide Act of 1947)	EPA	Required registration of all pesticides in U.S. commerce; allowed administrator to cancel or suspend registration under specified circumstances.

(Appendix continues)

Appendix (continued)

Legislation	Implementing agency	Key provisions
Marine Protection Act of 1972, PL 92-532	EPA	Regulated dumping of waste materials into the oceans and coastal waters.
Coastal Zone Management Act of 1972, PL 92-583	Office of Coastal Zone Management, Commerce Department	Authorized federal grants to the states to develop coastal zone management plans under federal guidelines.
Endangered Species Act of 1973, PL 93-205	Fish & Wildlife Service, Interior Department	Broadened federal authority to protect all "threatened" as well as "endangered" species; authorized grant program to assist state programs; required coordination among all federal agencies.
	Ford administration	
Safe Drinking Water Act of 1974, PL 93-523	EPA	Authorized federal government to set standards to safeguard the quality of public drinking water supplies and to regulate state programs for protecting underground water sources.
Toxic Substances Control Act of 1976, PL 94-469	EPA	Authorized pre-market testing of chemical substances; allowed EPA to ban or regulate the manufacture, sale, or use of any chemical presenting an "unreasonable risk of injury to health or environment"; prohibited most uses of PCBs.
Federal Land Policy and Management Act of 1976, PL 94-579	Bureau of Land Management, Interior Department	Gave Bureau of Land Management authority to manage public lands for long-term benefits; officially ended policy of conveying public lands into private ownership.

Resource Conservation and Recovery Act of 1976, PL 94-580	EPA	Required EPA to set regulations for hazardous-waste treatment, storage, transportation, and disposal; provided assistance for state hazardous-waste programs under federal guidelines.
National Forest Management Act of 1976, PL 94-588	U.S. Forest Service, Agriculture Department	Gave statutory permanence to national forest lands and set new standards for their management; restricted timber harvesting to protect soil and watersheds; limited clearcutting.
	Carter administration	
Surface Mining Control and Reclamation Act of 1977, PL 95-87	Interior Department	Established environmental controls over strip mining; limited mining on farmland, alluvial valleys, and slopes; required restoration of land to original contours.
Clean Air Act Amendments of 1977, PL 95-95	EPA	Amended and extended Clean Air Act; postponed deadlines for compliance with auto emission and air quality standards; set new standards for "prevention of significant deterioration" in clean air areas.
Clean Water Act Amendments of 1977, PL 95-217	EPA	Extended deadlines for industry and cities to meet treatment standards; set national standards for industrial pretreatment of wastes; increased funding for sewage treatment construction grants and gave states flexibility in determining priorities.
Public Utility Regulatory Policies Act of 1978, PL 95-617	Energy Department, states	Provided for Energy Department and Federal Energy Regulatory Commission regulation of electric and natural gas utilities and crude oil transportation systems in order to promote energy conservation and efficiency; allowed small cogeneration and renewable energy projects to sell power to utilities.

(Appendix continues)

Appendix (continued)

Legislation	Implementing agency	Key provisions
Alaska National Interest Lands Conservation Act of 1980, PL 96-487	Interior Department, Agriculture Department	Protected 102 million acres of Alaskan land as national wilderness, wildlife refuges, and parks.
Comprehensive Environmental Response, Compensation, and Liability Act of 1980 (Superfund), PL 96-510	EPA	Authorized federal government to respond to hazardous-waste emergencies and to clean up chemical dump sites; created $1.6 billion "Superfund"; established liability for cleanup costs.
	Reagan administration	
Nuclear Waste Policy Act of 1982, PL 97-425; Nuclear Waste Policy Act Amendments of 1987, PL 100-203	Energy Department	Established a national plan for the permanent disposal of highly radioactive nuclear waste and authorized the Energy Department to site, obtain a license for, construct, and operate geologic repositories for spent fuel from commercial nuclear power plants.
Resource Conservation and Recovery Act Amendments of 1984, PL 98-616	EPA	Revised and strengthened EPA procedures for regulating hazardous-waste facilities; authorized grants to states for management of solid and hazardous wastes; prohibited land disposal of certain hazardous liquid wastes; and required states to consider recycling in comprehensive solid-waste plans.
Food Security Act of 1985 (the "Farm Bill"), PL 99-198	Agriculture Department	Limited federal program benefits for producers of commodities on highly erodible land or converted wetlands; established a conservation reserve program; authorized Agriculture Department technical assistance for subsurface water quality preservation; and revised and extended the Soil and Water Conservation Act (1977) programs through the year 2008.

Safe Drinking Water Act of 1986, PL 99-339	EPA	Reauthorized the Safe Drinking Water Act of 1974 and revised EPA safe drinking water programs, including grants to states for drinking water standards enforcement and groundwater protection programs; accelerated EPA schedule for setting standards for maximum contaminant levels of eighty-three toxic pollutants.
Superfund Amendments and Reauthorization Act of 1986, PL 99-499	EPA	Provided $8.5 billion through 1991 to clean up the nation's most dangerous abandoned chemical dumps; set strict standards and timetables for cleaning up such sites; required that industry provide local communities with information on hazardous chemicals used or emitted.
Clean Water Act Amendments of 1987, PL 100-4	EPA	Amended the Federal Water Pollution Control Act of 1972 and extended and revised EPA water pollution control programs, including grants to states for construction of wastewater treatment facilities and implementation of mandated nonpoint-source pollution management plans; expanded EPA enforcement authority; established a national estuary program.
Global Climate Protection Act of 1987, PL 100-204	State Department	Authorized the State Department to develop an approach to the problems of global climate change; created an intergovernmental task force to develop U.S. strategy for dealing with the threat posed by global warming.
Ocean Dumping Act of 1988, PL 100-688	EPA	Amended the Marine Protection, Research, and Sanctuaries Act of 1972 to end all ocean disposal of sewage sludge and industrial waste by December 31, 1991; revised EPA regulation of ocean dumping by establishing dumping fees, permit requirements, and civil penalties for violations.

Appendix 2 Spending on Natural Resources and the Environment, Fiscal Years 1980-1990 (in millions of dollars)

Budget item	1980	1981	1982	1983	1984	1985	1986	1987	1988	1989 (Est.)	1990 Proposed
Water resources	4,085 (4,728)	4,079 (4,326)	3,913 (3,913)	4,608 (4,544)	3,781 (3,584)	4,087 (3,777)	3,678 (3,399)	4,107 (3,510)	4,295 (3,520)	4,336 (3,414)	4,141 (3,137)
Conservation and land management	1,302 (1,507)	1,364 (1,446)	902 (902)	1,883 (1,857)	1,389 (1,317)	1,446 (1,336)	1,430 (1,322)	1,721 (1,471)	2,650 (2,172)	3,648 (2,872)	633 (480)
Recreational resources	1,642 (1,900)	1,252 (1,328)	1,220 (1,220)	1,581 (1,559)	1,453 (1,377)	1,574 (1,455)	1,456 (1,346)	1,685 (1,440)	1,647 (1,350)	1,838 (1,447)	1,372 (1,039)
Pollution control and abatement	4,672 (5,407)	2,982 (3,162)	3,645 (3,645)	3,677 (3,626)	4,037 (3,826)	4,303 (3,977)	3,399 (3,141)	5,296 (4,526)	4,932 (4,043)	5,040 (3,968)	4,789 (3,628)
Other natural resources	1,395 (1,615)	1,494 (1,584)	1,583 (1,583)	1,547 (1,526)	1,622 (1,537)	1,934 (1,787)	1,761 (1,628)	1,770 (1,513)	1,852 (1,518)	1,965 (1,547)	1,774 (1,344)
Total [a]	13,096 (15,157)	11,171 (11,846)	11,263 (11,263)	13,297 (13,113)	12,282 (11,642)	13,344 (12,332)	11,724 (10,834)	14,578 (12,460)	15,375 (12,602)	16,826 (13,249)	12,709 (9,628)

Source: Office of Management and Budget, *Historical Tables, Budget of the United States Government, Fiscal Year 1990* (Washington, D.C.: U.S. Government Printing Office, 1989).

Note: The upper figure represents budget authority in nominal dollars. The lower figure in parentheses represents budget authority adjusted to 1982 dollars. Figures for 1988, 1989, and 1990 are deflated using an estimate of 5 percent per year. Amounts are adjusted to 1982 dollars using implicit price deflators for federal government purchases of nondefense goods and services as calculated by the Bureau of Economic Analysis, Department of Commerce.

[a] For comparison, the total budget authority for natural resources and the environment in 1972 was \$3.76 billion, or \$8.04 billion in 1982 dollars; by 1976 total authority had risen to \$6.05 billion, or \$9.42 billion in 1982 dollars.

Appendix 3 Budgets of Selected Environmental and Natural Resource Agencies (in millions of dollars)

	1975 (Nixon)		1980 (Carter)		1985 (Reagan)		1990 (Bush)	
Agency	proposed	actual	proposed	actual	proposed	actual	proposed [a]	actual
Environmental Protection Agency [b]	694.9 (1,146.7)	850.1 (1,402.9)	1,286.8 (1,489.3)	1,268.7 (1,468.4)	1,198.2 (1,107.4)	1,339.7 (1,238.1)	1,887.1 (1,429.6)	1,989.0 (1,506.8)
Bureau of Land Management	290.0 (478.5)	399.9 (659.9)	851.0 (985.0)	918.7 (1,063.3)	608.9 (562.8)	799.6 (739.0)	943.6 (714.8)	956.4 (724.5)
Fish and Wildlife Service	200.3 (330.5)	207.0 (341.6)	407.7 (471.9)	435.3 (503.8)	529.8 (489.6)	585.5 (541.1)	605.9 (459.0)	533.5 (404.2)
National Park Service	414.3 (683.6)	415.8 (686.1)	503.5 (582.8)	531.2 (614.8)	840.9 (777.2)	1,005.3 (929.1)	865.5 (655.7)	1,095.0 (829.5)
Office of Surface Mining	N/A	N/A	195.2 (225.9)	179.5 (207.8)	361.4 (334.0)	377.3 (348.7)	254.1 (192.5)	295.5 (223.9)
Forest Service	796.2 (1,313.9)	955.6 (1,576.9)	1,777.0 (2,056.7)	2,249.6 (2,603.7)	2,045.0 (1,890.0)	2,116.4 (1,956.0)	2,511.4 (1,902.6)	2,255.3 (1,708.6)
Council on Environmental Quality	2.5 (4.1)	2.5 (4.1)	3.1 (3.6)	3.1 (3.6)	0.7 (0.6)	0.7 (0.6)	0.9 (0.7)	1.5 (1.1)
Army Corps of Engineers	1,611.0 (2,658.4)	1,744.5 (2,878.7)	3,039.4 (3,517.8)	3,233.7 (3,742.7)	2,491.0 (2,302.2)	2,882.8 (2,664.3)	3,139.6 (2,378.5)	3,164.0 (2,397.0)

Sources: Office of Management and Budget, *Budget of the United States Government*, fiscal years 1975, 1977, 1980, 1982, 1985, 1987, and 1990; *Congressional Quarterly Weekly Report*, October 7, 1989, 2625 and October 28, 1989, 2872.

Note: The upper figure represents budget authority in nominal dollars; the president's proposed budget and the actual budget approved by Congress are shown. The lower figure in parentheses represents a constant level, with the numbers converted to 1982 dollars. Amounts are deflated to 1982 dollars using implicit price deflators for federal government purchases of nondefense goods and services as calculated by the Bureau of Economic Analysis, Department of Commerce. A 5 percent rate of deflation was applied for 1988 through 1990.

[a] The proposed fiscal 1990 budget is the Reagan administration's. The Bush budget for environmental programs in fiscal 1990 differed only slightly from the Reagan budget. The 1990 figures are the initial authorization approved by Congress for fiscal 1990. Some adjustments will be made as part of deficit reduction measures. The final budget will probably be 5 percent less.

[b] These figures exclude sewage treatment construction grants and Superfund allocations. Construction grant authority totaled $7.7 billion in 1975, $3.4 billion in 1980, $2.4 billion in 1985, and $1.2 billion was proposed for 1990. The figures decline because the grants program is being phased out. Superfund budget authority in 1985 (there was no budget in 1975 and 1980) was $606 million, and $1.7 billion was proposed for 1990.

Appendix 4 Budget Authority for EPA Research and Development (in millions of dollars)

Fiscal year	Nominal dollars	Constant dollars [a]	Percentage change from 1980, constant dollars
1980	$342.0	$395.8	—
1988	373.9	294.4	-25.6
1989 estimate	389.8	306.9	-22.5
1990 budget [b]	421.5	319.3	-19.0

Sources: Albert H. Teich and Kathleen M. Gramp, *R & D in the 1980s: A Special Report* (Washington, D.C.: American Association for the Advancement of Science, 1988); and the American Association for the Advancement of Science, *AAAS Report XIV: Research and Development, FY 1990* (Washington, D.C.: American Association for the Advancement of Science, 1989).

[a] Amounts are adjusted to 1982 dollars using implicit price deflators for federal government purchases of nondefense goods and services, as calculated by the Bureau of Economic Analysis, Department of Commerce. A 5 percent annual rate of deflation was assumed for 1988 through 1990.

[b] Submitted to Congress by President Ronald Reagan in January 1989.

Appendix 5 Employees in Selected Federal Agencies and Departments, Selected Years, 1977-1989

Agency/department	1977	1980	1983	1986	1989[a]
Environmental Protection Agency	11,694	13,867	12,054	13,852	15,385
excluding Superfund-related employees	—	—	11,329	12,209	12,635
Department of Interior	77,496	79,285	74,012	72,109	71,833
Army Corps of Engineers	31,243	32,718	30,102	29,343	30,398
Council on Environmental Quality	57	59	13	11	11

Sources: U.S. Civil Service Commission, *Federal Civilian Workforce Statistics* (Washington, D.C.: U.S. Government Printing Office, January 1977); and U.S. Office of Personnel Management, *Federal Civilian Workforce Statistics* (Washington, D.C.: U.S. Government Printing Office, January 1980, 1983, 1986, 1989).

Note: The data refer to the total number of employees in the department or agency in January of the year listed.

[a] Reagan budget.

Contributors

Douglas J. Amy is associate professor in the Department of Politics at Mount Holyoke College. He is the author of *The Politics of Environmental Mediation* (1987) and numerous articles and papers on policy analysis and environmental policy making.

Richard N. L. Andrews is professor of environmental sciences and engineering and director of the Institute for Environmental Studies at the University of North Carolina, Chapel Hill. Formerly chairman of the Natural Resources Policy and Management Program at the University of Michigan and a budget examiner at the U.S. Office of Management and Budget, he is the author of *Environmental Policy and Administrative Change* (1976) and of numerous journal articles on environmental policy, impact and risk assessments, and benefit-cost analysis.

Robert V. Bartlett is associate professor of political science at Purdue University. He is the author of *The Reserve Mining Controversy: Science, Technology, and Environmental Quality* (1980), coauthor of *A Study of Ways to Improve the Scientific Content and Methodology of Environmental Impact Analysis* (1983), and editor of *Policy Through Impact Assessment: Institutionalized Analysis as a Policy Strategy* (1989). His articles on environmental impact assessment and ecological rationality have appeared as chapters in edited volumes and in such journals as *Environmental Ethics, Natural Resources Journal,* and *The Environmental Professional.*

Lynton K. Caldwell is the Arthur F. Bentley Professor Emeritus of Political Science and professor emeritus of public and environmental affairs at Indiana University, Bloomington. He is the author of many articles and several books on environmental policy, including *Environment: A Challenge for Modern Society* (1970), *Science and the National*

Environmental Policy Act: Redirecting Policy Through Procedural Reform (1982), and *International Environmental Policy: Emergence and Dimensions* (1984).

A. Myrick Freeman III is senior fellow at Resources for the Future and professor of economics at Bowdoin College. He has also held appointments as visiting college professor at the University of Washington and Robert M. La Follette Visiting Distinguished Professor at the University of Wisconsin-Madison. He is the author of *The Benefits of Environmental Improvement: Theory and Practice*, and *Air and Water Pollution Control: A Benefit-Cost Assessment*. He is currently a member of the Clean Air Scientific Advisory Committee of the Environmental Protection Agency.

Michael E. Kraft is professor of political science and public affairs and the Herbert Fisk Johnson Professor of Environmental Studies at the University of Wisconsin-Green Bay. He has been a visiting distinguished professor in the environmental studies program at Oberlin College and a Robert M. La Follette Visiting Distinguished Professor at the University of Wisconsin-Madison. Among other works, he is coeditor and a contributing author of *Environmental Policy in the 1980s: Reagan's New Agenda* (1984), *Technology and Politics* (1988), and *Public Opinion and Nuclear Waste* (forthcoming 1991).

James P. Lester is professor of political science at Colorado State University. He is editor of *Environmental Politics and Policy: Theories and Evidence* (1989) and author of numerous articles and book chapters on environmental policy, hazardous waste politics, and public policy implementation. During the fall of 1989, he was a visiting scholar with the Department of Water and Environmental Studies at Linkoping University in Sweden.

Daniel A. Mazmanian is the director of the Center for Politics and Policy and the Luther Lee Professor of Government at the Claremont Graduate School. He is currently serving as president of the Policy Studies Organization. He has written numerous articles and several books, including *Can Organizations Change? Environmental Protection, Citizen Participation, and the Corps of Engineers* (1979), *Can Regulation Work? The Implementation of the 1972 California Coastal Initiative* (1983), and *The Implementation of Public Policy* (1983, 1989).

Robert Cameron Mitchell is a sociologist in the Graduate School of Geography at Clark University. His articles on environmental public opinion and the environmental movement have appeared in *Natural*

Resource Journal, Society, Public Opinion, Western Political Quarterly, and as chapters in several volumes. Most recently he is coauthor of *Using Surveys to Value Public Goods: The Contingent Valuation Method* (1988) and is currently writing a book on the U.S. environmental movement.

David Morell is president of Environmental Programs Information and Compliance Services, International, a consulting firm in Oakland, California. Author of five books and more than fifty articles, he has served as an office director in both the air and water divisions of the Environmental Protection Agency in Washington, D.C., and director of policy for the Hazardous Waste Program in the California Department of Health Services. Morell has taught environmental policy at Princeton and at the University of California, Berkeley.

Robert C. Paehlke is professor of political studies and environmental and resource studies at Trent University, Peterborough, Ontario. He is the author of *Environmentalism and the Future of Progressive Politics* (1989) and coeditor of *Managing Leviathan: Environmental Politics and the Administrative State* (1990). He is a founding editor of the Canadian journal *Alternatives: Perspectives on Society, Technology and Environment.*

Richard J. Tobin teaches courses in public and environmental policy in the Department of Political Science at the State University of New York at Buffalo. He is the author of *The Social Gamble: Determining Acceptable Levels of Air Quality* (1979), *The Expendable Future: Politics and the Protection of Biological Diversity* (1990), as well as many articles and book chapters on environmental policy and politics. During the period in which his chapter was written, he was engaged in research in Southeast Asia, first in Malaysia and then in the Philippines.

Norman J. Vig is professor of political science and codirector of the Technology and Policy Studies Program at Carleton College. He is the author of *Science and Technology in British Politics* (1968) and coeditor and a contributing author of *Politics in Advanced Nations* (1974), *Environmental Policy in the 1980s: Reagan's New Agenda* (1984), *Political Economy in Western Democracies* (1985), and *Technology and Politics* (1988).

David Vogel is professor of business and public policy at the Haas School of Business at the University of California, Berkeley. He has written extensively on business-government relations in the United States and on comparative environmental regulation. His most recent books are *Na-*

tional Styles of Regulation: Environmental Policy in Great Britain and the United States (1986) and *Fluctuating Fortunes: The Political Power of Business in America* (1989).

Geoffrey Wandesforde-Smith teaches environmental politics and law in the Department of Political Science and the Division of Environmental Studies at the University of California, Davis. He is cochair of the editorial policy committee of the *Environmental Impact Assessment Review* and a former senior fellow at the Environmental Institute of the Science Center, Berlin.

Lettie McSpadden Wenner is professor and chair of the Department of Political Science at Northern Illinois University. She is the author of *One Environment Under Law* (1976), *The Environmental Decade in Court* (1982), and numerous articles and book chapters on environmental policy and judicial politics. She is at work on a book on interest groups' influence on national energy and environmental policies.

INDEX